CHENG & TSUI

"Bringing Asia to the World"™

中文听说读写

INTEGRATED CHINESE

Simplified Characters

2

Textbook

4th Edition

Yuehua Liu and Tao-chung Yao
Nyan-Ping Bi, Liangyan Ge, Yaohua Shi

Original Edition by Tao-chung Yao and Yuehua Liu
Liangyan Ge, Yea-fen Chen, Nyan-Ping Bi, Xiaojun Wang, Yaohua Shi

Y0-CPC-010

CHENG & TSUI

"Bringing Asia to the World"™

Copyright © 2025, 2018, 2009, 2005, 1997 by
Cheng & Tsui Co., Inc.

Fourth Edition 2018
Third Edition 2009
Second Edition 2005
First Edition 1997

1st Printing, 2024

28 27 26 25 24   1 2 3 4 5

ISBN 978-1-62291-748-8
[Fourth Edition with Supplemental Readings,
Simplified Characters, Hardcover]

ISBN 978-1-62291-749-5
[Fourth Edition with Supplemental Readings,
Simplified Characters, Paperback]

Library of Congress Cataloging-in-Publication
Data [Third Edition]

Integrated Chinese = [Zhong wen ting shuo
du xie]. Traditional character edition. Level
1, part 2/ Yuehua Liu . . . [et. al]. – 3rd. ed.
p. cm.

Chinese and English.

Includes indexes.

Parallel title in Chinese characters.

– ISBN 978-0-88727-673-6 (trad. hbk.)
– ISBN 978-0-88727-672-9 (trad. pbk.)
– ISBN 978-0-88727-671-2 (simp. hbk.)
– ISBN 978-0-88727-670-5 (simp. pbk.)
1. Chinese language–Textbooks for foreign
speakers–English. I. Liu, Yuehua. II. Title: Zhong
wen ting shuo du xie.

PL1129.E5I683 2008

495.1–dc22

Printed in Canada

Publisher
JILL CHENG

Editorial Manager
BEN SHRAGGE

Editors
LEI WANG and MIKE YONG

Creative Director
CHRISTIAN SABOGAL

Designers
KATE PAPADAKI and LIZ YATES

Illustrator
KATE PAPADAKI

Photographs
© Adobe Stock
© Cheng & Tsui

Cheng & Tsui Co., Inc.
Phone (617) 988-2400 / (800) 554-1963
Fax (617) 426-3669
25 West Street
Boston, MA 02111-1213 USA
cheng-tsui.com

All rights reserved. No part of this publication
may be reproduced or transmitted in any form
or by any means, electronic or mechanical,
including photocopying, recording, scanning,
or any information storage or retrieval system,
without written permission from the publisher.

All trademarks and references mentioned in
this book are used for identification purposes
only and are the property of their respective
owners.

The *Integrated Chinese* series encompasses
textbooks, workbooks, character workbooks,
teacher's resources, audio, video, a digital
edition on Cheng & Tsui FluencyLink™, and
more. Visit cheng-tsui.com for more information
on *Integrated Chinese*.

This Fourth Edition of *Integrated Chinese* is dedicated to the memory of our dearest colleague and
friend, Professor Tao-chung (Ted) Yao.

Cheng & Tsui Editorial Board

Professor Shou-hsin Teng (Chief Editor)
Graduate Institue of Teaching Chinese as a
Second Language
National Taiwan Normal University

Professor Dana Scott Bourgerie
Department of Asian and Near Eastern
Languages
Brigham Young University

Professor Samuel Cheung
Department of Chinese
Chinese University of Hong Kong

Professor Hong Gang Jin
Faculty of Arts and Humanities
University of Macau

Professor Ying-che Li
Department of East Asian Languages and
Literatures
University of Hawaii

Former members of our Editorial Board

Professor Timothy Light (emeritus)
Western Michigan University

Professor Stanley R. Munro (emeritus)
University of Alberta

Professor Ronald Walton (in memoriam)
University of Maryland

Contents

Introduction

Volumes 1 and 2 of *Integrated Chinese* Fourth Edition have been updated to include a new Supplemental Reading Practice section. On FluencyLink™, the online course now has a Teacher View that integrates resources from the Teacher's Resources. The Student Course now incorporates both Workbook and new online-only activities into the instructional sequence.

Series Components

The IC series has been carefully conceptualized and developed to facilitate flexible delivery options that meet the needs of different instructional environments.

Component per Volume	Description	Includes
Print Textbook	• Ten engaging lessons • Ten supplemental readings • Vols. 1 and 2 available in Simplified or Traditional Characters • Vols. 3 and 4 available in Simplified with Traditional Characters	• Streaming Audio & Video on FluencyLink™ • Downloadable Audio on FluencyLink™
Print Workbook	• Vols. 1 and 2 available in Simplified or Traditional Characters • Vols. 3 and 4 available in Simplified with Traditional Characters	• Downloadable Audio on FluencyLink™
Print Character Workbook	• Simplified with Traditional Characters; Radical- and character-writing and stroke order practice	• Downloadable with FluencyLink™ subscription
eTextbook	• Same content and formats as Print Textbook (see above) • Embedded audio and video • Ability to highlight or add notes	• Available on FluencyLink™
FluencyLink™ Subscription: Student Online Course	• Upgraded student experience features interactive content from Textbook and Workbook with auto-graded activities, flashcards, video activities, and additional online-only practice	• eTextbook with Embedded Audio and Video • Interactive Workbook with Auto Feedback • Downloadable Character Workbook
FluencyLink™ Subscription: Teacher Online Course	• Upgraded teacher experience features integrated PPTs, Teaching Tips and Answer Keys alongside textbook pages	• All Components from the Student Course • Auto-gradeable activities • Customization Capabilities to Personalize • Integrated and Downloadable Teacher's Resources
Audio and Video	• Storyline video of textbook dialogues and narratives • Culture Minutes (Vols. 1 and 2) • Documentary-style segments (Vols. 3 and 4) • Normal and adjustable-speed audio	• Streaming and Downloadable Audio • Streaming Video

New Updates

Supplemental Reading Practice

To respond to increasing demand for readings that are accessible to Novice and Intermediate Chinese learners, we have added a new Supplemental Reading Section, referenced in each chapter's Lesson Wrap-Up.

Readings are culturally rich and level appropriate.

Use **supplemental vocabulary** to enhance reading comprehension.

Dating

恋爱综艺为什么这么受欢迎?
高书文

在恋综《最好的印象》里约会的大学生王可苹(左)和白朋(右)

最近几年，恋爱综艺(也就是恋综)在中国很受欢迎。现在除了有素人恋综和明星恋综以外，还有明星和素人约会的恋综。另外，有些大学生还会自己在学校里做"恋综"。那为什么有这么多人喜欢看这种节目呢？我们来听听几位平常喜欢看恋综的观众是怎么说的。

一位名叫文文的单身大学生告诉我们，"我可以单身，但是我喜欢的CP(英文 'couple' 的缩写) 一定要在一起！"她说她看到节目里别人约会，自己也觉得很甜。她看到节目里的人出去旅行，就觉得自己好像也去"旅行"了。跟文文比，刚工作的小东更喜欢看恋综里

> 我可以单身，但是我喜欢的CP一定要在一起！

的那些"冲突"。他说："那些冲突有的时候是因为谁得打扫和整理房间，有的时候是因为俩人都想跟同一个人约会……非常有意思！"他还说在恋综里他能找到跟自己很像的人，找到共鸣，而且还可以从节目里学到些东西，让自己的EQ更高。

因为这几年恋综很受欢迎，有的素人上完节目以后自己也成了"明星"。这让观众觉得，现在有的素人就是想给观众一个好印象，所以他们约会的时候就像演电影一样，不够真实。另外，这几年恋综越来越多，广电总局会不会觉得这是个问题？恋综还能受欢迎几年？现在，我们还不知道。

> ## Supplemental Vocabulary

No.	Word	Pinyin	Part of Speech	Definition
1	恋爱	liàn'ài	n/v	love, romantic relationship; to be in love
2	综艺	zōngyì	n	entertainment show (a broad category including reality TV, variety programs, etc.)
3	受欢迎	shòu huānyíng	adj	popular
4	素人	sùrén	n	ordinary person (non-celebrity)
5	明星	míngxīng	n	celebrity, star
6	约会	yuēhuì	n/v	date; to have a date
7	另外	lìngwài	conj	furthermore, in addition
8	节目	jiémù	n	program, show
9	观众	guānzhòng	n	audience, viewers, spectators
10	单身	dānshēn	adj	single
11	缩写	suōxiě	n/v	abbreviation; to abbreviate
12	要	yào	mv	need to, should, must
13	冲突	chōngtū	n	conflict, clash
14	共鸣	gòngmíng	n/v	resonance; to resonate
15	真实	zhēnshí	adj	true, real, genuine
16	广电总局	Guǎngdiàn Zǒngjú	pn	National Radio and Television Administration (in China)

> ## Reading Comprehension

A Skimming and Scanning: Skim the reading and try to get a basic sense of the content and purpose of the text. INTERPRETIVE

1 What genre of nonfiction writing does this reading belong to, and where might you come across it?

(a) movie teaser in a newspaper

(b) cultural commentary in a magazine

(c) coffee shop review in a travel guide

Reading strategies help make readings accessible.

The new Supplemental Reading section contains ten (10) level-appropriate readings. These informational and semi-authentic readings are accompanied by cultural context and scaffolded activities. The Sample Reading below is the sixth reading in Volume 2.

Added cultural information focuses on **practices and perspectives.**

Pinyin provides **additional support.**

<u>B</u> **Comprehension Check:** Mark the following statements true or false. INTERPRETIVE

1 This article focuses specifically on celebrity dating shows. T F
2 Wenwen likes watching the conflicts unfold in dating shows. T F
3 The author predicts that dating shows will remain popular for many more years. T F

Cultural and Societal Context

China's thriving entertainment industry produces a plethora of reality and variety shows to cater to the diverse interests of its audience. These shows encompass various genres, ranging from dating shows to escape room shows to rap competitions. Their devoted fans have given rise to many internet slang words and memes. One example of fandom internet language is 我可以单身，但是我喜欢的CP一定要在一起. This expression is commonly used by CP粉 (CP fěn; fans of character pairings and celebrity couples) to emphasize how important their favored pairings are to them. The terms CP and 粉 are also examples of the prevalence of English abbreviations and transliterations in Chinese internet language, particularly among younger generations.

> **Reflection**

<u>A</u> **Discussion:** Ask and answer the following questions with your classmates. INTERPERSONAL

1 你看过恋爱综艺节目或者别的真人秀 (zhēn rén xiù; reality show) 吗？你喜欢看真人秀吗？为什么？

2 如果有机会 (jīhuì; opportunity)，你想不想上真人秀 (zhēn rén xiù; reality show)？为什么？

<u>B</u> **Research and Reflect:** Investigate one of the questions below. Present your thoughts and findings in Chinese, using the supplemental vocabulary and/or consulting a dictionary for additional words as needed. PRESENTATIONAL

1 哪几种综艺节目现在在中国最受欢迎？如果你们国家 (guójiā; country) 也有这几种节目，它们和中国的节目有什么一样和不一样的地方？如果没有，你觉得这几种节目在你们国家会受欢迎吗？

2 请介绍几个中文网络流行语 (wǎngluò liúxíngyǔ; internet slang)，说说它们是什么意思、可以怎么用。

Thought-provoking questions foster **interpretive, interpersonal, and presentational** communication.

<u>C</u> **Further Exploration:** Extend your knowledge by looking into the following questions.

1 Consider the psychology of reality shows — how does watching them impact people's perceptions of self, relationships, and societal norms? What emotional factors contribute to their appeal?

2 The National Radio and Television Administration (广电总局) has played a key role in shaping the media landscape in China. One example is its support for including ordinary citizens in programs, which contributes to a more diverse representation of society in entertainment. Is there a comparable institution in your country? What do you see as the advantages and disadvantages of such regulatory bodies?

> **Pinyin of the Text**

Liàn'ài zōngyì wèishéme zhème shòu huānyíng?

Gāo Shūwén

Zuìjìn jǐ nián, liàn'ài zōngyì (yě jiù shì liàn zōng) zài Zhōngguó hěn shòu huānyíng. Xiànzài chúle yǒu sùrén liàn zōng hé míngxīng liàn zōng yǐwài, hái yǒu míngxīng hé sùrén yuēhuì de liàn zōng. Lìngwài, yǒu xiē dàxuéshēng hái huì zìjǐ zài xuéxiào lǐ zuò "liàn zōng". Nà wèishéme yǒu zhème duō rén xǐhuan kàn zhè zhǒng jiémù ne? Wǒmen lái tīng ting jǐ wèi píngcháng xǐhuan kàn liàn zōng de guānzhòng shì zěnme shuō de.

Yí wèi míng jiào Wénwen de dānshēn dàxuéshēng gàosu wǒmen, "Wǒ kěyǐ dānshēn, dànshì wǒ xǐhuan de CP (Yīngwén 'couple' de suōxiě) yídìng yào zài yìqǐ!" Tā shuō tā kàn dào jiémù lǐ biérén yuēhuì, zìjǐ yě juéde hěn tián. Tā kàn dào jiémù lǐ de rén chùqù lǐxíng, jiù juéde zìjǐ hǎoxiàng yě qù "lǚxíng" le. Gēn Wénwen bǐ, gāng gōngzuò de Xiǎo Dōng gèng xǐhuan kàn liàn zōng lǐ de nà xiē "chōngtū". Tā shuō, "Nà xiē chōngtū yǒude shíhou shì yīnwèi shéi děi dǎsǎo hé zhěnglǐ fángjiān, yǒude shíhou shì yīnwèi liǎ rén dōu xiǎng gēn tóng yí ge rén yuēhuì . . . Fēicháng yǒu yìsi!" Tā hái shuō zài liàn zōng lǐ tā néng zhǎo dào gēn zìjǐ hěn xiàng de rén, zhǎo dào gòngmíng, érqiě hái kěyǐ cóng jiémù lǐ xué dào nà xiē dōngxi, ràng zìjǐ de EQ gèng gāo.

Yīnwèi zhè jǐ nián liàn zōng hěn shòu huānyíng, yǒude sùrén shàng wán jiémù yǐhòu zìjǐ yě chéng le "míngxīng". Zhè ràng guānzhòng juéde, xiànzài yǒude sùrén shàng liàn zōng jiù shì xiǎng gěi guānzhòng yí ge hǎo yìnxiàng, suǒyǐ tāmen yuēhuì de shíhou jiù xiàng yǎn diànyǐng yíyàng, bú gòu zhēnshí. Lìngwài, zhè jǐ nián liàn zōng yuè lái yuè duō, Guǎngdiàn Zǒngjú huì bú huì juéde zhè shì ge wèntí? Liàn zōng hái néng shòu huānyíng jǐ nián? Xiànzài, wǒmen hái bù zhīdào.

A cameraman shoots a street scene for a Chinese reality TV show in Hong Kong

Student and Teacher Online Course

Our FluencyLink™ digital learning platform has been redesigned to make the user experience more integrated and intuitive. All screenshots are from the Teacher Online Course.

Organization and Navigation

Content **organized by lesson section** follows the book's instructional sequence.

Easily navigate to the page of your instructional focus.

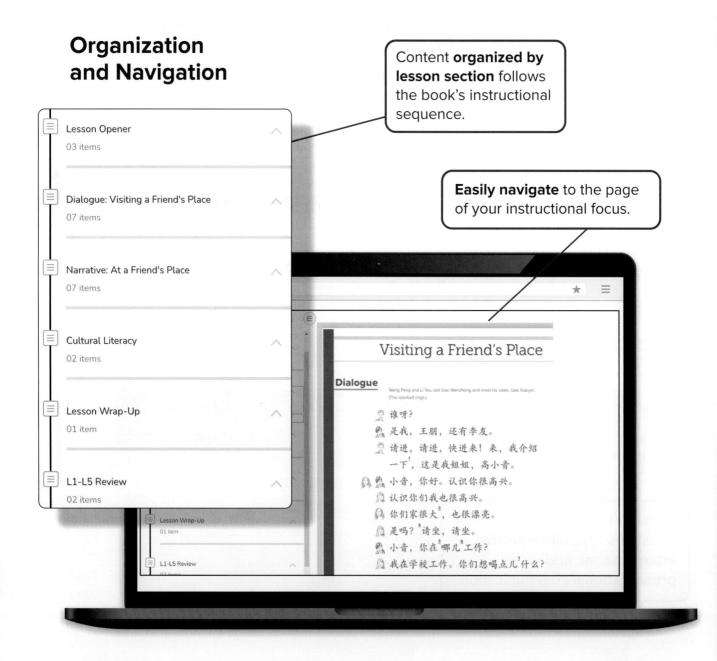

Lesson Opener
03 items

Dialogue: Visiting a Friend's Place
07 items

Narrative: At a Friend's Place
07 items

Cultural Literacy
02 items

Lesson Wrap-Up
01 item

L1-L5 Review
02 items

Lesson Wrap-Up
01 item

L1-L5 Review
02 items

Visiting a Friend's Place

Dialogue

Weng Peng and Li You visit Gao Wenzhong and meet his sister, Gao Xiaoyin. (The doorbell rings.)

谁呀？

是我，王朋，还有李友。

请进，请进，快进来！来，我介绍一下，这是我姐姐，高小音。

小音，你好。认识你很高兴。

认识你我也很高兴。

你们家很大，也很漂亮。

是吗？请坐，请坐。

小音，你在哪儿工作？

我在学校工作。你们想喝点儿什么？

Workbook Activities

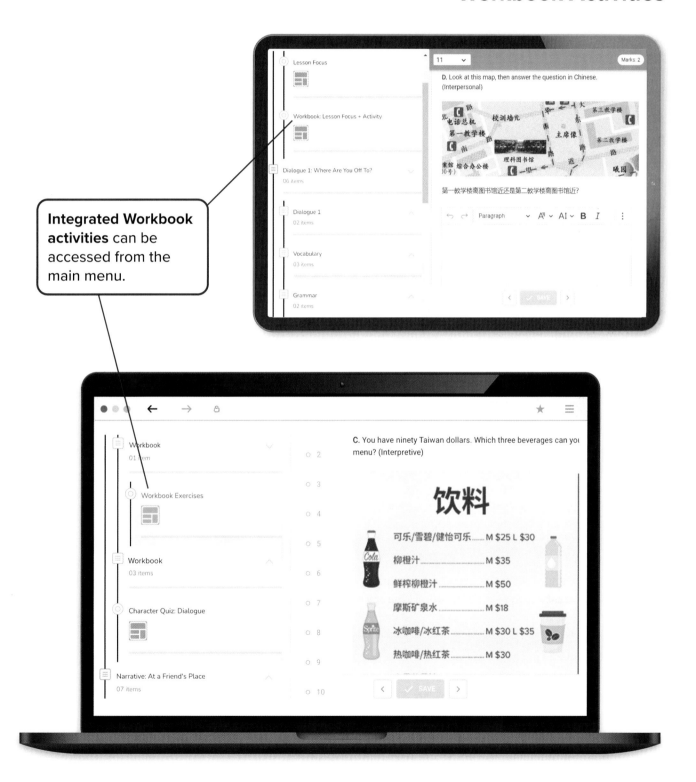

Integrated Workbook activities can be accessed from the main menu.

Preface*

The *Integrated Chinese* (IC) series is an internationally acclaimed Mandarin Chinese language course that delivers a cohesive system of print and digital resources for highly effective teaching and learning. First published in 1997, it is now the leading series of Chinese language learning resources in the United States and beyond. Through its holistic focus on the language skills of listening, speaking, reading, and writing, IC teaches novice and intermediate students the skills they need to function in Chinese.

What's New

It has been over eight years since the publication of the Third Edition of IC. We are deeply grateful for all the positive feedback, as well as constructive suggestions for improvement, from IC users. In the meantime, China and the world have seen significant transformations in electronic communications, commerce, and media. Additionally, the technology available to us is transforming the way teachers and students interact with content. The teaching of Chinese as a second language needs to keep pace with these exciting developments. Therefore, the time seems right to update IC across delivery formats.

In developing this latest edition of IC, we have consulted the American Council on the Teaching of Foreign Languages (ACTFL) *21st Century Skills Map for World Languages*. The national standards for foreign language learning in the 21st century focus on goals in five areas—communication, cultures, connections, comparisons, and communities. In addition to classifying the applicable **Language Practice** activities by communication mode (interpersonal, interpretive, and presentational), we have added a host of materials that address the 5 Cs. The delivery of IC via **Cheng & Tsui FluencyLink™,** Cheng & Tsui's online learning platform, elevates the teaching and learning experience by presenting multimedia and interactive content in a truly blended and integrated way.

New, visually rich supplementary modules that recur in each lesson have been introduced. These can be taught in any sequence to serve as prompts for classroom discussion and student reflection:

- **Get Real with Chinese** draws on realia to situate language learning in real-life contexts. Students are required to analyze, predict, and synthesize before coming to conclusions about embedded linguistic and cultural meaning. Photos and questions connect the classroom to authentic Chinese experiences. To familiarize students with both character sets, students are exposed to realia in simplified characters and realia in traditional characters.

- **Chinese Chat** provides opportunities for language practice in the digital environment. Realistic texting, microblogging, and social media scenarios show students how the younger generation has adapted Chinese to new communication technologies.

- **Characterize It!** encourages students to approach Chinese characters analytically. Additional activities are provided on FluencyLink™.

- While not a new segment, **How About You?** has been revamped for the Fourth Edition. This module encourages students to personalize their study of vocabulary and learn words and phrases that relate to their own interests and background. Questions now appear in both Chinese and English, while visual cues, which typically correspond to possible answers, promote vocabulary expansion and retention. Vocabulary items corresponding to the visual cues are listed in a separate index.

Moreover, to promote students' awareness of cultural diversity in a world of rapid globalization, we have included **Compare & Contrast** activities in the **Cultural Literacy** (formerly Culture Highlights) section. This section as a whole has been given a lavishly illustrated, magazine-style treatment to better engage students. Users who subscribe to FluencyLink™ will have access to additional cultural content related to the lesson themes.

We have also updated the **Grammar** section to include exercises tailored to each grammar point, so students can immediately put into practice the language forms they have just learned. Additional practice exercises for each grammar point are accessible via FluencyLink™.

Keeping It Casual (formerly That's How the Chinese Say It!) remains a review of functional expressions after Lessons 15 and 20 that encourages students to build their own personalized list of useful expressions.

Finally, the new **Lesson Wrap-Up** section includes context-based tasks that prepare students to communicate with native Chinese speakers. Also in this section are **Make It Flow!** exercises, which help students develop and apply

*Please note that this is the original fourth edition authors' Preface.

strategies to organize information coherently and cohesively in written and spoken discourse. We created this activity to address the common phenomenon of novice and intermediate students speaking in choppy, isolated sentences. The ultimate purpose of acquiring a language is communication, and a hallmark of effective communication is the ability to produce continuous discourse. The **Lesson Wrap-Up** activities are intended as assessment instruments for the **Can-Do Checklist**, which encourages students to measure their progress at the end of the lesson.

As previous users of IC will note, we have renamed the four-volume series. The new sequencing of Volumes 1 to 4 better reflects the flexibility of the materials and the diversity of our user groups and their instructional environments. However, we also recognize that Volumes 1 and 2 are often used together in the first year of language instruction, and Volumes 3 and 4 in the second. Thus, for ease of reference, we have retained the sequencing of the lessons from 1 to 20 in each half of the series.

As with the Third Edition, the Fourth Edition of IC features both traditional and simplified character versions of the Volume 1 and 2 textbooks and workbooks, and a combination of traditional and simplified characters in the Volume 3 and 4 textbooks and workbooks. However, in response to user feedback, we have updated the traditional characters to ensure they match the standard set used in Taiwan. For reference, we have consulted the Taiwan Ministry of Education's online *Revised Chinese Dictionary*.

The most significant change in the Fourth Edition is the incorporation of innovative educational technology. Users of the print edition have access to audio (available on FluencyLink), while subscribers to FluencyLink have access to streaming audio plus additional, interactive content.

Users who choose to subscribe to the FluencyLink online learning platform will have access to:

- The Workbook (with auto-grading)
- The fully-downloadable Character Workbook
- Audio (Textbook and Workbook)
- Audio recording for teacher feedback
- Video of the lesson texts
- Additional cultural content

In addition to student subscriptions, teacher subscriptions are also available for FluencyLink. The teacher subscription to FluencyLink conveniently makes connections between the Textbook and the additional resources provided in the Teacher's Resources, such as video activity sheets, quizzes, and answer keys.

A key feature of FluencyLink is coherence. The innovative instructional design provides an integrated user experience, with multiple options for integration and Single Sign-on (SSO). Learners can move seamlessly between the transmission, practice, application, and evaluation stages, navigating the content to suit their particular learning needs and styles. For more information and a free trial, please visit cheng-tsui.com.

Both in its print and digital versions, the new IC features a contemporary layout that adds clarity and rigor to its instructional design. Rich new visuals complement the text's revised, user-friendly language and up-to-date cultural content. We hope that students and teachers find the many changes and new features timely and meaningful.

Organizational Principles

In the higher education setting, the IC series often covers two years of instruction, with smooth transitions from one level to the next. The lessons first cover topics from everyday life, then gradually move to more abstract subject matter. The materials do not follow one pedagogical methodology, but instead blend several effective teaching approaches. Used in conjunction with FluencyLink, incorporating differentiated instruction, blended learning, and the flipped classroom is even easier. Here are some of the features of IC that distinguish it from other Chinese language resources:

Integrating Pedagogy and Authenticity

We believe that students should be taught authentic materials even in their first year of language instruction. Therefore, authentic materials (produced by native Chinese speakers for native Chinese speakers) are included in every lesson.

Integrating Traditional and Simplified Characters

We believe that students should learn both traditional and simplified Chinese characters. However, we also realize that teaching students both forms from day one could be overwhelming. In the higher education setting, the IC series often covers two years of instruction, with the first two volumes usually used in the first year of study, and the final two volumes in the second. Therefore, the first two volumes of IC are available in separate traditional and simplified versions, with the alternative character forms of the texts included in the Appendix.

By their second year of study, we believe that all students should be exposed to both forms of written Chinese. Accordingly, the final two volumes of IC include both traditional and simplified characters. Students in second-year Chinese language classes come from different backgrounds, and should be allowed to write in their preferred form. However, it is important that the learner write in one form only, and not a mix of both.

Integrating Teaching Approaches

Because no single teaching method can adequately train a student in all language skills, we employ a variety of approaches in IC. In addition to the communicative approach, we also use traditional methods such as grammar-translation and the direct method.

Users of FluencyLink can employ additional teaching approaches, such as differentiated learning and blended learning. Students can self-pace their learning, which is a very powerful instructional intervention. The product also facilitates breaking down direct instruction into more engaging "bites" of learning, which improves student engagement. Moreover, FluencyLink allows students to interact with the content at home and practice and apply their learning in the classroom with corrective teacher feedback, which has the potential to improve student outcomes. Additionally, teachers and learners do not need to follow the instructional flow of the underlying book. They can navigate using multiple pathways in flexible and customized ways and at varying paces for true individualized learning.

Acknowledgments

We would like to thank users around the world for believing in IC. We owe much of the continued success of IC to their invaluable feedback. Likewise, we would be remiss if we did not acknowledge the University of Notre Dame for sponsoring and inviting us to a one-day workshop on IC on April 9, 2016. Leading Chinese-language specialists from across the country shared their experiences with the IC authors. We are especially indebted to Professor Yongping Zhu, Chair of the Department of East Asian Languages and Cultures at Notre Dame, and his colleagues and staff for organizing the workshop.

Professors Fangpei Cai and Meng Li of the University of Chicago took time out from their busy teaching schedules to compile a detailed list of comments and suggestions. We are profoundly touched by their generosity. In completing this Fourth Edition, we have taken into consideration their and other users' recommendations for revision. Indeed, many of the changes are in response to user feedback. The authors are naturally responsible for any remaining shortcomings and oversights.

For two summers in a row, Professor Liangyan Ge's wife, Ms. Yongqing Pan, warmly invited the IC team to their home to complete the bulk of the work of revising the IC series. Words are inadequate to express our thanks to Ms. Pan for her gracious hospitality and her superb cooking day in and day out.

We are deeply grateful to our publisher Cheng & Tsui Company and to Jill Cheng in particular for her unswerving support for IC over the years. We would also like to express our heartfelt appreciation to our editor Ben Shragge and his colleagues for their meticulous attention to every aspect of this new edition.

As we look back on the evolution of IC, one person is never far from our thoughts. Without Professor Tao-chung Yao's commitment from its inception, IC would not have been possible. Sadly, Professor Yao passed away in September 2015. Throughout the summer, Professor Yao remained in close contact with the rest of the team, going over each draft of IC 1 with an eagle eye, providing us with the benefit of his wisdom by phone and email. This Fourth Edition of IC is a living tribute to his vision and guidance.

Note: Prefaces to the previous editions of IC are available at cheng-tsui.com.

Lesson Structure

All components of IC (Textbooks, Workbooks, and Teacher's Resources) are considered core and are designed to be used together to enhance teaching and learning. Recurrent lesson subsections are highlighted in the Textbook Elements column. Note that Supplementary Modules do not compose a separate section, but are rather discrete entities that appear throughout each lesson.

Section	Textbook Elements	Interactive Content	Workbooks	Teacher's Resources
Lesson Opener	• Learning Objectives state what students will be able to do by the end of the lesson • Relate & Get Ready helps students reflect on similarities and differences between Chinese culture and their own		• Opportunity for students to revisit learning objectives and self-assess	• Overview of language functions, vocabulary, grammar, pronunciation, and characters taught in the lesson • Sequencing recommendations and teaching aids
Text	• Two Chinese lesson texts demonstrate practical vocabulary and grammar usage • *Pinyin* versions of the texts provide pronunciation support • Language Notes elaborate on important structures and phrases in the lesson texts	• Audio builds receptive skills • Video provides insight into non-verbal cues and communication plus context through authentic settings	• Listening comprehension and speaking exercises based on the dialogues • Reading comprehension	• Strategies for teaching the lesson texts, plus question prompts • Dialogues as narratives • Pre- and post-video viewing activity worksheets and scripts
Vocabulary	• Vocabulary lists define and categorize new words from the lesson texts (proper nouns are listed last)	• Audio models proper pronunciation • Flashcards assist with vocabulary acquisition	• Handwriting and stroke order practice is provided in the Character Workbook • All exercises use lesson vocabulary to support acquisition	• Explanations, pronunciation tips, usage notes, and phrasal combinations • Vocabulary slideshows
Grammar	• Grammar points, which correspond to numbered references in the readings, explain and model language forms • Exercises allow students to practice the grammar points immediately	• Additional exercises deepen knowledge of the language	• Writing and grammar exercises based on grammar introduced in the lesson	• Explanations, pattern practice, and additional grammar notes • Grammar slideshows

Section	Textbook Elements	Interactive Content	Workbooks	Teacher's Resources
Language Practice	• Role-plays, pair activities, contextualized drills, and colorful cues prompt students to produce language		• Exercises and activities spanning the three modes of communication (interpersonal, interpretive, and presentational), plus *pinyin* and tone practice, to build communication and performance skills	• Student presentations, integrative practice, and additional practice activities • Additional activities categorized by macro-skill
Cultural Literacy	• Culture notes provide snapshots of contemporary and traditional Chinese-speaking cultures • Compare & Contrast draws connections between cultures	• Additional content further develops cultural literacy of the lesson theme	• Authentic materials to develop predictive skills	• Background notes expand on the section
Lesson Wrap-Up	• Make It Flow! develops students' ability to produce smooth discourse • Projects encourage review and recycling of lesson materials through different text types • Can-Do Checklist allows students to assess their fulfillment of the learning objectives			• Teaching tips for implementing self-diagnostic activities, answer keys for Make it Flow!, additional Make It Flow! exercises, and additional sample quizzes and tests • Slideshows that summarize content introduced in the lesson
Supplementary Modules	• How About You? encourages students to personalize their vocabulary • Get Real with Chinese teaches students to predict meaning from context • Characterize It! explores the structure of Chinese characters • Chinese Chat demonstrates how language is used in text messaging and social media	• Additional Characterize It! exercises increase understanding of characters		• Teaching tips and strategies for fully exploiting and implementing these new elements

Digital Assets

 Lesson Text, Vocabulary, Pronunciation
Audio

 Lesson Text, Culture Minute
Video

 **Characterize It!**
More characters

 Grammar
More exercises

 Vocabulary
Flashcards

 Cultural Literacy
Cultural Literacy

Scope and Sequence

Lesson	Learning Objectives	Grammar	Cultural Literacy
11 Weather	· Talk about the weather in basic terms · Compare weather in two places · Talk about what you can do in nice or bad weather · Present a simple weather forecast	1. Comparative sentences using 比 (bǐ) (I) 2. The particle 了 (le) (III): 了 as a sentence-final particle 3. The modal verb 会 (huì) (will) (II) 4. Adjective + （一）点儿 ([yì] diǎnr) (a bit) 5. The adverb 又 (yòu) (again) 6. Adjective/verb + 是 (shì) + adjective/verb + 可是／但是··· (kěshì/dànshì...)	· Place name transliteration · Weather · Units of measurement · Weather records
12 Dining	· Ask if there are seats available at a restaurant · Order some Chinese dishes · Describe your dietary preferences and restrictions · Ask for recommendations · Rush your order · Pay for your meal and get change	1. 一···也／都···不／没··· (yī...yě/dōu...bù/méi...) 2. 多／少 (duō/shǎo) + verb 3. Comparing 刚 (gāng) (just) and 刚才 (gāngcái) (just now) 4. Resultative complements (I) 5. 好 (hǎo) as a resultative complement 6. Adjective reduplication (I) 7. The verb 来 (lái)	· Four major schools of cooking · Utensils · Localization · Vegetarianism
13 Asking Directions	· Ask for and give directions · Identify locations by using landmarks as references · Describe whether two places are close to or far away from each other · State where you are heading and the reason for going there	1. Direction and location words 2. Comparative sentences using 没（有） (méi[yǒu]) 3. Indicating degree using 那么 (nàme) 4. 到 (dào) + place + 去 (qù) + action 5. The dynamic particle 过 (guo) 6. Verb reduplication (I) 7. Resultative complements (II) 8. 一···就··· (yī...jiù...) (as soon as...then...)	· Feng shui · Chinatown · Casual greetings · Urban planning
14 Birthday Party	· Ask a friend to go to a party with you · Suggest things to bring to a get-together · Thank people for gifts · Describe a duration of time · Talk about the year of your birth and your Chinese zodiac sign	1. Indicating an action in progress using 呢 (ne) 2. Verbal phrases and subject-predicate phrases used as attributives 3. Time duration (I) 4. Sentences with 是···的 (shì...de) (I) 5. 还 (hái) (still) 6. 又···又··· (yòu...yòu...) (both...and...)	· Chinese zodiac · Karaoke · Gift giving · Party etiquette

Lesson	Learning Objectives	Grammar	Cultural Literacy
15 Seeing a Doctor	• Describe common cold and allergy symptoms • Understand instructions on when and how often to take medications • Talk about why you do or don't want to see the doctor • Urge others to see a doctor when they are not feeling well	1. Indicating an extreme degree using 死 *(sǐ)* 2. Indicating the beginning of an action using 起来 *(qi lai)* 3. 次 *(cì)* for frequency 4. The 把 *(bǎ)* construction (I) 5. The preposition 对 *(duì)* (to, for) 6. 越来越··· *(yuè lái yuè...)* (more and more...) 7. The conjunction 再说 *(zàishuō)* (moreover)	• Chinese medicine • Seeing the doctor • Medical care • Hua Tuo
Keeping It Casual (L11–L15)	• Review functional expressions	1. 在 *(zài)* (to exist) 2. Complimentary expressions 3. 怎么了? *(Zěnme le?)* (What's the matter? What's wrong?) 4. 糟糕 *(zāogāo)* ([it's] awful/what a mess)	
16 Dating	• Describe how long you've known someone • Ask someone out on a date • Make arrangements to go out with friends • Accept or gently decline a date • End a phone conversation politely	1. Descriptive complements (II) 2. Potential complements (I) 3. 就 *(jiù)* (only, just) 4. Directional complements (II)	• Marriage • Dates • Saving face • Matchmaking corners
17 Renting an Apartment	• Describe your current and ideal dwellings • Name common pieces of furniture • State how long you have been living at your current residence • Explain why a place is or isn't right for someone • Discuss and negotiate rent, utilities, and security deposits	1. Verb + 了 *(le)* + numeral + measure word + noun + 了 *(le)* 2. 连···都/也··· *(lián... dōu/yě...)* 3. Potential complements (II) 4. Indicating an approximate number using 多 *(duō)* 5. Question pronouns using 都/也 *(dōu/yě)*	• Dorms • Apartments • Pets
18 Sports	• Name and discuss some popular sports • Talk about your exercise habits • Compare soccer and American football in simple terms	1. Duration of inactivity 2. 好/难 *(hǎo/nán)* + verb 3. Indicating continuation using 下去 *(xia qu)* 4. Duration of activity (II) 5. The particle 着 *(zhe)* 6. Passive-voice sentences using 被/叫/让 *(bèi/jiào/ràng)*	• Popular sports • Morning exercises • *Cuju* • Diet and weight

Lesson	Learning Objectives	Grammar	Cultural Literacy
19 Travel	· Talk about your plans for summer break · Describe what kind of city Beijing is · Describe your travel itinerary · Ask for discounts, compare airfares and routes, and book airplane tickets · Ask about seat assignments and request meal accommodations based on your dietary restrictions or preferences	1. 不得了 *(bùdéliǎo)* (extremely) 2. Question pronouns as indefinite references (whoever, whatever, etc.) 3. Numbers over one thousand 4. Comparative sentences using 比 *(bǐ)* (II)	· Rail travel · Travel agencies · Airlines · Attitudes toward travel
20 At the Airport	· Check in at the airport · Wish departing friends a safe journey and remind them to keep in touch · Greet guests at the airport · Compliment someone's language ability · Ask about someone's health · Take leave of someone	1. Comparing 的 *(de)*, 得 *(de)*, and 地 *(de)* 2. The 把 construction (II) 3. ···的时候 *(... de shíhou)* and ···以后 *(... yǐhòu)* compared 4. 还 *(hái)* + positive adjective 5. Kinship terms	· Flying domestic · Beijing roast duck
Keeping It Casual (L16–L20)	· Review functional expressions	1. 一言为定 *(yì yán wéi dìng)* (it's a deal, it's decided) 2. Good, very good, excellent, and extraordinary 3. Greetings 4. Farewells 5. Mealtime expressions	

Abbreviations of Grammatical Terms

adj	adjective	**pr**	pronoun
adv	adverb	**prefix**	prefix
conj	conjunction	**prep**	preposition
interj	interjection	**qp**	question particle
m	measure word	**qpr**	question pronoun
mv	modal verb	**t**	time word
n	noun	**v**	verb
nu	numeral	**vc**	verb plus complement
p	particle	**vo**	verb plus object
pn	proper noun		

Cast of Characters

Wang Peng
王朋

A Chinese freshman from Beijing. He has quickly adapted to American college life and likes to play and watch sports.

Li You
李友

Amy Lee, an American student from New York State. She and Wang Peng meet each other on the first day of classes and soon become good friends.

Gao Wenzhong
高文中

Winston Gore, an English student. His parents work in the United States. Winston enjoys singing, dancing, and Chinese cooking. He has a secret crush on Bai Ying'ai.

Bai Ying'ai
白英爱

Baek Yeung Ae, an outgoing Korean student from Seoul. She finds Wang Peng very "cool" and very "cute."

Gao Xiaoyin
高小音

Jenny Gore, Winston's older sister. She has already graduated from college, and is now a school librarian.

Chang Laoshi
常老师

Chang Xiaoliang, originally from China and in her forties. She has been teaching Chinese in the United States for ten years.

Wang Hong
王红

Wang Peng's younger sister. She is preparing to attend college in America.

Wang Peng's parents
王朋的父母

From Beijing, in their late forties.

Hailun
海伦

Helen, Gao Wenzhong's cousin. She has a one-year-old son, Tom.

Fei Xiansheng
费先生

Owen Fields, Gao Xiaoyin's high school classmate.

天气

Tiānqì

WEATHER

Learning Objectives	Relate & Get Ready

In this lesson, you will learn to:

- Talk about the weather in basic terms
- Compare weather in two places
- Talk about what you can do in nice or bad weather
- Present a simple weather forecast

In your own culture/community:

- What is the typical weather in spring, summer, autumn, and winter?
- Where do people get weather information?
- What weather-dependent outdoor sports are popular, if any?
- How do people feel about rain or snow?

Tomorrow's Weather Will Be Even Better!

Dialogue 1

Audio

Video

（高小音跟弟弟高文中聊到天气……）

 今天天气比[1]*昨天好，不下雪了[2]。

我约了朋友明天去公园滑冰，不知道
天气会[3]怎么样，冷不冷？

我刚才看了网上的天气预报，明天天气
比今天更好。不但不会下雪，而且[a]会
暖和一点儿[4]。

是吗？太好了！

你约了谁去滑冰？

白英爱。

你约了白英爱？可是她今天早上坐飞机
去纽约了。

真的啊？那我明天怎么办？

你还是在家看电视吧！

---

* Here and throughout the book, the blue lesson text and numbers correspond to explanations in the **Grammar section**.

 (Gāo Xiǎoyīn gēn dìdi Gāo Wénzhōng liáo dào tiānqì . . .)

 Jīntiān tiānqì bǐ^1 zuótiān hǎo, bú xià xuě le^2.

 Wǒ yuē le péngyou míngtiān qù gōngyuán huá bīng, bù zhīdào tiānqì huì^3 zěnmeyàng, lěng bu lěng?

 Wǒ gāngcái kàn le wǎng shang de tiānqì yùbào, míngtiān tiānqì bǐ jīntiān gèng hǎo. Búdàn bú huì xià xuě, érqiě^a huì nuǎnhuo yì diǎnr^4.

 Shì ma? Tài hǎo le!

 Nǐ yuē le shéi qù huá bīng?

 Bái Yīng'ài.

 Nǐ yuē le Bái Yīng'ài? Kěshì tā jīntiān zǎoshang zuò fēijī qù Niǔyuē le.

 Zhēn de a? Nà wǒ míngtiān zěnme bàn?

Nǐ háishi zài jiā kàn diànshì ba!

Language Note

a 不但 (búdàn)···, 而且 (érqiě)···

In a sentence with the 不但 (búdàn)···, 而且 (érqiě)··· (not only . . . , but also . . .) structure, the conjunction 而且 (érqiě) in the second clause is generally required, while the conjunction 不但 (búdàn) in the first clause is optional.

Vocabulary

Audio

Flashcards

No.	Word	Pinyin	Part of Speech	Definition
1	天气	tiānqì	n	weather
2	比	bǐ	prep/v	compared with (comparison marker); to compare [See Grammar 1.]
3	下雪	xià xuě	vo	to snow
4	约	yuē	v	to make an appointment
5	公园	gōngyuán	n	park
6	滑冰	huá bīng	vo	to ice skate
7	会	huì	mv	will [See Grammar 3.]
8	冷	lěng	adj	cold
9	刚才	gāngcái	t	just now, a moment ago
10	网上	wǎng shang		on the Internet
11	预报	yùbào	v/n	to forecast; forecast
12	更	gèng	adv	even more
13	不但···, 而且···	búdàn..., érqiě...	conj	not only..., but also...
14	暖和	nuǎnhuo	adj	warm
15	办	bàn	v	to handle, to do

You're in line to board your flight to Harbin, and you open up the weather app on your tablet. What are the chances that snow will fall during your trip? Can you identify any other details from the forecast?

GET Real WITH CHINESE

哈尔滨市

−20° 阴

今天有雪,天寒地冻,千万裹严实点!

湿度 79%　风力 2级

53 良

-15 | -24℃

明天 优
多云

今天 优
阵雪转多云

天气

15天预报

优

优

阵雪

多云

优

晴

轻

晴

你们那儿天气
怎么样?

Nǐmen nàr tiānqì zěnmeyàng?
How's the weather over there?

我们这儿 ＿＿＿＿＿＿＿。
Wǒmen zhèr ＿＿＿＿＿＿＿ .

See index for corresponding vocabulary or research another term.

How About You?

Grammar

Comparative sentences using 比 (bǐ) (I)

You can use the pattern below to compare two entities.

X + 比 (bǐ) + Y + adjective

A 李友比她大姐高。

Lǐ Yǒu bǐ tā dàjiě gāo.

Li You is taller than her oldest sister.

B 今天比昨天冷。

Jīntiān bǐ zuótiān lěng.

Today is colder than yesterday.

C 第十课的语法比第九课的语法容易。

Dì shí kè de yǔfǎ bǐ dì jiǔ kè de yǔfǎ róngyì.

The grammar in Lesson Ten is easier than the grammar in Lesson Nine.

There are two ways in which the basic comparative construction can be further modified: the first is by adding a qualifying expression after the adjective, as shown in the following pattern. Note that the modifying expression must be placed *after* the adjective, not before it.

X + 比 (bǐ) + Y + adjective + 一点儿 (yì diǎnr)/得多 (de duō)/多了 (duō le)

D 今天比昨天冷一点儿。

Jīntiān bǐ zuótiān lěng yì diǎnr.

Today is a little colder than yesterday.

[✗ 今天比昨天一点儿冷。]

E 明天会比今天冷得多。

Míngtiān huì bǐ jīntiān lěng de duō.

Tomorrow will be much colder than today.

F 纽约比这儿冷多了／冷得多。

Niǔyuē bǐ zhèr lěng duō le/lěng de duō.

New York is much colder than here.

[⊗ 纽约比这儿很冷。]

Note that "much colder" is 冷多了 *(lěng duō le)* or 冷得多 *(lěng de duō)*, not 很冷 *(hěn lěng)* (very cold).

The second way to modify the basic comparative construction is by adding the adverb 更 *(gèng)* or the adverb 还 *(hái) before* the adjective, as shown in the following pattern.

X + 比 *(bǐ)* + Y + 更 *(gèng)*/还 *(hái)* + adjective

G 昨天冷，今天比昨天更冷／今天比昨天还冷。

Zuótiān lěng, jīntiān bǐ zuótiān gèng lěng/jīntiān bǐ zuótiǎn hái lěng.

Yesterday was cold. Today is even colder than yesterday.

跟 *(gēn)* and 和 *(hé)* can also be used to form a comparative sentence, as shown in the pattern below.

X + 跟 *(gēn)*/和 *(hé)* + Y + (不)一样 *([bù] yíyàng)* + adjective

However, unlike a comparative sentence using 比 *(bǐ)*, a comparative sentence using 跟 *(gēn)* or 和 *(hé)* only indicates whether two entities do or don't exhibit an attribute to the same degree. Compare (H) with (I) and (J) with (K).

H 这个教室和那个教室一样大。

Zhè ge jiàoshì hé nà ge jiàoshì yíyàng dà.

This classroom and that classroom are the same size.

I 这个教室跟那个教室不一样大。

Zhè ge jiàoshì gēn nà ge jiàoshì bù yíyàng dà.

This classroom and that classroom are not the same size.

J 这个教室比那个教室大。

Zhè ge jiàoshì bǐ nà ge jiàoshì dà.

This classroom is larger than that classroom.

K 这个教室比那个教室大得多。

Zhè ge jiàoshì bǐ nà ge jiàoshì dà de duō.

This classroom is much larger than that classroom.

More exercises

EXERCISES

Turn the following sentences into comparative statements, inserting 比 where appropriate. Use exercise 1 as an example.

1 今天的天气好，昨天的天气不好。

→ 今天的天气比昨天的好。

2 我的衣服贵，你的衣服不贵。

3 一月冷，十二月不冷。

2 | **The particle 了 *(le)* (III): 了 as a sentence-final particle**

When 了 *(le)* occurs at the end of a sentence, it usually indicates a change of status or the realization of a new situation. [See also Grammar 5, Lesson 5, and Grammar 5, Lesson 8, Volume 1.]

A 下雪了。

Xià xuě le.

It's snowing (now).

B 妹妹累了。

Mèimei lèi le.

My sister is tired (now).

C 我昨天没有空儿，今天有空儿了。

Wǒ zuótiān méiyǒu kòngr, jīntiān yǒu kòngr le.

I didn't have time yesterday, but I do today.

D 你看，公共汽车来了。

Nǐ kàn, gōnggòng qìchē lái le.

Look, the bus is here.

When used in this sense, 了 *(le)* can still be used at the end of a negative sentence.

E 我没有钱了，不买了。

Wǒ méiyǒu qián le, bù mǎi le.

I don't have any money left. I won't buy it anymore.

To negate 有 (*yǒu*) (to have), use 没 (*méi*), rather than 不 (*bù*).

EXERCISES

More exercises

Answer the questions using 了 to suggest a change in state. Use exercise 1 as an example.

1 四月了，你们那儿冷吗？（不冷）

→ 我们这儿不冷了。

2 已经十二点半了，你饿不饿？（饿）

3 这种样子的裤子你们上个星期没有中号的，
这个星期呢？（有）

---

3   **The modal verb 会 (*huì*) (will) (II)**

会 (*huì*) (will) indicates an anticipated event or action. [See also Grammar 9, Lesson 8.]

A 白老师现在不在办公室，可是他明天会在。

Bái lǎoshī xiànzài bú zài bàngōngshì, kěshì tā míngtiān huì zài.

Teacher Bai is not in the office now, but he will be tomorrow.

B Q: 你明年做什么？   A: 我明年会去英国学英文。

Nǐ míngnián zuò shénme?   *Wǒ míngnián huì qù Yīngguó xué Yīngwén.*

What are you going to do next year?   I'm going to Britain to study English next year.

C 他说他晚上会给你发短信。

Tā shuō tā wǎnshang huì gěi nǐ fā duǎnxìn.

He said he'll send you a text message in the evening.

The negative form of 会 (*huì*) is 不会 (*bú huì*).

D 小王觉得不舒服，今天不会来滑冰了。

Xiǎo Wáng juéde bù shūfu, jīntiān bú huì lái huá bīng le.

Little Wang is not feeling well. He won't come ice skating today after all.

E 她这几天特别忙，晚上不会去听音乐会。

Tā zhè jǐ tiān tèbié máng, wǎnshang bú huì qù tīng yīnyuèhuì.

She's very busy these days. She won't be going to the concert tonight.

F 天气预报说这个周末不会下雪。

Tiānqì yùbào shuō zhè ge zhōumò bú huì xià xuě.

The weather forecast says that it won't snow this weekend.

More exercises

EXERCISES

Answer the questions using 会 or 不会 where appropriate. Use exercise 1 as an example.

1 你明天会去看电影吗？（我明天很忙……）

→ 我明天很忙，不会去看电影。

2 明天会下雪吗？（明天天气很好……）

3 你今年夏天会去中国学习中文吗？（我今年夏天不在美国学校上课……）

4 | Adjective + （一）点儿 *([yì] diǎnr)* **(a bit)**

The expression （一）点儿 *([yì] diǎnr)* (a bit) can be placed after an adjective to indicate slight qualification. 一 *(yī)* is often omitted in casual speech.

A 前几天我很不高兴，可是昨天考试考得很好，我高兴点儿了。

Qián jǐ tiān wǒ hěn bù gāoxìng, kěshì zuótiān kǎo shì kǎo de hěn hǎo, wǒ gāoxìng diǎnr le.

I was very unhappy a few days ago, but I did very well on the exam yesterday. I am a little bit happier now.

B 我妹妹比我姐姐高一点儿。

Wǒ meìmei bǐ wǒ jiějie gāo yì diǎnr.

My younger sister is a little taller than my older sister.

C 你得快点儿，看电影要晚了。

Nǐ děi kuài diǎnr, kàn diànyǐng yào wǎn le.

You'd better hurry up or you'll be late for the movie.

D 今天比昨天冷点儿。

Jīntiān bǐ zuótiān lěng diǎnr.

Today is a bit colder than yesterday.

E 老师，请您说话说得慢一点儿。

Lǎoshī, qǐng nín shuō huà shuō de màn yì diǎnr.

Teacher, please speak a little more slowly.

（一）点儿 (*[yì] diǎnr*) does not precede the adjective. The following sentences are incorrect:

[❌ 我妹妹比我姐姐一点儿高。]

[❌ 今天比昨天一点儿冷。]

[❌ 老师，请您说话说得一点儿慢。]

EXERCISES

Paraphrase the sentences using 得多/多了 or 一点儿 where appropriate. Use exercise 1 as an example.

More exercises

1 今天有点儿冷，昨天不冷。

→ 今天比昨天冷一点儿。

2 坐地铁很快，坐公共汽车很慢。

3 这家商店的东西很便宜，那家商店的东西很贵。

Language Practice

Let's compare

INTERPERSONAL

In pairs, role-play two friends shopping. Compare the colors, styles, and prices of these two pairs of shoes and help each other decide which pair to buy.

size: 8
$90

size: 8.5
$100

Afterwards, you wear your new shoes on a blind date. Use the prompts to tell each other your preferences and opinions, e.g.:

好吃 *(hǎochī)* (good to eat, delicious)

我喜欢吃美国菜。我觉得美国菜比中国菜好吃。你呢？

Wǒ xǐhuan chī Měiguó cài. Wǒ juéde Měiguó cài bǐ Zhōngguó cài hǎochī. Nǐ ne?

1		好喝 *hǎohē*	(delicious to drink)
2		容易 *róngyì*	
3		快 *kuài*	

A new you

PRESENTATIONAL

Little Zhang has decided to change his old habits in order to lead a healthier lifestyle. Based on the images, describe how he does things differently these days using 了 *(le)*, e.g.:

 ❌ (past) ✅ (present)

他以前不吃早饭，现在吃早饭了。

Tā yǐqián bù chī zǎofàn, xiànzài chī zǎofàn le.

1 ✅ (past) ❌ (present)

2 ✅ (past) ❌ (present)

3 ❌ (past) ✅ (present)

What about you? Share a list of lifestyle changes that you would like to make.

C | **Super-fan** | INTERPERSONAL

In pairs, show how much of a fan you are of the IC characters. Answer the questions affirmatively by using 不但…而且… (*búdàn . . . érqiě . . .*) and add that they possess other qualities or capacities.

Q: 王朋帅吗？
Wáng Péng shuài ma?

高
gāo

A: 王朋不但很帅，而且很高。
Wáng Péng búdàn hěn shuài, érqiě hěn gāo.

Q: 王朋喜欢看球吗？
Wáng Péng xǐhuan kàn qiú ma?

打球
dǎ qiú

A: 王朋不但喜欢看球，而且喜欢打球。
Wáng Péng búdàn xǐhuan kàn qiú, érqiě xǐhuan dǎ qiú.

1 Q: 高文中高吗？
Gāo Wénzhōng gāo ma?

帅
shuài

A: _____

Q: 高文中喜欢唱歌吗？
Gāo Wénzhōng xǐhuan chàng gē ma?

跳舞
tiào wǔ

A: _____

2 Q: 白英爱写字写得快吗？

Bái Yīng'ài xiě zì xiě de kuài ma?

A: _____

漂亮

piàoliang

Q: 白英爱会说英文吗？

Bái Yīng'ài huì shuō Yīngwén ma?

A: _____

中文

Zhōngwén

3 Q: 李友的衣服好看吗？

Lǐ Yǒu de yīfu hǎokàn ma?

A: _____

便宜

piányi

Q: 李友常常复习生词语法吗？

Lǐ Yǒu chángcháng fùxí shēngcí yǔfǎ ma?

A: _____

预习

yùxí

D | **Weather forecast** | PRESENTATIONAL

Use the images below to give a weather report to the class, e.g.:

北京

Běijīng

天气预报说北京明天会下雪。

Tiānqì yùbào shuō Běijīng míngtiān huì xià xuě.

1 北京

Běijīng

2 纽约

Niǔyuē

3 纽约

Niǔyuē

Dating dilemma

INTERPERSONAL

You can't make up your mind: "Who should I go out with, Student A or Student B?" Student A has many good qualities. Your friend argues that Student B at least equals Student A, perhaps even surpasses him/her. Or your friend reminds you that Student B is better than Student A in some other way. Use ···跟···一样··· (. . . gēn . . . yíyàng . . .) or 比 (bǐ) to compare the two based on their attributes, e.g.:

You   我觉得Student A 很帅／漂亮。

Wǒ juéde Student A *hěn shuài/piàoliang.*

Friend   可是Student B 跟 Student A一样帅／漂亮。

Kěshì Student B *gēn* Student A *yíyàng shuài/piàoliang.*

不，不，不，Student B比 Student A帅／漂亮多了。

Bù, bù, bù, Student B *bǐ* Student A *shuài/piàoliang duō le.*

1 高
gāo

2 酷
kù

3 学习　好
xuéxí　hǎo

4 打球打得好
dǎ qiú dǎ de hǎo

5 跳舞跳得好
tiào wǔ tiào de hǎo

Then give a conclusion about whom you should go out with, using ···比 (bǐ)···好 (hǎo).

More characters

❶ 冷 ❷ 冰

What do the characters mean?

What is the common radical?

What does the radical mean?

How does the radical relate to the overall meaning of the characters?

Chinese Chat

The IC cast is discussing plans to go ice skating on WeChat. Which of the characters are planning to go?

9:41 PM   85%

< 朋友们

7:20 PM

明天我想去滑冰。谁想一起去?

我!

我也想去，可是我现在在纽约……

明天天气很好，那我也去吧!

The Weather Here Is Awful!

Dialogue 2

（高文中在网上找白英爱聊天儿。）

英爱，纽约那么好玩儿，你怎么在网上，没出去？

这儿的天气非常糟糕。

怎么了？[a]

昨天下大雨，今天又[5]下雨了。

这个周末这儿天气很好，你快一点儿回来吧。

这个周末纽约也会暖和一点儿。我下个星期有一个面试，还不能回去。

我在加州找了一个工作，你也去吧。加州冬天不冷，夏天不热，春天和秋天更舒服。

加州好是好[6]，可是我更喜欢纽约。

Audio

Video

Language Note

a 怎么了？ *(Zěnme le?)*
This question may be asked upon encountering an unusual situation.

Pinyin Dialogue

(Gāo Wénzhōng zài wǎng shang zhǎo Bái Yīng'ài liáo tiānr.)

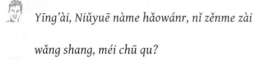 Yīng'ài, Niǔyuē nàme hǎowánr, nǐ zěnme zài

wǎng shang, méi chū qu?

Zhèr de tiānqì fēicháng zāogāo.

Zěnme le?[a]

Zuótiān xià dà yǔ, jīntiān yòu[5] xià yǔ le.

Zhè ge zhōumò zhèr tiānqì hěn hǎo, nǐ kuài yì

diǎnr huí lai ba.

Zhè ge zhōumò Niǔyuē yě huì nuǎnhuo yì diǎnr.

Wǒ xià ge xīngqī yǒu yí ge miànshì, hái bù néng

huí qu.

Wǒ zài Jiāzhōu zhǎo le yí ge gōngzuò, nǐ yě qù

ba. Jiāzhōu dōngtiān bù lěng, xiàtiān bú rè,

chūntiān hé qiūtiān gèng shūfu.

Jiāzhōu hǎo shi hǎo[6], kěshì wǒ gèng xǐhuan

Niǔyuē.

Vocabulary

No.	Word	Pinyin	Part of Speech	Definition
1	那么	nàme	pr	(indicating degree) so, such
2	好玩儿	hǎowánr	adj	fun, amusing, interesting
3	非常	fēicháng	adv	very, extremely, exceedingly
4	糟糕	zāogāo	adj	in a terrible mess, how terrible
5	下雨	xià yǔ	vo	to rain
6	又	yòu	adv	again [See Grammar 5.]
7	面试	miànshì	v/n	to interview; interview (for a job or school admission)
8	回去	huí qu	vc	to go back, to return
9	冬天	dōngtiān	n	winter
10	夏天	xiàtiān	n	summer
11	热	rè	adj	hot
12	春天	chūntiān	n	spring
13	秋天	qiūtiān	n	autumn, fall
14	舒服	shūfu	adj	comfortable
15	加州	Jiāzhōu	pn	California

Audio

Flashcards

You see these decorations alongside a neighbor's door in Chinatown. What season is being celebrated?

Calligraphy courtesy of Zhongli Zhang

GET Real WITH CHINESE

如果天气不好，
你想在家做什么？

Rúguǒ tiānqì bù hǎo, nǐ xiǎng zài jiā zuò shénme?

If the weather is bad, what would you like to do at home?

我想在家 ＿＿＿＿＿＿＿。
Wǒ xiǎng zài jiā ＿＿＿＿＿＿.

See index for corresponding vocabulary or research another term.

Grammar

5 | **The adverb 又 *(yòu)* (again)**

又 *(yòu)* (again) indicates the recurrence of an action.

A　昨天早上下雪，今天早上又下雪了。

Zuótiān zǎoshang xià xuě, jīntiān zǎoshang yòu xià xuě le.

It snowed yesterday morning, and snowed again this morning.

B　妈妈上个星期给我打电话，这个星期又给我打电话了。

Māma shàng ge xīngqī gěi wǒ dǎ diànhuà, zhè ge xīngqī yòu gěi wǒ dǎ diànhuà le.

My mom called me last week, and she called me again this week.

C　他昨天复习了第八课的语法，今天又复习了。

Tā zuótiān fùxí le dì bā kè de yǔfǎ, jīntiān yòu fùxí le.

He reviewed the grammar in Lesson Eight yesterday, and reviewed it again today.

If the verb is 是 *(shì)* or a modal verb, 又 *(yòu)* is required regardless of the timing of the action.

D　明天又是星期一了。

Míngtiān yòu shì xīngqīyī le.

Tomorrow is Monday again.

E　妹妹上个星期买了很多衣服，明天又要去买衣服。

Mèimei shàng ge xīngqī mǎi le hěn duō yīfu, míngtiān yòu yào qù mǎi yīfu.

My younger sister bought a lot of clothes last week. She'll go clothes shopping again tomorrow.

Like 又 *(yòu)*, 再 *(zài)* also signifies the recurrence of an action, but refers to the future.

F 同学们刚才练习打球练习得不错，不过老师说明天得再练习。

Tóngxué men gāngcái liànxí dǎ qiú liànxí de búcuò, búguò lǎoshī shuō míngtiān děi zài liànxí.

The students did well practicing playing ball just now, but the teacher said that they need to keep practicing tomorrow.

G 我昨天去跳舞了，我想明天晚上再去跳舞。

Wǒ zuótiān qù tiào wǔ le, wǒ xiǎng míngtiān wǎnshang zài qù tiào wǔ.

I went dancing yesterday. I'd like to go dancing again tomorrow night.

More exercises

EXERCISES

Using 又, combine the sentences to create a new one to indicate that something happened again. Use exercise 1 as an example.

1 昨天我妈妈给我打电话了。

今天我妈妈给我打电话了。

→ 今天我妈妈又给我打电话了。

2 我们上个星期考试了。我们这个星期考试了。

3 这里昨天下雪了。这里今天下雪了。

6
> **Adjective/verb + 是** *(shì)* **+ adjective/verb +**
> **可是/但是···** *(kěshì/dànshì . . .)*

Sentences in this pattern usually imply that the speaker accepts the validity of a certain point of view but wishes to offer an alternative perspective or emphasize a different aspect of the matter.

A Q: 滑冰难不难？

Huá bīng nán bu nán?

Is ice skating difficult?

A: 滑冰难是难，可是很有意思。

Huá bīng nán shì nán, kěshì hěn yǒu yìsi.

It is difficult, but it is very interesting.

B Q: 在高速公路上开车，你紧张吗？

Zài gāosù gōnglù shang kāi chē, nǐ jǐnzhāng ma?

Do you get nervous driving on the highway?

A: 紧张是紧张，可是也很好玩儿。

Jǐnzhāng shì jǐnzhāng, kěshì yě hěn hǎowánr.

I do get nervous, but I find it a lot of fun, too.

C Q: 明天学校开会，你去不去？

Míngtiān xuéxiào kāi huì, nǐ qù bu qù?

There's a meeting at school tomorrow. Are you going?

A: 我去是去，可是会晚一点儿。

Wǒ qù shì qù, kěshì huì wǎn yì diǎnr.

I am going, but I'll be a little bit late.

D Q: 你喜欢这张照片吗？

Nǐ xǐhuan zhè zhāng zhàopiàn ma?

Do you like this photo?

A: 喜欢是喜欢，可是这张照片太小了。

Xǐhuan shì xǐhuan, kěshì zhè zhāng zhàopiàn tài xiǎo le.

I do, but this picture is too small.

This pattern can be used only when the adjective or verb in it has already been mentioned, e.g., 难 (*nán*) in (A), 紧张 (*jǐnzhāng*) in (B), 去 (*qù*) in (C), and 喜欢 (*xǐhuan*) in (D). In this regard, it is different from the pattern 虽然…可是/但是… (*suīrán … kěshì/dànshì …*).

EXERCISES

In pairs, take turns completing the exchanges using 是···可是/但是··· where appropriate. Use exercise 1 as an example.

1　**Student A**　坐公共汽车很麻烦。（很便宜）

　　Student B　坐公共汽车麻烦是麻烦，可是很便宜。

2　**Student A**　打车去机场很方便。（很贵）

　　Student B　＿＿＿＿＿＿＿＿＿＿＿＿＿＿＿。

3　**Student A**　这件衬衫大小很合适。（样子不好）

　　Student B　＿＿＿＿＿＿＿＿＿＿＿＿＿＿＿。

Chinese Chat

Your friend is chatting with you to arrange an outing. How would you reply?

Language Practice

Depends on the weather	INTERPERSONAL

When you plan something and the weather does not cooperate, what do you do? In pairs, take turns suggesting alternatives using 还是···吧··· (háishi ... ba ...) and see if you can settle on plans.

Student A 我想出去玩儿，可是下雨了。

Wǒ xiǎng chū qu wánr, kěshì xià yǔ le.

Student B 别出去了！还是在家看电视吧。

Bié chū qu le! Háishi zài jiā kàn diànshì ba.

1 Student A 我想去买点儿东西，可是雪下得很大。

Wǒ xiǎng qù mǎi diǎnr dōngxi, kěshì xuě xià de hěn dà.

Student B _____

2 Student A 我想出去看朋友，可是天气很糟糕。

Wǒ xiǎng chū qu kàn péngyou, kěshì tiānqì hěn zāogāo.

Student B _____

3 Student A 我想去公园打球，但是太热。

Wǒ xiǎng qù gōngyuán dǎ qiú, dànshì tài rè.

Student B _____

Same old, same old

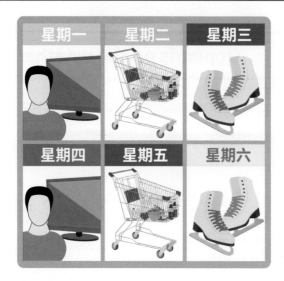

Based on the above calendar, recap what Little Zhang did last week by using 又 (yòu), e.g.:

小张星期一看电视，星期四又看电视了。

Xiǎo Zhāng xīngqīyī kàn diànshì, xīngqīsì yòu kàn diànshì le.

1  **2**

Two sides to every coin

In pairs, take turns reminding each that there is another side to consider by using
…是…，可是… (… *shì* … , *kěshì* …), e.g.:

加州　　漂亮

Jiāzhōu　　*piàoliang*

Student A　加州很漂亮。

　　　　　Jiāzhōu hěn piàoliang.

Student B　加州漂亮是漂亮，可是东西太贵了。

　　　　　Jiāzhōu piàoliang shì piàoliang, kěshì dōngxi tài guì le.

1 纽约
   Niǔyuē

   有意思
   yǒu yìsi

2 坐地铁
   zuò dìtiě

   便宜
   piányi

3 坐公共汽车
   zuò gōnggòng qìchē

   慢
   màn

4 北京的冬天
   Běijīng de dōngtiān

   下雪
   xià xuě

Weather report PRESENTATIONAL

It's winter, and you're the newly hired weatherperson at the student TV station. Report on the weather in Beijing for the next three days. Describe which days will be colder/warmer and how the weather will change. After finishing up your report, compare the weather in Beijing with the weather in your town.

next Monday

28°F

next Tuesday

37°F

next Wednesday

40°F

What do the characters mean?

What is the common radical?

What does the radical mean?

How does the radical relate to the overall meaning of the characters?

Characterize it!

❶ 春   ❷ 暖

More characters

Continue to explore

A section of the Great Wall near Beijing

Peach blossoms in Wuyuan, Jiangxi Province

波士顿
Bōshìdùn
BOSTON

伦敦
Lúndūn
LONDON

柏林
Bólín
BERLIN

PLACE NAME TRANSLITERATION

Some Chinese names for places in the West were invented by early Chinese immigrants, for example, San Francisco was dubbed 旧金山 (*Jiùjīnshān*) (lit. Old Gold Mountain) after gold was discovered in Victoria, Australia. For a period of time, Melbourne was called 新金山 (*Xīnjīnshān*) (lit. New Gold Mountain). However, the vast majority of Chinese names for places in the West are transliterations. California, for instance, is transliterated as 加利福尼亚州 (*Jiālìfúníyàzhōu*), which is often shortened to 加州 (*Jiāzhōu*). The character 州 (*zhōu*) means "state." Today, Melbourne is known by its transliteration 墨尔本 (*Mò'ěrběn*) as well.

Weather

Across China, climatic conditions differ dramatically. In general terms, the north is cold and snowy in winter; the south, hot and wet in summer. 重庆 (Chóngqìng), 武汉 (Wǔhàn), and 南京 (Nánjīng), are nicknamed the "Three Furnaces on the Yangtze River" for their scorching hot summer temperatures. Some cities are known for being temperate year-round—昆明 (Kūnmíng), for instance, is famous for being like spring all year, 四季如春 (sìjì rú chūn). In the lower Yangtze (长江) (Chángjiāng) valley, the rainy season called 梅雨 (méi yǔ) starts in mid-June and lasts until early July, bringing copious rain and high humidity. 梅 (méi) (plum) is a homophone of 霉 (méi) meaning "mold." In southern China, the rainy season generally starts in July and ends in August, swelling nearly all rivers to flood levels. In winter, the warmth and resorts of the island of 海南 (Hǎinán) provide a respite to tourists from the north, while many southerners brave the cold in the northern city of 哈尔滨 (Hā'ěrbīn) for its annual ice sculpture festival.

A snow-covered house in Xuexiang Village, Heilongjiang Province

UNITS OF MEASUREMENT

China uses the metric system: thus, temperatures are given in Celsius, distances in kilometers, and weights in kilograms in China. However, on occasion, people do still use traditional Chinese units of measurement such as the 里 (lǐ), equal to half a kilometer or 0.311 miles, and the 斤 (jīn), equal to half a kilogram or 1.102 pounds. The 里 (lǐ) is referred to in a famous Chinese proverb from the Tao Te Ching, 道德经 (Dàodéjīng), attributed to Laozi: 千里之行，始于足下 (qiān lǐ zhī xíng, shǐ yú zú xià) (A journey of a thousand li begins with a single step).

COMPARE & CONTRAST

The traditional Chinese calendar, which is strictly speaking a lunisolar calendar, is divided into twenty-four solar terms called 节气 (jiéqì). One term, 冬至 (dōngzhì) (winter solstice), marks the longest night of the year in the Northern Hemisphere. Traditionally, people eat dumplings (饺子) (jiǎozi), in the north, and wonton (馄饨) (húntun) and glutinous rice balls (汤圆) (tāngyuán) in the south. It is also the day to make ritual offerings to one's ancestors and visit the graves of deceased relatives. Is the December solstice observed in any special way in your culture? Are there any foods or traditions associated with it?

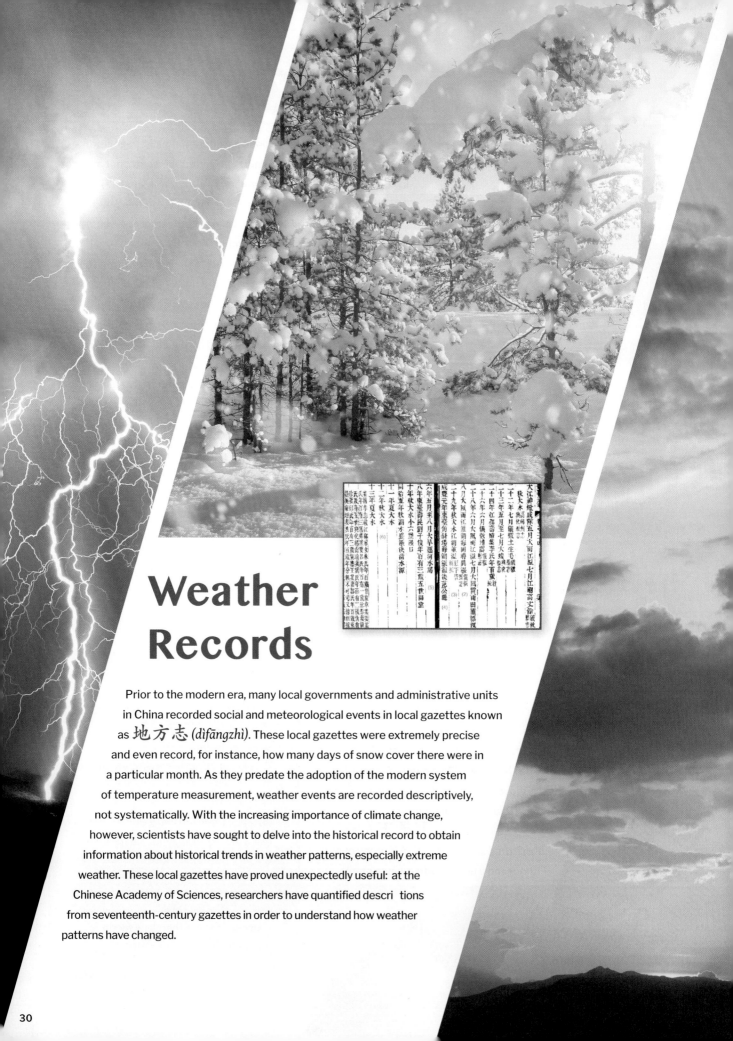

Weather Records

Prior to the modern era, many local governments and administrative units in China recorded social and meteorological events in local gazettes known as 地方志 (dìfāngzhì). These local gazettes were extremely precise and even record, for instance, how many days of snow cover there were in a particular month. As they predate the adoption of the modern system of temperature measurement, weather events are recorded descriptively, not systematically. With the increasing importance of climate change, however, scientists have sought to delve into the historical record to obtain information about historical trends in weather patterns, especially extreme weather. These local gazettes have proved unexpectedly useful: at the Chinese Academy of Sciences, researchers have quantified descri tions from seventeenth-century gazettes in order to understand how weather patterns have changed.

Lesson Wrap-Up

Rearrange the sentences below into a logical sequence. Then combine the sentences into a coherent narrative. Replace nouns with pronouns and change periods to commas where appropriate. Delete identical subject pronouns. Add the connective devices 而且 (érqiě) and 所以 (suǒyǐ), the location word 这儿 (zhèr), and the time word 晚上 (wǎnshang) where desirable.

_____ 晚上高文中在网上跟白英爱聊天。

_____ 高文中告诉白英爱学校那边的天气很好。

  1   白英爱昨天来纽约找工作。

_____ 高文中让白英爱快点回去。

_____ 纽约今天又下雨了。

_____ 白英爱说纽约的天气非常糟糕。

_____ 纽约昨天下大雨了。

_____ 白英爱说纽约的天气周末也会好一点。

_____ 白英爱说下星期一她有一个面试。

_____ 白英爱说她不能回去。

Pretend that you are a Chinese cable TV weatherperson and give a national two-day weather forecast to the class or make a video and share it with your classmates. Look up the two-day weather forecasts for five cities in five different regions of your country—e.g., New England, Florida, the Midwest, the Pacific Northwest, and California—for any two-day period. Is there any rain or snow in the forecasts? How do the temperatures compare across the two-day period?

Interview

Interview a friend about what the seasons are like in his/her hometown.

你家那儿的冬天怎么样？冷不冷？常常下雪吗？

冬天可以做什么？

你家那儿的春天呢？长不长？舒服不舒服？

夏天热不热？常常下雨吗？

夏天可以做什么？

秋天天蓝不蓝？

你喜欢你家那儿的春天、夏天、秋天还是冬天？为什么？

Supplemental Reading Practice

For additional reading practice that builds on the vocabulary introduced in this lesson, turn to the supplemental readings that begin on page 419.

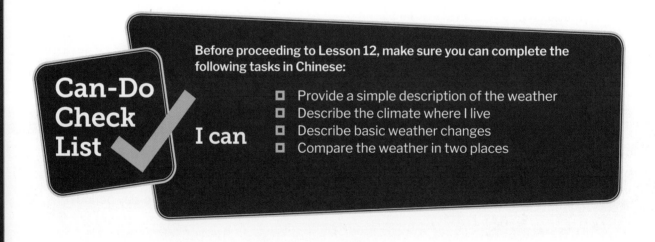

Can-Do Check List ✔ **I can**

Before proceeding to Lesson 12, make sure you can complete the following tasks in Chinese:

- ☐ Provide a simple description of the weather
- ☐ Describe the climate where I live
- ☐ Describe basic weather changes
- ☐ Compare the weather in two places

吃饭

Chī fàn

DINING

Learning Objectives

In this lesson, you will learn to:

- Ask if there are seats available at a restaurant
- Order some Chinese dishes
- Describe your dietary preferences and restrictions
- Ask for recommendations
- Rush your order
- Pay for your meal and get change

Relate & Get Ready

In your own culture/community:

- Do people order and eat their own dishes, or do they share their dishes with others?
- Do people prefer hot or cold beverages with their meals?
- How do most people pay for their meals: in cash or with a credit card?

Dining Out

Dialogue 1

（在饭馆儿……）

请进，请进。

人怎么这么^a多？好像一个位子^b都没[1]有了。

服务员，请问，还有没有位子？

有，有，有。那张桌子没有人。

……

两位想吃点儿什么？

王朋，你点菜吧。

好。先给我们两盘饺子，要素的。

除了饺子以外，还要什么？

李友，你说呢？

还要一盘家常豆腐，不要放肉，我吃素。

我们的家常豆腐没有肉。

还要两碗^c酸辣汤，请别放味精，少[2]放点儿盐。有小白菜吗？

对不起，小白菜刚[3]卖完[4]。

那就不要青菜了。

那喝点儿什么呢?

我要一杯冰茶。李友,你喝什么?

我很渴,请给我一杯可乐,多放点儿冰。

好,两盘饺子,一盘家常豆腐,两碗酸辣汤,一杯冰茶,一杯可乐,多放冰。还要别的吗?

不要别的了,这些够^d了。服务员,我们都饿了,请上菜快一点儿^e。

没问题,菜很快就能做好⁵。

(Zài fànguǎnr . . .)

 Qǐng jìn, qǐng jìn.

 Rén zěnme zhème^a duō? Hǎoxiàng yí ge wèizi^b

dōu méi[1] yǒu le.

 Fúwùyuán, qǐng wèn, hái yǒu méiyǒu wèizi?

 Yǒu, yǒu, yǒu. Nà zhāng zhuōzi méiyǒu rén.

. . .

 Liǎng wèi xiǎng chī diǎnr shénme?

 Wáng Péng, nǐ diǎn cài ba.

 Hǎo. Xiān gěi wǒmen liǎng pán jiǎozi, yào sù de.

 Chúle jiǎozi yǐwài, hái yào shénme?

 Lǐ Yǒu, nǐ shuō ne?

 Hái yào yì pán jiācháng dòufu, bú yào fàng ròu,

wǒ chī sù.

 Wǒmen de jiācháng dòufu méiyǒu ròu.

 Hái yào liǎng wǎn^c suānlàtāng, qǐng bié fàng

wèijīng, shǎo[2] fàng diǎnr yán. Yǒu xiǎo báicài ma?

 Duìbuqǐ, xiǎo báicài gāng[3] mài wán[4].

 Nà jiù bú yào qīngcài le.

 Nà hē diǎnr shénme ne?

 Wǒ yào yì bēi bīngchá. Lǐ Yǒu, nǐ hē shénme?

 Wǒ hěn kě, qǐng gěi wǒ yì bēi kělè, duō fàng

diǎnr bīng.

 Hǎo, liǎng pán jiǎozi, yì pán jiācháng dòufu, liǎng

wǎn suānlàtāng, yì bēi bīngchá, yì bēi kělè, duō

fàng bīng. Hái yào bié de ma?

 Bú yào bié de le, zhè xiē gòu^d le. Fúwùyuán,

wǒmen dōu è le, qǐng shàng cài kuài yì diǎnr^e.

 Méi wèntí, cài hěn kuài jiù néng zuò hǎo[5].

---

a 这么 *(zhème/zème)*

In Beijing, 这么 *(zhème)* is commonly pronounced as *zème*.

b 位子 *(wèizi)* **and** 椅子 *(yǐzi)*

Seat is 位子 *(wèizi)*; chair is 椅子 *(yǐzi)*.

c 碗 *(wǎn)*

Nouns for objects that contain things can function as measure words, as in 一碗饭 *(yì wǎn fàn)* (a bowl of rice), 一杯水 *(yì bēi shuǐ)* (a glass of water), and 一盘饺子 *(yì pán jiǎozi)* (a plate of dumplings). When these words are used as nouns rather than as measure words, some have to take a suffix such as 子 *(zi)*, as in 杯子 *(bēizi)* (cup), 盘子 *(pánzi)* (plate), and 瓶子 *(píngzi)* (bottle). Note that these words are defined in the vocabulary list according to the part of speech in which they appear in the text.

d 够 *(gòu)*

When used as an adjective, 够 *(gòu)* can only be a predicate; it cannot come before the noun being modified. Thus you can say 我的钱不够 *(Wǒ de qián bú gòu)* (I don't have enough money), but never ❌ 我没有够钱. In an affirmative statement, 够 *(gòu)* usually cannot be modified by 很 *(hěn)*. Additionally, 够 *(gòu)* can be used after a verb as a complement, e.g.: 玩（儿）够了 *(wán[r] gòu le)* (to have played enough) and 买够了 *(mǎi gòu le)* (to have bought enough).

e **Topic-comment sentences**

请上菜快一点儿 *(qǐng shàng cài kuài yì diǎnr)* is a topic-comment sentence. [See also Grammar 1, Lesson 10, Volume 1.] 上菜 *(shàng cài)* is known information and the topic of the sentence. 快一点儿 *(kuài yì diànr)* is new information, hence the word order.

Vocabulary

Audio

Flashcards

No.	Word	Pinyin	Part of Speech	Definition
1	饭馆（儿）	fànguǎn(r)	n	restaurant
2	好像	hǎoxiàng	adv	to seem, to be like
3	位子	wèizi	n	seat
4	服务员	fúwùyuán	n	waiter, attendant
	服务	fúwù	v	to serve, to provide service
5	桌子	zhuōzi	n	table
6	点菜	diǎn cài	vo	to order food
7	盘	pán	n	plate, dish
8	饺子	jiǎozi	n	dumplings (with vegetable and/or meat filling)
9	素	sù	adj	vegetarian (lit. plain)
10	家常	jiācháng	n	home-style
11	豆腐	dòufu	n	tofu, bean curd
12	放	fàng	v	to put, to place
13	肉	ròu	n	meat
14	碗	wǎn	n	bowl
15	酸辣汤	suānlàtāng	n	hot-and-sour soup
	酸	suān	adj	sour
	辣	là	adj	spicy, hot
	汤	tāng	n	soup
16	味精	wèijīng	n	monosodium glutamate (MSG)
17	盐	yán	n	salt
18	小白菜	xiǎo báicài	n	baby bok choy
19	刚	gāng	adv	just [See Grammar 3.]

素菜

酸辣白菜	¥20
蒜蓉青菜	¥18
拍黄瓜	¥18
麻婆豆腐	¥22
凉拌豆腐	¥20

荤菜

酸辣肥牛	¥48
水煮肉片	¥68
红烧肉	¥38
椒盐牛仔骨	¥48
糖醋鱼	¥45

汤类

¥18

面类

GET Real WITH CHINESE

No.	Word	Pinyin	Part of Speech	Definition
20	卖完	*mài wán*	vc	to be sold out [See Grammar 4.]
	完	*wán*	c	finished
21	青菜	*qīngcài*	n	green, leafy vegetable
22	冰茶	*bīngchá*	n	iced tea
	冰	*bīng*	n	ice
23	渴	*kě*	adj	thirsty
24	些	*xiē*	m	(measure word for an indefinite amount), some
25	够	*gòu*	adj	enough
26	饿	*è*	adj	hungry
27	上菜	*shàng cài*	vo	to serve food

去中餐馆吃饭，你想点什么菜？

Qù Zhōngcānguǎn chī fàn, nǐ xiǎng diǎn shénme cài?

What dishes would you like to order at a Chinese restaurant?

How About You?

我想点 ＿＿＿＿＿＿ 。

Wǒ xiǎng diǎn ＿＿＿＿＿＿ .

See index for corresponding vocabulary or research another dish.

Grammar

---

1 | 一···也/都···不/没··· *(yī . . . yě/dōu . . . bù/méi . . .)*

These structures are used for emphatic negation; they express the meaning "not at all" or "not even one."

> Subject + 一 + measure word + object + 也/都 + 不/没（有） (+ verb)
> *(yī)*   *(yě/dōu)* *(bù/méi[yǒu])*

A 小李一个朋友也没有。

Xiǎo Lǐ yí ge péngyou yě méiyǒu.

Little Li doesn't have a single friend.

B 爸爸今天一杯茶都没喝。

Bàba jīntiān yì bēi chá dōu méi hē.

My father didn't have a single cup of tea today.

> Topic (object) + subject + 一 + measure word + 也/都 + 不/没 + verb
> *(yī)*   *(yě/dōu)* *(bù/méi)*

C 这些衬衫我一件也不喜欢。

Zhè xiē chènshān wǒ yí jiàn yě bù xǐhuan.

I don't like any of these shirts.

D 哥哥的鞋，弟弟一双都不能穿。

Gēge de xié, dìdi yì shuāng dōu bù néng chuān.

The younger brother cannot wear a single pair of his older brother's shoes.

> Subject + 一点儿 + object + 也/都 + 不/没 + verb
> *(yì diǎnr)*   *(yě/dōu)* *(bù/méi)*

E 他去了商店，可是一点儿东西也没买。

Tā qù le shāngdiàn, kěshì yì diǎnr dōngxi yě méi mǎi.

He went to the store, but didn't buy anything at all.

F 妈妈做菜一点儿味精都不放。

Māma zuò cài yì diǎnr wèijīng dōu bú fàng.

Mom doesn't use any MSG in her cooking.

If the noun after 一 (yī) is countable, a proper measure word should be used between 一 (yī) and the noun, as in (A), (B), (C), and (D). If the noun is uncountable, the phrase 一点儿 (yì diǎnr) is usually used instead, as in (E) and (F).

The following sentences are incorrect:

[❌ 小李没有一个朋友。]

[❌ 这些衬衫我不喜欢一件。]

[❌ 他东西没买一点儿。]

The construction 一点儿 (yìdiǎnr) + 也/都 (yě/dōu) + 不/没 (bù/méi) can also be used before an adjective to express emphatic negation, as in (G), (H), and (I).

G 这儿的冬天一点儿也不冷。

Zhèr de dōngtiān yì diǎnr yě bù lěng.

Winter here isn't cold at all.

H 那个学校一点儿也不漂亮。

Nà ge xuéxiào yì diǎnr yě bú piàoliang.

That school is not pretty at all.

I 这杯冰茶一点都不好喝。

Zhè bēi bīngchá yì diǎnr dōu bù hǎohē.

This glass of iced tea doesn't taste good at all.

EXERCISES

More exercises

Make the sentences more emphatic by using the 一···也/都···不/没··· structure and appropriate measure words. Use exercise 1 as an example.

1   她不喜欢这个饭馆儿的菜。

→ 这个饭馆儿的菜她一个都不喜欢。

2   我今年没有买衣服。

3   小王昨天没有预习中文生词。

多 / 少 (duō/shǎo) + verb

The way the two adjectives 多 (duō) and 少 (shǎo) are used is non-typical of adjectives in general. To express doing something "more" or "less," place 多 (duō) or 少 (shǎo) before the verb.

A 爸爸告诉妈妈做菜的时候少放盐，
多放点儿糖。

Bàba gàosu māma zuò cài de shíhou shǎo fàng yán, duō fàng diǎnr táng.

Dad asked Mom to add less salt and more sugar when cooking.

B 上中文课得多说中文，少说英文。

Shàng Zhōngwén kè děi duō shuō Zhōngwén, shǎo shuō Yīngwén.

In Chinese class, one should speak more Chinese and less English.

The "多 / 少 (duō/shǎo) + verb" construction is sometimes used to denote a deviation from the correct amount or number.

C 你多找了我一块钱。

Nǐ duō zhǎo le wǒ yí kuài qián.

You gave me one dollar too many.

D 老师说要写五十个字，我写了四十五个，
少写了五个。

Lǎoshī shuō yào xiě wǔshí ge zì, wǒ xiě le sìshíwǔ ge, shǎo xiě le wǔ ge.

The teacher told us to write fifty characters. I wrote forty-five. I was five short.

EXERCISES

Fill in the blanks with 多 or 少. Use exercise 1 as an example.

More exercises

1 医生说我们得少喝可乐，多喝水。

2 爸爸希望我 ＿＿＿＿ 吃青菜 ＿＿＿＿ 吃肉。

3 这双鞋一百七十五块，我给了售货员两百块，
她找了我三十五块，＿＿＿＿ 找了十块。

As an adverb, 刚 (gāng) (just) denotes that an action or change in situation took place in the very recent past.

A   我哥哥刚从中国来，在这儿一个朋友都没有。

Wō gēge gāng cóng Zhōngguó lái, zài zhèr yí ge péngyou dōu méiyǒu.

My older brother just came from China. He doesn't have a single friend here.

B   我刚洗完澡，舒服极了。

Wǒ gāng xǐ wán zǎo, shūfu jí le.

I just showered, and feel great.

刚才 (gāngcái) (just now) is a time word that refers to the period just moments before.

C   Q: 你知道王朋在哪儿吗？

Nǐ zhīdào Wáng Péng zài nǎr ma?

Do you know where Wang Peng is?

   A: 他刚才在这儿，我不知道他去哪儿了。

Tā gāngcái zài zhèr, wǒ bù zhīdao tā qù nǎr le.

He was here a moment ago. I don't know where he went.

D   弟弟刚才吃了十五个饺子，喝了两碗酸辣汤。

Dìdi gāngcái chī le shíwǔ ge jiǎozi, hē le liǎng wǎn suānlàtāng.

My younger brother ate fifteen dumplings and two bowls of hot-and-sour soup a moment ago.

Although 刚 (gāng) and 刚才 (gāngcái) are similar in meaning, they are classified as different parts of speech and are therefore used differently. First, unlike 刚才 (gāngcái), 刚 (gāng) cannot be followed by 不 (bù) or 没 (méi).

E   Q: 你刚才为什么没说？

Nǐ gāngcái wèishénme méi shuō?

Why didn't you say anything a moment ago?

A: 我刚才不想说。

Wǒ gāngcái bù xiǎng shuō.

I didn't want to say anything a moment ago.

[❌ 你刚为什么没说？]
[❌ 我刚不想说。]

Second, sentences that include 刚才 (*gāngcái*) often end with 了 (*le*). By contrast, sentences that include 刚 (*gāng*) cannot end with 了 (*le*).

F Q: 你刚才去哪儿了？老师要你去办公室找他。

Nǐ gāngcái qù nǎr le? Lǎoshī yào nǐ qù bàngōngshì zhǎo tā.

Where were you a moment ago? The teacher wanted you to go to his office.

A: 我刚才去图书馆了。

Wǒ gāngcái qù túshūguǎn le.

I went to the library just now.

G Q: 明天的考试你开始准备了吗？

Míngtiān de kǎoshì nǐ kāishǐ zhǔnbèi le ma?

Have you started preparing for tomorrow's test?

A: 刚开始准备。

Gāng kāishǐ zhǔnbèi.

I just started.

[❌ 刚开始准备了。]

EXERCISES

Fill in the blanks with 刚 or 刚才. Use exercise 1 as an example.

1　高文中 ＿＿＿ 从英国来。

　　→ 高文中刚从英国来。

2　她 ＿＿＿ 给我发了一个短信。

3　你 ＿＿＿ 吃完饭，现在别去洗澡。

More
exercises

Resultative complements (I)

Following a verb, an adjective or another verb can be used to denote the result of the action, hence the term resultative complement.

| A | 小白菜卖完了。 |

Xiǎo báicài mài wán le.

The baby bok choy is sold out.

| B | 你找错钱了。 |

Nǐ zhǎo cuò qián le.

You gave me the wrong change.

| C | 那个人是谁你看清楚了吗? |

Nà ge rén shì shéi nǐ kàn qīngchu le ma?

Did you see clearly who that person was?

(清楚 *[qīngchu]* [clear] [See Dialogue 2.])

| D | 太好了，这个字你写对了。 |

Tài hǎo le, zhè ge zì nǐ xiě duì le.

Great! You wrote this character correctly.

Generally, the negative form of a resultative complement is formed by placing 没 *(méi)* (no, not) or 没有 *(méiyǒu)* (have not) before the verb.

| E | 小白菜没卖完。 |

Xiǎo báicài méi mài wán.

The baby bok choy isn't sold out.

| F | 那个人我没看清楚。 |

Nà ge rén wǒ méi kàn qīngchu.

I didn't see clearly who that person was.

| G | 糟糕，这个字你没有写对。 |

Zāogāo, zhè ge zì nǐ méiyǒu xiě duì.

Yikes! You didn't write this character correctly.

The use of an adjective as a resultative complement is not random. It is advisable to take the combination of the verb and the complement as a whole unit.

EXERCISES

Fill in the blanks with the appropriate resultative complement: 完, 到, 错, 对, or 懂.
Use exercise 1 as an example.

1   你说错了，她的名字不是王小英。

2   你说 ＿＿＿ 了，白英爱是韩国人。

3   老师的话你听 ＿＿＿ 了吗？

---

5 | **好 (hǎo) as a resultative complement**

好 (hǎo) can serve as a complement following a verb to signify the completion of an action
and readiness to start another.

A   饭做好了，快来吃吧。

Fàn zuò hǎo le, kuài lái chī ba.

The food is ready. Come and eat.

B   功课做好了，我要睡觉了。

Gōngkè zuò hǎo le, wǒ yào shuì jiào le.

My homework is done, and I'm going to bed.

C   衣服我已经帮你买好了，明天晚会
你就可以穿了。

Yīfu wǒ yǐjīng bāng nǐ mǎi hǎo le, míngtiān wǎnhuì nǐ jiù kěyǐ chuān le.

I've already bought clothes for you. You can wear them to the party tomorrow night.

EXERCISES

Fill in the blanks with the appropriate verbs: 看, 做, 买, or 准备, and add 好 to indicate
that one is ready for the next action. Use exercise 1 as an example.

1   饭做好了，可以吃饭了。

2   电影票 ＿＿＿＿＿＿ 了，我们进去吧。

3   ＿＿＿＿＿＿ 了吗？可以开始考试了吗？

Language Practice

A | **I'll pass** | PRESENTATIONAL

Your friend is hard to please and doesn't like any of the items he/she sees while out shopping with you. In pairs, discuss his/her shopping haul using 一···也/都···不/没··· (yì... yě/dōu... bù/méi), e.g.:

那儿的衬衫他/她都不喜欢，一件都没买。

Nàr de chènshān tā dōu bù xǐhuan, yí jiàn dōu méi mǎi.

1   **2**   **3**   **4**   **5**

B | **One of those days** | PRESENTATIONAL

Everything went wrong for Wang Peng today. Li You, on the other hand, had a great day today. Recap what happened to them to the class using 了 (le), e.g.:

Wang Peng rode the wrong bus.

王朋今天坐错车了。

Wáng Péng jīntiān zuò cuò chē le.

1 Wang Peng wore the wrong clothes.

2 Wang Peng did the wrong homework.

3 Li You understood what the teacher said.

4 Li You finished her homework.

5 Li You saw her good friend Bai Ying'ai.

Getting it done

In pairs, take turns asking each other whether you have finished one task and are ready for the next one, using 好 (hǎo), e.g.:

练习   汉字

liànxí   *Hànzì*

Q: 你汉字练习好了吗?

Nǐ Hànzì liànxí hǎo le ma?

A: 汉字我练习好了。 (affirmative)

Hànzì wǒ liànxí hǎo le.

A: 我练习汉字没练习好。/
汉字我没练习好。 (negative)

Wǒ liànxí Hànzì méi liànxí hǎo./Hànzì wǒ méi liànxí hǎo.

1 做   中文功课

zuò   *Zhōngwén gōngkè*

2 复习   生词语法

fùxí   *shēngcí yǔfǎ*

3 准备   考试

zhǔnbèi   *kǎoshì*

Characterize it!

What do the characters mean?
What is the common radical?
What does the radical mean?
How does the radical relate to the overall meaning of the characters?

❶ 饭   ❷ 馆   ❸ 饺   ❹ 饿

More characters

What do Chinese-language teachers hope for from their students? Form complete sentences using 多 (duō) or 少 (shǎo), e.g.:

老师希望学生：   *Lǎoshī xīwàng xuésheng:*

多来上课   *duō lái shàng kè*

老师希望学生多来上课。   *Lǎoshī xīwàng xuésheng duō lái shàng kè.*

1 多预习课文

duō yùxí kèwén

2 多听录音

duō tīng lùyīn

3 多复习生词语法

duō fùxí shēngcí yǔfǎ

4 多练习写汉字

duō liànxí xiě Hànzì

5 上课少说英文

shàng kè shǎo shuō Yīngwén

6 少玩儿

shǎo wánr

Then, in pairs, come up with your own list of what you or would like your teacher to do more or less, using 学生希望老师······ *(xuésheng xīwàng lǎoshī...)*.

> **Chinese Chat**
>
> Li You just posted a restaurant review on Dianping（大众点评）*(Dàzhòng diǎnpíng)*, a popular Chinese review app. What dishes do you think she would recommend?

 李友
★★★★☆   口味:4   环境:5   服务:4   人均:¥35

酸辣汤太好喝了！家常豆腐也很好吃，一点儿味精都没放。不过素饺子不太好吃······

10-22 心美小馆   赞 (9)   回应 (2)   收藏   举报

At the Dining Hall

Dialogue 2

（今天是星期四，学生餐厅有中国菜，
师傅是上海人。）

师傅[a]，请问今天晚饭有什么好吃的？

我们今天有糖醋鱼，甜甜的[6]、酸酸的，
好吃极了[b]，你买一个吧。

好。今天有没有红烧牛肉？

没有。你已经要鱼了，别吃肉了。来[7]个
凉拌黄瓜吧？

好。再来一碗米饭。一共多少钱？

糖醋鱼，四块五，凉拌黄瓜，一块七；
一碗米饭，五毛钱。一共六块七。

师傅，糟糕，我忘了带饭卡了。这是十块钱。

找你三块三。

师傅，钱你找错了，多找了我一块钱。

对不起，我没有看清楚。

没关系[c]。

下个星期四再来。

好，再见。

Pinyin Dialogue

(*Jīntiān shì xīngqīsì, xuéshēng cāntīng yǒu
Zhōngguó cài, shīfu shì Shànghǎi rén.*)

 Shīfu[a], qǐng wèn jīntiān wǎnfàn yǒu shénme hàochī de?

 *Wǒmen jīntiān yǒu tángcùyú, tián tián de[6], suān
suān de, hǎochī jí le[b], nǐ mǎi yí ge ba.*

 Hǎo. Jīntiān yǒu méiyǒu hóngshāo niúròu?

 *Méiyǒu. Nǐ yǐjīng yào yú le, bié chī ròu le. Lái[7] ge
liángbàn huánggua ba?*

 Hǎo. Zài lái yì wǎn mǐfàn. Yígòng duōshao qián?

 *Tángcùyú, sì kuài wǔ, liángbàn huánggua, yí kuài
qī; Yì wǎn mǐfàn, wǔ máo qián. Yígòng liù kuài qī.*

 *Shīfu, zāogāo, wǒ wàng le dài fànkǎ le. Zhè shì shí
kuài qián.*

 Zhǎo nǐ sān kuài sān.

 Shīfu, qián nǐ zhǎo cuò le, duō zhǎo le wǒ yí kuài qián.

 Duìbuqǐ, wǒ méiyǒu kàn qīngchu.

 Méi guānxi[c].

 Xià ge xīngqīsì zài lái.

 Hǎo, zàijiàn.

Language Notes

a 师傅 *(shīfu)*

The term 师傅 *(shīfu)* (master worker) is commonly
used in Mainland China for addressing strangers,
particularly taxi drivers, chefs, and other skilled service
workers. [See also Cultural Literacy, Lesson 9, Volume 1.]

b 极了 *(jí le)*

When used after an adjective or verb, 极了 *(jí le)*
usually indicates a superlative degree, as in
今天热极了 *(Jīntiān rè jí le)* (It is extremely hot today)
and 他高兴极了 *(Ta gāoxìng jí le)* (He is overjoyed).

c 没关系 *(méi guānxi)*

To respond to 对不起 *(duìbuqǐ)*, it is common
to say 没关系 *(méi guānxi)* (it doesn't matter).

Vocabulary

No.	Word	Pinyin	Part of Speech	Definition
1	师傅	shīfu	n	master worker
2	好吃	hǎochī	adj	delicious
3	糖醋鱼	tángcùyú	n	sweet-and-sour fish
	糖	táng	n	sugar
	醋	cù	n	vinegar
4	甜	tián	adj	sweet
5	酸	suān	adj	sour
6	极	jí	adv	extremely
7	红烧	hóngshāo	v	to braise in soy sauce (to red-cook)
8	牛肉	niúròu	n	beef
	牛	niú	n	cow, ox
9	鱼	yú	n	fish
10	凉拌	liángbàn	v	(of food) cold "blended," cold tossed
11	黄瓜	huánggua	n	cucumber
12	米饭	mǐfàn	n	cooked rice
13	忘	wàng	v	to forget
14	带	dài	v	to bring, to take, to carry, to come with
15	饭卡	fànkǎ	n	meal card
16	错	cuò	adj	wrong

Audio

Flashcards

This is an order slip from a cafe in Taiwan. Did this group of customers all want coffee? How many cold and hot beverages did they order? Did they make any special requests?

1	冰珍珠奶茶 半糖	65
3	熱拿鐵咖啡	225
1	冰拿鐵咖啡	75
1	熱卡布奇諾	75
	合計：	440

GET Real WITH CHINESE

No.	Word	Pinyin	Part of Speech	Definition
17	清楚	*qīngchu*	adj	clear
18	没关系	*méi guānxi*		it doesn't matter
19	上海	*Shànghǎi*	pn	Shanghai

你希望能在学校餐厅吃到什么菜？

Nǐ xīwàng néng zài xuéxiào cāntīng chī dào shénme cài?

What dishes would you like to be able to eat at the school cafeteria?

我希望 _____。

Wǒ xīwàng _____.

See index for corresponding vocabulary or research another term.

Grammar

Adjective reduplication (I)

Some Chinese adjectives can be reduplicated. When monosyllabic adjectives are reduplicated, the accent usually falls on the second occurrence. Reduplication of adjectives often suggests an approving and appreciative attitude on the speaker's part when they are attributives and predicates.

A 王朋高高的，很帅。

Wáng Péng gāo gāo de, hěn shuài.

Wang Peng is tall and handsome.

B 可乐凉凉的，很好喝。

Kělè liáng liáng de, hěn hǎo hē.

The cola is nicely cold and tasty.

C 酸辣汤酸酸的、辣辣的，非常好喝。

Suānlàtāng suān suān de, là là de, fēicháng hǎo hē.

The hot-and-sour soup is a bit sour and a bit hot; it tastes great.

Reduplication of adjectives usually does not appear in negative form.

EXERCISES

Paraphrase the sentences by repeating the adjectives to show your approval or appreciation. Use exercise 1 as an example.

More exercises

1 这碗汤　　辣　　很好喝

　　→ 这碗汤辣辣的，很好喝。

2 冰咖啡　　凉　　很好喝

3 红烧牛肉　甜　　很好吃

The verb 来 (lái)

In colloquial Chinese, the verb 来 (lái) can serve as a substitute for certain verbs, mostly in imperative sentences.

A

Q: 先生，你们想吃点儿什么？

Xiānsheng, nǐmen xiǎng chī diǎnr shénme?

Sir, what would you like?

A: 来一盘糖醋鱼，一碗酸辣汤，和一碗米饭。

Lái yì pán tángcùyú, yì wǎn suānlàtāng, hé yì wǎn mǐfàn.

Give us a plate of sweet-and-sour fish, a bowl of hot-and-sour soup, and a bowl of rice, please.

At a concert, when the singer has sung the last song:

B

再来一个！

Zài lái yí ge!

Encore!

The use of 来 (lái) in this sense is rather limited. It is usually used at restaurants, stores, and parties, especially when buying small things or coaxing someone to sing another song and so on.

Language Practice

Try the special

PRESENTATIONAL

Role-play as a waiter in a restaurant. Use the images below to make recommendations to the class, e.g.:

我们的青菜好吃极了。

Wǒmen de qīngcài hǎochī jí le.

 1

2

3

 4

5

Now, role-play as a customer and complain about the food, e.g., it's too expensive, sour, sweet, spicy . . . Note: the opposites of 好吃 (*hǎochī*) and 好喝 (*hǎohē*) are 难吃 (*nánchī*) and 难喝 (*nánhē*).

| How do you pronounce the characters? |
| What is the common component? |
| How do you pronounce the common component? |
| How does the component relate to the pronunciation of the characters? |

Characterize it!

❶ 请 ❷ 精 ❸ 清

More characters

May I take your order?

Pretend you and your classmates are in a restaurant in China, and the waiter is taking your order. The easiest way to place an order in a Chinese restaurant is to use 来 (lái), e.g.:

Q: 您想喝点儿什么?

Nín xiǎng hē diǎnr shénme?

 x2 A: 服务员，来两杯冰茶。

Fúwùyuán, lái liǎng bēi bīngchá.

1 x3

2  x1

3  x1

4  x2

5 x2

It doesn't agree with me

Tell the waiter that you have a special diet and would like the chef not to use certain ingredients or seasonings, e.g.:

我不吃盐，请师傅一点儿盐都不要/别放。

Wǒ bù chī yán, qǐng shīfu yìdiǎnr yán dōu bú yào/bié fàng.

1 MSG

2 meat

3 vinegar

4 sugar

At your service

You're helping your friend to prepare for an interview for a part-time job at a restaurant. In groups, brainstorm and create a protocol cheat sheet on how to greet and seat customers, recommend dishes, address customers' dietary restrictions, ensure customer satisfaction, etc. Compare each group's suggestions and vote for the best.

Q: 如果客人问："服务员，还有没有位子？"服务员说什么？

Rúguǒ kèrén wèn: "Fúwùyuán, hái yǒu méiyǒu wèizi?" Fúwùyuán shuō shénme?

A: 服务员说："有，有，有，那儿有位子。"

Fúwùyuán shuō: "Yǒu, yǒu, yǒu, nàr yǒu wèizi."

Chinese Chat

A customer is texting your restaurant to place a takeout order. How would you respond?

9:48 PM   85%

心美小馆

我想点餐。
15 minutes ago

…
13 minutes ago

姓张。一个家常豆腐，一碗酸辣汤，一碗米饭。
12 minutes ago

…
10 minutes ago

豆腐卖完了？那有什么好吃的素菜？
8 minutes ago

…
7 minutes ago

好，一共多少钱？能刷卡吗？
6 minutes ago

…
5 minutes ago

什么时候能做好？
3 minutes ago

…
1 minute ago

Send

文化

Continue
to explore

Cantonese cuisine

FOUR
MAJOR SCHOOLS OF
Cooking

Shandong cuisine

The term 中国菜 (Zhōngguó cài) encompasses the great variety of Chinese cuisine. There are said to be four major schools of cooking: 鲁菜 (Lǔcài), from northern Shandong Province; 川菜 (Chuāncài), from Sichuan Province; 粤菜 (Yuècài), from Guangdong Province; and 淮扬菜 (Huáiyángcài), from the lower Yangtze Valley. Chinese restaurants typically specialize in one particular style, but some are more eclectic.

Traditionally, the Chinese meal is built around a staple (主食) (zhǔshí)—historically, this typically would have been rice in the south, whereas in the north, it often would have been noodles (面条) (miàntiáo), dumplings (饺子) (jiǎozi), or Chinese steamed bread (馒头) (mántou).

Huaiyang cusine

Sichuanese cuisine

Utensils

In traditional Chinese food culture, knives (刀) *(dāo)* typically belong in the kitchen, not at the dining table. The cook preempts the diner's need for a knife by cutting up food, especially meat, into small pieces before cooking. Most Chinese people prefer to eat with chopsticks (筷子) *(kuàizi)*.

59

COMPARE & CONTRAST

1 In China as in many other countries, there are regional differences in cuisine. Can you think of any similar regional differences in your own country?

2 In what ways are Chinese restaurants in China different from those in your country? How do diners in China feel about ice-cold beverages? For Chinese diners, is it not a meal without soup? How about desserts and fortune cookies?

Localization

Since the 1990s, American fast food restaurants such as KFC (肯德基) *(Kěndéjī)*, McDonald's (麦当劳) *(Màidāngláo)*, and Pizza Hut (必胜客) *(Bìshèngkè)* have flourished in Chinese cities. The dubious reputation of American fast food as "fattening" has not scared many Chinese customers away. The success of these American restaurants in China has been, at least in part, due to their efforts at adapting to local tastes. KFC, for instance, offers soy milk (豆浆) *(dòujiāng)* and deep-fried dough sticks (油条) *(yóutiáo)* for breakfast, while McDonald's has chicken rolls (鸡肉卷) *(jīròujuǎn)* on the menu.

Vege
tarian
ism

Historically, vegetarianism (吃素) *(chī sù)* in China has been related to the practice of Buddhism. According to orthodox standards, 吃素 entails abstaining from not only meat but also pungent vegetables and herbs such as onions, garlic, and chives. Many vegetarian dishes, however, try to emulate the texture and flavor of meat. This is why Buddhist temple dishes regularly feature "mock chicken" and "mock duck." Nowadays, people in China become vegetarian for a wide variety of reasons, like health, that are unrelated to religious practices.

Lesson Wrap-Up

Rearrange the sentences below into a logical sequence. Then combine the sentences into a coherent narrative. Replace nouns with pronouns and change periods to commas where appropriate. Delete identical subject pronouns. Add the connective devices 后来 (hòulái), 就 (jiù), 除了…以外 (chúle … yǐwài), 还… (hái …), 可是 (kěshì), and 就 (jiù) where necessary.

_____ 饭馆里好像一个位子都没有了。

_____ 李友又要了两碗酸辣汤。

_____ 小白菜已经卖完了。

_____ 王朋和李友看到有一张桌子没有人。

_____ 王朋和李友点了两盘素饺子。

_____ 王朋和李友还点了一盘家常豆腐。

__1__ 昨天王朋和李友去一家中国饭馆吃饭。

_____ 饭馆里吃饭的人很多。

_____ 李友觉得点的菜够了。

_____ 李友觉得不用点别的了。

_____ 王朋和李友坐了下来。

_____ 李友还想点小白菜。

_____ 李友让服务员上菜快一点儿。

Role-Play

Student A   You have a part-time job working as a server at a Chinese restaurant. Welcome customers to the restaurant. Find out what they would like to drink first. Take their orders. Suggest a dish that they can share. Assure them that the food will be prepared according to their dietary restrictions.

Student B   Customer, vegetarian, does not like MSG, likes tofu, likes dumplings; would like a Coke while waiting for the food.

Student C   Customer, loves meat, does not like salty food, likes dumplings; would like tea while waiting for the food.

Presentation

Make a slideshow presentation about your favorite Chinese dish. Include these points:

- Ingredients: 这个菜里有哪些材料 *(cáiliào)* (ingredient)？
- Seasonings: 这个菜里有哪些调料 *(tiáoliào)* (seasoning)？
- Flavors of the dish: 这个菜甜不甜，辣不辣……？
- Reason for liking the dish: 我喜欢这个菜，因为……

Supplemental Reading Practice

For additional reading practice that builds on the vocabulary introduced in this lesson, turn to the supplemental readings that begin on page 419.

Can-Do Check List

I can

Before proceeding to Lesson 13, make sure you can complete the following tasks in Chinese:

- ☐ Ask if there are seats available
- ☐ Name some Chinese dishes and place an order
- ☐ Tell the waiter my dietary preferences and restrictions
- ☐ Ask for recommendations
- ☐ Pay my bill
- ☐ Get correct change after payment

Lesson 13

第十三课

Dì shísān kè

问路

Wèn lù

ASKING DIRECTIONS

Learning Objectives

In this lesson, you will learn to:

- Ask for and give directions
- Identify locations by using landmarks as references
- Describe whether two places are close to or far away from each other
- State where you are heading and the reason for going there

Relate & Get Ready

In your own culture/community:

- Besides "hello," "how are you," and "what's up," what are some common greetings?
- What phrases do people often use when giving directions?

Where Are You Off To?

Dialogue 1

Audio

Video

（白英爱刚下课……）

小白，下课了？上哪儿去^a？

您好，常老师。我想去学校的电脑中心，不知道怎么走，听说就在运动场旁边[1]。

电脑中心没有[2]运动场那么[3]远。你知道学校图书馆在哪里^b吗？

知道，离王朋的宿舍不远。

电脑中心离图书馆很近，就在图书馆和学生活动中心中间。

常老师，您去哪儿呢？

我想到学校书店去买书[4]。

书店在什么地方^c？

就在学生活动中心里边。我们一起走吧。

好。

(Bái Yīng'ài gāng xià kè . . .)

 Xiǎo Bái, xià kè le? Shàng nǎr qu^a?

 Nín hǎo, Cháng lǎoshī. Wǒ xiǎng qù xuéxiào de

diànnǎo zhōngxīn, bù zhīdào zěnme zǒu, tīngshuō

jiù zài yùndòngchǎng *pángbiān*[1].

 Diànnǎo zhōngxīn *méiyǒu*[2] yùndòngchǎng nàme[3]

yuǎn. Nǐ zhīdào xuéxiào túshūguǎn zài nǎli^b ma?

 Zhīdào, lí Wáng Péng de sùshè bù yuǎn.

 Diànnǎo zhōngxīn lí túshūguǎn hěn jìn,

jiù zài túshūguǎn hé xuéshēng huódòng

zhōngxīn zhōngjiān.

 Cháng lǎoshī, nín qù nǎr ne?

 Wǒ xiǎng *dào xuéxiào shūdiàn qù mǎi shū*[4].

 Shūdiàn zài shénme dìfang^c?

 Jiù zài xuéshēng huódòng zhōngxīn lǐbian.

Wǒmen yìqǐ zǒu ba.

 Hǎo.

Language Notes

a 上哪儿去 (shàng nǎr qu)

This is a more casual way of asking 去哪儿 (qù nǎr).

b 哪里 (nǎli)

This is a question word meaning "where." It is interchangeable with 哪儿 (nǎr). People in northern China, especially in Beijing, end many words with the 儿 (ér) sound. For example, some people say 明儿 (míngr) for "tomorrow" instead of 明天 (míngtiān), and 这儿 (zhèr) for "here" instead of 这里 (zhèli).

c 什么地方 (shénme dìfang)

This phrase literally means "what place." It is generally interchangeable with 哪儿 (nǎr) or 哪里 (nǎli).

Vocabulary

Audio

Flashcards

No.	Word	Pinyin	Part of Speech	Definition
1	上	*shàng*	v	to go [colloq.]
2	中心	*zhōngxīn*	n	center
3	听说	*tīngshuō*	v	to be told, to hear of
4	运动	*yùndòng*	n	sports
5	场	*chǎng*	n	field
6	旁边	*pángbiān*	n	side [See Grammar 1.]
7	远	*yuǎn*	adj	far
8	离	*lí*	prep	away from
9	近	*jìn*	adj	near
10	活动	*huódòng*	n	activity
11	中间	*zhōngjiān*	n	middle
12	书店	*shūdiàn*	n	bookstore
13	地方	*dìfang*	n	place
14	里边	*lǐbian*	n	inside [See Grammar 1.]

你下课以后想
上哪儿去？

Nǐ xià kè yǐhòu xiǎng shàng nǎr qu?

Where are you going after class?

我想 ＿＿＿＿＿＿＿＿＿。

Wǒ xiǎng ＿＿＿＿＿＿＿＿＿.

How About You?

See index for corresponding vocabulary or research another term.

Grammar

<u>1</u> **Direction and location words**

The direction words 上／下／前／后／左／右／东／南／西／北／里／外／旁 (*shàng/xià/qián/hòu/zuǒ/yòu/dōng/nán/xī/běi/lǐ/wài/páng*) are often combined with suffixes such as 边 (*biān*), 面 (*miàn*), and 头 (*tóu*). As shown below, such compounds become location words.

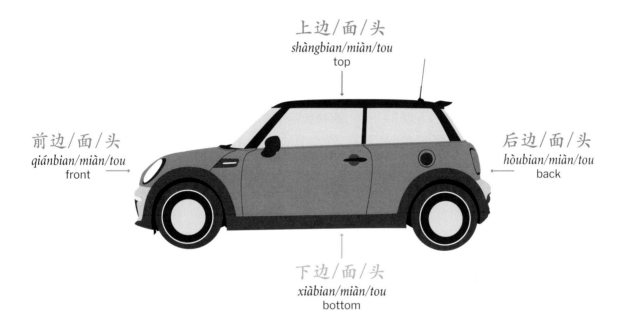

上边／面／头
shàngbian/miàn/tou
top

前边／面／头
qiánbian/miàn/tou
front

后边／面／头
hòubian/miàn/tou
back

下边／面／头
xiàbian/miàn/tou
bottom

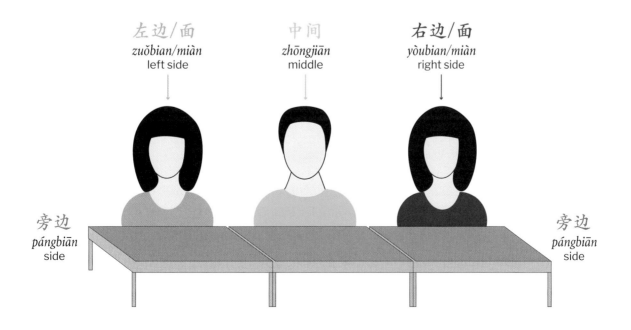

左边／面
zuǒbian/miàn
left side

中间
zhōngjiān
middle

右边／面
yòubian/miàn
right side

旁边
pángbiān
side

旁边
pángbiān
side

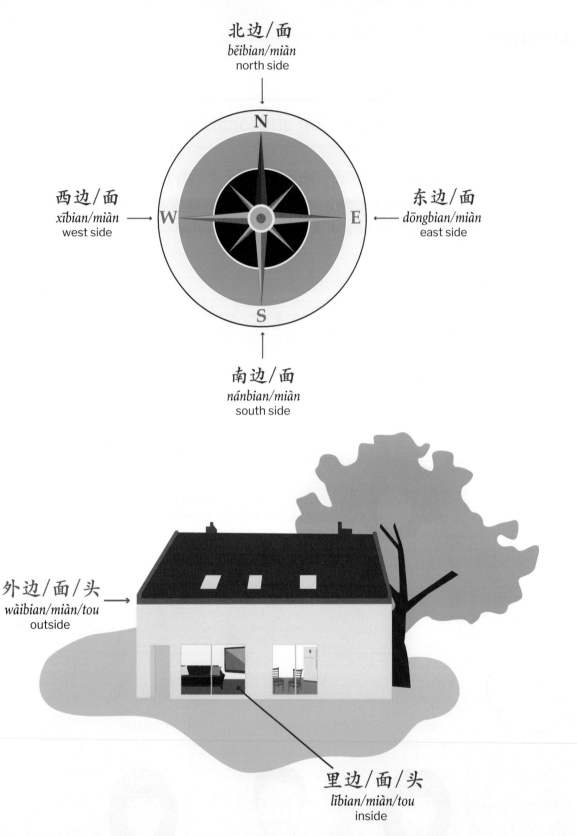

北边/面
běibian/miàn
north side

西边/面
xībian/miàn
west side

东边/面
dōngbian/miàn
east side

南边/面
nánbian/miàn
south side

外边/面/头
wàibian/miàn/tou
outside

里边/面/头
lǐbian/miàn/tou
inside

The direction word 上 (*shàng*) (on) or 里 (*lǐ*) (in) can be combined with a noun to form a location expression, as in (A). Other examples include 桌子上 (*zhuōzi shang*) (on the table), 衣服上 (*yīfu shang*) (on the clothes), 书上 (*shū shang*) (in/on the book), 学校里 (*xuéxiào li*) (in the school), 办公室里 (*bàngōngshì li*) (in the office), 教室里 (*jiàoshì li*) (in the classroom), and 电视里 (*diànshì li*) (on TV). Note that 里 (*lǐ*) cannot be used after some proper nouns, such as countries or cities, as shown in (B).

A 学校里有很多学生。

Xuéxiào li yǒu hěn duō xuésheng.

There are many students at school.

B 北京有很多学生。

Běijīng yǒu hěn duō xuésheng.

There are many students in Beijing.

[✕ 北京里有很多学生。]

The combination of a direction word plus 边 *(biān)*/面 *(miàn)*/头 *(tóu)* can follow a noun to indicate a location, e.g., 图书馆（的）旁边 *(túshūguǎn [de] pángbiān)* (near the library), 学校（的）里面 *(xuéxiào [de] lǐmiàn)* (inside the school), 桌子（的）上头 *(zhuōzi [de] shàngtou)* (on the table), 教室（的）外面 *(jiàoshì [de] wàimiàn)* (outside the classroom), and 城市（的）北边 *(chéngshì [de] běibian)* (north of the city). In these expressions, the particle 的 *(de)* following the noun is optional.

GET Real WITH CHINESE

You see this sign while touring Sun Moon Lake. What is it pointing toward, and would you want to make this part of your itinerary?

EXERCISES

Complete the sentences with the appropriate location words: 上边/头, 前面/头, 后面/头, 里面/头, or 中间. Use exercise 1 as an example.

1 教室 ＿＿＿ 有很多学生。

→ 教室里面有很多学生。

2 桌子 ＿＿＿ 有三本书。

3 图书馆和电脑中心的 ＿＿＿ 是宿舍。

2 | **Comparative sentences using 没（有）(méi[yǒu])**

Besides using 比 (bǐ), another way to make a comparison is to use 没（有） (méi[yǒu]). The two are opposites in meaning, as shown in the table below. In a comparative sentence using 没有 (méiyǒu), the pronoun 那么 (nàme) is sometimes added to the sentence, as seen in (C) and (D).

X 比 (bǐ) Y 大 (dà)   X > Y

= Y 没有 (méiyǒu) X 大 (dà)   Y < X

A 我比弟弟高。   or 弟弟没有我高。

Wǒ bǐ dìdi gāo.   *Dìdi méiyǒu wǒ gāo.*

I am taller than my younger brother.   My younger brother is not as tall as I am.

B 上海比北京热。   or 北京没有上海热。

Shànghǎi bǐ Běijīng rè.   *Běijīng méiyǒu Shànghǎi rè.*

Shanghai is hotter than Beijing.   It is not as hot in Beijing as in Shanghai.

C 他哥哥比他姐姐喜欢买东西。

Tā gēge bǐ tā jiějie xǐhuan mǎi dōngxi.

His older brother likes shopping more than his older sister does.

_{or} 他姐姐没有他哥哥那么喜欢买东西。

Tā jiějie méiyǒu tā gēge nàme xǐhuan mǎi dōngxi.

His older sister does not like shopping as much as his older brother does.
(His older sister might like shopping too, but not as much as his older brother.)

D 她比我喜欢刷卡买东西。

Tā bǐ wǒ xǐhuan shuā kǎ mǎi dōngxi.

She likes to use credit cards for shopping more than I do.

_{or} 我没有她那么喜欢刷卡买东西。

Wǒ méiyǒu tā nàme xǐhuan shuā kǎ mǎi dōngxi.

I don't like to use credit cards for shopping as much as she does.
(I do use credit cards for shopping, but she likes to use them more than I do.)

EXERCISES

Paraphrase the sentences by inserting 没有 where appropriate. Use exercise 1 as an example.

More exercises

1 王老师说话不快，李老师说话快。

   → 王老师说话没有李老师快。

2 那篇课文没有意思，这篇课文有意思。

3 红色的鞋不贵，黑色的鞋贵。

---

3 | **Indicating degree using 那么** *(nàme)*

那么 *(nàme)* is often placed before adjectives or verbs such as 想 *(xiǎng)*, 喜欢 *(xǐhuan)*, 会 *(huì)*, 能 *(néng)*, and 希望 *(xīwàng)*, to denote a high degree, as in (A). 没有…那么… *(méiyǒu … nàme …)* means "not reaching the point of," as in (B), (C), (D), and (E).

A 你那么不喜欢发短信，就别发了吧。

Nǐ nàme bù xǐhuan fā duǎnxìn, jiù bié fā le ba.

Since you dislike sending text messages so much, stop doing it then.

B 弟弟没有哥哥那么帅，那么酷。

Dìdi méiyǒu gēge nàme shuài, nàme kù.

The younger brother is not as handsome and cool as the older brother.

C 坐地铁没有坐公共汽车那么麻烦。

Zuò dìtiě méiyǒu zuò gōnggòng qìchē nàme máfan.

Taking the subway is not as much of a hassle as taking the bus.

D 这件衣服没有那件衣服那么舒服。

Zhè jiàn yīfu méiyǒu nà jiàn yīfu nàme shūfu.

This outfit is not as comfortable as that one.

E 这个电脑没有那个电脑那么新。

Zhè gè diànnǎo méiyǒu nà gè diànnǎo nàme xīn.

This computer is not as new as that one.

By using 那么 *(nàme)*, the speaker attributes a certain quality or characteristic to something or somebody. By stating that the younger brother does not reach the same level of handsomeness and coolness as the older brother, for instance, (B) confirms that the older brother is handsome and cool.

More
exercises

EXERCISES

Paraphrase the sentences by inserting 没有···那么··· where appropriate. Use exercise 1 as an example.

1 那件衣服比这件衣服便宜。

→ 这件衣服没有那件衣服那么便宜。

2 我弟弟比我喜欢打球。

3 写中文比说中文难。

到 (dào) + place + 去 (qù) + action

In this structure, the combination of "到 (dào) + place + 去 (qù) + action" denotes the purpose of going somewhere. It is the same as "去 (qù) + place + action."

A
我要到电脑中心去上网。
or 我要去电脑中心上网。

Wǒ yào dào diànnǎo zhōngxīn qù shàng wǎng. or Wǒ yào qù diànnǎo zhōngxīn shàng wǎng.

I want to go to the computer center to use the Internet.

B
他到朋友的宿舍去聊天儿了。
or 他去朋友的宿舍聊天儿了。

Tā dào péngyou de sùshè qù liáo tiānr le. or Tā qù péngyou de sùshè liáo tiānr le.

He went to his friend's dorm to chat.

C
我们到公园去滑冰吧。
or 我们去公园滑冰吧。

Wǒmen dào gōngyuán qù huábīng ba. or Wǒmen qù gōngyuán huábīng ba.

Let's go ice skating in the park.

EXERCISES

Rephrase the following sentences with 到…去…. Use exercise 1 as an example.

More exercises

1   我要去图书馆看书。
    → 我要到图书馆去看书。

2   王朋要去商店买东西。

3   我们周末要去朋友家吃饭。

Language Practice

Lost and found

INTERPERSONAL

Little Peng can't find anything in his room; his mom has to tell him where everything is. In pairs, role-play Little Peng, who cannot find anything and keeps asking "Where is my . . . ?" and his mother, who has to tell him where everything is. Use direction and location words, e.g.:

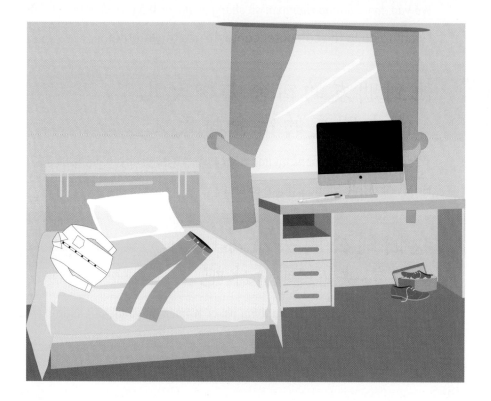

Q: 我的电脑呢?
Wǒ de diànnǎo ne?

A: 你的电脑在桌子上。
Nǐ de diànnǎo zài zhuōzi shang.

1 　　2 　　3 　　4

B

This and that

PRESENTATIONAL

Based on the given clues, use 没有⋯（那么）⋯ (méiyǒu . . . [nàme] . . .) to make comparisons, e.g.:

今天没有昨天（那么）暖和。

Jīntiān méiyǒu zuótiān (nàme) nuǎnhuo.

1 6′ 1″   5′ 11″

2

3

4

5

C

Near and far

INTERPERSONAL

In pairs, locate each city on the map and form a question-and-answer about whether the city is close to or far away from where you live, e.g.:

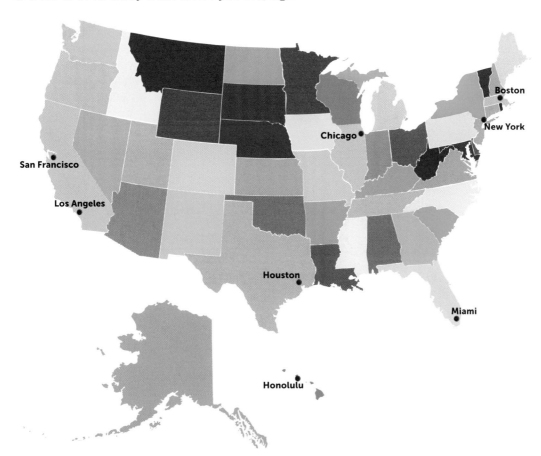

Q: 纽约离我们这儿远吗？

Niǔyuē lí wǒmen zhèr yuǎn ma?

A: 纽约离我们这儿很远/不远/很近。

Niǔyuē lí wǒmen zhèr hěn yuǎn/bù yuǎn/hěn jìn.

1 Boston   **3** Houston   **5** Miami   **7** Honolulu
2 Chicago   **4** Los Angeles   **6** San Francisco

D | **Hot spots and cool places** | INTERPERSONAL

In pairs, role-play a friend coming to visit your school and make suggestions for showing him/her around. Pick a place and an activity depicted below, and use the "到 *(dào)* + place + 去 *(qù)* + action" or "去 *(qù)* + place + action" patterns to discuss possible itineraries, e.g.:

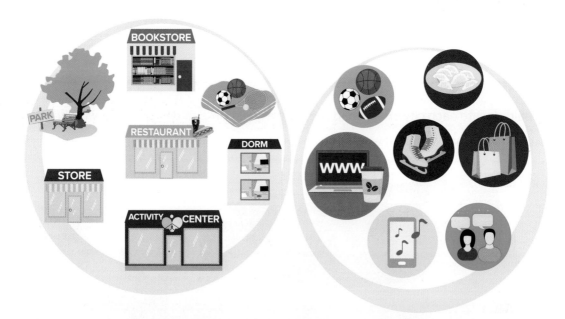

Student A 我们到公园去滑冰，好吗？ /
我们去公园滑冰，好吗？

Wǒmen dào gōngyuán qù huá bīng, hǎo ma?/Wǒmen qù gōngyuán huá bīng, hǎo ma?

Student B 好，什么时候去？ (affirmative)

Hǎo, shénme shíhou qù?

Student B 我们还是……吧。 (negative)

Wǒmen háishi . . . ba.

Inside scoop

You're interning at a local market research company and have been asked to survey students' consumer behaviors. Collect the results and make a presentation to your class.

1 你喜欢到哪儿去跳舞？

Nǐ xǐhuan dào nǎr qù tiào wǔ?

2 你周末晚上常常到哪儿去吃饭？

Nǐ zhōumò wǎnshang chángcháng dào nǎr qù chī fàn?

3 你喜欢到哪儿去看电影？

Nǐ xǐhuan dào nǎr qù kàn diànyǐng?

4 你常常到哪儿去买衣服？

Nǐ chángcháng dào nǎr qù mǎi yīfu?

Chinese Chat

The student union just published a new post on Weibo. Where do you think people on campus will be headed tonight?

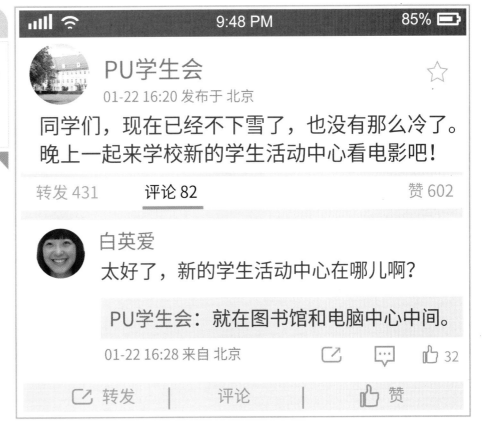

9:48 PM 85%

PU学生会 ☆
01-22 16:20 发布于 北京

同学们，现在已经不下雪了，也没有那么冷了。晚上一起来学校新的学生活动中心看电影吧！

转发 431   评论 82   赞 602

白英爱
太好了，新的学生活动中心在哪儿啊？

PU学生会：就在图书馆和电脑中心中间。

01-22 16:28 来自 北京   32

转发 | 评论 | 赞

Going to Chinatown

Dialogue 2

Audio

Video

（高文中找王朋去中国城吃饭……）

我们去中国城吃中国饭吧！

我没去过[5]中国城，不知道中国城在哪儿。

没问题[a]，你开车，我告诉你怎么走。

你有谷歌地图吗？拿给我看看[6]。

手机在宿舍里，我忘了带了。

没有地图，走错了怎么办？

没有地图没关系，中国城我去过很多次，不用地图也能找到[7]。你从这儿一直往南开，到第三个路口，往西一拐[b]就[8]到了。

哎，我不知道东南西北[c]。

那你一直往前开，到第三个红绿灯，往右一拐就到了。

（到了第三个路口……）

不对，不对。你看，这个路口只能往左拐，不能往右拐。

那就是下一个路口。往右拐，再往前开。到了，到了，你看见了吗？前面有很多中国字。

那不是中文，那是日文，我们到了小东京了。

是吗？那我们不吃中国饭了，吃日本饭吧！

(Gāo Wénzhōng zhǎo Wáng Péng qù Zhōngguóchéng chī fàn.)

 Wǒmen qù Zhōngguóchéng chī Zhōngguó fàn ba!

 Wǒ méi qù guo [5] Zhōngguóchéng, bù zhīdào Zhōngguóchéng zài nǎr.

 Méi wèntí [a], nǐ kāi chē, wǒ gàosù nǐ zěnme zǒu.

 Nǐ yǒu Gǔgē dìtú ma? Ná gěi wǒ kàn kan [6].

 Shǒujī zài sùshè li, wǒ wàng le dài le.

 Méiyǒu dìtú, zǒu cuò le zěnmebàn?

 Méiyǒu dìtú méi guānxi, Zhōngguóchéng wǒ qù guo hěn duō cì, bú yòng dìtú yě néng zhǎo dào [7].
Nǐ cóng zhèr yìzhí wǎng nán kāi, dào dì sān ge lùkǒu, wǎng xī yì guǎi [b] jiù [8] dào le.

 Āi, wǒ bù zhīdào dōng nán xī běi [c].

 Nà nǐ yìzhí wǎng qián kāi, dào dì sān ge hónglǜdēng, wǎng yòu yì guǎi jiù dào le.
(Dào le dì sān ge lùkǒu . . .)

 Bú duì, bú duì. Nǐ kàn, zhè ge lùkǒu zhǐ néng wǎng zuǒ guǎi, bù néng wǎng yòu guǎi.

 Nà jiù shì xià yí ge lùkǒu. Wǎng yòu guǎi, zài wǎng qián kāi. Dào le, dào le, nǐ kàn jiàn le ma? Qiánmiàn yǒu hěn duō Zhōngguó zì.

 Nà bú shì Zhōngwén, nà shì Rìwén, wǒmen dào le Xiǎo Dōngjīng le.

 Shì ma? Nà wǒmen bù chī Zhōngguó fàn le, chī Rìběn fàn ba.

a 没问题 (*méi wèntí*) vs. 没关系 (*méi guānxi*)

You can use 没问题 (*méi wèntí*) (no problem) to assure someone that their request will be met or a problem will be solved, e.g.: 开车送你去机场? 没问题! (*Kāi chē sòng nǐ qù jīchǎng? Méi wèntí!*) (Drive you to the airport? No problem!). 没关系 (*méi guānxi*) (it doesn't matter), on the other hand, downplays the severity or impact of an issue, and is often used in response to someone's apology for a minor mistake.

b 拐 (*guǎi*)

拐 (*guǎi*), in the sense of "to turn," is used mainly in northern China. In the south, 转 (*zhuǎn*) is more common. It is also the more formal substitute for 拐 (*guǎi*) in the north.

c 东南西北 (*dōng nán xī běi*)

Chinese speakers customarily mention the four directions in a set sequence, 东南西北 (*dōng nán xī běi*) or 东西南北 (*dōng xī nán běi*). Unlike in English, intermediate directions are given with east or west first. Hence, for southeast and northeast, one says 东南 (*dōng nán*) and 东北 (*dōng běi*), never ⊗ 南东 (*nán dōng*) or ⊗ 北东 (*běi dōng*). Similarly, for southwest and northwest, one says 西南 (*xī nán*) and 西北 (*xī běi*), never ⊗ 南西 (*nán xī*) or ⊗ 北西 (*běi xī*). The speaker means he can't tell which way is east, south, etc.

Vocabulary

No.	Word	Pinyin	Part of Speech	Definition
1	中国城	Zhōngguóchéng	n	Chinatown
	城	chéng	n	town, city
2	过	guo	p	(particle used after a verb to indicate a past experience) [See Grammar 5.]
3	地图	dìtú	n	map
4	拿	ná	v	to take, to get
5	次	cì	m	(measure word for frequency)
6	从	cóng	prep	from
7	一直	yìzhí	adv	straight, continuously
8	往	wǎng	prep	towards
9	南	nán	n	south
10	路口	lùkǒu	n	intersection
11	西	xī	n	west
12	拐	guǎi	v	to turn
13	哎	āi	excl	(exclamatory particle to express surprise or dissatisfaction)
14	东	dōng	n	east
15	北	běi	n	north
16	前	qián	n	forward, ahead
17	红绿灯	hónglǜdēng	n	traffic light
	灯	dēng	n	light
18	右	yòu	n	right
19	左	zuǒ	n	left

Audio

Flashcards

大型车

摩托车

靠右

You're taking a bus from Beijing to Zhangjiakou to go skiing, and you see this sign as you look out the window. What message does the sign have for motorcyclists and for drivers of large buses and trucks?

GET
Real
WITH CHINESE

No.	Word	Pinyin	Part of Speech	Definition
20	前面	*qiánmiàn*	n	ahead, in front of
21	谷歌	*Gǔgē*	pn	Google
22	日文	*Rìwén*	pn	Japanese (language)
23	东京	*Dōngjīng*	pn	Tokyo
24	日本	*Rìběn*	pn	Japan

你的中文教室在
图书馆的哪边？

Nǐ de Zhōngwén jiàoshì zài túshūguǎn de nǎ bian?

Where is your Chinese classroom located relative to the library?

How About You?

我的中文教室在 _____。

Wǒ de Zhōngwén jiàoshì zài _____.

See index for corresponding vocabulary or refer to Language Note c to combine the cardinal directions.

Grammar

The dynamic particle 过 (guo)

The dynamic particle 过 (guo) is used to denote a past experience or occurrence that has not continued to the present but, typically, has a bearing on the present.

A 我在中国城工作过一年，所以我知道怎么走。

Wǒ zài Zhōngguóchéng gōngzuò guo yì nián, suǒyǐ wǒ zhīdào zěnme zǒu.

I worked in Chinatown for a year, so I know how to get there.

[The fact that the speaker worked in Chinatown for a year is the reason why he/she knows how to get there.]

B 我见过李友，（所以知道）她很高。

Wǒ jiàn guo Lǐ Yǒu, (suǒyǐ zhīdào) tā hěn gāo.

I've met Li You before, (so I know) she is tall.

C Q: 运动场远不远，你知道吗？

Yùndòngchǎng yuǎn bu yuǎn, nǐ zhīdào ma?

Do you know if the sports field is far from here?

A: 运动场我去过，（所以我知道）不远，很近。

Yùndòngchǎng wǒ qù guo, (suǒyǐ wǒ zhīdào) bù yuǎn, hěn jìn.

I've been to the sports field, (so I know) it is not far away. It's very close.

In this kind of sentence, expressions of time are often either unspecific or completely absent. If there is no time expression, the implied time for the action or event is 以前 (yǐqián) (before, previously). Sometimes 以前 (yǐqián) can appear in the sentence as well.

D 我以前去过中国城，知道怎么走。

Wǒ yǐqián qù guo Zhōngguóchéng, zhīdào zěnme zǒu.

I've been to Chinatown before. I know how to get there.

E 以前我们见过面，可是没说过话。

Yǐqián wǒmen jiàn guo miàn, kěshì méi shuō guo huà.

We've met before, but we've never spoken to each other.

An expression indicating a specific time can also occasionally appear in a sentence with 过 (guo).

F Q: 你见过李小姐吗？

Nǐ jiàn guo Lǐ xiǎojiě ma?

Have you ever met Miss Li?

A: 见过，上个月还见过她。

Jiàn guo, shàng ge yuè hái jiàn guo tā.

Yes. I saw her as recently as last month.

More exercises

EXERCISES

Use 过 to find out whether someone has or hasn't done something.
Use exercise 1 as an example.

1 你妈妈　　去　　英国

　　→　你妈妈去过英国吗？

2 你　　　　吃　　素饺子

3 你爸爸　　喝　　酸辣汤

6 | **Verb reduplication (I)**

Like adjectives [see Grammar 6, Lesson 12], verbs can also be reduplicated in imperative sentences. Verb reduplication softens the tone of a request or suggestion.

A 老师，您再说说什么时候用"了"，好吗？

Lǎoshī, nín zài shuō shuo shénme shíhou yòng "le," hǎo ma?

Teacher, would you say a bit more about when to use "le," please?

B 妈，您看看，我这样写对不对？

Mā, nín kàn kan, wǒ zhèyàng xiě duì bu duì?

Mom, take a look—did I write this correctly or not?

C 我用用你的电脑可以吗？

Wǒ yòng yong nǐ de diànnǎo kěyǐ ma?

Could I use your computer for a minute?

D 你帮我找找我的笔，好吗？

Nǐ bāng wǒ zhǎo zhao wǒ de bǐ, hǎo ma?

Could you help me look for my pen for a second?

E 你考完试，我们一起去公园走走，
聊聊天儿。

Nǐ kǎo wán shì, wǒmen yìqǐ qù gōngyuán zǒu zou, liáo liao tiānr.

After your exam, let's take a walk in the park and have a chat.

If a sentence includes both a modal verb and an action verb, only the action verb can be reduplicated.

F 她想看看我的新手机。

Tā xiǎng kàn kan wǒ de xīn shǒujī.

She wants to take a look at my new cell phone.

EXERCISES

Repeat the verb to soften the tone of voice. Use exercise 1 as an example.

More
exercises

1 你看，这件衣服我穿合适不合适？（看）
   → 你看看，这件衣服我穿合适不合适？

2 你说，他那么做对不对？（说）

3 王朋，我用你的笔，行吗？（用）

7

Resultative complements (II)

Let's review all the resultative complements that you have come across so far, and learn some new ones that can be formed from the verbs and complements you already know.

完 (*wán*):

A 看完

kàn wán

finish reading, finish watching

B 吃完

chī wán

finish eating

C 喝完

hē wán

finish drinking

D 考完

kǎo wán

finish taking a test

E 买完

mǎi wán

finish buying

F 卖完

mài wán

finish selling, sell out

到 (*dào*):

G 找到

zhǎo dào

find (something or someone) successfully

H 看到

kàn dào

see (something or someone)

I 听到

tīng dào

hear (something or someone)

J 买到

mǎi dào

buy (something) successfully

见 (jiàn):

K 看见

kàn jiàn

see (something or someone)—
same as 看到 (*kàn dào*)

L 听见

tīng jiàn

hear (something or someone)—
same as 听到 (*tīng dào*)

好 (hǎo):

M 做好

zuò hǎo

complete doing something (and now be ready for the next action)

N 买好

mǎi hǎo

complete buying something (and now be ready for the next action)

O 准备好

zhǔnbèi hǎo

prepare something (and now be ready for the next action)

错 (cuò):

P 买错

mǎi cuò

buy the wrong thing

S 说错

shuō cuò

say (something) incorrectly

Q 找错

zhǎo cuò

give the wrong change, find
the wrong person or thing

T 走错

zǒu cuò

go the wrong way

R 写错

xiě cuò

write (something) incorrectly

懂 (dǒng):

U 听懂

tīng dǒng

comprehend what
one hears

V 看懂

kàn dǒng

comprehend what
one reads or sees

清楚 (qīngchu):

W 看清楚

kàn qīngchu

see (something) clearly

X 听清楚

tīng qīngchu

hear (something) clearly

会 (huì):

Y 学会

xué huì

acquire a skill (to do something that one was previously unable to do)

Collocations such as these, made up of a verb and a resultative complement, are best learned as set phrases. Some resultative complements are semantically related to the verb. For instance, in the sentence 我昨天看见她了 *(Wǒ zuótiān kàn jiàn tā le)* (I saw her yesterday), the complement is semantically related to 看 *(kàn)*, the verb of the sentence. Some resultative complements are semantically related to the object. In the sentence 我写错了两个字 *(Wǒ xiě cuò le liǎng ge zì)* (I wrote two characters incorrectly), for instance, it is the object "characters" 字 *(zì)* that are "wrong" 错 *(cuò)*. Some resultative complements are related to the subject, e.g., in the sentence 我学会了 *(Wǒ xué huì le)* (I have learned it), the complement 会 *(huì)* is semantically related to 我 *(wǒ)*, the subject of the sentence.

More
exercises

EXERCISES

Fill in the blanks with the appropriate complements. Use exercise 1 as an example.

完　懂　错　清楚　对　到

1　我没有买到电影票。

2　你听＿＿＿了，她不叫李文英。

3　这篇课文你看＿＿＿了吗？

8

一···就··· (yī...jiù...) (as soon as ... then ...)

This structure combines two habitual or two one-time actions. In a habitual situation, whenever the first action occurs, the second action immediately follows.

A

他一上课就想睡觉。

Tā yí shàng kè jiù xiǎng shuì jiào.

He feels sleepy every time class starts.

B

小张平常只吃青菜，一吃肉就不舒服。

Xiǎo Zhāng píngcháng zhǐ chī qīngcài, yì chī ròu jiù bù shūfu.

Little Zhang normally eats only vegetables. He feels sick whenever he eats meat.

C

李律师一累就喝咖啡。

Lǐ lǜshī yí lèi jiù hē kāfēi.

Attorney Li drinks coffee whenever he feels tired.

In a one-time situation, the second action takes place as soon as the first is completed:

D

我们一进饭馆儿，服务员就告诉我们没位子了。

Wǒmen yí jìn fànguǎnr, fúwùyuán jiù gàosù wǒmen méi wèizi le.

As soon as we entered the restaurant, the waiter told us there were no seats available.

E

这课的语法很容易，我一看就懂。

Zhè kè de yǔfǎ hěn róngyì, wǒ yí kàn jiù dǒng.

The grammar in this lesson was very easy (to understand). I understood it as soon as I read it.

F 活动中心离这儿不远，到第二个路口，
往右一拐就到了。

Huódòng zhōngxīn lí zhèr bù yuǎn, dào dì èr ge lùkǒu, wǎng yòu yì guǎi jiù dào le.

The activity center is not far from here. Turn right at the second intersection, and you'll be there.

More
exercises

EXERCISES

In pairs, ask and answer the following questions. Use exercise 1 as an example.

1 你一起床就做什么？（洗澡）

 → 我一起床就洗澡。

2 你一吃完早饭就做什么？（去学校上课）

3 你一做完功课就做什么？（听音乐）

Characterize it!

More
characters

❶ ❷ ❸ ❹ ❺

| What do the characters mean? |
| What is the common radical? |
| What does the radical mean? |
| How does the radical relate to the overall meaning of the characters? |

Language Practice

Have you ever?

INTERPERSONAL

In pairs, form a question-and-answer about whether your partner has tried the following things. Ask a follow-up question if the answer is affirmative. Ask if he/she wishes to try them if the answer is negative. Use 过 (guo) to denote the past experience, e.g.:

Q: 你打过球吗？

Nǐ dǎ guo qiú ma?

A: 我打过（球）。

Wǒ dǎ guo (qiú).

Q: 你觉得打球有意思吗？

Nǐ juéde dǎ qiú yǒu yìsi ma?

A: 我觉得打球很有意思／没有意思。

Wǒ juéde dǎ qiú hěn yǒu yìsi/méiyǒu yìsi.

1   2    3

Then find out how adventurous an eater your partner is. Use 过 (guo) to ask whether they have tried a certain dish, e.g.:

Student A 你吃过家常豆腐吗？

Nǐ chī guo jiācháng dòufu ma?

Student B 我没吃过。家常豆腐好吃吗？

Wǒ méi chī guo. Jiācháng dòufu hǎochī ma?

Student A 我觉得（家常豆腐）很好吃／不好吃。

Wǒ juéde (jiācháng dòufu) hěn hǎochī/bù hǎochī.

4   5   6

G | **One thing after another** | INTERPERSONAL

In pairs, take turns asking questions about each other's habits. Use 一···就··· (yī . . . jiù . . .) to denote the sequence.

1 Q: 你平常一吃完早饭就做什么？

Nǐ píngcháng yì chī wán zǎofàn jiù zuò shénme?

A: _____

2 Q: 你平常一下中文课就做什么？

Nǐ píngcháng yí xià Zhōngwénkè jiù zuò shénme?

A: _____

3 Q: 你平常一高兴就做什么？

Nǐ píngcháng yì gāoxìng jiù zuò shénme?

A: _____

4 Q: 你昨天早上一起床就做什么了？

Nǐ zuótiān zǎoshang yì qǐ chuáng jiù zuò shénme le?

A: _____

5 Q: 你昨天一回家就做什么了？

Nǐ zuótiān yì huí jiā jiù zuò shénme le?

A: _____

Location, location, location

Locate the following places using landmarks and direction and location words, e.g.:

Q: 请问图书馆在哪儿?

Qǐng wèn túshūguǎn zài nǎr?

A: 图书馆在运动场（的）北边。/
图书馆在教室和咖啡馆（的）中间。

Túshūguǎn zài yùndòngchǎng (de) běibian./
Túshūguǎn zài jiàoshì hé kāfēiguǎn (de) zhōngjiān.

1 公园

gōngyuán

2 餐厅

cāntīng

3 运动场

yùndòngchǎng

4 公共汽车站

gōnggòng qìchē zhàn

Getting there from here

In pairs, use the map from the previous exercise to ask for and give directions with your partner, e.g.:

公园 → 老师办公室

gōngyuán ⟶ lǎoshī bàngōngshì

Q: 从公园到老师办公室怎么走?

Cóng gōngyuán dào lǎoshī bàngōngshì zěnme zǒu?

A: 你从公园出来，上五行路，往北走，到第一个路口，往东拐，一直走，到第三个路口往左一拐，就到了。/
老师办公室就在你（的）右边儿。

Nǐ cóng gōngyuán chū lai, shàng Wǔxínglù, wǎng běi zǒu, dào dì yī ge lùkǒu, wǎng dōng guǎi, yìzhí zǒu, dào dì sān ge lùkǒu wǎng zuǒ yì guǎi, jiù dào le./
Lǎoshī bàngōngshì jiù zài nǐ (de) yòubianr.

1 电脑中心 → 运动场

diànnǎo zhōngxīn ⟶ yùndòngchǎng

2 学生宿舍 → 公共汽车站

xuéshēng sùshè ⟶ gōnggòng qìchē zhàn

3 书店 → 花店

shūdiàn ⟶ huādiàn (florist)

You're exchanging WeChat messages with a friend to confirm whe e you'll meet. What would you type?

Lola

8:23 PM

你在哪儿?

我们不是约在运动中心见面吗? 你在哪儿?

…

你听错了! 是运动中心，不是运动场……

…

不远。往东一直走，到第三个红绿灯往左一拐就到了。

哪儿是东? 还是你来找我吧! 😊

Characterize it!

What do the characters mean?

What is the common radical?

What does the radical mean?

How does the radical relate to the overall meaning of the characters?

❶ 城　❷ 地　❸ 场

More characters

文化
Continue
to explore

FENG SHUI

Many Chinese people would prefer to have their houses face south, 坐北朝南 (zuò běi cháo nán) (situated in the north and facing south). Just look at the palaces of the Forbidden City in Beijing! In terms of 风水 (fēngshuǐ) (lit. wind and water), the ages-old Chinese practice of harmonizing human existence with nature, south is the most auspicious direction for one's home to face because it balances yin, 阴 (yīn), and yang, 阳 (yáng), and optimizes the flow f qi, 气 (qì) (lit. air), a metaphysical life force. This is hardly surprising, considering that in the northern hemisphere facing south allows for maximum sun and light exposure.

COMPARE & CONTRAST

1 Many Chinese people prefer south-facing homes. Is home orientation a big deal in your culture? Which direction do you prefer your windows to face?

2 The so-called Four Symbols (四象) (Sìxiàng) are four Chinese mythological animals, each with its own cardinal direction. They are the Blue Dragon (青龙) (Qīnglóng) of the east, Vermilion Bird (朱雀) (Zhūquè) of the south, White Tiger (白虎) (Báihǔ) of the west, and Black Turtle (玄武) (Xuánwǔ) of the north. Culturally, they have been important in China, Korea, Japan, and Vietnam, and they appear in modern popular entertainment such as manga and anime. Are there similar ideas in your culture?

A courtyard in a traditional house in Pingyao, Shanxi Province

Chinatown

中国城 (*Zhōngguóchéng*) (Chinatown), also known as 唐人街 (*Tángrénjiē*) (lit. street for the people of Tang, Tang referring to the Tang dynasty in Chinese history), were originally ethnic enclaves for Chinese immigrants in large metropolitan areas in the United States and other countries. However, with the mingling of immigrants from across Asia, especially East Asia, many Chinatowns are becoming increasingly "pan-Asian" rather than specifically Chinese. However, Chinatowns remain a meaningful window on Chinese culture.

Casual greetings

In Chinese culture, people commonly greet each other by asking a casual question about the routine activity that the other person is engaged in at the moment. Thus, upon seeing a friend on her way to a grocery store, you could ask 买菜呀？ (*Mǎi cài ya?*) (Going grocery shopping, eh?). Running into a fellow student who is leaving a classroom, you could ask 下课了？ (*Xià kè le?*) (Just had your class?). As the situation is usually very obvious, the speaker does not expect, and is not interested in, an elaborate answer. Nor are these questions considered intrusive or personal.

A view of Beijing from north of the Forbidden City

URBAN

PLANNING

Beijing is essentially laid out around a symmetrical grid of large, straight thoroughfares, at the center of which is the Forbidden City. The urban planning principles that undergird the city of Beijing are based on Chinese cosmology. "The sky is round and the earth square" (天圆地方) *(tiān yuán dì fāng)*, as the familiar saying goes. Situating the emperor, known as "the Son of Heaven" (天子) *(Tiānzǐ)* at the center of the square capital was therefore highly symbolic. The emperor performed his most important ceremonial duties enthroned in the Hall of Supreme Harmony facing the south. The influence of Beijing's Ming-era planning persists into the present: the names of many subway stations, such as 东直门 *(Dōngzhímén)* and 西直门 *(Xizhímén)*, refer to old gates in the demolished Beijing city wall.

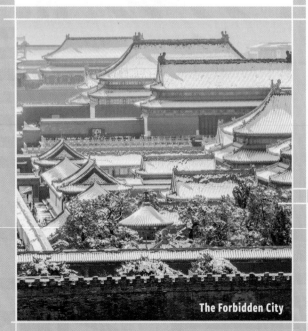

The Forbidden City

Lesson Wrap-Up

Rearrange the following sentences into a logical sequence. Then combine the sentences into a coherent narrative. Replace nouns with pronouns and change periods to commas where appropriate. Delete identical subject pronouns. Add the connective devices 这个时候 (zhè ge shíhou), 就 (jiù), and 所以 (suǒyǐ) where appropriate.

_____白英爱看见常老师来了。

_____白英爱问常老师。

__1__白英爱要去学校的电脑中心。

_____常老师告诉白英爱电脑中心就在图书馆和学生活动中心中间。

_____白英爱现在知道去电脑中心怎么走了。

_____白英爱不知道去电脑中心怎么走。

_____常老师告诉白英爱电脑中心离图书馆很近。

_____白英爱知道图书馆离王朋住的地方不远。

Skit

As you come out of the student activity center, you see a Chinese visitor looking lost. Greet him/her in Chinese and find out where he/she would like to go. The Chinese visitor is very glad that you speak Chinese. He/she thinks your campus is nice-looking and tells you where he/she is from. He/she is trying to find the library. Explain how to get to the library from the student activity center. Offer to walk there with him/her. The Chinese visitor thanks you and asks you about your school. At the entrance to the library, he/she thanks you again, and you say goodbye to each other.

Asking Directions

You are home on break. A Chinese friend is coming to stay with you for a couple of days. He/she calls you from the road. He/she is lost, but thinks that he/she is only several blocks from your house. Decide where your friend is and tell him/her how to get to your house. Incorporate the useful expressions 一直往东/西/南/北开 (yìzhí wǎng dōng/xī/nán/běi kāi), 到第 X 个路口 (dào dì x ge lùkǒu), 往左/右拐 (wǎng zuǒ/yòu guǎi), 然后··· (ránhòu . . .), and ···就到了 (. . . jiù dào le). Optional: After you've recorded your directions, exchange your recording with a classmate. Listen to each other's recordings and draw a map indicating the driving route. Exchange maps and let each other know how the other person did.

Supplemental Reading Practice

For additional reading practice that builds on the vocabulary introduced in this lesson, turn to the supplemental readings that begin on page 419.

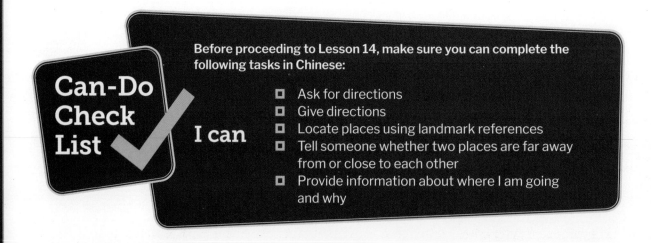

Can-Do Check List

I can

Before proceeding to Lesson 14, make sure you can complete the following tasks in Chinese:

- ☐ Ask for directions
- ☐ Give directions
- ☐ Locate places using landmark references
- ☐ Tell someone whether two places are far away from or close to each other
- ☐ Provide information about where I am going and why

第十四课

Dì shísì kè

生日晚会

Shēngrì wǎnhuì

BIRTHDAY PARTY

Learning Objectives

In this lesson, you will learn to:

- Ask a friend to go to a party with you
- Suggest things to bring to a get-together
- Thank people for gifts
- Describe a duration of time
- Talk about the year of your birth and your Chinese zodiac sign

Relate & Get Ready

In your own culture/community:

- How are birthdays usually celebrated?
- What do people bring to a birthday party?
- Are there any gift-giving taboos?
- Are people supposed to open gifts in front of the gift giver?

Let's Go to a Party!

Dialogue 1

Audio

Video

（李友给王朋打电话。）

王朋，你做什么呢[1]？

我看书呢。

今天高小音过生日[a]，晚上我们在她家开舞会，你能去吗？

能去。几点？

七点。我们先吃饭，吃完饭再唱歌跳舞。

有哪些人？

小音和她的男朋友、小音的表姐[b]、白英爱、你妹妹王红，听说还有小音的中学同学。

你要送给小音什么生日礼物？

我买了一本书送给她。

那我带什么东西？

饮料或者水果都可以。

那我带一些饮料，再买一把花儿。

小音爱吃水果，我再买一些苹果、梨和西瓜吧。

你住的地方[2]离小音家很远，水果很重，我开车去接你，我们一起去吧。

好，我六点半在楼下等你。

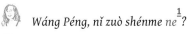

(Lǐ Yǒu gěi Wáng Péng dǎ diànhuà.)

Wáng Péng, nǐ zuò shénme ne[1]?

Wǒ kàn shū ne.

Jīntiān Gāo Xiǎoyīn guò shēngrì[a], wǎnshang wǒmen zài tā jiā kāi wǔhuì, nǐ néng qù ma?

Néng qù. Jǐ diǎn?

Qī diǎn. Wǒmen xiān chī fàn, chī wán fàn zài chàng gē tiào wǔ.

Yǒu nǎ xiē rén?

Xiǎoyīn hé tā de nánpéngyou, Xiǎoyīn de biǎojiě[b], Bái Yīng'ài, nǐ mèimei Wáng Hóng, tīngshuō hái yǒu Xiǎoyīn de zhōngxué tóngxué.

Nǐ yào sòng gěi Xiǎoyīn shénme shēngrì lǐwù?

Wǒ mǎi le yì běn shū sòng gěi tā.

Nà wǒ dài shénme dōngxi?

Yǐnliào huòzhě shuǐguǒ dōu kěyǐ.

Nà wǒ dài yì xiē yǐnliào, zài mǎi yì bǎ huār.

Xiǎoyīn ài chī shuǐguǒ, wǒ zài mǎi yì xiē píngguǒ, lí hé xīgua ba.

Nǐ zhù de dìfang[2] lí Xiǎoyīn jiā hěn yuǎn, shuǐguǒ hěn zhòng, wǒ kāi chē qù jiē nǐ, wǒmen yìqǐ qù ba.

Hǎo, wǒ liù diǎn bàn zài lóu xià děng nǐ.

Language Notes

a 过 *(guò)*

Apart from 过生日 *(guò shēngrì)* (to celebrate one's birthday), the verb 过 *(guò)* (to live [a life], to observe [a holiday], to celebrate [a festival]) appears in many other expressions, such as 过年 *(guò nián)* (to celebrate the New Year), 过节 *(guò jié)* (to celebrate a festival), and 过日子 *(guò rìzi)* (to live one's life, to live from day to day).

b 表姐 *(biǎojiě)* and 堂姐 *(tángjiě)*

The kinship term 表姐 *(biǎojiě)* is more narrowly defined than its translation "older female cousin" would suggest. Your "older female cousin" is a 表姐 *(biǎojiě)* if she is a daughter of your father's sister or your mother's sister or brother. But if she is your paternal uncle's daughter, she is a 堂姐 *(tángjiě)*, not a 表姐 *(biǎojiě)*. Therefore, your 堂姐 *(tángjiě)* typically shares your family name. For more Chinese kinship terms, see Grammar 5 in Lesson 20.

Vocabulary

Audio

Flashcards

No.	Word	Pinyin	Part of Speech	Definition
1	过	guò	v	to live (a life), to observe (a holiday), to celebrate (a festival), to pass
2	舞会	wǔhuì	n	dance party, ball
3	表姐	biǎojiě	n	older female cousin
4	中学	zhōngxué	n	middle school, secondary school
5	送	sòng	v	to give as a gift
6	礼物	lǐwù	n	gift, present
7	本	běn	m	(measure word for books)
8	饮料	yǐnliào	n	beverage
9	水果	shuǐguǒ	n	fruit
10	把	bǎ	m	(measure word for things with handles, for handfuls of things)
11	花	huā	n	flower
12	爱	ài	v	to love, to like, to be fond of
13	苹果	píngguǒ	n	apple
14	梨	lí	n	pear
15	西瓜	xīgua	n	watermelon
16	住	zhù	v	to live (in a certain place)
17	重	zhòng	adj	heavy, serious
18	接	jiē	v	to catch, to meet, to welcome

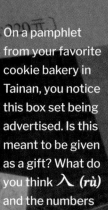

On a pamphlet from your favorite cookie bakery in Tainan, you notice this box set being advertised. Is this meant to be given as a gift? What do you think 入 *(rù)* and the numbers indicate?

GET Real WITH CHINESE

超值分享包 | 7種口味〔NT110元〕

{ **18入綜合禮盒** }
煎·餅·禮·盒·系·列

F r i e d C o o k i e s

小瓦煎燒9入 / 海苔煎餅4入 /
格子煎餅4入 / 檸檬捲心5入 /
草莓捲心5入

每盒 / 〔NT220元〕

No.	Word	Pinyin	Part of Speech	Definition
19	楼	*lóu*	n	multi-story building, floor (of a multi-level building)
20	王红	*Wáng Hóng*	pn	a personal name

你爱吃什么水果?

Nǐ ài chī shénme shuǐguǒ?
What fruits do you like to eat?

我爱吃 ＿＿＿＿＿＿。
Wǒ ài chī ＿＿＿＿＿＿.

See index for corresponding vocabulary or research another term.

Grammar

Indicating an action in progress using 呢 (ne)

呢 (ne) at the end of a sentence indicates that the action denoted by the verb is in progress. In this sense, it is similar to 在 (zài). However, 在 (zài) is not used at the end of a sentence, but before the verb.

A

你写什么呢?

Nǐ xiě shénme ne?

What are you writing?

B

你找什么呢?

Nǐ zhǎo shénme ne?

What are you looking for?

呢 (ne) can also be used in conjunction with 在 (zài).

C

你在写什么呢?

Nǐ zài xiě shénme ne?

What are you writing?

D

你在找什么呢?

Nǐ zài zhǎo shénme ne?

What are you looking for?

在 (zài) by itself can indicate that an action is in progress; therefore, the 呢 (ne) in (C) and (D) can be omitted.

在 (zài) can also be preceded by 正 (zhèng). The phrase 正在 (zhèngzài) further emphasizes that the action is ongoing.

E

我昨天给他打电话的时候,
他正在做功课呢。

Wǒ zuótiān gěi tā dǎ diànhuà de shíhou, tā zhèngzài zuò gōngkè ne.

When I called him yesterday, he was right in the middle of doing his homework.

F

别去找他, 他正在睡觉呢。

Bié qù zhǎo tā, tā zhèngzài shuì jiào ne.

Don't go looking for him. He's sleeping at the moment.

EXERCISES

Complete the sentences with 正在…呢. Use exercise 1 as an example.

1 我回家的时候

妈妈（做饭）

→ 我回家的时候，妈妈正在做饭呢。

2 姐姐给我打电话的时候

我（听音乐）

3 老师进教室的时候

小高（复习生词）

Chinese Chat

In a group chat, you and two friends are trying to plan a party. How would you respond?

< Messages　**Group**　Contact

明天的舞会我准备音乐。谁带饮料、水果？

我带些梨和苹果吧。

…

谢谢二位！别忘了舞会八点开始。明天见。

Send

2 Verbal phrases and subject-predicate phrases used as attributives

In Chinese, attributives, often followed by the particle 的 (de), always appear before what they modify. Verbs, verbal phrases, and subject-predicate phrases can all serve as attributives.

A 吃的东西

chī de dōngxi

things to eat

B 穿的衣服

chuān de yīfu

clothes to wear, or clothes being worn

C 新买的饭卡

xīn mǎi de fànkǎ

newly bought meal card

D 昨天来的同学

zuótiān lái de tóngxué

classmate/classmates who came yesterday

E 以前认识的朋友

yǐqián rènshi de péngyou

friend/friends one previously got to know

F 我妈妈做的豆腐

wǒ māma zuò de dòufu

the tofu dish my mother makes/made

G 老师给我们的功课

lǎoshī gěi wǒmen de gōngkè

the homework the teacher assigned us

H 朋友送的苹果

péngyou sòng de píngguǒ

apples given by a friend

I 请你跳舞的那个人

qǐng nǐ tiào wǔ de nà gè rén

that person who asked you to dance

J 我妹妹喜欢去的那个很酷的地方

wǒ mèimei xǐhuan qù de nà ge hěn kù de dìfang

that very cool place that my younger sister loves to go to

EXERCISES

Modify the nouns with a verb phrase or subject-predicate phrase. Use exercise 1 as an example.

More exercises

1 笔（我刚买）→ 我刚买的笔
2 书（你送给我）
3 衣服（哥哥新买）
4 朋友（昨天认识）

What do the characters mean?
What is the common radical?
What does the radical mean?
How does the radical relate to the overall meaning of the characters?

Characterize it!

❶ 礼 ❷ 视 ❸ 票 ❹ 祝

More characters

Language Practice

A — In the midst

INTERPERSONAL

In pairs, form a question-and-answer about what these people are doing. Use 呢 (ne) to indicate the action is in progress, e.g.:

Q: 她（在）做什么呢？

Tā (zài) zuò shénme ne?

A: 她（在）喝汤呢。

Tā (zài) hē tāng ne.

 1 2 3 4 5

Then ask your partner what he/she was doing last night at 7:00 and 9:00.

B — Oh, that one!

PRESENTATIONAL

Combine the two short sentences into one, using the highlighted verb and phrase to form an attributive. Add 的 (de) where appropriate, e.g.:

他买了一件衣服。那件衣服很贵。

Tā mǎi le yí jiàn yīfu. Nà jiàn yīfu hěn guì.

他买的那件衣服很贵。

Tā mǎi de nà jiàn yīfu hěn guì.

1 他写了一个字。那个字很漂亮。

Tā xiě le yí ge zì. Nà ge zì hěn piàoliang.

2 她买了一件衬衫。那件衬衫是中号的。

Tā mǎi le yí jiàn chènshān. Nà jiàn chènshān shì zhōng hào de.

3 我哥哥给了我一枝笔。那枝笔是黑色的。

Wǒ gēge gěi le wǒ yì zhī bǐ. Nà zhī bǐ shì hēisè de.

4 妹妹带了一些水果。那些水果很贵。

Mèimei dài le yì xiē shuǐguǒ. Nà xiē shuǐguǒ hěn guì.

5 表姐卖了一些花。那些花很漂亮。

Biǎojiě mài le yì xiē huā. Nà xiē huā hěn piàoliang.

C | **Who's who?** | INTERPERSONAL

Help your new classmate match people in your class to their names, using a verb phrase or subject-predicate phrases as an attributive. Add 的 (de) where appropriate, e.g.:

Q: Jamal是谁？

Jamal *shì shéi?*

A: Jamal是那个穿蓝色衬衫的学生。

Jamal *shì nà ge chuān lánsè chènshān de xuésheng.*

Q: Katy是谁？

Katy *shì shéi?*

A: Katy是那个正在看书的女孩。

Katy *shì nà ge zhèngzài kàn shū de nǚ hái.*

Then quiz the new classmate, e.g.:

Q: 那个穿蓝色衬衫的学生是谁？

Nà ge chuān lánsè chènshān de xuésheng shì shéi?

A: 那个穿蓝色衬衫的学生是Jamal。

Nà ge chuān lánsè chènshān de xuésheng shì Jamal.

Birthday Bash

Dialogue 2

Audio

Video

（在高小音家……）

王朋，李友，快进来。

小音，祝你生日快乐！这是送给你的生日礼物。

谢谢！……太好了！我一直想买这本书。带这么多东西，你们太客气了。

哥哥，李友，你们来了[a]。

啊[b]。小红，你怎么样？

我很好。每天都在学英文。

小红，你每天练习英文练习多长时间[3]？

三个半钟头[c]。还看两个钟头的英文电视。

哎，你们两个是什么时候到的[4]？

刚到。

白英爱没跟你们一起来吗？

她还[5]没来？我以为[d]她已经来了。

王朋，李友，来，我给你们介绍一下，这是我表姐海伦，这是她的儿子汤姆。

你好，海伦。

你好，王朋。文中和小音都说你又聪明[e]又用功[6]。

哪里，哪里。你的中文说得真好，是在哪儿学的？

在暑期班[f]学的。

哎，汤姆长[g]得真可爱！你们看，他笑了。他几岁了？

刚一岁，是去年生的，属狗。

你们看，他的脸圆圆的，眼睛大大的，鼻子高高的，嘴不大也不小，长得很像海伦。

妈妈这么漂亮，儿子长大一定也很帅。

来，来，来，我们吃蛋糕吧。

等等白英爱吧。她最爱吃蛋糕。

(Zài Gāo Xiǎoyīn jiā . . .)

 Wáng Péng, Lǐ Yǒu, kuài jìn lai.

 Xiǎoyīn, zhù nǐ shēngrì kuàilè! Zhè shì sòng gěi nǐ de shēngrì lǐwù.

 Xièxiè! . . . Tài hǎo le! Wǒ yìzhí xiǎng mǎi zhè běn shū. Dài zhème duō dōngxi, nǐmen tài kèqi le.

 Gēge, Lǐ Yǒu, nǐmen lái le<u>ᵃ</u>.

 À<u>ᵇ</u>. Xiǎo Hóng, nǐ zěnmeyàng?

 Wǒ hěn hǎo. Měi tiān dōu zài xué Yīngwén.

 Xiǎo Hóng, nǐ měi tiān liànxí Yīngwén liànxí duō cháng shíjiān³?

 Sān ge bàn zhōngtóu<u>ᶜ</u>. Hái kàn liǎng ge zhōngtóu de Yīngwén diànshì.

 Āi, nǐmen liǎng ge shì shénme shíhou dào de⁴?

 Gāng dào.

 Bái Yīng'ài méi gēn nǐmen yìqǐ lái ma?

 Tā hái⁵ méi lái? Wǒ yǐwéi<u>ᵈ</u> tā yǐjīng lái le.

 Wáng Péng, Lǐ Yǒu, lái, wǒ gěi nǐmen jièshào yí xià, zhè shì wǒ biǎojiě Hǎilún, zhè shì tā de érzi Tāngmǔ.

 Nǐ hǎo, Hǎilún.

 Nǐ hǎo, Wáng Péng. Wénzhōng hé Xiǎoyīn dōu shuō nǐ yòu cōngming<u>ᵉ</u> yòu yònggōng⁶.

 Nǎli, nǎli. Nǐ de Zhōngwén shuō de zhēn hǎo, shì zài nǎr xué de?

 Zài shǔqī bān<u>ᶠ</u> xué de.

 Āi, Tāngmǔ zhǎng<u>ᵍ</u> de zhēn kě'ài! Nǐmen kàn, tā xiào le. Tā jǐ suì le?

Gāng yí suì, shì qùnián shēng de, shǔ gǒu.

Nǐmen kàn, tā de liǎn yuán yuán de, yǎnjing dà dà de, bízi gāo gāo de, zuǐ bú dà yě bù xiǎo, zhǎng de hěn xiàng Hǎilún.

Māma zhème piàoliang, érzi zhǎng dà yídìng yě hěn shuài.

Lái, lái, lái, wǒmen chī dàngāo ba.

Děng děng Bái Yīng'ài ba. Tā zuì ài chī dàngāo.

a 你们来了。 *(Nǐmen lái le.)*

This sentence, equivalent to "You're here," not only acknowledges the visitors' arrival, but also serves as a casual greeting. [See also Cultural Literacy, Lesson 13.]

b 啊 *(a/à)*

Different from 啊 *(a)* in Dialogue 2 of Lesson 6, where it is pronounced in the neutral tone as a sentence-final particle, 啊 *(à)* here is pronounced in the fourth tone as an answer to someone else's greeting.

c 钟头 *(zhōngtóu)*

This is the colloquial equivalent of 小时 *(xiǎoshí)* (hour). [See also Vocabulary, Lesson 15.]

d 以为 *(yǐwéi)*

This is often used to signify an understanding or judgment that has proved to be erroneous, e.g.: 我以为你吃素 *(Wǒ yǐwéi nǐ chī sù)* (I thought you were vegetarian).

e 聪明 *(cōngming)*

聪 *(cōng)* literally means "able to hear well," and 明 *(míng)* means "able to see clearly," among other things. Therefore, 聪明 *(cōngming)* describes someone who is sharp or bright.

f 班 *(bān)* vs. 课 *(kè)*

These two words denote two different concepts that are represented by the same word, "class," in English. While 课 *(kè)* refers to an educational course or a meeting time for the course, 班 *(bān)* means a group of students taking a course together. Thus you would say 我今天有电脑课 *(Wǒ jīntiān yǒu diànnǎo kè)* (I have a computer class today), but 我的电脑班有二十个人 *(Wǒ de diànnǎo bān yǒu èrshí ge rén)* (There are twenty people in my computer class).

g 长 *(zhǎng/cháng)*

This character has two different meanings and pronunciations. As a verb, it is pronounced *"zhǎng,"* meaning "to grow." When used as an adjective, it is pronounced *cháng*, meaning "long."

Vocabulary

Audio

Flashcards

No.	Word	Pinyin	Part of Speech	Definition
1	钟头	zhōngtóu	n	hour
2	以为	yǐwéi	v	to assume erroneously
3	聪明	cōngming	adj	smart, bright, clever
4	用功	yònggōng	adj	hardworking, diligent, studious
5	暑期	shǔqī	n	summer term
6	班	bān	n	class
7	长	zhǎng	v	to grow, to appear
8	可爱	kě'ài	adj	cute, lovable
9	去年	qùnián	t	last year
10	属	shǔ	v	to belong to
11	狗	gǒu	n	dog
12	脸	liǎn	n	face
13	圆	yuán	adj	round
14	眼睛	yǎnjing	n	eye
15	鼻子	bízi	n	nose
16	嘴	zuǐ	n	mouth
17	像	xiàng	v	to be like, to look like, to take after
18	长大	zhǎng dà	vc	to grow up
19	一定	yídìng	adj/adv	certain, definite; certainly, definitely
20	蛋糕	dàngāo	n	cake
21	最	zuì	adv	most, (of superlative degree) -est

It's your birthday! You're having a party, and one of your friends has brought over a delicious selection of bubble tea (珍珠奶茶) (*zhēnzhū nǎichá*). What fla ors did she bring?

GET **Real** WITH **CHINESE**

No.	Word	Pinyin	Part of Speech	Definition
22	海伦	*Hǎilún*	pn	Helen
23	汤姆	*Tāngmǔ*	pn	Tom

给朋友过生日开舞会，你会准备些什么东西？

Gěi péngyou guò shēngrì kāi wǔhuì, nǐ huì zhǔnbèi xiē shénme dōngxi?

What would you prepare for a friend's birthday party?

How About You?

我会准备 _____。

Wǒ huì zhǔnbèi _____ .

See index for corresponding vocabulary or research another term.

Grammar

3 | **Time duration (I)**

To indicate the duration of an action, the following structure is used:

Subject + verb + (object + verb) + (了) (le) + duration of time

A 老高想在上海住一年。

Lǎo Gāo xiǎng zài Shànghǎi zhù yì nián.

Old Gao would like to live in Shanghai for a year.

B 我每天在书店工作三个钟头。

Wǒ měi tiān zài shūdiàn gōngzuò sān ge zhōngtóu.

I work at a bookstore for three hours every day.

C 昨天下雪下了一天。

Zuótiān xià xuě xià le yì tiān.

It snowed for a whole day yesterday.

D 你上暑期班上了多长时间？

Nǐ shàng shǔqī bān shàng le duō cháng shíjiān?

How long were you in summer school for?

Sentences in this pattern must be in the affirmative. If the verb takes an object, the verb has to be repeated, as in (C) and (D). If the verb has an object, the following alternative pattern can be used to express the same idea.

Subject + verb + (了) (le) + duration of time + (的) (de) + object

E 昨天下了一天（的）雪。

Zuótiān xià le yì tiān (de) xuě.

It snowed for a whole day yesterday.

F 我上了四个星期（的）暑期班。

Wǒ shàng le sì ge xīngqī (de) shǔqī bān.

I was at summer school for four weeks.

[⊗ 我四个星期上了暑期班。]

The phrase for the length of time must not be put before the verb.

EXERCISES

Complete the sentences with the phrases provided to indicate the duration of an action. Use exercise 1 as an example.

1 我昨天上中文课　　　　　　半个钟头

→ 我昨天上中文课上了半个钟头。/

我昨天上了半个钟头的中文课。

2 我妹妹每天听音乐　　　　　一个半钟头

3 我上个星期在图书馆工作　　三天

<u>4</u>　　　　**Sentences with 是…的** *(shì … de)* **(I)**

To describe or inquire about the time, the place, the manner, or the initiator of an action that we know already happened, use the 是…的 *(shì … de)* structure. The use of 是 *(shì)*, however, is optional.

A　Q: 你去过北京吗？　　　　　　　A: 我去过北京。

Nǐ qù guo Běijīng ma?　　　　　　*Wǒ qù guo Běijīng.*

Have you been to Beijing?　　　　　Yes, I've been to Beijing.

Having confirmed that the respondent has been to Beijing in the past, the questioner now wants to find out when, how, and with whom the respondent went to Beijing:

Q: 你（是）跟谁一起去的？

Nǐ (shì) gēn shéi yìqǐ qù de?

With whom did you go?

A: 我（是）跟我表姐一起去的。

Wǒ (shì) gēn wǒ biǎojiě yìqǐ qù de.

I went with my cousin.

Q: 你们（是）什么时候去的？

Nǐmen (shì) shénme shíhou qù de?

When did you go?

A: 我们（是）寒假去的。

Wǒmen (shì) hánjià qù de.

We went over winter break.

Q: 你们（是）怎么去的？

Nǐmen (shì) zěnme qù de?

How did you get there?

A: 我们（是）坐飞机去的。

Wǒmen (shì) zuò fēijī qù de.

We flew.

B Q: 你看过这本书吗？

Nǐ kàn guo zhè běn shū ma?

Have you read this book?

A: 看过。

Kàn guo.

Yes, I have.

Q: （是）什么时候看的？

(Shì) shénme shíhou kàn de?

When did you read it?

[The questioner knows that the action 看 (kàn) already took place.]

A: （是）上个周末看的。

(Shì) shàng ge zhōumò kàn de.

I read it last weekend. (It was last weekend that I read it.)

C　你这条裤子真好看。（是）在哪儿买的？

Nǐ zhè tiáo kùzi zhēn hǎokàn. (Shì) zài nǎr mǎi de?

These pants of yours look great. Where did you get them?

[Most people buy pants (as opposed to making them at home, for example), so the action 买 (mǎi) is assumed.]

D　Q: 你吃饭了吗？

Nǐ chī fàn le ma?

Have you eaten yet?

A: 吃了。

Chī le.

Yes, I have.

[The action 吃 (chī) is now known.]

Q: （是）在哪儿吃的？

(Shì) zài nǎr chī de?

Where did you eat?

A: （是）在学生餐厅吃的。

(Shì) zài xuéshēng cāntīng chī de.

In the student cafeteria.

E　Q: 你学过电脑吗？

Nǐ xué guo diànnǎo ma?

Have you ever studied computer science?

A: 学过。

Xué guo.

Yes, I have.

Q:（是）跟谁学的？

(Shì) gēn shéi xué de?

Who did you study with?

A:（是）跟王老师学的。

(Shì) gēn Wáng lǎoshī xué de.

With Teacher Wang.

是 *(shì)* cannot be omitted in negative statements.

F **Q:** 你是在中国学的中文吗？

Nǐ shì zài Zhōngguó xué de Zhōngwén ma?

Did you study Chinese in China?

A: 我不是在中国学的，是在美国学的。

Wǒ bú shì zài Zhōngguó xué de, shì zài Měiguó xué de.

No, I didn't study Chinese in China. I studied it in the U.S.

G **Q:** 小李是昨天走的吗？

Xiǎo Lǐ shì zuótiān zǒu de ma?

Did Little Li leave yesterday?

A: 她不是昨天走的，好像是上个星期走的。

Tā bú shì zuótiān zǒu de, hǎoxiàng shì shàng ge xīngqī zǒu de.

No, she didn't leave yesterday. I think she left last week.

Characterize it!

What do the characters mean?

What is the common radical?

What does the radical mean?

How does the radical relate to the overall meaning of the characters?

① 本 **②** 果 **③** 楼 **④** 梨

More characters

EXERCISES

In pairs, form questions-and-answers by using the given question cue words and bracketed answers. Use 是…的 where appropriate. Use exercise 1 as an example.

1   你去纽约

去过吗？（去过）　　什么时候？（去年）

跟谁一起？（同学）　　怎么去？（坐飞机）

→Q: 你去过纽约吗？

A: 去过。

Q: （是）什么时候去的？

A: （是）去年去的。

Q: （是）跟谁一起去的？

A: （是）跟同学一起去的。

Q: （是）怎么去的？

A: （是）坐飞机去的。

2   你看中国电影

看过吗？（看过）　　在哪儿？（学校）

什么时候？（上个星期）跟谁一起？（小王）

3   你吃红烧牛肉

吃过吗？（吃过）　　在哪儿？（中国饭馆）

什么时候？（前天）　　跟谁一起？（弟弟）

---

5 | 还 *(hái)* **(still)**

还 *(hái)*, as an adverb, can mean "still."

A   上午十一点了，他还在睡觉。

Shàngwǔ shíyī diǎn le, tā hái zài shuì jiào.

It's 11:00 a.m. He's still sleeping.

B 今天的功课我还没写完。

Jīntiān de gōngkè wǒ hái méi xiě wán.

I'm still not done with today's homework.

C 这个语法老师教了，可是我还不懂。

Zhè ge yǔfǎ lǎoshī jiāo le, kěshì wǒ hái bù dǒng.

The teacher went over this grammar point, but I still don't understand it.

EXERCISES

Complete the sentences by inserting 还 where appropriate. Use exercise 1 as an example.

More exercises

1 已经晚上十点了，弟弟没回家
   → 已经晚上十点了，弟弟还没回家。

2 他在电话里说了三次，我听不清楚

3 这课的课文我看了一个钟头，不懂

---

6 | 又⋯⋯又⋯⋯ *(yòu . . . yòu . . .)* **(both . . . and . . .)**

When two adjectives are joined in this structure, they must both be either positive or negative in meaning. For example, in 又聪明又用功 *(yòu cōngming yòu yònggōng)* (smart and hardworking) both adjectives are positive in meaning, while in 又多又难 *(yòu duō yòu nán)* (too much and difficult), both adjectives are negative in meaning.

EXERCISES

Combine the adjectives by inserting 又⋯⋯又⋯⋯ where appropriate. Use exercise 1 as an example.

More exercises

1 聪明   用功 → 又聪明又用功

2 高   大

3 饿   累

Language Practice

D	**Where did you get that?** `INTERPERSONAL`

You love something your classmate has or is wearing. You want to find out whether he/she bought it, and if so, where and when it was bought. Use the 是⋯的 *(shì . . . de)* structure when necessary, e.g.:

你的手机真酷⋯⋯

Nǐ de shǒujī zhēn kù . . .

（是）你买的还是别人送的？

(Shì) nǐ mǎi de háishi biérén sòng de?

（是）什么时候买的？

(Shì) shénme shíhou mǎi de?

（是）在哪儿买的？

(Shì) zài nǎr mǎi de?

1   **2**   **3**

E `INTERPERSONAL`	**Older or younger** `PRESENTATIONAL`

Interview your classmates to find out everyone's birthplace, birth year, and Chinese zodiac sign. Then report to the class how many classmates are older than you, how many are younger than you, how many were born in the same state/province/city as you were, and which zodiac sign is most common in the class. Use the 是⋯的 *(shì . . . de)* structure when necessary.

1 你是在哪儿生的？

Nǐ shì zài nǎr shēng de?

3 你属什么？

Nǐ shǔ shénme?

2 你是哪一年生的？

Nǐ shì nǎ yì nián shēng de?

Wanderlust

INTERPERSONAL

In pairs, discuss where you have traveled. Take turns asking each other the questions below. Use the 是···的 (shì . . . de) structure when necessary.

1 你去过 (a city or country) 吗?

Nǐ qù guo (a city or country) ma?

2 你（是）什么时候去的?

Nǐ (shì) shénme shíhou qù de?

3 你（是）跟谁一起去的?

Nǐ (shì) gēn shéi yìqǐ qù de?

4 你（是）怎么去的?

Nǐ (shì) zěnme qù de?

G

Tight schedule

INTERPERSONAL

Imagine that you've signed up to go on a whirlwind tour of China during summer break. You just got your itinerary, and the travel schedule looks very intense. The trip leaders have scheduled each day down to the minute. In pairs, form a question-and-answer about how much time you'll have for each activity, e.g.:

Q: 你每天洗澡洗多长时间?

Nǐ měi tiān xǐ zǎo xǐ duō cháng shíjiān?

7:30 a.m.–7:35 a.m.　A: 我每天洗澡洗五分钟。

Wǒ měi tiān xǐ zǎo xǐ wǔ fēnzhōng.

1

1:30 p.m.–2:30 p.m.

2

5:30 p.m.–6:00 p.m.

3

11:00 p.m.–5:00 a.m.

Ask your partner about how much time he/she typically spends eating dinner every day.

| INTERPERSONAL | **Last night** | PRESENTATIONAL |

Survey your classmates about how they spent their time last night. Use the "subject + verb + (object + verb) + (了) + duration of time" or "subject + verb + (了) + duration of time + (的) + object" structure to indicate the duration of an action, e.g.:

Q: Emily, 你昨天晚上做什么了?

Emily, *nǐ zuótiān wǎnshang zuò shénme le?*

A: 我昨天晚上看电视了。

Wǒ zuótiān wǎnshang kàn diànshì le.

Q: 你昨天晚上看电视看了多长时间?

Nǐ zuótiān wǎnshang kàn diànshì kàn le duō cháng shíjiān?

A: 我昨天晚上看电视看了半个钟头。/

我昨天晚上看了半个钟头的电视。

Wǒ zuótiān wǎnshang kàn diànshì kàn le bàn ge zhōngtóu. /

Wǒ zuótiān wǎnshàng kàn le bàn gè zhōngtóu de diànshì.

Then share your findings with the class.

Emily昨天晚上看电视看了半个钟头。

Emily *zuótiān wǎnshang kàn diànshì kàn le bàn ge zhōngtóu.*

| INTERPERSONAL | **Puppy love** | PRESENTATIONAL |

In pairs, describe this dog's features and comment on how cute it is.

| INTERPERSONAL | **Party planner** | PRESENTATIONAL |

Find out among your classmates whose birthday is coming up by asking 谁的生日快到了？ *(Shéi de shēngrì kuài dào le?)* (Whose birthday is coming up?). Everyone should take a turn asking that person what he/she likes to eat, drink, and do. Then work as a class to plan a birthday party together, and decide who will bring what to the party. In Chinese, note down the day of the party and the things you were assigned to bring.

Chinese Chat

On Facebook, Gao Wenzhong just posted about a party he's throwing. What are his friends going to bring?

高文中
November 12 at 12:50 pm

谢谢大家今天晚上来我家给我姐过生日！你们都准备带些什么呀？

👍 Like   💬 Comment   ➤ Share

👍❤ 52

王红 我买了饺子。
November 12 at 12:52 pm · Like 👍 12 · Reply

王朋 我带冰茶、可乐和花。
November 12 at 1:12 pm · Like 👍 10 · Reply

李友 水果和礼物！
November 12 at 1:31 pm · Like 👍 6 · Reply

海伦 我自己做的日本菜。
November 12 at 2:50 pm · Like 👍 15 · Reply

文化 Continue to explore

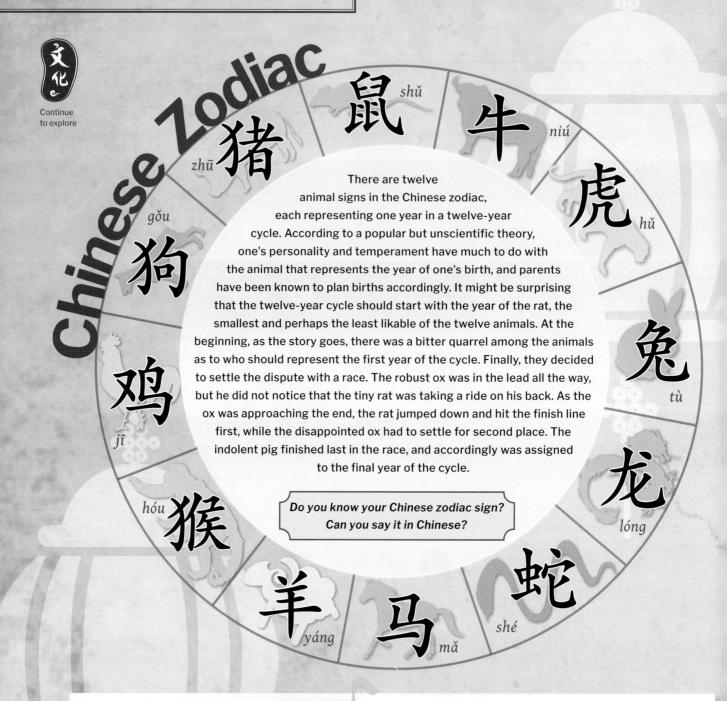

Chinese Zodiac

鼠 shǔ
牛 niú
虎 hǔ
兔 tù
龙 lóng
蛇 shé
马 mǎ
羊 yáng
猴 hóu
鸡 jī
狗 gǒu
猪 zhū

There are twelve animal signs in the Chinese zodiac, each representing one year in a twelve-year cycle. According to a popular but unscientific theory, one's personality and temperament have much to do with the animal that represents the year of one's birth, and parents have been known to plan births accordingly. It might be surprising that the twelve-year cycle should start with the year of the rat, the smallest and perhaps the least likable of the twelve animals. At the beginning, as the story goes, there was a bitter quarrel among the animals as to who should represent the first year of the cycle. Finally, they decided to settle the dispute with a race. The robust ox was in the lead all the way, but he did not notice that the tiny rat was taking a ride on his back. As the ox was approaching the end, the rat jumped down and hit the finish line first, while the disappointed ox had to settle for second place. The indolent pig finished last in the race, and accordingly was assigned to the final year of the cycle.

Do you know your Chinese zodiac sign? Can you say it in Chinese?

KARAOKE

A common way for people sing for fun in China is to sing karaoke, 卡拉OK (kǎlā'OK). Originally from Japan, karaoke has become a popular activity in Mainland China and Taiwan. Some young people regularly go to karaoke bars, known as KTVs, to have a good time or celebrate someone's birthday. They can order food and beverages and reserve private rooms for their parties. More recently, another way people sing for fun is on social media apps, or even specialized singing apps.

Gift Giving

The Chinese usually express their appreciation for gifts profusely, typically by saying 你太客气了！*(Nǐ tài kèqi le!)* (You're too kind!). However, to avoid giving the impression of greediness, most Chinese people would refrain from opening a present immediately in front of the gift giver. Flowers can make good gifts, but on happy occasions, one should avoid bouquets of white flowers, which are typically for funerals. Another taboo is giving a clock to an elderly person as a present, because the phrase 送钟 *(sòng zhōng)* (to give a clock as a present) sounds ominously like 送终 *(sòng zhōng)*, which means to bid farewell to a deceased person.

COMPARE & CONTRAST

1 What would you say to a friend giving you a present? Would you open it right away? If you gave a present to a Chinese friend and he/she didn't open it right away, how would you feel? What would be culturally appropriate to say to him/her?

2 In the past, on a child's first birthday, his/her parents would organize a special ceremony called 抓周 *(zhuā zhōu)* (grabbing test). Various objects—a book, a writing brush, a carpenter's tool, cosmetics, etc. —would be spread out before the child, and parents, grandparents, and other relatives would wait with bated breath to see which object the child would pick up, as the child's choice was supposed to indicate his/her character and inclinations. Additionally, when a baby is one month old, many parents hold a special banquet called 满月酒 *(mǎnyuèjiǔ)*. What special milestone celebrations are held for children in your culture?

Potluck dinner parties are not very common in China. Chinese hosts and hostesses typically prepare everything for their guests, and do not count on them to bring anything. However, visitors can still bring something as a token of appreciation, such as fruit.

Party Etiquette

Lesson Wrap-Up

Make It Flow!

The following sentences are arranged in a logical order. Combine the sentences into a coherent narrative. Substitute nouns with pronouns and change periods to commas where necessary. Avoid unnecessary repetitions of subject pronouns. Add the connective devices 只有 (zhǐyǒu), 先 (xiān), 然后 (ránhòu), 这个时候 (zhè ge shíhou), and 最后 (zuìhòu) where appropriate.

晚上王朋和李友到了高小音家。大家都来了。白英爱还没来。大家祝小音生日快乐。大家一起聊天。王朋问妹妹小红每天练习中文练习多长时间。王红说每天练习中文练习三个半钟头。王红说每天还看两个钟头的英文电视。小音给王朋和李友介绍她的表姐海伦。海伦中文说得非常好。海伦是在暑期班学的中文。海伦有一个儿子。海伦的儿子叫汤姆。汤姆属狗。汤姆刚一岁。汤姆长得很像海伦。汤姆很可爱。小音让大家吃蛋糕。

Skit

Student A Persuade your friend to go to a party with you. Tell him/her when and where the party is, who else will be there, and what kind of food and music he/she can expect.

Student B You're not sure if you want to go. You have an exam next Monday and you didn't do well on the last one. You want to study and review. Are there other reasons for your lack of interest?

Student A How can you get your friend to agree to go to the party with you?

Email

Tell a friend about the party you went to last weekend. Who was there? When did it start and what was it for? Describe somebody you met there. What did he/she look like? What did you talk about? How were the food and music? When did you get home? Did you have fun?

Supplemental Reading Practice

For additional reading practice that builds on the vocabulary introduced in this lesson, turn to the supplemental readings that begin on page 419.

Can-Do Check List ✓ **I can**

Before proceeding to Lesson 15, make sure you can complete the following tasks in Chinese:

- ☐ Ask a friend to a party
- ☐ Offer a ride and set up a place and time for a pickup
- ☐ Talk about the duration of an action
- ☐ Thank someone for his/her gift
- ☐ Discuss my birth year and Chinese zodiac sign
- ☐ Describe facial features in simple terms

看病

Kàn bìng

SEEING A DOCTOR

Learning Objectives

In this lesson, you will learn to:

- Describe common cold and allergy symptoms
- Understand instructions on when and how often to take medications
- Talk about why you do or don't want to see the doctor
- Urge others to see a doctor when they are not feeling well

Relate & Get Ready

In your own culture/community:

- Can you see a doctor without an appointment?
- Do you have to pay an office visit fee before seeing a doctor?
- Is medication commonly prescribed and dispensed in the same place?
- Apart from medication, what other treatments might a doctor recommend?
- Is everyone covered by health insurance?

My Stomach Is Killing Me!

Dialogue 1

Audio

Video

（病人去医院看病……）

医生，我肚子疼死[1]了。

你昨天吃什么东西了？

我姐姐上个星期过生日，蛋糕没吃完。昨天晚上我吃了几口，夜里肚子就疼起来[2]了，今天早上上了好几次[3]厕所。

你把[4]蛋糕放在哪儿了？

放在冰箱里了。

放了几天了？

五、六天[a]了。

发烧吗？

不发烧。

你躺下。先检查一下。

……

你吃蛋糕把肚子吃坏了。

得打针吗？

不用打针，吃这种药^b就可以。一天三次，一次两片。

医生，一天吃几次？请您再说一遍。

一天三次，一次两片。

好！饭前^c吃还是饭后吃？

饭前饭后都可以。不过，你最好二十四小时不要吃饭。

那我要饿死了。不行，这个办法不好！

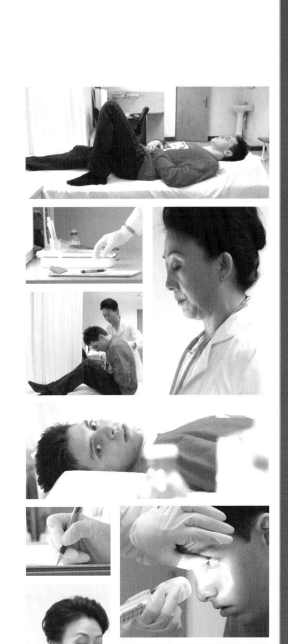

(Bìngrén qù yīyuàn kàn bìng . . .)

Yīshēng, wǒ dùzi téng sǐ[1] le.

Nǐ zuótiān chī shénme dōngxi le?

Wǒ jiějie shàng ge xīngqī guò shēngrì, dàngāo méi

chī wán. Zuótiān wǎnshang wǒ chī le jǐ kǒu, yè li

dùzi jiù téng qi lai[2] le, jīntiān zǎoshang shàng le

hǎo jǐ cì[3] cèsuǒ.

Nǐ bǎ[4] dàngāo fàng zài nǎr le?

Fàng zài bīngxiāng lǐ le.

Fàng le jǐ tiān le?

Wǔ, liù tiān[a] le.

Fā shāo ma?

Bù fā shāo.

Nǐ tǎng xia. Xiān jiǎnchá yí xià.

. . .

Nǐ chī dàngāo bǎ dùzi chī huài le.

Děi dǎ zhēn ma?

Búyòng dǎ zhēn, chī zhè zhǒng yào[b] jiù kěyǐ.

Yì tiān sān cì, yí cì liǎng piàn.

Yīshēng, yì tiān chī jǐ cì? Qǐng nín zài shuō

yí biàn.

Yì tiān sān cì, yí cì liǎng piàn.

Hǎo! Fàn qián[c] chī háishi fàn hòu chī?

Fàn qián fàn hòu dōu kěyǐ. Búguò, nǐ zuìhǎo èrshí

sì xiǎoshí bú yào chī fàn.

Nà wǒ yào è sǐ le. Bù xíng, zhè ge bànfǎ bù hǎo!

a 五、六天 *(wǔ, liù tiān)*

Approximate numbers can be expressed by two numbers in succession, e.g.: 五十六、七岁 *(wǔshí liù, qī suì)* (fifty-six or fifty-seven years old), 十八、九块钱 *(shí bā, jiǔ kuài qián)* (eighteen or nineteen dollars), 三、四天 *(sān, sì tiān)* (three or four days), and 两、三枝笔 *(liǎng, sān zhī bǐ)* (two or three pens). However, the numbers nine and ten cannot be used this way since in speech, it would be difficult to distinguish 九、十天 *(jiǔ, shí tiān)* from 九十天 *(jiǔshí tiān)* (ninety days).

b 吃药 *(chī yào)*

"To take medicine" is 吃药 *(chī yào)* (lit. to eat medicine). A more formal expression is 服药 *(fú yào)*, which commonly appears in prescriptions and prescription instructions.

c 前 *(qián)* **and** 后 *(hòu)*

前 *(qián)* (before) in 饭前 *(fàn qián)* (before meals) and 后 *(hòu)* (after) in 饭后 *(fàn hòu)* (after meals) are the shortened forms of 以前 *(yǐqián)* (before) and 以后 *(yǐhòu)* (after), respectively.

Vocabulary

No.	Word	Pinyin	Part of Speech	Definition
1	病人	bìngrén	n	patient
	病	bìng	n/v	illness; to get sick
2	医院	yīyuàn	n	hospital
3	看病	kàn bìng	vo	to see a doctor
4	肚子	dùzi	n	belly, abdomen, stomach
5	疼死	téng sǐ	adj + c	really painful [See Grammar 1.]
	疼	téng	adj	aching
	死	sǐ	v/c	to die; (a complement indicating an extreme degree)
6	夜里	yè li	n	at night
7	好几	hǎo jǐ		quite a few
8	厕所	cèsuǒ	n	restroom, toilet
9	把	bǎ	prep	(indicating disposition, arrangement, or settlement of something) [See Grammar 4.]
10	冰箱	bīngxiāng	n	refrigerator
11	发烧	fā shāo	vo	to have a fever
12	躺下	tǎng xia	vc	to lie down
	躺	tǎng	v	to lie, to recline
13	检查	jiǎnchá	v	to examine
14	吃坏	chī huài	vc	to get sick because of bad food
	坏	huài	adj	bad
15	打针	dǎ zhēn	vo	to get an injection
	针	zhēn	n	needle

Audio

Flashcards

While browsing the bookstore at Beijing Capital International Airport, this title catches your eye. What do you think the book is about? Who is it written for?

GET Real WITH CHINESE

No.	Word	Pinyin	Part of Speech	Definition
16	药	*yào*	n	medicine
17	片	*piàn*	m	(measure word for tablets, slices, etc.)
18	遍	*biàn*	m	(measure word for complete courses of an action or instances of an action)
19	最好	*zuìhǎo*	adv	had better
20	小时	*xiǎoshí*	n	hour
21	办法	*bànfǎ*	n	method, way (of doing something)

你怎么了？哪儿不舒服？

Nǐ zěnme le? Nǎr bù shūfu?

What's wrong with you? Where's the discomfort?

How About You?

我 _____ 。

Wǒ _____ .

See index for corresponding vocabulary or research another term.

Grammar

---

1   **Indicating an extreme degree using 死 (sǐ)**

Placed after an adjective, 死 (sǐ) can serve as a complement to indicate an extreme degree of the condition described by the adjective.

A   打针疼死了。

Dǎ zhēn téng sǐ le.

Getting shots is extremely painful.

B   我饿死了。

Wǒ è sǐ le.

I'm starving.

C   今天热死了。

Jīntiān rè sǐ le.

It's awfully hot today.

死 (sǐ) often follows adjectives with a pejorative meaning, and the combination carries a negative connotation, as shown in the examples above. However, 高兴 (gàoxìng) (happy) 死了 (sǐ le) is one of few exceptions.

D   知道了这件事，他高兴死了。

Zhīdào le zhè jiàn shì, tā gāoxìng sǐ le.

He was incredibly happy when he found out about this.

Most adjectives with a positive meaning cannot be followed by 死 (sǐ). People, therefore, seldom say:

[✖ 他跟他的女朋友好死了。]

Note that when 死 (sǐ) is used as a resultative complement, it can literally mean "to die."

E 听说那个地方有人饿死了。

Tīngshuō nà ge dìfang yǒu rén è sǐ le.

I heard people had died of hunger in that place.

More exercises

EXERCISES

Complete the sentences by inserting 死了 where appropriate. Use exercise 1 as an example.

1   这儿的夏天   热

      → 这儿的夏天热死了。

2   今天的考试   难

3   我中午没有时间吃饭   饿

2   Indicating the beginning of an action using 起来 *(qi lai)*

起来 *(qi lai)* indicates the moment when something static becomes dynamic: that is, it signifies the beginning of an action or state. Note that if there is an object when the 起来 *(qi lai)* structure is used, the object is placed between 起 *(qi)* and 来 *(lai)*, as in (B) and (C).

A 我们一见面就聊起来了。

Wǒmen yí jiàn miàn jiù liáo qi lai le.

We started to chat as soon as we met.

B 他一回家就玩儿起手机来了。

Tā yì huí jiā jiù wánr qi shǒujī lai le.

He started to play with his cell phone as soon as he got home.

C 下了课以后，学生们打起球来。

Xià le kè yǐhòu, xuésheng men dǎ qi qiú lai.

The students started playing ball once class was over.

EXERCISES

Complete the sentences with 起来. Use exercise 1 as an example.

1   小明上完课　　就看电子邮件

→ 小明上完课，就看起电子邮件来了。

2   他刚吃完晚饭　就看书

3   弟弟一回到家　就打电话

---

3 | 次 (cì) for frequency

次 (cì) is the measure word most frequently used to express how many times an action is performed. The "number + 次 (cì)" combination follows the verb.

A   上午我打了两次电话。/
上午我打电话打了两次。

Shàngwǔ wǒ dǎ le liǎng cì diànhuà./
Shàngwǔ wǒ dǎ diànhuà dǎ le liǎng cì.

I made two phone calls this morning.

B   我昨天吃了三次药。

Wǒ zuótiān chī le sān cì yào.

I took medicine three times yesterday.

If the object represents a person or a place, 次 (cì) can go either between the verb and the object or after the object, as in (C) and (D).

C   去年我去了一次中国。/
去年我去了中国一次。

Qùnián wǒ qù le yí cì Zhōngguó./Qùnián wǒ qù le Zhōngguó yí cì.

Last year I went to China once.

D 昨天我找了三次王医生。/
昨天我找了王医生三次。

Zuótiān wǒ zhǎo le sān cì Wáng yīshēng./Zuótiān wǒ zhǎo le Wáng yīshēng sān cì.

I went looking for Dr. Wang three times yesterday.

If the object is a personal pronoun, however, 次 *(cì)* must follow the object.

E 我昨天找了他两次，他都不在。

Wǒ zuótiān zhǎo le tā liǎng cì, tā dōu bú zài.

Yesterday I went looking for him twice, but he wasn't around either time.

遍 *(biàn)* is another measure word for occurrences of actions, but it pertains to the entire course of an action from beginning to end.

F 请你念一遍课文。

Qǐng nǐ niàn yí biàn kèwén.

Please read the text (from beginning to end) once.

More exercises

EXERCISES

Complete the sentences with 次 or 遍. Use exercise 1 as an example.

1 今天小明洗澡　　　　两
→ 今天小明洗了两次澡。/
　 今天小明洗澡洗了两次。

2 我每天念课文　　　　一

3 小明上个星期找老师　两

The 把 (bǎ) construction (I)

Sentences with 把 (bǎ) are common in Chinese. The basic construction is as follows:

Subject + 把 (bǎ) + object + verb + other element (complement/ 了 [le], etc.)

In the 把 (bǎ) construction, what follows 把 (bǎ) and precedes the verb serves as both the object of 把 (bǎ) and the object of the verb. In general, a sentence with the 把 (bǎ) construction emphasizes the subject's disposition of or impact upon the object, with the result of the disposition or impact indicated by the element following the verb.

A 我把你要的书找到了。

Wǒ bǎ nǐ yào de shū zhǎo dào le.

I've found the books that you wanted.

[The resultative complement 到 (dào) serves as the "other element."]

In (A), the subject 我 (wǒ) exerts an impact on the book through the action of 找 (zhǎo), of which 到 (dào) is the result.

B 你把这个字写错了。

Nǐ bǎ zhè ge zì xiě cuò le.

You wrote this character wrong.

[The resultative complement 错 (cuò) serves as the "other element."]

In (B), the subject 你 (nǐ) exerts an impact on the character through the action of 写 (xiě), of which 错 (cuò) is the result.

C 请把那条裤子给我。

Qǐng bǎ nà tiáo kùzi gěi wǒ.

Please pass me that pair of pants.

[The indirect object 我 (wǒ) serves as the "other element."]

D 你再把这篇课文看看。

Nǐ zài bǎ zhè piān kèwén kàn kan.

Would you take another look at this text?

[The reduplicated verb 看 (kàn) serves as the "other element."]

E 把这片药吃了！

Bǎ zhè piàn yào chī le!

Take this tablet of medicine!

F 你怎么把女朋友的生日忘了？

Nǐ zěnme bǎ nǚpéngyou de shēngrì wàng le?

How did you manage to forget your girlfriend's birthday?

[In (E) and (F), the particle 了 *(le)* serves as the "other element."]

(C), (D), and (E) suggest what the listener is requested to do to the objects (the pants, the text, and the medicine). The "other element" can be a complement as in (A) and (B), an indirect object as in (C), a reduplicated verb as in (D), or the particle 了 *(le)* as in (E) and (F).

In the 把 *(bǎ)* construction, the object is often something already known to both the speaker and the listener. For example, 你要的书 *(nǐ yào de shū)* in (A), 这个字 *(zhè ge zì)* in (B), 那条裤子 *(nà tiáo kùzi)* in (C), and 女朋友的生日 *(nǚpéngyou de shēngrì)* in (F) are all things that are already known. Compare the following two sentences:

G 老王给了小张一些钱。

Lǎo Wáng gěi le Xiǎo Zhāng yì xiē qián.

Old Wang gave Little Zhang some money.

H 老王把钱给小张了。

Lǎo Wáng bǎ qián gěi Xiǎo Zhāng le.

Old Wang gave the money to Little Zhang.

The object in (G), "some money," is unspecified. However, in (H), the speaker expects the listener to know what money is being referred to.

A sentence must use the 把 *(bǎ)* construction when the subject is given, the object is known to both the speaker and listener, and the verb is followed by a complement in the form of a prepositional phrase with 在 *(zài)* or 到 *(dào)*.

I 你把笔放在桌子上。

Nǐ bǎ bǐ fàng zài zhuōzi shang.

Put the pen on the desk.

[✖ 你放笔在桌子上。]

J 请你把这个电脑送到律师的办公室。

Qǐng nǐ bǎ zhè ge diànnǎo sòng dào lǜshī de bàngōngshì.

Please deliver this computer to the attorney's office.

[✖ 请你送这个电脑到律师的办公室。]

EXERCISES

Rearrange these words to form new sentences with 把. Use exercise 1 as an example.

1　小明　放　杯子　在　　桌子上

→ 小明把杯子放在桌子上。

2　请你　给　我　　看看　你家的照片

3　你　　给　老师　功课

More
exercises

Characterize it!

What do the characters mean?
What is the common radical?
What does the radical mean?
How does the radical relate to the overall meaning of the characters?

❶ 　❷ 　❸

More
characters

Language Practice

A | Edge case   PRESENTATIONAL

Based on the images given below, indicate an extreme degree of the condition by using
死 (sǐ), e.g.:

他渴死了。

Tā kě sǐ le.

 1    **2**    **3**

B | Routine inspection   INTERPERSONAL

In pairs, discuss your daily routine for studying Chinese and what happened yesterday.
Use the "number + 次/遍 (cì/biàn)" construction, e.g.:

听录音

tīng lùyīn

Q: 你每天听几遍/次录音? or
你每天听录音听几遍/次?

Nǐ měi tiān tīng jǐ biàn/cì lùyīn? or Nǐ měi tiān tīng lùyīn tīng jǐ biàn/cì?

A: 我每天听两遍/两次录音。 or
我每天听录音听两遍/两次。

Wǒ měi tiān tīng liǎng biàn/liǎng cì lùyīn. or Wǒ měi tiān tīng lùyīn tīng liǎng biàn/liǎng cì.

Q: 昨天呢?

Zuótiān ne?

A: 我昨天听了两遍/两次录音。 or
我昨天听录音听了两遍/两次。

Wǒ zuótiān tīng le liǎng biàn/liǎng cì lùyīn. or Wǒ zuótiān tīng lùyīn tīng le liǎng biàn/liǎng cì.

1 念课文

niàn kèwén

2 复习生词语法

fùxí shēngcí yǔfǎ

3 写汉字

xiě Hànzì

<u>C</u>
Moving day

In pairs, role-play a friend helping another friend on moving day. Form a question-and-answer about where things should go by using the 把 (*bǎ*) construction, e.g.:

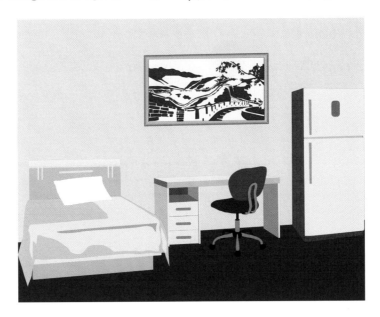

Q: 把纸和笔放在什么地方?

Bǎ zhǐ hé bǐ fàng zài shénme dìfang?

A: 请把纸和笔放在桌子上。

Qǐng bǎ zhǐ hé bǐ fàng zài zhuōzi shang.

1 　　**2** 　　**3** 　　**4**

You don't look well

Your classmate is concerned about you and wants to know what's wrong. Based on the images, form a question-and-answer to discuss what's ailing you, e.g.:

Q: 你怎么了?

Nǐ zěnme le?

A: 我头疼。

Wǒ tóu téng.

1

2

3

Chinese Chat

Your friend is messaging to check in with you. How would you reply?

Ying Wang
Active Now • Messenger

你怎么了? 今天怎么没去上课?

...

是吗? 吃药了吗?

...

还是找个医生给你检查一下吧。

...

要不要我开车带你去看病?

...

那你多喝水、早点儿睡。有事儿给我发短信。

Allergies

Dialogue 2

（王朋这几天好像生病了……）

Audio

Video

王朋，你怎么了？眼睛怎么红红的，感冒了吗？

没感冒。我也不知道怎么了，最近这几天身体很不舒服。眼睛又红又痒。

你一定是对[5]什么过敏了。

我想也是，所以去药店买了一些药。已经吃了四、五种了，花了不少钱，都没有用。

把你买的药拿出来给我看看。

这些就是。

这些药没有用。为什么不去看病？你没有健康保险吗？

我有保险。可是我这个学期功课很多，看病太花时间。

那你也得赶快去看病[a]。要不然病会越来越[6]重。

我想再吃点儿别的药试试[b]。我上次生病，没去看医生[a]，休息了两天，最后也好了。

不行，不行，你太懒了。再说[7]，你不能自己乱吃药。走，我跟你看病去。

(Wáng Péng zhè jǐ tiān hǎoxiàng shēng bìng le . . .)

Wáng Péng, nǐ zěnme le? Yǎnjing zěnme hóng

hóng de, gǎnmào le ma?

Méi gǎnmào. Wǒ yě bù zhīdào zěnme le, zuìjìn zhè jǐ

tiān shēntǐ hěn bù shūfu. Yǎnjing yòu hóng yòu yǎng.

Nǐ yídìng shì duì[5] shénme guòmǐn le.

Wǒ xiǎng yě shì, suǒyǐ qù yàodiàn mǎi le yì xiē

yào. Yǐjīng chī le sì, wǔ zhǒng le, huā le bù shǎo

qián, dōu méiyǒu yòng.

Bǎ nǐ mǎi de yào ná chū lai gěi wǒ kàn kan.

Zhè xiē jiù shì.

Zhè xiē yào méiyǒu yòng. Wèishénme bú qù kàn

bìng? Nǐ méiyǒu jiànkāng bǎoxiǎn ma?

Wǒ yǒu bǎoxiǎn. Kěshì wǒ zhè ge xuéqī gōngkè

hěn duō. Kàn bìng tài huā shíjiān.

Nà nǐ yě děi gǎnkuài qù kàn bìng[a]. Yàobùrán bìng

huì yuè lái yuè[6] zhòng.

Wǒ xiǎng zài chī diǎnr bié de yào shì shi[b]. Wǒ

shàng cì shēng bìng, méi qù kàn yīshēng[a], xiūxi le

liǎng tiān, zuìhòu yě hǎo le.

Bù xíng, bù xíng, nǐ tài lǎn le. Zàishuō[7], nǐ bù

néng zìjǐ luàn chī yào. Zǒu, wǒ gēn nǐ kàn bìng qu.

a 看病 (kàn bìng) vs. 看医生 (kàn yīshēng)

The two phrases 看病 (kàn bìng) and 看医生 (kàn yīshēng) are interchangeable, although in northern China, 看病 (kàn bìng) is much more common than 看医生 (kàn yīshēng).

b 试试 (shì shi)

试试 (shì shi) can be used when trying most things. But when tasting or trying any food or drink, you say 我尝尝 (Wǒ cháng chang) (Let me taste it) instead of 我试试 (Wǒ shì shi) (Let me try it).

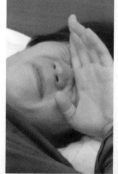

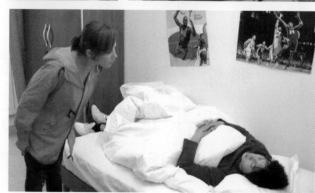

Vocabulary

No.	Word	Pinyin	Part of Speech	Definition
1	生病	*shēng bìng*	vo	to get sick
2	感冒	*gǎnmào*	v	to have a cold
3	身体	*shēntǐ*	n	body, health
4	痒	*yǎng*	adj	itchy
5	过敏	*guòmǐn*	v	to be allergic to
6	药店	*yàodiàn*	n	pharmacy
7	健康	*jiànkāng*	adj/n	healthy; health
8	保险	*bǎoxiǎn*	n/adj	insurance; secure
9	赶快	*gǎnkuài*	adv	right away, quickly, in a hurry
10	要不然	*yàobùrán*	conj	otherwise
11	越来越	*yuè lái yuè*	adv	more and more [See Grammar 6.]
12	上次	*shàng cì*		last time
13	休息	*xiūxi*	v	to take a break, to rest
14	懒	*lǎn*	adj	lazy
15	再说	*zàishuō*	conj	moreover [See Grammar 7.]
16	乱	*luàn*	adv	randomly, arbitrarily, messily

Audio

Flashcards

你对什么过敏？

Nǐ duì shénme guòmǐn?

What are you allergic to?

我对 _____ 。

Wǒ duì _____ .

See index for corresponding vocabulary or research another term.

GET Real WITH CHINESE

You see this thermometer inside a window in Qiqihar, one of the northernmost cities in China. What warning does it have for when the temperature dips below 18°C?

Grammar

<table>
<tr><td>5</td><td>The preposition 对 (duì) (to, for)</td></tr>
</table>

The preposition 对 (duì) (to, for) indicates a person or thing that is affected by someone or something else. Its English translation varies depending on the context.

A 这种药对感冒很有用。

Zhè zhǒng yào duì gǎnmào hěn yǒu yòng.

This medicine is very effective for colds.

B 电脑对他练习发音很有用。

Diànnǎo duì tā liànxí fāyīn hěn yǒu yòng.

The computer is very useful for his pronunciation practice.

C 你一定（是）对什么东西过敏了。

Nǐ yídìng (shì) duì shénme dōngxi guòmǐn le.

You must be allergic to something.

EXERCISES

Rearrange the words to form new sentences with 对. Use exercise 1 as an example.

More exercises

1 这本书 很有用 找工作
   → 这本书对找工作很有用。

2 小王   过敏   鱼

3 这种药 没有用 感冒

越来越··· (yuè lái yuè...) (more and more...)

The structure 越来越··· (yuè lái yuè...) (more and more...) denotes a progressive change over time.

A　李友的中文越来越好。

Lǐ Yǒu de Zhōngwén yuè lái yuè hǎo.

Li You's Chinese is getting better and better.

B　天气越来越暖和了。

Tiānqì yuè lái yuè nuǎnhuo le.

The weather is becoming warmer and warmer.

C　表姐考试考得越来越糟糕。

Biǎojiě kǎo shì kǎo de yuè lái yuè zāogāo.

My cousin is doing worse and worse on her exams.

More exercises

EXERCISES

Complete the sentences by inserting 越来越 where appropriate. Use exercise 1 as an example.

1　健康保险　　　贵

　　→ 健康保险越来越贵了。

2　老王的身体　　好

3　天气　　　　　冷

The conjunction 再说 (zàishuō) (moreover)

The expression 再说 (zàishuō) (moreover) introduces an additional reason for an action taken or decision made. It is different from 再 + 说 (zài + shuō) (to say again).

A Q: 你为什么不去纽约?

Nǐ wèishénme bú qù Niǔyuē?

Why aren't you going to New York?

A: 我没有时间，再说也没有钱。

Wǒ méiyǒu shíjiān, zàishuō yě méiyǒu qián.

I don't have the time, and besides, I don't have the money.

B 我不喜欢今天晚上的舞会，音乐不好，再说人也太少。

Wǒ bù xǐhuan jīntiān wǎnshang de wǔhuì, yīnyuè bù hǎo, zàishuō rén yě tài shǎo.

I didn't like the dance party tonight. The music was lousy. Besides, there were too few people there.

Like 再说 (zàishuō), 而且 (érqiě) (moreover, in addition) also conveys the idea of "furthermore," "additionally," etc., but the clause that follows it may or may not be explanatory in nature. Compare the following sentences:

C Q: 你为什么不去纽约?

Nǐ wèishénme bú qù Niǔyuē?

Why aren't you going to New York?

A: 我没有时间，而且也没有钱。

Wǒ méiyǒu shíjiān, érqiě yě méiyǒu qián.

I don't have the time. Besides, I don't have the money.

Note: In (C), 而且 (érqiě) can be replaced with 再说 (zàishuō).

D 这是王先生，他不但是我的老师，
而且也是我的朋友。

Zhè shì Wáng xiānsheng, tā búdàn shì wǒ de lǎoshī, érqiě yě shì wǒ de péngyou.

This is Mr. Wang. He is not only my teacher but also my friend.

Note: In (D), 而且 (*érqiě*) cannot be replaced with 再说 (*zàishuō*).

[⊗ 这是王先生，他不但是我的老师，
再说也是我的朋友。]

EXERCISES

Answer the questions with 再说. Use exercise 1 as an example.

More exercises

1   Q: 你今天晚上为什么不去看电影？
   （我明天有考试）
   （电影票卖完了）

   A: 我明天有考试，再说电影票也卖完了。

2   Q: 你为什么不去上你哥哥的那个大学？
   （那个大学太远）
   （我不喜欢跟他在一个学校学习）

   A: _____

3   Q: 你知道小王寒假为什么不回家吗？
   （他说飞机票太贵）
   （他父母去外国了）

   A: _____

Language Practice

| INTERPERSONAL | **Allergies! Allergies! Allergies!** | PRESENTATIONAL |

Survey your classmates about whether anyone is allergic to the following items.
Use 对 (duì)···过敏 (guòmǐn), e.g.:

Q: Dmitri, 你对味精过敏吗？

Dmitri, *nǐ duì wèijīng guòmǐn ma?*

A: 我对味精过敏。／我对味精不过敏。

Wǒ duì wèijīng guòmǐn./Wǒ duì wèijīng bú guòmǐn.

1    **2**   **3**

Then tally who's allergic to what, e.g.:

Dmitri、 Maya、 ······对味精过敏。

Dmitri, Maya, . . . , *duì wèijīng guòmǐn.*

F | **Free advice** | PRESENTATIONAL |

How would you help incoming Chinese language students avoid falling into bad study habits?
Use 要不然 (yàobùrán) to give advice, e.g.:

你得多练习写汉字，要不然你的汉字不好看。

Nǐ děi duō liànxí xiě Hànzì, yàobùrán nǐ de Hànzì bù hǎokàn.

Then use 要不然 (yàobùrán) to give incoming students some advice on how to take care
of themselves at college, e.g.:

如果身体不舒服，你就得去看病，要不然病会
越来越重。

Rúguǒ shēntǐ bù shūfu, nǐ jiù děi qù kàn bìng, yàobùrán bìng huì yuè lái yuè zhòng.

What's your take?

In pairs, form a question-and-answer about how your study of Chinese is progressing. Use 越来越 (yuè lái yuè) to indicate a progressive change, e.g.:

生词　多 vs. 少

shēngcí　　duō vs. *shǎo*

Q: 你觉得生词越来越多还是越来越少？

　　Nǐ juéde shēngcí yuè lái yuè duō háishi yuè lái yuè shǎo?

A: 我觉得生词越来越多／少。

　　Wǒ juéde shēngcí yuè lái yuè duō/shǎo.

1 功课　多 vs. 少

　　gōngkè　　duō vs. *shǎo*

2 课文　长 vs. 短

　　kèwén　　cháng vs. *duǎn*

3 考试　难 vs. 容易

　　kǎoshì　　nán vs. *róngyì*

4 语法　难 vs. 容易

　　yǔfǎ　　nán vs. *róngyì*

And not only that

In pairs, form a question-and-answer about why you didn't do certain things. Use 再说 (zàishuō) to introduce an additional reason, e.g.:

Q: 你今天为什么没吃早饭？

　　Nǐ jīntiān wèishénme méi chī zǎofàn?

A: 我没时间，再说我也不饿。

　　Wǒ méi shíjiān, zàishuō wǒ yě bú è.

1 Q: 你为什么不运动？

　　　Nǐ wèishénme bú yùndòng?

　　A: _____

2 Q: 你为什么寒假没回家看爸爸妈妈？

　　　Nǐ wèishénme hánjià méi huí jiā kàn bàba māma?

　　A: _____

3 Q: 你为什么学中文？

Nǐ wèishénme xué Zhōngwén?

A: _____

4 Q: 你为什么上这个学校？

Nǐ wèishénme shàng zhè ge xuéxiào?

A: _____

Chinese Chat

Your friend just published a post on haodf.com (好大夫在线) *(Hǎo dàifu zàixiàn)*, a popular medical consultation and scheduling website in China. What's ailing him, and what does the doctor suggest?

李新
状态：就诊前

> 患
>
> 医生，上周我眼睛特别红，这几天刚好，可是现在鼻子又特别痒 …… 吃了很多又贵又难吃的药都没用。我是感冒了还是过敏了？
>
> 来自好大夫APP (下载APP与医生一对一免费沟通)

高朋 大夫

> 医
>
> 别乱吃药，我得先给你检查一下，快来医院看病。

Characterize it!

What do the characters mean?	
What is the common radical?	
What does the radical mean?	
How does the radical relate to the overall meaning of the characters?	

❶ 　**❷** 　**❸**

More characters

文化
e

Continue
to explore

Chinese Medicine

Before the seventeenth-century introduction of Western medicine (西医) (*Xīyī*) by European missionaries, people in China had relied on traditional Chinese medicine (中医) (*Zhōngyī*). Its treatment modalities—acupuncture, herbal medicine, massage, etc.—remain well-respected options for treating various ailments in China, and many people opt for traditional medicine either in conjunction with or instead of Western medicine. Traditional Chinese medicine is by no means a panacea. However, some of its practices have found popularity in the West despite misgivings among medical professionals. Other practices have been confirmed by modern science: sweet wormwood (*Artemisia annua*) or 青蒿 (*qīnghāo*) has been used to treat fevers for more than two millennia. In the search for a drug to treat malaria, the Chinese chemist Tu Youyou consulted a text from the fourth century and succeeded in isolating the plant's active compound, artemisinin or 青蒿素 (*qīnghāosù*), in the 1970s. Artemisinin is now one of the main drugs used in the treatment of malaria, and for her work, Tu was awarded the Nobel Prize in 2015.

COMPARE & CONTRAST

There are a variety of alternative medical treatments in China, including moxibustion (艾灸) (*ài jiǔ*), in which dried mugwort is burned on the skin; acupuncture (针灸) (*zhēnjiǔ*), in which specialized needles are inserted into the body at particular points; and cupping (拔罐) (*bá guàn*), in which a vacuum is created on the skin with the use of glass cups. All of these practices are believed to facilitate the flow f qi through the body. Are alternative medical treatments used in your culture or community, and if so, how is their efficacy pe ceived?

Seeing *the* Doctor

In China, consulting a doctor requires the payment of a registration fee, 挂号费 (*guàhào fèi*), typically under fifty yuan (about seven dollars). Consulting someone designated as a "senior expert," 专家 (*zhuānjiā*), however, can require a registration fee as high as several hundred yuan. Patients typically pay upfront for tests.

Injections, 打针 (*dǎ zhēn*), and intravenous infusions, which are 打点滴 (*dǎ diǎndī*) in Taiwan and 输液 (*shū yè*) in Mainland China, are somewhat common treatments in Chinese hospitals and clinics compared to their use in Western hospitals, and are sometimes used even for ailments like colds.

Most outpatients in China pick up prescriptions from a pharmacy within the hospital itself. However, prescription medication can also be obtained from independent pharmacies.

Medical Care

Employees of all state-owned enterprises and institutions in China were entitled to free medical care until the 1980s. This became a huge financial burden on the government, and the practice was discontinued with the government's initiation of healthcare reform in the 1990s. China currently provides basic medical insurance to over 95% of its population, although the type and source of insurance varies depending on employment and location. The basic medical insurance can also be supplemented with commercial health insurance.

Hua Tuo

Hua Tuo (华佗) (Huà Tuó), a famed physician who lived during the second century, is credited as the first in China to introduce anesthesia during surgery, using a concoction called 麻沸散 (máfèisǎn) before the operation. Following this, the modern Chinese term for anesthesia is 麻醉 (mázuì), literally "numb and inebriated." Hua Tuo also wrote a manual of qigong exercises, 五禽戏 (Wǔ Qín Xì) ("Games of Five Beasts"), based on his studies of the tiger, deer, bear, monkey, and crane. The pronunciation of Hua Tuo in ancient Chinese sounded similar to gada, Sanskrit for sickness and related to Agada, one of eight branches of Indian medicine. Some scholars have speculated that many stories of Hua Tuo's medical feats are in fact of Indian origin.

Lesson Wrap-Up

Rearrange the following sentences into a logical sequence. Then combine the sentences into a coherent narrative. Substitute nouns with pronouns and change periods to commas where appropriate. Avoid unnecessary repetitions of subject pronouns. Add the connective devices 就 (jiù), ⋯以后 (. . . yǐhòu), and 还 (hái) where appropriate.

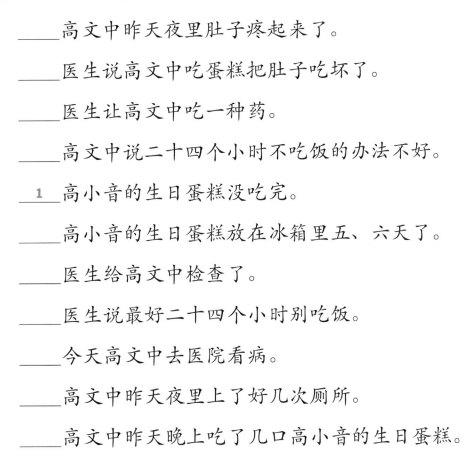

_____ 高文中昨天夜里肚子疼起来了。

_____ 医生说高文中吃蛋糕把肚子吃坏了。

_____ 医生让高文中吃一种药。

_____ 高文中说二十四个小时不吃饭的办法不好。

__1__ 高小音的生日蛋糕没吃完。

_____ 高小音的生日蛋糕放在冰箱里五、六天了。

_____ 医生给高文中检查了。

_____ 医生说最好二十四个小时别吃饭。

_____ 今天高文中去医院看病。

_____ 高文中昨天夜里上了好几次厕所。

_____ 高文中昨天晚上吃了几口高小音的生日蛋糕。

You went to a friend's birthday party last Friday. You met a lot of interesting people. You liked the music and the food. You had a good time, but got sick. The doctor asks you what's wrong. You have a stomachache. The doctor wants to know what and how much you ate and drank last night. Depending on your answer, the doctor will examine you, see if you have a fever, and determine if you need injections or medication. If you need medicine, find out how many times a day you need to take it and whether you need to take it before or after you eat.

Social Media

It's hay fever season. On a social media platform, post about allergy symptoms and remedies to help Chinese students on your campus deal. Explain how to distinguish allergy and cold symptoms, referring to the template below.

中国同学们，你们好！最近，你们是不是……？

过敏：

感冒：

怎么办：多……，多……，少……，少……

Supplemental Reading Practice

For additional reading practice that builds on the vocabulary introduced in this lesson, turn to the supplemental readings that begin on page 419.

Can-Do Check List ✔

I can

Before proceeding to Lesson 16, make sure you can complete the following tasks in Chinese:

- ☐ Tell a doctor about my cold symptoms
- ☐ Ask a doctor if a shot or medicine is needed for treatment
- ☐ Follow and repeat a doctor's instructions on when and how often to take medicine
- ☐ Tell people about my allergies and briefly describe my symptoms

Keeping It Casual (Lessons 11–15)

Before you progress to the next half of the text, we'll review how some of the functional expressions from Lessons 11–15 are used in casual Chinese. After you complete the review, note any other casual expressions you would like to learn; then share the list with your teacher.

<u>1</u>

> ## 在 (zài) (to exist)

When you think someone else might have something of yours, ask 我的⋯⋯在你那儿吗? (Wǒ de . . . zài nǐ nàr ma?) instead of 你有我的⋯⋯吗? (Nǐ yǒu wǒ de . . . ma?).

A | **Bai Ying'ai**

老师，我的功课在您那儿吗？

Lǎoshī, wǒ de gōngkè zài nín nàr ma?

Teacher, do you have my homework?

Teacher Chang

我已经还给你了。

Wǒ yǐjīng huán gěi nǐ le.

I gave it to you already.

[还给 *(huán gěi)*, to return something (to someone)]

Bai Ying'ai

是吗？对不起，我再找找。

Shì ma? Duìbuqǐ, wǒ zài zhǎo zhao.

Oh, you did? Sorry, I'll look for it again.

B | **Daughter**

妈，我的绿色衬衫在您那儿吗？

Mā, wǒ de lǜ sè chènshān zài nín nàr ma?

Mom, do you have my green shirt?

Mother

在我这儿。给你吧。

Zài wǒ zhèr. Gěi nǐ ba.

Yes, I have it. Here you are.

C **Wang Peng**

我的书还在你那儿吗？昨天你拿去看了。

Wǒ de shū hái zài nǐ nàr ma? Zuótiān nǐ ná qù kàn le.

Do you still have my book? You took it to read yesterday.

Gao Wenzhong

哦，还在我家，我回去拿。

Ò, hái zài wǒ jiā, wǒ huí qu ná.

Yeah, it's still at my place. I'll go get it.

2 | Complimentary expressions

Note the different expressions that are used to compliment men, women, and children.

A 那个小孩真可爱。

Nà ge xiǎohái zhēn kě'ài.

That little kid is really cute.

B 她长得真好看！

Tā zhǎng de zhēn hǎokàn!

She's really beautiful!

C 李友长得很漂亮。

Lǐ Yǒu zhǎng de hěn piàoliang.

Li You looks very pretty.

D 王朋真帅。

Wáng Péng zhēn shuài.

Wang Peng is really handsome.

E 那个班的学生都很酷。

Nà ge bān de xuésheng dōu hěn kù.

The students in that class are all very cool.

3 | 怎么了？(Zěnme le?) (What's the matter? What's wrong?)

You can ask 怎么了？ *(Zěnme le?)* upon finding someone under unusual circumstances or showing signs of concern, anxiety, or pain.

A   **Little Gao**

你怎么了？怎么这么不高兴？

Nǐ zěnme le? Zěnme zhème bù gāoxìng?

What's the matter? Why are you so unhappy?

         Mr. Fei

我的女朋友不爱我了。

Wǒ de nǚpéngyou bú ài wǒ le.

My girlfriend doesn't love me anymore.

B   **Li You**

怎么了？眼睛怎么这么红？

Zěnme le? Yǎnjīng zěnme zhème hóng?

What's wrong? Why are your eyes so red?

         Wang Peng

没什么。我可能对什么东西过敏了。

Méi shénme. Wǒ kěnéng duì shénme dōngxi guòmǐn le.

It's nothing. I may be allergic to something.

4 | 糟糕 (zāogāo) ([it's] awful/what a mess)

Say this when you realize you've forgotten something important or something consequential has gone wrong.

A   **Gao Wenzhong**

糟糕，我的信用卡不见了。

Zāogāo, wǒ de xìnyòngkǎ bú jiàn le.

Shoot! My credit card has disappeared.

         Wang Peng

快给你爸爸打电话吧。

Kuài gěi nǐ bàba dǎ diànhuà ba.

Hurry, call your dad.

B

Li You

糟糕，快要考试了，我还没准备好。

Zāogāo, kuài yào kǎo shì le, wǒ hái méi zhǔnbèi hǎo.

Drat. It's almost time for the test. I am not ready yet.

Bai Ying'ai

你没听说吗？今天不考试了。

Nǐ méi tīngshuō ma? Jīntiān bù kǎo shì le.

Didn't you hear? There's no test today.

Li You

是吗？那太好了！……为什么？

Shì ma? Nà tài hǎo le! . . . Wèishénme?

Really? That's great! . . . How come?

Bai Ying'ai

老师病了。

Lǎoshī bìng le.

The teacher is sick.

糟糕，快要考试了，我还没准备好。

约会

Yuēhuì

DATING

Learning Objectives

In this lesson, you will learn to:

- Describe how long you've known someone
- Ask someone out on a date
- Make arrangements to go out with friends
- Accept or gently decline a date
- End a phone conversation politely

Relate & Get Ready

In your own culture/community:

- Is it socially acceptable to call a person you only met once and whose phone number you obtained indirectly?
- Is it impolite to decline a date without providing an excuse?
- How do you end a phone conversation without being rude?

Seeing a Movie

Dialogue 1

王朋跟李友在同^a一个学校学习，他们认识已经快半年了。王朋常常帮李友练习说中文。他们也常常一起出去玩儿，每次都玩儿得¹很高兴。李友对王朋的印象^b很好，王朋也很喜欢李友，他们成了好朋友。

这个周末学校演一个中国电影^c，我们一起去看，好吗？

好啊！不过，听说看电影的人很多，买得到²票吗？

票已经买好了，我费了很大的力气才买到。

好极了！我早^d就想看中国电影了。还有别人跟我们一起去吗？

没有，就³我们俩^e。

好。什么时候？

后天晚上八点。

看电影以前，我请你吃晚饭。

太好了！一言为定^f。

Wáng Péng gēn Lǐ Yǒu zài tóng^a *yí ge xuéxiào xuéxí, tāmen rènshi yǐjīng kuài bàn nián le. Wáng Péng chángcháng bāng Lǐ Yǒu liànxí shuō Zhōngwén. Tāmen yě chángcháng yìqǐ chū qu wánr, měi cì dōu wánr de*¹ *hěn gāoxìng. Lǐ Yǒu duì Wáng Péng de yìnxiàng*^b *hěn hǎo, Wáng Péng yě hěn xǐhuan Lǐ Yǒu, tāmen chéng le hǎo péngyou.*

Zhè ge zhōumò xuéxiào yǎn yí ge Zhōngguó diànyǐng^c, *wǒmen yìqǐ qù kàn, hǎo ma?*

*Hǎo a! Búguò, tīngshuō kàn diànyǐng de rén hěn duō, mǎi de dào*² *piào ma?*

Piào yǐjīng mǎi hǎo le, wǒ fèi le hěn dà de lìqi cái mǎi dào.

Hǎo jí le! Wǒ zǎo^d *jiù xiǎng kàn Zhōngguó diànyǐng le. Hái yǒu bié rén gēn wǒmen yìqǐ qù ma?*

*Méiyǒu, jiù*³ *wǒmen liǎ*^e.

Hǎo. Shénme shíhou?

Hòutiān wǎnshang bā diǎn.

Kàn diànyǐng yǐqián, wǒ qǐng nǐ chī wǎnfàn.

Tài hǎo le! Yì yán wéi dìng^f.

Language Notes

a 同 *(tóng)*

This word cannot be used as a predicate. Even as an attributive, its usage is very limited.

b 印象 *(yìnxiàng)*

Compare 李友对王朋的印象很好 *(Lǐ Yǒu duì Wáng Péng de yìnxiàng hěn hǎo)* (Li You has a very good impression of Wang Peng) and 李友给王朋的印象很好 *(Lǐ Yǒu gěi Wáng Péng de yìnxiàng hěn hǎo)* (Li You made a very good impression on Wang Peng).

c 演电影 *(yǎn diànyǐng)*

The phrase 演电影 *(yǎn diànyǐng)* (to show a film) is interchangeable with 放电影 *(fàng diànyǐng)*. In addition, 演电影 *(yǎn diànyǐng)* can also mean "to act in a film."

d 早 *(zǎo)*

The primary meaning of 早 *(zǎo)* is "early," but in an extended sense it can also mean "a long time ago" or "early on."

e 俩 *(liǎ)*

This is a colloquial equivalent of 两个 *(liǎng ge)*.

f 一言为定 *(yì yán wéi dìng)*

This phrase literally means "achieving certainty with one word" and is one of many four-character idioms that have their origins in classical Chinese and continue to be used by many native speakers of the language.

Vocabulary

No.	Word	Pinyin	Part of Speech	Definition
1	同	*tóng*	adj	same
2	印象	*yìnxiàng*	n	impression
3	成	*chéng*	v	to become
4	演	*yǎn*	v	to show (a film), to perform
5	费	*fèi*	v	to spend, to take (effort)
6	力气	*lìqi*	n	strength, effort
7	就	*jiù*	adv	just, only (indicating a small number)
8	俩	*liǎ*	nu+m	(coll.) two
9	后天	*hòutiān*	t	the day after tomorrow
10	一言为定	*yì yán wéi dìng*		that settles it, that's settled, it's decided

周末你想约朋友
出去做什么？

Zhōumò nǐ xiǎng yuē péngyou chūqu zuò shénme?

What would you like to ask your friends to do over the weekend?

我想约朋友去＿＿＿＿＿＿＿＿。

Wǒ xiǎng yuē péngyou ＿＿＿＿＿＿＿.

How About You?

See index for corresponding vocabulary or research another term.

C **Student A** 这本书我考试要用，你今天看得完吗？

Zhè běn shū wǒ kǎoshì yào yòng, nǐ jīntiān kàn de wán ma?

I need this book for an exam. Can you finish reading this book today?

Student B 这本书我今天看不完，你先用吧，我以后再看。

Zhè běn shū wǒ jīntiān kàn bu wán, nǐ xiān yòng ba, wǒ yǐhòu zài kàn.

I can't finish this book today. You use it first; I'll read it later.

D 那个字怎么写，我想不起来了。

Nà ge zì zěnme xiě, wǒ xiǎng bu qǐ lái le.

I can't remember how to write that character.
[See Dialogue 2 for 想不起来 (xiǎng bu qǐ lái).]

E 健康保险太贵，我买不起。

Jiànkāng bǎoxiǎn tài guì, wǒ mǎi bu qǐ.

Health insurance is too expensive. I can't afford it.

Potential complements usually appear in negative sentences. They are used in affirmative sentences much less often. In affirmative sentences, we normally use the "能 (néng) + verb + resultative/directional complement" structure:

F 今天的功课不多，我很快就能做完。

Jīntiān de gōngkè bù duō, wǒ hěn kuài jiù néng zuò wán.

There isn't much homework today. I can finish it very quickly.

G 这个中国电影的中文不难，我能看懂。

Zhè ge Zhōngguó diànyǐng de Zhōngwén bù nán, wǒ néng kàn dǒng.

The language in this Chinese movie isn't difficult. I can understand it.

Potential complements can be used to ask questions. In these situations, we can answer affirmatively using potential complements.

H Q: 这条中文短信你看得懂吗?

Zhè tiáo Zhōngwén duǎnxìn nǐ kàn de dǒng ma?

Can you understand this Chinese text message?

A: 我看得懂。

Wǒ kàn de dǒng.

Yes, I can understand it.

I Q: 二十个饺子你吃得完吃不完?

Èrshí ge jiǎozi nǐ chī de wán chī bu wán?

Can you eat twenty dumplings or not?

A: 我吃得完。

Wǒ chī de wán.

Yes, I can.

Potential complements are an important feature of Chinese. They are often the only way to convey the idea that the absence of certain conditions prevents a result from being achieved. Potential complements have a unique function that cannot be fulfilled by the "不能 *(bù néng)* + verb + resultative/directional complement" construction. Sometimes we have to use potential complements in negative sentences. If we used the "不能 *(bù néng)* + verb + resultative/directional complements" construction, the sentence would be incorrect.

[⊗ 老师说得太快,我不能听清楚。]

Sometimes the meaning would change:

J 门太小,我进不去。

Mén tài xiǎo, wǒ jìn bu qù.

The door is too narrow. I can't go in.

K 里面正在开会,你不能进去!

Lǐmiàn zhèngzài kāi huì, nǐ bù néng jìnqu!

They are having a meeting inside. You can't go in.

A potential complement cannot be used in a 把 *(bǎ)* sentence, either.

[⊗ 我把今天的功课做不完。]

EXERCISES

Answer the questions in the negative with a potential complement. Use exercise 1 as an example.

More exercises

1　你下午三点能回来/回得来吗?

　　→ 我下午有课，三点回不来。

2　你能看懂/看得懂这本中文书吗?

3　你今天能写完/写得完一百个汉字吗?

SHANGHAI SYMPHONY HALL
上海交响乐团音乐厅

"回味肖邦"
肖邦音乐套曲中国首演及钢琴作品音乐会

剧场　主厅
日期　2016-11-04
时间　19:30

区域　H区 双号
座位　1排 8座
票价　280元

SSOS161030000004

上海交响乐团音乐厅 SHANGHAI SYMPHONY HALL 上海市复兴中路1380号 NO. 1380 MIDDLE FUXING ROAD, SHANGHAI

GET Real WITH CHINESE

What kind of event is this ticket for? What other information can you identify?

就 (jiù) (only, just)

When used before a noun, pronoun, or verb, 就 (jiù) means "only" or "just." Often, the noun, pronoun, or verb can be modified by a numeral-measure word combination.

A　我们班人很少，就七个学生。

Wǒmen bān rén hěn shǎo, jiù qī ge xuésheng.

Our class is small, with just seven students.

B　今天功课很少，就写五个汉字。

Jīntiān gōngkè hěn shǎo, jiù xiě wǔ ge Hànzì.

There's little homework today. We only have to write five characters.

C　我们一家五口，就我对味精过敏。

Wǒmen yì jiā wǔ kǒu, jiù wǒ duì wèijīng guòmǐn.

There are five people in our family. Only I am allergic to MSG.

D　今天我就有一节课。

Jīntiān wǒ jiù yǒu yì jié kè.

Today I have only one class.

More exercises

EXERCISES

Complete the sentences by inserting 就 where appropriate. Use exercise 1 as an example.

1　我们的电脑班很小　　　　二十个学生

→ 我们的电脑班很小，就二十个学生。

2　这个城市的中国饭馆很多　　我去过两家

3　弟弟这个月没花很多钱　　　两百块

Chinese Chat

A friend is messaging you to make plans. How would you respond?

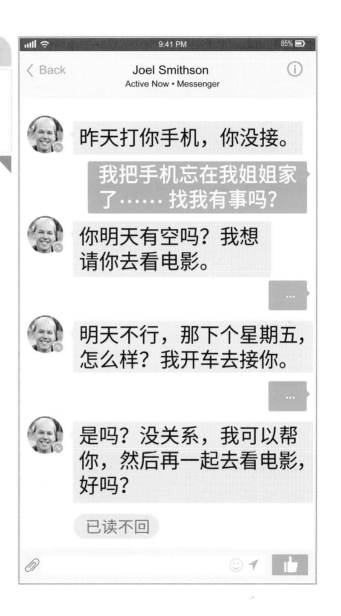

Language Practice

A	How did you feel?	INTERPERSONAL

In pairs, ask each other questions about how the following activities affect or affected you, e.g.:

Student A 你昨天晚上写汉字写得累不累？

Nǐ zuótiān wǎnshang xiě Hànzì xiě de lèi bu lèi?

Student B 我昨天晚上写汉字写得很累/不累。你呢？

Wǒ zuótiān wǎnshang xiě Hànzì xiě de hěn lèi/bú lèi. Nǐ ne?

1 你每天上课上得累不累？

Nǐ měi tiān shàng kè shàng de lèi bu lèi?

2 你昨天晚上睡觉睡得舒服不舒服？

Nǐ zuótiān wǎnshang shuì jiào shuì de shūfu bu shūfu?

3 你上个周末玩儿得高兴不高兴？

Nǐ shàng ge zhōumò wánr de gāoxìng bu gāoxìng?

B	First day	INTERPERSONAL

In pairs, form a question-and-answer about your partner's first day of school. Use 得 (de) or 不 (bu) to indicate whether you achieved the desired result or not, e.g.:

Q: 你找得到找不到你的教室？

Nǐ zhǎo de dào zhǎo bu dào nǐ de jiàoshì?

A: 我找得到我的教室。／我找不到我的教室。

Wǒ zhǎo de dào wǒ de jiàoshì./Wǒ zhǎo bu dào wǒ de jiàoshì.

1 你买得到买不到你要的书？

Nǐ mǎi de dào mǎi bu dào nǐ yào de shū?

2 你听得懂听不懂中文老师说的话？

Nǐ tīng de dǒng tīng bu dǒng Zhōngwén lǎoshī shuō de huà?

3 你看得清楚看不清楚老师写的字？

Nǐ kàn de qīngchu kàn bu qīngchu lǎoshī xiě de zì?

C | **Bring it on** | INTERPERSONAL

In pairs, form a question-and-answer about whether you and your partner would be up to the challenge of an eating or drinking competition involving the following items and quantities. Use 得 *(de)* or 不 *(bu)*, e.g.:

x30

Q: 你吃得完吃不完三十个热狗？

Nǐ chī de wán chī bu wán sānshí ge règǒu?

A: 我吃得完三十个热狗。/
我吃不完三十个热狗。

Wǒ chī de wán sānshí ge règǒu./Wǒ chī bu wán sānshí ge règǒu.

1  x100　　**2**  x10　　**3** x15　　**4**  x20　　**5** x25

How do you pronounce the characters?
What is the common component?
How do you pronounce the common component?
How does the component relate to the pronunciation of the characters?

Characterize it!

❶ 　❷ 　❸

吗　妈　码

More characters

IC fan quiz

In pairs, form a question-and-answer to test how much of an IC fan you are. Use 就 (jiù) to indicate exceptions, e.g.:

Q: 他们都有弟弟吗？

Tāmen dōu yǒu dìdi ma?

A: 不，就高小音一个人有弟弟。

Bù, jiù Gāo Xiǎoyīn yí ge rén yǒu dìdi.

1 他们都会滑冰吗？

Tāmen dōu huì huá bīng ma?

2 他们都吃素吗？

Tāmen dōu chī sù ma?

3 他们都爱吃蛋糕吗？

Tāmen dōu ài chī dàngāo ma?

4 他们都不会说英文吗？

Tāmen dōu bú huì shuō Yīngwén ma?

Turning Down an Invitation

Dialogue 2

（费先生给李友打电话……）

喂，请问李友小姐在吗？

我就是。请问你是哪一位？

我姓费，你还记得[a]我吗？

姓费？

你还记得上个月高小音的生日舞会吗？我就是最后请你跳舞的那个人。你再想想。想起来了吗？

对不起，我想不起来。

我是高小音的中学同学。

是吗？你是怎么知道我的电话号码的？

是小音告诉我的。

费先生，你有事吗？

这个周末你有空儿吗？我想请你去跳舞。

这个周末不行，下个星期我有三个考试。

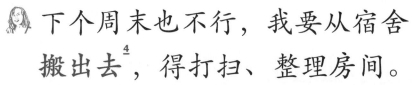 没关系，下个周末怎么样？你考完试，我们好好儿[b]玩儿玩儿。

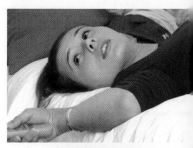

 下个周末也不行，我要从宿舍搬出去[4]，得打扫、整理房间。

你看下下个周末，好不好？

 对不起，下下个周末更不行了，我要跟我的男朋友去纽约旅行。

……那……

 费先生，对不起，我的手机没电了。再见！

 喂……喂……

(Fèi xiānsheng gěi Lǐ Yǒu dǎ diànhuà . . .)

Wéi, qǐng wèn Lǐ Yǒu xiǎojiě zài ma?

Wǒ jiù shì. Qǐng wèn nǐ shì nǎ yí wèi?

Wǒ xìng Fèi, nǐ hái jìde[a] *wǒ ma?*

Xìng Fèi?

Nǐ hái jìde shàng ge yuè Gāo Xiǎoyīn de shēngrì

wǔhuì ma? Wǒ jiù shì zuìhòu qǐng nǐ tiào wǔ de

nà ge rén. Nǐ zài xiǎng xiang. Xiǎng qi lai le ma?

Duìbuqǐ, wǒ xiǎng bu qǐ lái.

Wǒ shì Gāo Xiǎoyīn de zhōngxué tóngxué.

Shì ma? Nǐ shì zěnme zhīdào wǒ de diànhuà

hàomǎ de?

Shì Xiǎoyīn gàosu wǒ de.

Fèi xiānsheng, nǐ yǒu shì ma?

Zhè ge zhōumò nǐ yǒu kòngr ma? Wǒ xiǎng qǐng

nǐ qù tiào wǔ.

Zhè ge zhōumò bù xíng, xià ge xīngqī wǒ yǒu sān

ge kǎoshì.

Méi guānxi, xià gè zhōumò zěnmeyàng? Nǐ kǎo

wán shì, wǒmen hǎohāor[b] *wánr wanr.*

Xià ge zhōumò yě bù xíng, wǒ yào cóng sùshè

bān chu qu[4]*, děi dǎsǎo, zhěnglǐ fángjiān.*

Nǐ kàn xià xià ge zhōumò, hǎo bu hǎo?

Duìbuqǐ, xià xià ge zhōumò gèng bù xíng le, wǒ

yào gēn wǒ de nánpéngyou qù Niǔyuē lǚxíng.

. . . Nà . . .

Fèi xiānsheng, duìbuqǐ, wǒ de shǒujī méi diàn le.

Zàijiàn!

Wéi . . . wéi . . .

a 记得 *(jìde)*

While 记得 *(jìde)* pertains to the continuous state of remembering, 想起来 *(xiǎng qi lai)* refers to the mental act of retrieving information from your memory. Thus you can say: 我记得他上过我的课，可是我想不起来他叫什么名字。 *(Wǒ jìde tā shàng guo wǒ de kè, kěshì wǒ xiǎng bu qi lai tā jiào shénme míngzi)* (I remember that he took my class, but I can't recall his name at the moment).

b 好好儿 *(hǎohāor)*

This colloquial expression means "all out, to one's heart's content" and often precedes a verb to serve as an adverbial, e.g.: 考试以后我要去纽约好好儿玩儿玩儿 *(Kǎo shì yǐhòu wǒ yào qù Niǔyuē hǎohāor wánr wanr)* (After the test I want to go to New York and have a great time). Note the different tone for the reduplicated syllable 好 *(hǎo)*.

Vocabulary

Audio

Flashcards

No.	Word	Pinyin	Part of Speech	Definition
1	记得	jìde	v	to remember
	记	jì	v	to record
2	想	xiǎng	v	to think
3	想起来	xiǎng qi lai	vc	to remember, to recall
4	号码	hàomǎ	n	number
5	搬	bān	v	to move
6	打扫	dǎsǎo	v	to clean up (a room, apartment or house)
	扫	sǎo	v	to sweep
7	整理	zhěnglǐ	v	to put in order
8	房间	fángjiān	n	room
9	旅行	lǚxíng	v	to travel
10	电	diàn	n	electricity

周末我想请你去
跳舞，有空吗？

*Zhōumò wǒ xiǎng qǐng nǐ qù tiào wǔ,
yǒu kòng ma?*

I'd like to take you dancing this weekend.
Are you free?

对不起，周末不行，
我得 _____。

*Duìbuqǐ, zhōumò bù xíng,
wǒ děi _____ .*

How About You?

See index for corresponding vocabulary or research another term.

Grammar

<table>
<tr><td>4</td><td>Directional complements (II)</td></tr>
</table>

Directional complements indicate the direction in which a person or an object moves. A directional verb such as 上 *(shang)* (to go up), 下 *(xia)* (to go down), 进 *(jin)* (to go in), 出 *(chu)* (to go out), 回 *(hui)* (to return), 过 *(guo)* (to go over, to pass), 起 *(qi)* (to rise), 开 *(kai)* (to part from), 到 *(dao)* (to arrive), 来 *(lai)* (to come), and 去 *(qu)* (to go) can be placed after another verb to become what is known as a "simple directional complement."

Simple directional complements:

Pattern A1
Subject + verb + place word/noun (phrase) + 来/去
(lai/qu)

A 她下楼来。

Tā xià lóu lai.

She comes downstairs.

B 她上楼去。

Tā shàng lóu qu.

She goes upstairs.

C 请你买一些水果来。

Qǐng nǐ mǎi yì xiē shuǐguǒ lai.

Please buy some fruit (and bring it) here. (anticipated action)

D 你给他送一点儿吃的东西去。

Nǐ gěi tā sòng yì diǎnr chī de dōngxi qu.

Take some food to him. (anticipated action)

E 妹妹给爸爸拿了一杯咖啡来。

Mèimei gěi bàba ná le yì bēi kāfēi lai.

My younger sister brought Dad a cup of coffee. (completed action)

F 他买来了一些水果。

Tā mǎi lai le yì xiē shuǐguǒ.

He bought and brought over some fruit. (completed action)

G 他给朋友送去了一些花。

Tā gěi péngyou sòng qu le yì xiē huā.

He sent some flowers to his friend. (completed action)

When the object of the verb is a location word as in (A) and (B), the sentence can only appear in Pattern A1. When the object is a regular noun and the action is not completed, the sentence often appears in Pattern A1 as well, as in (C) and (D). If the action is completed, the sentence can appear either in Pattern A1 or in Pattern A2. It is, therefore, a good idea to memorize Pattern A1 as the failsafe form.

Pattern B
Subject + verb + 上/下/进/出/回/过/起/开/到/来/去 + place word/noun
(shang / xia / jin / chu / hui / guo / qi / kai / dao / lai / qu)

H 他走上楼。

Tā zǒu shang lóu.

He walks upstairs.

[The sentence doesn't indicate whether the speaker is upstairs or downstairs.]

I 老师走进教室。

Lǎoshī zǒu jin jiàoshì.

The teacher walks into the classroom.

[The sentence doesn't indicate whether the speaker is in the classroom or not.]

J 请你拿出一张纸。

Qǐng nǐ ná chu yì zhāng zhǐ.

Please take out a piece of paper. (anticipated action)

K 妈妈买回了一些水果。

Māma mǎi hui le yì xiē shuíguǒ.

Mom bought some fruit. (completed action)

In Pattern B, note that when the directional complement is 上/下/进/出/回/过/起/开/到 (shang/xia/jin/chu/hui/guo/qi/kai/dao), regardless if the object is a place word or an ordinary noun, if the action is completed or not, the object comes after the directional complement.

When a simple directional complement—上/下/进/出/回/过/起/到 (shang/xia/jin/chu/hui/guo/qi/dao)—is combined with 来(lai) or 去 (qu), we have what is called a "compound directional complement," again with two basic patterns.

Compound directional complements:

Pattern A
Subject + verb + 上/下/进/出/回/过/起/到 + place word/noun + 来/去
(shang / xia / jin / chu / hui / guo / qi / dao)   *(lai / qu)*

L 她走下楼来。

Tā zǒu xia lóu lai.

She walks downstairs.

[The speaker is downstairs.]

M 老师走进教室来/去。

Lǎoshī zǒu jin jiàoshì lai/qu.

The teacher walks into the classroom.

[With 来 (lai), the speaker is in the classroom; with 去 (qu), the speaker is outside the classroom.]

N 弟弟跳上床来/去。

Dìdi tiào shang chuáng lai/qu.

My little brother jumps onto the bed.

[With 来 (lai), the speaker is on the bed; with 去 (qu), the speaker is not on the bed.]

O 请你买回一些梨来。

Qǐng nǐ mǎi hui yì xiē lí lai.

Please buy some pears and bring them back here. (anticipated action)

P 请大家都拿起笔来。

Qǐng dàjiā dōu ná qi bǐ lai.

Everyone, please pick up a pen. (anticipated action)

Q 他拿出了一张纸来。

Tā ná chu le yì zhāng zhǐ lai.

He took out a piece of paper. (completed action)

> ### Pattern B
> **Subject + verb + 上/下/进/出/回/过/起 + 来/去 + noun**
> *(shang/xia/jin/chu/hui/guo/qi)*   *(lai/qu)*

R 他买回来了一些水果。

Tā mǎi hui lai le yì xiē shuǐguǒ.

He bought some fruit (and brought it back here). (completed action)

S 妹妹拿出来一件新买的衣服。

Mèimei ná chu lai yí jiàn xīn mǎi de yīfu.

My younger sister took out a jacket she just bought.

As in the case of the simple directional compounds, when the object is a location word, the sentence appears only in Pattern A, as in (L), (M), and (N). If the object is a regular noun and the action is not completed, the sentence often appears in Pattern A as well, as in (O) and (P). If the action is completed, the sentence can appear either in Pattern A or in Pattern B as in (Q), (R), and (S). Again, it is not a bad idea to memorize Pattern A as the failsafe form.

EXERCISES

Reference the parenthetical information to complete the sentences with a directional complement. Use exercise 1 as an example.

More exercises

1 他很快地　　走下楼　　（说话人在楼下）
　→ 他很快地走下楼来。

2 你快一点儿　跑上楼　　（说话人在楼下）

3 我看见他刚才 走进你的房间
　（说话人在房间外边）

Characterize it!

| What do the characters mean? |
| What is the common radical? |
| What does the radical mean? |
| How does the radical relate to the overall meaning of the characters? |

❶ 搬　❷ 打　❸ 扫

More characters

请勿打扰

请打扫房间

GET Real WITH CHINESE

You're staying at a hotel in Xi'an, and would like to get your room cleaned while you head out for some sightseeing. Which of these door hangers should you use?

Language Practice

| E | **What do you think?** | PRESENTATIONAL |

Having bought or done something, you want to get your friends' opinions, e.g.:

这是我刚买的鞋，你看看怎么样？

Zhè shì wǒ gāng mǎi de xié, nǐ kàn kan zěnmeyàng?

1

2

3  [See also Language Note b, Dialogue 2, Lesson 15.]

4  [See also Language Note b, Dialogue 2, Lesson 15.]

| F | **Charades** | PRESENTATIONAL |

Choose a classmate you admire, then have the rest of your class guess who it is by saying things like 她/他就是……的那个人 (*Tā jiù shì . . . de nà ge rén*). See how many such sentences are required before someone guesses correctly.

By any chance, could I . . .

Try to soften your tone by repeating the verb.

1   You would like to see your partner's family picture.

2   You want your partner to have a look at the characters you have written.

3   You want to listen to your partner's recording.

4   You want to use your partner's cell phone.

5   You want your partner to help you look for your book.

6   You hope your partner will practice Chinese with you.

Chinese Chat

Li You just updated her status on Weibo and Mr. Fei left some comments. What do you think Li You is hinting at?

李友
01-22 16:20 来自华为 Mate 9

虽然今天很冷，但是我心里暖暖的。

转发 2   评论 4   赞 8

小费   👍 2   💬
01-22 16:28

为什么啊？

李友：因为和朋友看了一个非常好
　　　看的中国电影……

小费：那下周我们也一起去看电影
　　　吧？

李友：糟糕，今天的功课又多又难，
　　　可能做不完……不聊了……

↗ 转发　|　转发　|　👍 赞

文化

Continue
to explore

Marriage

Until the first half of the twentieth century, arranged marriages were the norm in China, and divorces were rare. Love marriages are now the ideal. People are free to date, marry, and divorce. Nevertheless, upon finding that their children have reached a certain age without having acquired a boyfriend or girlfriend, some parents opt to take matters into their own hands and arrange a few blind dates, 相亲 (xiāng qīn), for their offspring. In premodern China, intimate contact between unmarried young men and women was strictly prohibited. Traditionally, Chinese people shied away from public displays of affection, and even as recently as the 1980s, one seldom saw couples holding hands on the street. Today, although there has been debate over what counts as appropriate public behavior, public displays of affection have become much more common.

COMPARE & CONTRAST

1 In China and elsewhere, a tendency toward avoiding direct, blunt language in the context of dating can result in white lies to avoid hurting people's feelings. In one common scenario in Chinese romantic comedies, a girl calls a boy for help with her computer as a way to get to know him better. In another scenario, a girl arranges to get a call in the middle of a bad date, and then leaves in a hurry on the pretext of an emergency. In your culture/community, how common are white lies in the context of dating? In your opinion, are white lies essential or detrimental to ensuring that things with your date are on an even keel?

2 *If You Are the One,* 非诚勿扰 (*Fēi Chéng Wù Rǎo*), is a popular Chinese dating show that first aired on Chinese TV in January 2010. It broke ratings records and attracted attention from the international press. The format of the program is based on the Australian dating show *Take Me Out*. Episodes of *If You Are the One* with English subtitles can be found on the Internet. Watch an episode and check out the English-language coverage of the success and controversy of the show. How does the episode compare with similar programs in your country?

Dates

Seeing movies is part of the nightlife in Chinese cities, especially for people going out on dates. Karaoke clubs, upscale restaurants, theme parks, and game centers are also top spots for couples to visit.

SAVING FACE

Chinese people are typically very concerned about face, 面子 (*miànzi*)—both for themselves and others. Consequently, excuses are often provided when turning down requests and offers, and blunt rejections are avoided.

MATCHMAKING
CORNERS

Some Chinese parents anxious to find love matches for their children congregate in parks on weekends. People's Park in Shanghai, for instance, is famous for having a matchmaking corner (相亲角) (xiāngqīnjiǎo). On pieces of paper suspended from long strings, parents advertise their eligible children. Visitors to the park will find swarms of parents scrutinizing descriptions of age, height, job, income, personality, and so on in hopes of identifying a suitable mate for their son or daughter. For a fee, parents can advertise their children for five months. Sociologists cite the gender imbalance and high-achieving young women's difficulty in finding spouses as some of the reasons for parents' taking the matter into their own hands.

The matchmaking corner in People's Park, Shanghai

Lesson Wrap-Up

Make It Flow!

Rearrange the sentences into a logical sequence. Then combine the sentences into a coherent narrative. Avoid repeating unnecessarily identical elements. Substitute nouns with pronouns and change periods to commas where appropriate. Add the connective devices 已经 (yǐjīng), 也 (yě), 才 (cái), 早就…了 (zǎo jiù … le), and 还 (hái) where appropriate.

_____王朋和李友常常一起出去玩儿。

_____王朋很喜欢李友。

_____这个周末学校演一个中国电影。

__1__王朋和李友在同一个学校学习。

_____王朋费了很大力气买到两张票。

_____李友说想看中国电影。

_____王朋说"好极了，一言为定"。

_____王朋和李友在同一个学校学习快半年了。

_____李友对王朋的印象很好。

_____李友很高兴。

_____李友说看电影以前请王朋吃饭。

_____王朋常常帮助李友练习中文。

_____王朋要请李友去看电影。

Skit

You want to ask a classmate out. Find out if he/she would like to have lunch or go to a movie or concert with you. How would you start? The direct approach: I like you. Would you like to . . . ? The indirect approach: There is a very interesting film/concert/great new restaurant. Let your schoolmate know why he/she would enjoy the film/concert/new restaurant. Find out if he/she would like to go with you. You know he/she is free. Hopefully, the answer is yes!

Dating Profile

Your best friend is too busy to date, so you decide to help him/her out. Create a profile for your friend. Describe his/her personality, hobbies, background, and goals. Share the profile in class and see if you can make a connection for your friend.

Supplemental Reading Practice

For additional reading practice that builds on the vocabulary introduced in this lesson, turn to the supplemental readings that begin on page 419.

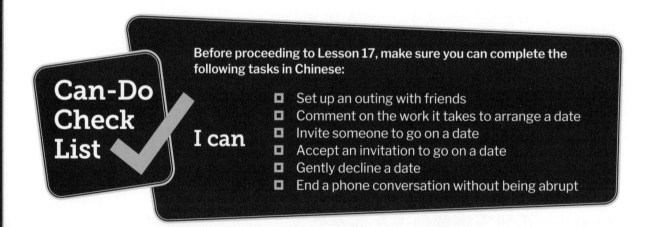

Can-Do Check List ✔ I can

Before proceeding to Lesson 17, make sure you can complete the following tasks in Chinese:

- ☐ Set up an outing with friends
- ☐ Comment on the work it takes to arrange a date
- ☐ Invite someone to go on a date
- ☐ Accept an invitation to go on a date
- ☐ Gently decline a date
- ☐ End a phone conversation without being abrupt

租房子

Zū fángzi

RENTING AN APARTMENT

Learning Objectives

In this lesson, you will learn to:

- Describe your current and ideal dwellings
- Name common pieces of furniture
- State how long you have been living at your current residence
- Explain why a place is or isn't right for someone
- Discuss and negotiate rent, utilities, and security deposits

Relate & Get Ready

In your own culture/community:

- How do you find an apartment o rent?
- What are typical living arrangements for young adults?
- What are the pros and cons of living in a dorm vs. in an apartment?
- Do leases include clauses for security deposits and pets? What other issues do leases cover?

Finding a Better Place

Narrative

Audio

Video

王朋在学校的宿舍住了两个学期了[1]。他觉得宿舍太吵，睡不好觉，房间太小，连电脑都[2]放不下[3]，再说也没有地方可以做饭，很不方便，所以准备下个学期搬出去住。他找房子找了一个多[4]月了，可是还没有找到合适的。刚才他在报纸上看到了一个广告，说学校附近有一套公寓出租，离学校很近，走路只要五分钟，很方便。公寓有一个[a]卧室，一个厨房，一个卫生间[b]，一个客厅，还带家具。王朋觉得这套公寓可能对他很合适。

Wáng Péng zài xuéxiào de sùshè zhù le liǎng ge xuéqī le[1]. Tā juéde sùshè tài chǎo, shuì bu hǎo jiào, fángjiān tài xiǎo, lián diànnǎo dōu[2] fàng bu xià[3], zàishuō yě méi-yǒu dìfang kěyǐ zuò fàn, hěn bù fāngbiàn, suǒyǐ zhǔnbèi xià ge xuéqī bān chu qu zhù. Tā zhǎo fángzi zhǎo le yí ge duō[4] yuè le, kěshì hái méiyǒu zhǎo dào héshì de. Gāng-cái tā zài bàozhǐ shang kàn dào le yí ge guǎnggào, shuō xuéxiào fùjìn yǒu yí tào gōngyù chūzū, lí xuéxiào hěn jìn, zǒu lù zhǐ yào wǔ fēnzhōng, hěn fāngbiàn. Gōngyù yǒu yí ge[a] wòshì, yí ge chúfáng, yí ge wèishēngjiān[b], yí ge kètīng, hái dài jiājù. Wáng Péng juéde zhè tào gōngyù kěnéng duì tā hěn héshì.

Language Notes

a 个 (gè) vs. 间 (jiān)

When speaking more formally, people prefer 间 (jiān) as the measure word for rooms, e.g.: 一间卧室 (yì jiān wòshì), 一间厨房 (yì jiān chúfáng), 一间卫生间 (yì jiān wèishēngjiān), 一间客厅 (yì jiān kètīng), and 一间教室 (yì jiān jiàoshì).

b 卫生间 (wèishēngjiān)

卫生间 (wèishēngjiān) (lit. hygiene room) is the most frequently used term for the bathroom in Mainland China. In public places 卫生间 (wèishēngjiān) simply means "restroom." Other Chinese terms for "bathroom" and "restroom" include 浴室 (yùshì) (bathroom with a shower or bathtub); 厕所 (cèsuǒ) (toilet, public restroom with no bathing facilities); 洗手间 (xǐshǒujiān) (restroom or bathroom); and 化粧室 (huàzhuāngshì) (bathroom) (lit. powder room), which is used mainly in Taiwan, especially for bathrooms in restaurants and department stores. Occasionally, some Chinese speakers refer to the restroom euphemistically as 一号 (yī hào) (lit. Number One).

Vocabulary

Audio

Flashcards

No.	Word	Pinyin	Part of Speech	Definition
1	吵	*chǎo*	v/adj	to quarrel; noisy
2	连	*lián*	prep	even
3	做饭	*zuò fàn*	vo	to cook, to prepare a meal
4	报纸	*bàozhǐ*	n	newspaper
5	广告	*guǎnggào*	n	advertisement
6	附近	*fùjìn*	n	vicinity, neighborhood, nearby area
7	套	*tào*	m	(measure word for things that come in a set/sets)
8	公寓	*gōngyù*	n	apartment
9	出租	*chūzū*	v	to rent out
10	走路	*zǒu lù*	vo	to walk
11	分钟	*fēnzhōng*	n	minute
12	卧室	*wòshì*	n	bedroom
13	厨房	*chúfáng*	n	kitchen
14	卫生间	*wèishēngjiān*	n	bathroom
15	客厅	*kètīng*	n	living room
16	家具	*jiājù*	n	furniture
17	可能	*kěnéng*	mv/adj	may; possible

In China, advertisements for apartments and rooms for rent may be posted on community bulletin boards or even pasted right on the wall of the building. What aspects of this room for rent would attract you as a potential tenant?

单人房分租

只限女性，不养宠物。不抽烟，无不良嗜好。公寓位于莲湖区劳动路。房间干净、安静，交通便利。月租1200元（水、电、网费全包）。

感兴趣请加我QQ2345xxxxx。

你希望你的客厅里有什么家具？

Nǐ xīwàng nǐ de kètīng lǐ yǒu shénme jiājù?

What furniture do you hope to have in your living room?

我希望我的客厅里有 _____。

Wǒ xīwàng wǒ de kètīng lǐ yǒu _____.

See index for corresponding vocabulary or research another term.

Grammar

> **Verb + 了** *(le)* **+ numeral + measure word + noun + 了** *(le)*

This structure usually implies that the action has been continuing for some time and will likely last into the future. For example, 王朋在学校的宿舍住了两个学期了 *(Wáng Péng zài xuéxiào de sùshè zhù le liǎng ge xuéqī le)* means that Wang Peng has been living on campus for two semesters up to this moment and will continue to live there.

A   Q: 你开出租汽车开了几年了？

Nǐ kāi chūzū qìchē kāi le jǐ nián le?

How many years have you been driving a cab for?

A: 一年半了。

Yì nián bàn le.

For a year and a half now.

B   弟弟写电子邮件写了半个钟头了，不知道还要写多长时间。

Dìdi xiě diànzǐ yóujiàn xiě le bàn ge zhōngtóu le, bù zhīdào hái yào xiě duō cháng shíjiān.

My younger brother has been writing emails for half an hour. Who knows how much longer he'll be at it.

The following two sentences differ in meaning:

C   他病了三天了。

Tā bìng le sān tiān le.

He has been sick for three days.

[His illness has continued for three days and he currently remains sick.]

D　他病了三天。

Tā bìng le sān tiān.

He was sick for three days.

[He recovered from the illness on the fourth day.]

However, the new sentence pattern with the additional sentence-final 了 (le) can be followed by another clause that suggests that the action will likely cease.

E　这本书我已经看了两遍了，不想再看了。

Zhè běn shū wǒ yǐjīng kàn le liǎng biàn le, bù xiǎng zài kàn le.

I've read this book twice already and don't want to read it again.

This structure can be used in reference to both time and quantity:

F　衣服我已经买了三件了，再买两件就够了。

Yīfu wǒ yǐjīng mǎi le sān jiàn le, zài mǎi liǎng jiàn jiù gòu le.

I've already bought three pieces of clothing. I'll buy two more and that'll be plenty.

G　我打扫房子打扫了一上午了，想休息一下。

Wǒ dǎsǎo fángzi dǎsǎo le yí shàngwǔ le, xiǎng xiūxi yí xià.

I've been cleaning the house all morning. I'd like to take a break.

EXERCISES

More exercises

Paraphrase the sentences to describe the time duration using the ⋯ 了 ⋯ 了 structure where appropriate. Use exercise 1 as an example.

1　小高八点开始吃早饭。
　　现在九点，他还在吃早饭。
　　→　小高吃早饭吃了一个小时了。

2　老李昨天晚上十点睡觉。
　　现在上午十点，他还在睡觉。

3　小王五月开始找房子。
　　现在是七月，他还在找房子。

连…都/也… (lián … dōu/yě …)

连 (lián) is an intensifier which is always used in conjunction with 都/也 (dōu/yě).

A 我姐姐的孩子很聪明，连日语都会说。

Wǒ jiějie de háizi hěn cōngming, lián Rìyǔ dōu huì shuō.

My sister's child is really smart. She can even speak Japanese.

B 我弟弟的公寓里连一件家具也没有。

Wǒ dìdi de gōngyù lǐ lián yí jiàn jiājù yě méiyǒu.

There isn't even a single piece of furniture in my younger brother's apartment.

C 你怎么连药都忘了吃？

Nǐ zěnme lián yào dōu wàng le chī?

How could you even forget to take your medicine?

D 昨天学的生词我连一个也不记得了。

Zuótiān xué de shēngcí wǒ lián yí ge yě bú jìde le.

I can't recall even a single new word we learned yesterday.

What follows 连 (lián) usually represents an extreme case: the biggest or smallest, the best or worst, the most difficult or easiest, etc. (A), for instance, implies that Japanese is very difficult. If a child can speak such a difficult language as Japanese, then the child must be very intelligent. Similarly, if my younger brother doesn't have a single piece of furniture in his apartment, it must look very bare.

EXERCISES

Rewrite the sentences to intensify the information in parentheses using the 连…都/也… structure where appropriate. Use exercise 1 as an example.

1 小白的公寓没有（厨房）。

→ 小白的公寓连厨房都没有。

2 我妹妹（星期天）去图书馆看书。

3 小王忘了（女朋友的电话号码）。

More exercises

3

Potential complements (II)

The "verb + 不下 (bu xià)" structure suggests that a location or container in question does not have the capacity to accommodate a certain number of people or things.

A 这个客厅大是大，不过坐不下二十个人。

Zhè ge kètīng dà shi dà, búguò zuò bu xià èrshí ge rén.

This living room is pretty spacious, but it still isn't large enough to seat twenty people.

B 这张纸写不下八百个字。

Zhè zhāng zhǐ xiě bu xià bābǎi ge zì.

This piece of paper isn't big enough to write eight hundred characters on.

C 这个冰箱放不下两个西瓜。

Zhè ge bīngxiāng fàng bu xià liǎng ge xīguā.

This refrigerator isn't big enough for two watermelons.

EXERCISES

More exercises

In pairs, form a question-and-answer about the capacity of a space using 得下 and 不下 where appropriate. Use exercise 1 as an example.

1   这个教室   坐三十个学生

   → Q: 这个教室坐得下三十个学生吗？

       A: 这个教室坐得下/坐不下三十个学生。

2   小高   喝五瓶可乐

3   这套公寓   住六个人

Indicating an approximate number using 多 (duō)

多 (duō) can be placed after a number to indicate an approximate number. The combination indicates not an exact number but a general numeric range, e.g., 十多个 (shí duō ge) means more than ten but fewer than twenty; it could be eleven, twelve, thirteen, etc.

If the concept represented by the noun is not divisible into smaller units, and the number is ten or a multiple of ten, 多 (duō) precedes the measure word.

A 二十多个人

èrshí duō ge rén

more than twenty people

B 三十多个学生

sānshí duō ge xuésheng

more than thirty students

C 一百多张纸

yì bǎi duō zhāng zhǐ

more than one hundred sheets of paper

However, if the concept represented by the noun can be divided into smaller units (e.g., 一块钱 = 十毛, 一个星期 = 七天 [yí kuài qián = shí máo, yí ge xīngqī = qī tiān]), there are two possibilities. If the number is not ten or a multiple of ten, 多 (duō) should be used after the measure word, e.g., 七块多钱 (qī kuài duō qián) (more than seven dollars but less than eight), 一个多星期 (yí ge duō xīngqī) (more than one week but less than two). If the number is ten or a multiple of ten, 多 (duō) can be used either before the measure word, e.g., 十多块钱 (shí duō kuài qián) (more than ten dollars but less than twenty) or after the measure word, e.g., 十块多钱 (shí kuài duō qián) (more than ten dollars but less than eleven), but these two options represent different numeric ranges.

D 这枝笔一块多钱。

Zhè zhī bǐ yí kuài duō qián.

This pen is one dollar something.

(The price is more than one dollar but less than two.)

E 我们班有二十多个学生。

Wǒmen bān yǒu èrshí duō ge xuésheng.

There are over twenty students in our class.

(There are more than twenty students but fewer than thirty.)

F 妹妹感冒十多天了。

Mèimei gǎnmào shí duō tiān le.

My younger sister has had a cold for more than ten days.

(The number of days is between ten and twenty.)

G 他昨天买了四十多个梨。

Tā zuótiān mǎi le sìshí duō ge lí.

He bought over forty pears yesterday.

(The number is between forty and fifty.)

H 他昨天买礼物花了一百多块钱。

Tā zuótiān mǎi lǐwù huā le yìbǎi duō kuài qián.

He bought over one hundred dollars' worth of gifts yesterday.

(He spent more than one hundred dollars but less than two hundred.)

I **Student A** 这双黑鞋十多块钱。

Zhè shuāng hēi xié shí duō kuài qián.

This pair of black shoes is over ten dollars.

(The price is more than ten dollars but less than twenty.)

Student B 这双咖啡色的鞋十块多钱。

Zhè shuāng kāfēi sè de xié shí kuài duō qián.

This pair of brown shoes is a little bit over ten dollars.

(The price is more than ten dollars but less than eleven.)

J **Student A** 这家饭馆儿的师傅和服务员认识十年多了。

Zhè jiā fànguǎnr de shīfu hé fúwùyuán rènshi shí nián duō le.

The chef and the waiter at this restaurant have known each other for ten years and some months.

(The length of time is longer than ten years but shorter than eleven.)

Student B 我以为他们认识十多年了。

Wǒ yǐwéi tāmen rènshi shí duō nián le.

I thought they had known each other for a dozen years or so.

(The length of time is between ten and twenty years.)

More exercises

EXERCISES

Translate the approximate number using 多 where appropriate. Use exercise 1 as an example.

1 over one hundred books

→ 一百多本书

2 more than fifty students

3 over two hundred and fifty Chinese characters but fewer than two hundred and sixty

Chinese Chat

Bai Ying'ai just posted a review on Airbnb. Would you consider staying at the same place after reading her review?

65条评价 ★★★★⯪

搜索评价

概述

准确性	★★★★★	位置	★★★★⯪
沟通交流	★★★★★	入住	★★★★★
清洁度	★★★★★	性价比	★★★★⯪

白英爱

我在这个公寓住了两天了。公寓带家具；离公园、商店、地铁站都很近，做什么都非常方便。冰箱里每天都有水果和饮料，这样连早饭都不用出去吃了！

👍有用

Language Practice

<table>
<tr><td>A</td><td>**Time flies**</td><td>INTERPERSONAL</td></tr>
</table>

In pairs, ask a partner the following questions.

1 你学中文学了多长时间了?

Nǐ xué Zhōngwén xué le duō cháng shíjiān le?

2 你在这个学校学习了多长时间了?

Nǐ zài zhè ge xuéxiào xuéxí le duō cháng shíjiān le?

3 你在你现在住的地方住了多长时间了?

Nǐ zài nǐ xiànzài zhù de dìfang zhù le duō cháng shíjiān le?

Based on your partner's situation, you may also want to ask how long he/she has been working, involved in his/her hobbies, etc.

<table>
<tr><td>B</td><td>**Space cadet**</td><td>PRESENTATIONAL</td></tr>
</table>

Little Bai is absent-minded and often forgetful. Based on the statements given below, recap what he forgot to do using 连···都/也··· (lián . . . dōu/yě . . .), e.g.:

He even forgot to bring a pen with him when he had to take a test.

考试的时候，他连笔都/也忘了带了。

Kǎo shì de shíhòu, tā lián bǐ dōu/yě wàng le dài le.

1 He even forgot his mother's birthday.

2 He didn't even remember his own phone number.

3 He even forgot to bring money when he was treating his friends to dinner.

Little Bai just moved, and is getting fed up with his new apartment. Describe what his apartment is like using 连···都／也··· (lián ... dōu/yě ...), e.g.:

The apartment doesn't even have a kitchen.

公寓连厨房都／也没有。

Gōngyù lián chúfáng dōu/yě méiyǒu.

4 His bathroom doesn't even have (running) water.

5 His bedroom is so tiny that even a bed cannot be placed in it.

6 His living room is so small that it cannot even seat five people.

Little Bai is also behind the times. Describe what he doesn't know using 连···都／也··· (lián ... dōu/yě ...), e.g.:

He doesn't even know how to use a computer.

小白连电脑都／也不会用。

Xiǎo Bái lián diànnǎo dōu/yě bú huì yòng.

7 He doesn't know how to use a cell phone.

8 He doesn't know how to send email.

9 He doesn't know how to use a credit card.

C | **Sizing up** | INTERPERSONAL |

In pairs, ask a partner how spacious his/her apartment/room, living room, classroom, refrigerator, desk, etc. are. Use the proper verb for each question, e.g.:

Q: 你的公寓／房间住得下多少／几个人？
Nǐ de gōngyù/fángjiān zhù de xià duōshao/jǐ ge rén?

A: 我的公寓／房间住得下两个人。
Wǒ de gōngyù/fángjiān zhù de xià liǎng ge rén.

1

2

3

4

5

Calling about an Apartment for Rent

Dialogue

（王朋打电话问租房子的事儿……）

喂，请问你们是不是^a 有公寓出租？

有啊，一房一厅^b，非常干净，还带家具。

有什么家具？

客厅里有一套沙发、一张饭桌跟四把椅子。卧室里有一张床、一张书桌和一个书架。

你们那里安静不安静？

非常安静。

每个月房租多少钱？

八百五十元。

八百五十美元？人民币差不多是……有一点儿贵，能不能便宜点儿？

那你不用付水电费。

要不要付押金？

要多付一个月的房租当押金，搬出去的时候还给你。另外，我们公寓不准养宠物。

没关系，我对养宠物没有兴趣[c]，什么宠物都[5]不养。

那太好了。你今天下午来看看吧。

好。

Language Notes

a 是不是… *(shì bu shì …)*

Here, this means "Is it true that . . ."

b 一房一厅 *(yì fáng yì tīng)*/一室一厅 *(yí shì yì tīng)*

Both expressions refer to an apartment with one bedroom and one living room. By the same token, you may refer to a two-bedroom apartment with a living room as 两房一厅 *(liǎng fáng yì tīng)* or 两室一厅 *(liǎng shì yì tīng)*.

c 有兴趣 *(yǒu xìngqù)* **vs.** 有意思 *(yǒu yìsi)*

Do not confuse 有兴趣 *(yǒu xìngqù)* with 有意思 *(yǒu yìsi)*. While 有兴趣 *(yǒu xìngqù)* is a verb phrase that describes someone who is interested (in something), 有意思 *(yǒu yìsi)* is an adjective describing someone or something that is interesting.

(Wáng Péng dǎ diànhuà wèn zū fángzi
de shìr . . .)

 Wéi, qǐng wèn nǐmen shì bú shì[a] yǒu gōngyù

chūzū?

 Yǒu a, yì fáng yì tīng[b], fēicháng gānjìng, hái dài

jiājù.

 Yǒu shénme jiājù?

 Kètīng li yǒu yí tào shāfā, yì zhāng fànzhuō gēn

sì bǎ yǐzi. Wòshì li yǒu yì zhāng chuáng, yì zhāng

shūzhuō hé yí ge shūjià.

 Nǐmen nàlǐ ānjìng bu ānjìng?

 Fēicháng ānjìng.

 Měi ge yuè fángzū duōshao qián?

 Bābǎi wǔshí yuán.

 Bābǎi wǔshí Měiyuán? Rénmínbì chàbuduō shì . . .

Yǒu yì diǎnr guì, néng bu néng piányi diǎnr?

 Nà nǐ búyòng fù shuǐ diàn fèi.

 Yào bu yào fù yājīn?

 Yào duō fù yí ge yuè de fángzū dāng yājīn, bān

chu qu de shíhou huán gěi nǐ. Lìngwài, wǒmen

gōngyù bù zhǔn yǎng chǒngwù.

 Méi guānxi, wǒ duì yǎng chǒngwù méiyǒu

xìngqù[c], shénme chǒngwù dōu[5] bù yǎng.

 Nà tài hǎo le. Nǐ jīntiān xiàwǔ lái kàn kan ba.

 Hǎo.

Vocabulary

Audio

Flashcards

No.	Word	Pinyin	Part of Speech	Definition
1	一房一厅	yì fáng yì tīng		one bedroom and one living room
2	干净	gānjìng	adj	clean
3	沙发	shāfā	n	sofa
4	饭桌	fànzhuō	n	dining table
5	椅子	yǐzi	n	chair
6	书桌	shūzhuō	n	desk
7	书架	shūjià	n	bookcase, bookshelf
8	那里	nàli	pr	there
9	安静	ānjìng	adj	quiet
10	房租	fángzū	n	rent
11	元	yuán	m	(measure word for the basic Chinese monetary unit), yuan
12	美元	Měiyuán	n	American dollar (USD)
13	人民币	Rénmínbì	n	renminbi (RMB, Chinese currency)
	人民	rénmín	n	the people
	币	bì	n	currency
14	差不多	chàbuduō	adv/adj	almost, nearly; similar
15	费	fèi	n	fee, expenses
16	押金	yājīn	n	security deposit
17	当	dāng	v	to serve as, to be

No.	Word	Pinyin	Part of Speech	Definition
18	还	*huán*	v	to return (something)
19	另外	*lìngwài*	conj	furthermore, in addition
20	准	*zhǔn*	v	to allow, to be allowed
21	养	*yǎng*	v	to raise
22	宠物	*chǒngwù*	n	pet
23	兴趣	*xìngqù*	n	interest

你（想）养什么宠物?

Nǐ (xiǎng) yǎng shénme chǒngwù?
What pets do you (want to) raise?

我（想）养 ＿＿＿＿＿＿＿＿。
Wǒ (xiǎng) yǎng ＿＿＿＿＿＿＿ .

See index for corresponding vocabulary or research another term.

Characterize it!

What do the characters mean?
What is the common radical?
What does the radical mean?
How does the radical relate to the overall meaning of the characters?

❶ 椅   ❷ 桌   ❸ 架

More characters

Grammar

Question pronouns using 都/也 (dōu/yě)

A question pronoun can appear in a statement. When it is followed by 都/也 (dōu/yě), it simply means "all" or "none" in the sense that everything in question is either included or excluded.

A   Q: 你想喝点儿什么饮料？

Nǐ xiǎng hē diǎnr shénme yǐnliào?

What beverage would you like to drink?

A: 谢谢，我不渴，什么都不想喝。

Xièxie, wǒ bù kě, shénme dōu bù xiǎng hē.

Thanks. I'm not thirsty. I don't feel like drinking anything.

B   这些公寓我哪套都不租。

Zhè xiē gōngyù wǒ nǎ tào dōu bù zū.

I'm not renting any of these apartments.

C   中国我什么地方都没去过。

Zhōngguó wǒ shénme dìfang dōu méi qù guo.

I haven't been anywhere in China.

D   我什么宠物都不养。养宠物太麻烦了！

Wǒ shénme chǒngwù dōu bù yǎng. Yǎng chǒngwù tài máfan le!

I don't keep any pets. Keeping pets is too much trouble!

E　在这个城市，哪儿也吃不到糖醋鱼。

Zài zhè ge chéngshì, nǎr yě chī bu dào tángcùyú.

You can't find sweet-and-sour fish anywhere in this city.

F　Q: 在舞会上你认识了谁？

Zài wǔhuì shang nǐ rènshi le shéi?

Who did you get to know at the dance party?

　　A: 我谁都没认识。

Wǒ shéi dōu méi rènshi.

I didn't get to know anybody.

G　你明天几点跟我见面都行。

Nǐ míngtiān jǐ diǎn gēn wǒ jiàn miàn dōu xíng.

You can meet with me anytime tomorrow.

H　这些药我哪种都试过，对我的过敏都没有用。

Zhè xiē yào wǒ nǎ zhǒng dōu shì guo, duì wǒ de guòmǐn dōu méiyǒu yòng.

I've tried all of these medicines; none are effective for my allergies.

EXERCISES

Rewrite the sentences to intensify the statement using the "interrogative pronoun + 都 / 也" structure where appropriate. Use exercise 1 as an example.

More exercises

1　我不养宠物。　(not any)

　　→ 我什么宠物都不养。

2　我昨天没有买衣服。　(not any)

3　小高不认识这里的人。　(not anyone)

Language Practice

| **Polar extremes** | PRESENTATIONAL |

Aisha and Mona are twins, but they couldn't be more different: Aisha is easygoing and Mona is difficult. Describe how they differ from each other using 都 / 也 *(dōu/yě)*, e.g.:

Aisha likes all colors. Mona hates all colors.

Aisha 什么颜色都喜欢。 Mona 什么颜色都不喜欢。

Aisha *shénme yánsè dōu xǐhuan.* Mona *shénme yánsè dōu bù xǐhuan.*

1 Aisha eats all sorts of fruits and vegetables. Mona eats no fruits and vegetables at all.

2 Aisha has been to all kinds of places. Mona hasn't been anywhere.

3 Aisha is happy all the time. Mona is unhappy all the time.

4 Everyone thinks Aisha is cool. Everyone thinks Mona is no fun.

**GET
Real
WITH CHINESE**

You're looking to rent an apartment in Quincy, a Massachusetts city with a large Chinese population. You want an apartment near Quincy Center. Which apartment has the best location?

房屋出租

Quincy: 2房1廳, 1廚房, 近巴士站 .... 月租

2房1廳, 1廚房, 有車位, 近地鐵 $1,450

排屋, 2房大廳, 有後院, 1.5浴, 有車位, 近地鐵 $1,500

全新, 750方呎, 2房1廳, 近地鐵 $1,700

4房2廳, 1廚房, 有車位, 近市中心 $1,900

Waltham: 公寓, 2房2廳, 2全浴. 新廚房, 有車位 $2,000

Weymouth: 翻新2房, 1廚房, 700方呎, 有車位 $1,800

Somerville: 3房1廳, 1廚房, 近地鐵 $1,300

.... $2,300

57
地皮
可以建
Hawke...

1241
複式公
全海景, 不
房, 廚房,
大睡房, 大

218 Integrated Chinese 2 | Textbook

Behind the façade

Take a look at the floor plan of this apartment. Name the rooms and describe what's in each of them.

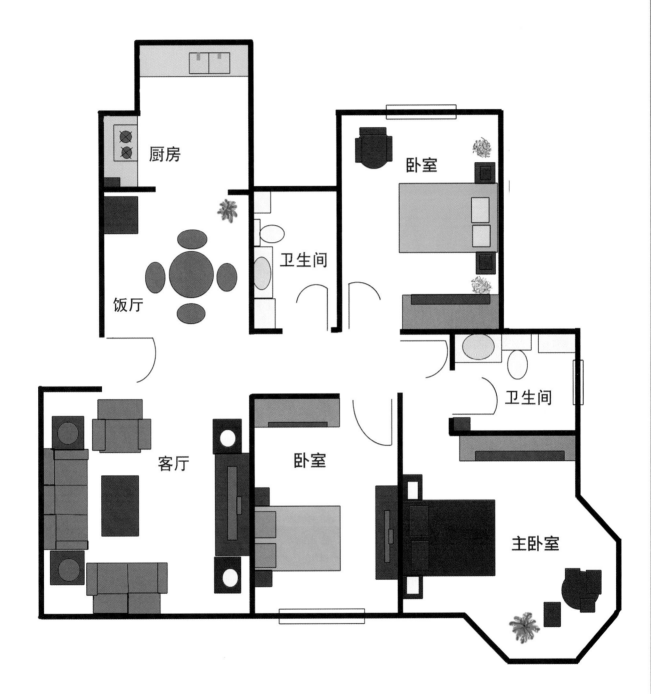

In my room

In pairs, describe the room in the picture, i.e., what's in it and how things are positioned. Don't forget the person and the dog.

On campus or off?

As a journalist for the student newspaper, you've been tasked with surveying the student body about the pros and cons of living in the dorms or off campus. Find an interviewee and report back to the class on what he/she thinks about where they live and whether they want to stay or move, e.g.:

Carlos 觉得他的公寓/宿舍对他很/不合适。
所以他不想/想搬出去。因为……

Carlos *juéde tā de gōngyù/ sùshè duì tā hěn/bù héshì.*

Suǒyǐ tā bù xiǎng/xiǎng bān chu qu. Yīnwèi . . .

Characterize it!

What do the characters mean?

What is the common radical?

What does the radical mean?

How does the radical relate to the overall meaning of the characters?

❶ 安　❷ 客　❸ 室　❹ 寓

More characters

< Messages　　李明　　Contact

您好！我叫李明。我朋友小张告诉我您有公寓出租，让我给您发短信。

…

请问公寓里有几个卧室？有没有自己的卫生间和厨房？带不带家具？

…

离地铁站或者公共汽车站近吗？

…

好，谢谢您。您告诉我在哪儿，我下午去看看。

…

📷 iMessage　　　　　Send

Chinese Chat

A prospective tenant is texting you to inquire about your apartment for rent. How would you reply?

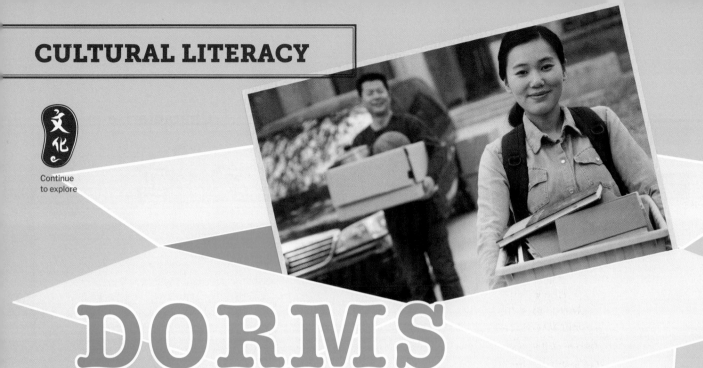

文化

Continue
to explore

DORMS

Until the late 1990s, college students in China were required to live in dorms on campus, with six or seven to a room and possibly dozens sharing a common bathroom at the end of the hallway. Because there was no place to cook in the dorms, everyone ate in the on-campus student dining halls, 学生餐厅 *(xuéshēng cāntīng)*. Living conditions for students have improved substantially since the late 1990s. At some colleges, students who can afford it now have the option of renting apartments off campus. Foreign students generally live in special dorms, two to a room, but some choose to live with host families or rent their own apartments.

Apartments

Renting an apartment in a Chinese city is not difficult. Listings can be found online and in local newspapers. You can also call or stop by one of the many intermediary companies, 中介公司 *(zhōngjiè gōngsī)*—agencies that match apartment owners with potential tenants.

Housing development has been a pillar of the Chinese economy for the last two decades, and living conditions for a significant portion of the urban population have improved enormously. However, while some have profited dramatically from the real estate market, skyrocketing prices in many cities have made housing prohibitively expensive for those of average means, leading to a widening gap between rich and poor. Many middle-class people feel crushed by heavy mortgages and refer to themselves as "slaves to houses," 房奴 *(fángnú)*. Meanwhile, in other areas, growth in the housing market has outpaced demand, leading to entire neighborhoods of finished but empty buildings. One example of this "ghost city" phenomenon is Ordos in Inner Mongolia, where thousands of newly built apartments go unlit at night.

Pets

Traditionally, people in China have had a special love for keeping songbirds as pets, in addition to cats and dogs. In 1983, amid fears of rabies, Beijing officially banned non-working dogs, as well as six other animals, from within city limits; this ban was only lifted in the early 1990s. Nowadays, only dogs under thirty-five centimeters (about fourteen inches) in height are permitted in Beijing, though exceptions are made for service dogs. Nevertheless, dogs are now extremely popular and have become much-loved members of many households. Cats are also popular pets, and in the countryside they sometimes also serve the practical purpose of keeping the mouse population under control.

COMPARE & CONTRAST

1 Some landlords in China often ask for a deposit and several months' rent in advance. Therefore, phrases like 押一付三 *(yā yī fù sān)* and 押一付二 *(yā yī fù èr)* are sometimes seen in rental ads. What do they mean? Are there similar practices in your country?

2 Among the large population of pet owners closely bonded with their pets, the term 毛小孩（儿）*(máo xiǎohái[r])* (lit. furry kid) is catching on. There are now pet-friendly hotels and restaurants, as well as tour packages tailored to the needs of pet owners. How pet-friendly is your community? How do people feel about pets in stores and restaurants?

3 With the rise of home ownership as a symbol of financial security, many parents of daughters have come to believe in home ownership as a prerequisite for prospective sons-in-law. For such parents, the notion of a married couple living in rented accommodation is unacceptable. Hence, many grooms, with or without family help, feel obligated to purchase homes before getting married. Although this pressure is intended to ensure security for the couple, it can be a terrible burden. In your culture/community, is there a relationship between housing and marriage? Is the bride's or the groom's family typically responsible for paying for the wedding? How are owning and renting perceived by most people?

Lesson Wrap-Up

Make It Flow!

The following sentences are in a logical sequence. Combine them into a coherent narrative. Avoid repeating unnecessarily identical elements. Substitute the nouns with designated pronouns such as 那个人 (*nà ge rén*) and change periods to commas where appropriate. Add the adverb 还 (*hái*) and the conjunction 不过 (*búguò*) where appropriate.

王朋给出租房子的人打电话。王朋问出租房子的人有没有公寓出租。出租房子的人说有公寓出租。出租房子的人说公寓一室一厅。出租房子的人说公寓非常干净。出租房子的人说公寓带家具。王朋问公寓带什么家具。出租房子的人告诉王朋公寓带什么家具。出租房子的人告诉王朋公寓房租多少钱。出租房子的人告诉王朋公寓不能养宠物。王朋听了以后觉得公寓好像不错。王朋下午想去看看公寓。

Skit

You need to find an affordable apartment in New York City this summer, so you decide to check out Chinatown. You look through the ads in the Chinese-language newspapers and write down several phone numbers. The first landlord that you call has a furnished apartment on Mercer Street. You want to find out how you can get to work from the apartment by subway or by bus (you'll be working on Manhattan's west side), how the apartment is furnished, the noise level, how much the deposit and rent are, whether utilities are included, etc.

Advertisement

You're studying in China and looking for a roommate. Based on this lesson's Chinese rental ads, write an ad for your apartment. Where is it located? How many bedrooms does it have? Is it furnished? Are pets allowed? Is it near a university or sports center? What type of roommate are you looking for? Don't forget to include your contact information. Your teacher will circulate or "publish" all the ads submitted. Which ad would attract your attention?

Supplemental Reading Practice

For additional reading practice that builds on the vocabulary introduced in this lesson, turn to the supplemental readings that begin on page 419.

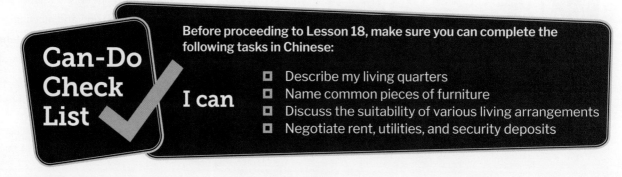

Can-Do Check List

I can

Before proceeding to Lesson 18, make sure you can complete the following tasks in Chinese:

- ☐ Describe my living quarters
- ☐ Name common pieces of furniture
- ☐ Discuss the suitability of various living arrangements
- ☐ Negotiate rent, utilities, and security deposits

运动

Yùndòng

SPORTS

Learning Objectives

In this lesson, you will learn to:

- Name and discuss some popular sports
- Talk about your exercise habits
- Compare soccer and American football in simple terms

Relate and Get Ready

In your own culture/community:

- Do people exercise regularly?
- Are most people sports fans?
- Which sports are most popular?
- Are there many sports programs on TV?
- Which is more popular, American football or soccer?

Getting in Shape

Dialogue 1

Audio

Video

（高文中跟王朋聊天儿……）

你看，我的肚子越来越大了。

你平常吃得那么多，又ᵃ不运动，当然越来越胖了。

那怎么办呢？

如果怕胖，你一个星期运动两、三次，每次半个小时，肚子就会小了。

我两年没运动了¹，做什么运动呢？

最简单的运动是跑步。

冬天那么冷，夏天那么热，跑步太难受²了。

你打网球吧。

打网球得买网球拍、网球鞋，你知道，网球拍、网球鞋贵极了！

找几个人打篮球吧。买个篮球很便宜。

那每次都得打电话约人，麻烦死了。

你去游泳吧。不用找人，也不用花很多钱，什么时候去都可以。

游泳？我怕水，太危险了，淹死了怎么办？

我也没办法了。你不愿意运动，那就胖下去[3]吧。

(Gāo Wénzhōng gēn Wáng Péng liáo tiānr . . .)

 Nǐ kàn, wǒ de dùzi yuè lái yuè dà le.

 Nǐ píngcháng chī de nàme duō, yòu[a] bú yùndòng,

dāngrán yuè lái yuè pàng le.

 Nà zěnme bàn ne?

 Rúguǒ pà pàng, nǐ yí ge xīngqī yùndòng liǎng, sān

cì, měi cì bàn ge xiǎoshí, dùzi jiù huì xiǎo le.

 Wǒ liǎng nián méi yùndòng le[1], zuò shénme

yùndòng ne?

 Zuì jiǎndān de yùndòng shì pǎo bù.

 Dōngtiān nàme lěng, xiàtiān nàme rè, pǎo bù tài

nánshòu[2] le.

 Nǐ dǎ wǎngqiú ba.

 Dǎ wǎngqiú děi mǎi wǎngqiú pāi, wǎngqiú xié, nǐ

zhīdao wǎngqiú pāi, wǎngqiú xié guì jí le!

 Zhǎo jǐ ge rén dǎ lánqiú ba. Mǎi ge lánqiú hěn

piányi.

 Nà měi cì dōu děi dǎ diànhuà yuē rén, máfan sǐ le.

 Nǐ qù yóu yǒng ba. Búyòng zhǎo rén, yě búyòng

huā hěn duō qián, shénme shíhou qù dōu kěyǐ.

 Yóu yǒng? Wǒ pà shuǐ, tài wēixiǎn le, yān sǐ le

zěnme bàn?

 Wǒ yě méi bànfǎ le. Nǐ bú yuànyì yùndòng, nà jiù

pàng xia qu[3] ba.

a 又 *(yòu)*

又 *(yòu)* can indicate a recurrence of an action or a state over the course of time, e.g.: 我昨天看了一个电影，今天又看了一个 *(Wǒ zuótiān kàn le yí ge diànyǐng, jīntiān yòu kàn le yí ge)* (I watched a movie yesterday, and I watched another one today). 又 *(yòu)* can also suggest the augmentation or exacerbation of certain conditions or circumstances, as in this excerpt from the dialogue: 你平常吃得那么多，又不运动，当然越来越胖了 *(Nǐ píngcháng chī de nàme duō, yòu bú yùndòng, dāngrán yuè lái yuè pàng le)* (You usually eat so much, and on top of that you don't exercise; no wonder you're putting on more and more weight).

Vocabulary

No.	Word	Pinyin	Part of Speech	Definition
1	当然	dāngrán	adv	of course
2	胖	pàng	adj	fat
3	怕	pà	v	to fear, to be afraid of
4	简单	jiǎndān	adj	simple
5	跑步	pǎo bù	vo	to jog
	跑	pǎo	v	to run
6	难受	nánshòu	adj	hard to bear, uncomfortable [See Grammar 2.]
7	网球	wǎngqiú	n	tennis
8	拍	pāi	n	racket
9	篮球	lánqiú	n	basketball
10	游泳	yóu yǒng	vo	to swim
11	危险	wēixiǎn	adj	dangerous
12	淹死	yān sǐ	vc	to drown
13	愿意	yuànyì	mv	to be willing

你喜欢做什么运动?

Nǐ xǐhuan zuò shénme yùndòng?
What sports do you like to play?

我喜欢 ＿＿＿＿＿＿＿＿。
Wǒ xǐhuan ＿＿＿＿＿＿＿ *.*

See index for corresponding vocabulary or research another term.

GET
Real
WITH **CHINESE**

As you walk along the edge of a river in Hangzhou, you see this sign. What is its message?

Grammar

1 | **Duration of inactivity**

Time expression + 没 (méi) + verb + (了) (le)

This structure indicates that an action has not been or was not performed for a certain period of time.

A 他三天没上网了。

Tā sān tiān méi shàng wǎng le.

He hasn't been online for three days.

[✖ 他没上网三天了。]

B 我两年没检查身体了。

Wǒ liǎng nián méi jiǎnchá shēntǐ le.

I haven't had a check-up in two years.

C 我的狗病了，一天没吃东西了。

Wǒ de gǒu bìng le, yì tiān méi chī dōngxi le.

My dog is sick; she hasn't eaten anything for a day.

D 妹妹上个月特别忙，三个星期没回家。

Mèimei shàng ge yuè tèbié máng, sān ge xīngqī méi huí jiā.

My younger sister was especially busy last month, and she didn't come home for three weeks.

E 去年寒假我去英国旅行，一个月没吃中国菜。

Qùnián hánjià wǒ qù Yīngguó lǚxíng, yí ge yuè méi chī Zhōngguó cài.

I went on a trip to the UK over winter break last year, and didn't eat any Chinese food for a month.

Note that there is a difference between this construction and its affirmative counterpart. Compare:

F   **Student A**   我学了两年中文了。

Wǒ xué le liǎng nián Zhōngwén le.

I have been studying Chinese for two years.

Student B   是吗？我两年没学中文了。

Shì ma? Wǒ liǎng nián méi xué Zhōngwén le.

Really? I haven't studied Chinese for two years.

More
exercises

EXERCISES

Complete the sentences to indicate the duration of inactivity, using the "Time expression + 没 + verb + (了)" structure where appropriate. Use exercise 1 as an example.

1   小李付房租　　两个月

　　→ 小李两个月没付房租了。

2   小王买衣服　　半年

3   王朋打球　　　三个星期

---

2   ⬚ **好/难** *(hǎo/nán)* **+ verb** ⬚

Some verbs can be preceded by 好 *(hǎo)* (fine, good, nice) or 难 *(nán)* (difficult); the resulting compounds become adjectives. In this case, 好 *(hǎo)* usually means "easy" while 难 *(nán)* means "difficult."

A   好受　　　难受

hǎoshòu　*nánshòu*

easy to bear　hard to bear

C   好走　　　难走

hǎozǒu　*nánzǒu*

easy to walk on　hard to walk on

B   好写　　　难写

hǎoxiě　*nánxiě*

easy to write　hard to write

D   好说　　　难说

hǎoshuō　*nánshuō*

easy to say　difficult to say

E	好懂	难懂
	hǎodǒng	*nándǒng*
	easy to understand	hard to understand

F	好唱	难唱
	hǎochàng	*nánchàng*
	easy to sing	hard to sing

In other compounds, however, 好 (*hǎo*) suggests that the action represented by the verb is pleasant, while 难 (*nán*) means the opposite.

G	好吃	难吃	**I**	好听	难听
	hǎochī	*nánchī*		*hǎotīng*	*nántīng*
	delicious	unappetizing		pleasant to listen to	unpleasant to listen to

H	好看	难看
	hǎokàn	*nánkàn*
	pretty	ugly

EXERCISES

Fill in the blanks using the "好／难 + verb" structure. The verbs are in parentheses. Use exercise 1 as an example.

More exercises

1　我喜欢妈妈做的菜，因为妈妈做的菜都很_____。（吃）

　　→ 我喜欢妈妈做的菜，因为妈妈做的菜都很好吃。

2　弟弟买的衬衫很便宜，可是很_____。（看）

3　这种咖啡虽然贵，可是真的非常_____。（喝）

Indicating continuation using 下去 (xia qu)

下去 (xia qu) signifies the continuation of an action that is in progress.

A   说下去。

Shuō xia qu.

Go on speaking.

B   你别念下去了，我一点儿也不喜欢听。

Nǐ bié niàn xia qu le, wǒ yì diǎnr yě bù xǐhuan tīng.

Please stop reading. I don't like listening to that at all.

C   中文很有意思，我想学下去。

Zhōngwén hěn yǒu yìsi, wǒ xiǎng xué xia qu.

Chinese is very interesting. I'd like to continue learning it.

D   你已经跑了一个多小时了，再跑下去，
要累死了。

Nǐ yǐjīng pǎo le yí ge duō xiǎoshí le, zài pǎo xia qu, yào lèi sǐ le.

You've already been running for more than an hour; if you keep running, you'll be exhausted.

More
exercises

EXERCISES

Fill in the blanks to indicate the continuation of an action or situation using the verbs in the parentheses and 下去. Use exercise 1 as an example.

1   你唱歌真好听，＿＿＿＿＿＿吧。（唱）
    → 你唱歌真好听，唱下去吧。

2   我很喜欢我的公寓，
    想在这儿＿＿＿＿＿＿。（住）

3   你跑步跑了两个小时了，
    不能再＿＿＿＿＿＿了。（跑）

Language Practice

A | **What's the matter?** | PRESENTATIONAL

Gao Wenzhong is not feeling well. Describe what he has been through using the structure
"time expression + 没 (méi) + V + 了 (le)," e.g.:

睡觉 ✖ 三天

shuì jiào ✖ sān tiān

高文中三天没睡觉了。

Gāo Wénzhōng sān tiān méi shuì jiào le.

1 吃东西 ✖ 两天

chī dōngxi ✖ liǎng tiān

2 喝东西 ✖ 一天

hē dōngxi ✖ yì tiān

3 上课 ✖ 一个星期

shàng kè ✖ yí ge xīngqī

What do the characters mean?	
What is the common radical?	
What does the radical mean?	
How does the radical relate to the overall meaning of the characters?	

Characterize it!

❶ 　❷ 　❸

More characters

Silent treatment

Wang Peng and Li You had a fight. The two of them haven't seen each other, called, texted, or chatted online for a while now. In pairs, form a question-and-answer about their strained relationship based on the images, e.g.:

a week

Q: 李友多长时间没跟王朋见面了？

Lǐ Yǒu duō cháng shíjiān méi gēn Wáng Péng jiàn miàn le?

A: 李友一个星期没跟王朋见面了。

Lǐ Yǒu yí ge xīngqī méi gēn Wáng Péng jiàn miàn le.

1 5 days

2 6 days

3 7 days

Chinese Chat

Gao Wenzhong is chatting with Wang Peng on LINE. Describe Gao Wenzhong's future exercise plans.

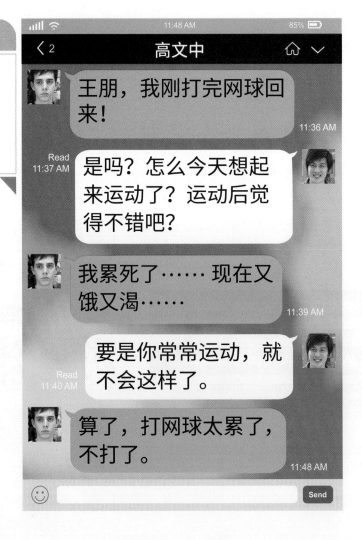

11:48 AM   85%

〈 2   高文中   ⌂ ⌄

王朋，我刚打完网球回来！
11:36 AM

Read 11:37 AM
是吗？怎么今天想起来运动了？运动后觉得不错吧？

我累死了⋯⋯ 现在又饿又渴⋯⋯
11:39 AM

Read 11:40 AM
要是你常常运动，就不会这样了。

算了，打网球太累了，不打了。
11:48 AM

Send

Open for comment

In pairs, use the "好／难 (hǎo/nán) + verb" structure to discuss with your partner and find out whether you have similar or different opinions based on the images, e.g.:

Q: 你觉得哪种茶好喝，哪种茶难喝？

Nǐ juéde nǎ zhǒng chá hǎohē, nǎ zhǒng chá nánhē?

A: 我觉得 (name of a tea) 很好喝。
我觉得 (name of a tea) 很难喝。

Wǒ juéde (name of a tea) hěn hǎohē. Wǒ juéde (name of a tea) hěn nánhē.

1 　　**2** 　　**3**

Then report your findings to the class. If the two of you share the same opinion, you can say:

Anya 跟我一样，我们都觉得……

Anya *gēn wǒ yíyàng, wǒmen dōu juéde . . .*

If you don't share the same opinion, then you can say:

Anya 跟我不一样，她觉得……我觉得……

Anya *gēn wǒ bù yíyàng, tā juéde . . . wǒ juéde . . .*

Watching American Football

Dialogue 2

Audio

Video

王朋的妹妹王红刚从北京来，要在美国上[a]大学，现在住在高小音家里学英文。为了[b]提高英文水平，她每天都看两个小时的电视[4]。

快把电视打开，足球比赛开始了。

是吗？我也喜欢看足球赛[c]。……这是什么足球[d]啊？怎么不是圆的？

这不是国际[e]足球，这是美式足球。

足球应该用脚踢，为什么那个人用手抱着[5]跑呢？

美式足球可以用手。

你看，你看，那么多人都压在一起，下面的人不是要被[6]压坏[f]了吗？

别担心，他们的身体都很棒，而且还穿特别的运动服，没问题。

我看了半天[g]也看不懂。还是看别的吧。

你在美国住半年就会喜欢了。我男朋友看美式足球的时候，常常连饭都忘了吃。

(*Wáng Péng de mèimei Wáng Hóng gāng cóng Běijīng lái, yào zài Měiguó shàng*[a] *dàxué, xiànzài zhù zài Gāo Xiǎoyīn jiā li xué Yīngwén. Wèile*[b] *tígāo Yīngwén shuǐpíng, tā měi tiān dōu kàn liǎng ge xiǎoshí de diànshì*[4]*.*)

 Kuài bǎ diànshì dǎ kāi, zúqiú bǐsài kāishǐ le.

 Shì ma? Wǒ yě xǐhuan kàn zúqiú sài[c] *... Zhè shì shénme zúqiú*[d] *a? Zěnme bú shì yuán de?*

 Zhè bú shì guójì[e] *zúqiú, zhè shì Měishì zúqiú.*

 Zúqiú yīnggāi yòng jiǎo tī, wèishénme nà ge rén yòng shǒu bào zhe[5] *pǎo ne?*

 Měishì zúqiú kěyǐ yòng shǒu.

 Nǐ kàn, nǐ kàn, nàme duō rén dōu yā zài yìqǐ, xiàmiàn de rén bú shì yào bèi[6] *yā huài*[f] *le ma?*

 Bié dān xīn, tāmen de shēntǐ dōu hěn bàng, érqiě hái chuān tèbié de yùndòngfú, méi wèntí.

 Wǒ kàn le bàntiān[g] *yě kàn bu dǒng. Háishi kàn bié de ba.*

 Nǐ zài Měiguó zhù bànnián jiù huì xǐhuan le. Wǒ nánpéngyou kàn Měishì zúqiú de shíhou, chángcháng lián fàn dōu wàng le chī.

Language Notes

a 上 (*shàng*)

This is a versatile verb. To board a car or plane is 上车/飞机 (*shàng chē/fēijī*), and to go to the bathroom is 上厕所 (*shàng cèsuǒ*). In this lesson, 上学 (*shàng xué*) means "to go to school" in colloquial Mandarin, so you can say 上小学/中学/大学 (*shàng xiǎoxué/zhōngxué/dàxué*) for attending elementary school/middle school/college.

b 为了 (*wèile*)

This usually appears in the first clause of a complex sentence, e.g.: 为了学好中文，他每天听两个小时录音 (*Wèile xué hǎo Zhōngwén, tā měi tiān tīng liǎng ge xiǎoshí lùyīn*) (In order to learn Chinese well, he listens to recordings for two hours every day).

c 赛 (*sài*)

This is short for 比赛 (*bǐsài*).

d 足球 (*zúqiú*)

This term literally means "football" and refers to soccer, not American football. To avoid confusion, Chinese speakers refer to American football as 美式足球 (*Měishì zúqiú*) (American-style football) or 美式橄榄球 (*Měishì gǎnlǎn qiú*) (lit. American-style olive ball). Rugby is known as 英式橄榄球 (*Yīngshì gǎnlǎn qiú*).

e **Adjectives as attributes**

Certain adjectives, such as 国际 (*guójì*), 男 (*nán*), 女 (*nǚ*), and 黑白 (*hēibái*), can only function as attributives and not as predicates.

f 压坏 (*yā huài*)

压坏 (*yā huài*) in this context means "to be crushed and injured." 坏 (*huài*) indicates the result of 压 (*yā*).

g 半天 (*bàntiān*)

This does not always mean exactly "a half day" as the word literally suggests. Rather, it often denotes a comparatively long stretch of time.

Vocabulary

Audio

Flashcards

No.	Word	Pinyin	Part of Speech	Definition
1	上大学	*shàng dàxué*	vo	to attend college/university
2	为了	*wèile*	prep	for the sake of
3	提高	*tígāo*	v	to improve, to raise, to heighten
4	水平	*shuǐpíng*	n	level, standard
5	足球	*zúqiú*	n	soccer, football
6	比赛	*bǐsài*	n/v	game, match, competition; to compete
7	国际	*guójì*	adj	international
8	美式	*Měishì*	adj	American-style
9	应该	*yīnggāi*	mv	should, ought to
10	脚	*jiǎo*	n	foot
11	踢	*tī*	v	to kick
12	手	*shǒu*	n	hand
13	抱	*bào*	v	to hold or carry in the arms
14	压	*yā*	v	to press, to hold down, to weigh down
15	被	*bèi*	prep	by [See Grammar 6.]
16	担心	*dān xīn*	vo	to worry
17	棒	*bàng*	adj	fantastic, super [colloq.]

You see this TV drama being advertised in the Taipei Metro. What do you think it's about?

GET Real WITH CHINESE

No.	Word	Pinyin	Part of Speech	Definition
18	运动服	*yùndòngfú*	n	sportswear, athletic clothing
19	半天	*bàntiān*		half a day, a long time

你喜欢看什么运动比赛?

Nǐ xǐhuan kàn shénme yùndòng bǐsài?

What sports games do you enjoy watching?

我喜欢看 ＿＿＿＿＿＿＿。

Wǒ xǐhuan kàn ＿＿＿＿＿＿＿ .

See index for corresponding vocabulary or research another term.

Grammar

Duration of activity (II)

As we learned in Grammar 3, Lesson 14, when a sentence contains both a time expression indicating the duration of an action and an object, it needs to be formed in one of these two patterns: repetition of the verb (*) or placement of the time expression before the object, often with 的 *(de)* (**). Let's look at some more examples and see how they differ from those in Grammar 1 of this lesson.

A　她每天听录音听一个小时。*

Tā měi tiān tīng lùyīn tīng yí ge xiǎoshí.

她每天听一个小时（的）录音。**

Tā měi tiān tīng yí ge xiǎoshí (de) lùyīn.

She listens to the audio for an hour every day.

B　她每天下午游泳游四十分钟。*

Tā měi tiān xiàwǔ yóu yǒng yóu sìshí fēnzhōng.

她每天下午游四十分钟（的）泳。**

Tā měi tiān xiàwǔ yóu sìshí fēnzhōng (de) yǒng.

She swims for forty minutes every afternoon.

C　她每天看英文报纸看两个小时，所以英文越来越好了。*

Tā měi tiān kàn Yīngwén bàozhǐ kàn liǎng ge xiǎoshí, suǒyǐ Yīngwén yuè lái yuè hǎo le.

她每天看两个小时（的）英文报纸，所以英文越来越好了。**

Tā měi tiān kàn liǎng ge xiǎoshí (de) Yīngwén bàozhǐ, suǒyǐ Yīngwén yuè lái yuè hǎo le.

She reads English-language newspapers for two hours every day, so her English is getting better and better.

EXERCISES

Indicate the time duration of the action by repeating the verbs or placing the time expression before the object. Use exercise 1 as an example.

1　我昨天跳舞　　　　　　　　两个小时
　　→ 我昨天跳舞跳了两个小时。/
　　我昨天跳了两个小时（的）舞。

2　她每天看中文书　　　　　　三个小时

3　老王昨天下午睡觉　　　　　四十分钟

---

5 | **The particle 着 (zhe)**

着 (zhe) signifies the continuation of an action or a state. Its function is descriptive. When 着 (zhe) is used between two verbs, the one that precedes 着 (zhe) signifies the accompanying action, while the second verb signifies the main action.

A　老师站着教课，学生坐着听课。

Lǎoshī zhàn zhe jiāo kè, xuésheng zuò zhe tīng kè.

While the teacher stood lecturing, the students sat listening.

B　我喜欢躺着听音乐。

Wǒ xǐhuan tǎng zhe tīng yīnyuè.

I like to listen to music while lying down.

C　美式足球可以抱着球跑。

Měishì zúqiú kěyǐ bào zhe qiú pǎo.

In American football, you can run while holding the ball in your hands.

着 (zhe) is normally used after a verb to indicate a continuing action or a state. 在 (zài) is normally used before a verb to indicate an ongoing action.

Lesson 18 | Sports | Grammar　243

D Q: 学生们在做什么呢?

Xuésheng men zài zuò shénme ne?

What are the students doing?

A: 在运动。

Zài yùndòng.

They're exercising.

在 (zài) in (D) cannot be replaced with 着 (zhe). Likewise, 着 (zhe) in the earlier sentences cannot be replaced with 在 (zài).

More exercises

EXERCISES

Form sentences to signify the accompanying action by using 着. Use exercise 1 as an example.

1 老王　看　电视　坐
→ 老王坐着看电视。

2 弟弟　吃　饭　　站

3 老师　上　课　　坐

---

6 | **Passive-voice sentences using** 被/叫/让 *(bèi/jiào/ràng)*

A sentence in the passive voice can be constructed with 被 *(bèi)*, 叫 *(jiào)*, or 让 *(ràng)*, using the following structure:

> Receiver of the action + 被 *(bèi)*/叫 *(jiào)*/让 *(ràng)* + agent of the action +
> verb + other element (complement/ 了 *[le]*, etc.)

A 我的功课被/叫/让狗吃了。

Wǒ de gōngkè bèi/jiào/ràng gǒu chī le.

My homework was eaten by my dog.

B 你买的那些书被/叫/让你的女朋友
拿去了。

Nǐ mǎi de nà xiē shū bèi/jiào/ràng nǐ de nǚpéngyou ná qù le.

The books that you bought were taken away by your girlfriend.

C 糟糕，你的网球拍被/叫/让我压坏了。

Zāogāo, nǐ de wǎngqiú pāi bèi/jiào/ràng wǒ yā huài le.

Oh gosh, your tennis racket was crushed into pieces [by me].

D 你看，我的梨被/叫/让你的西瓜
压坏了。

Nǐ kàn, wǒ de lí bèi/jiào/ràng nǐ de xīgua yā huài le.

Take a look. My pears were crushed by your watermelon.

In Chinese, the passive voice is not used as often as it is in English. It often carries a negative connotation, and is typically used in situations that are unpleasant for the receiver of the action or in situations where something is lost. As in the 把 (bǎ) structure (see Lesson 13), the verb is usually followed by another element, such as a complement or 了 (le).

In a passive-voice sentence with 被 (bèi)/叫 (jiào)/让 (ràng), the agent of the action does not always have to be specified. If the agent of the action is someone that is not identifiable or need not be identified, the agent can simply be referred to as 人 (rén) (someone, people).

E 我的信用卡被/叫/让人拿走了。

Wǒ de xìnyòngkǎ bèi/jiào/ràng rén ná zǒu le.

My credit card was taken away by someone.

With 被 (bèi), the agent of the action can be omitted from the sentence:

F 同学们在教室里又唱又跳，他快被
吵死了。

Tóngxué men zài jiàoshì li yòu chàng yòu tiào, tā kuài bèi chǎo sǐ le.

His classmates are singing and dancing in the classroom.
He is being driven to distraction by the noise.

被 (bèi) sometimes can be used in a positive sense, but we will not discuss this in detail here.

EXERCISES

Form sentences in the passive voice using 被/叫/让 and 了.
Use exercise 1 as an example.

1　他的车　　　女朋友开回家
→ 他的车被女朋友开回家了。

2　她买的水果　她妹妹吃完

3　小李的书　　小高拿到教室去

Language Practice

Packed schedule

PRESENTATIONAL

Based on the prompts, summarize who did what for how long yesterday. Repeat the verb or place the time expression before the object to indicate the duration of the action, e.g.:

费先生昨天跳舞跳了三个小时。 /
费先生昨天跳了三个小时（的）舞。

Fèi xiānsheng zuótiān tiào wǔ tiào le sān ge xiǎoshí./

Fèi xiānsheng zuótiān tiào le sān ge xiǎoshí (de) wǔ.

1  7:00 a.m.–8:00 a.m.

2  7:30 a.m.–8:15 a.m.

3   11:00 a.m.–12:00 p.m.

4   10:00 a.m.–12:30 p.m.

5   4:00 p.m.–6:30 p.m.

All in the technique

In groups, discuss traditional or innovative ways you can think of to improve Chinese proficiency. Then present each group's study strategies to the class, e.g.:

Q: 怎么才能提高中文水平?

Zěnme cái néng tígāo Zhōngwén shuǐpíng?

A: 为了提高中文水平,你应该每天听两个小时(的)录音。 / 为了提高中文水平,你应该每天听录音听两个小时。

Wèile tígāo Zhōngwén shuǐpíng, nǐ yīnggāi měi tiān tīng liǎng ge xiǎoshí (de) lùyīn.
Wèile tígāo Zhōngwén shuǐpíng, nǐ yīnggāi měi tiān tīng lùyīn tīng liǎng ge xiǎoshí.

1

2

3

What's going on?

Describe what the IC characters are doing using the "verb + 著 (zhe)" structure, e.g.:

王朋和李友站着聊天儿。
高文中坐着看电视。

Wáng Péng hé Lǐ Yǒu zhàn zhe liáo tiānr.

Gāo Wénzhōng zuò zhe kàn diànshì.

1

2

3

4

G — That's unfortunate

PRESENTATIONAL

Use the 被 *(bèi)*/叫 *(jiào)*/让 *(ràng)* structure to describe what happened to Little Gao yesterday.

1. His homework was eaten by his dog.
2. His coffee was drunk by his sister.
3. His credit card was taken away from him by his mother.
4. His car was driven to school by his brother.
5. The birthday gift that he was going to give to his friend was crushed by the sofa.

Have any of these ever happened to you? Do you have any similar experiences that you could share with your class?

H — Fitness queen/king!

INTERPERSONAL   **PRESENTATIONAL**

Survey your class for a research project about physical activity.

1. Do you exercise?
2. If so, how often do you exercise? If not, how long have you not been exercising?
3. If so, how long do you exercise each time? If not, when do you plan to start exercising, if ever?
4. What sports do you play, if any, and why do you like them?
5. Are there sports that you don't like to play? Why not?

Compare each other's information and report to the class who the fitness queen/king is. Possible sentence patterns include: _____ 运动得最多，是我们的运动天王！(_____ *yùndòng de zuì duō, shì wǒmen de yùndòng tiānwáng!*)

Characterize it!

| What do the characters mean? |
| What is the common radical? |
| What does the radical mean? |
| How does the radical relate to the overall meaning of the characters? |

 ❶ 跑   ❷ 踢   ❸ 跳

More characters

文化

Co...
to exp...

POPULARSPORTS

In recent decades, China has consolidated its status as the leading sports power in Asia. In some sports, such as table tennis and diving, China has enjoyed a dominant position in the world. One of the most popular sports in China, as in many other countries, is soccer, but despite this, China's national soccer team is second-rate at best. What Chinese speakers call "football," 足球 *(zúqiú)*, is actually soccer in American English. American football is not common there.

COMPARE & CONTRAST

1 Chinese athletics have been a national success story, and sports victories in China have been emotionally viewed as symbols of Chinese modernization. Chinese athletes began to "win glory for the country," 为国争光 *(wèi guó zhēng guāng)*, in the 1950s. In step with development, China has emerged as an athletic powerhouse, particularly at the Olympic Games. In your view, what common desires are satisfied by identification with a local or national sports team? Are there similar ties between sports and pride in your community/country?

2 China's athletic prowess is fueled by the country's extensive network of sports schools, which supply a steady stream of highly trained gymnasts, divers, and swimmers, as well as ping-pong, badminton, volleyball, basketball, and soccer players, to the national teams through a system based on that used in the former Soviet Union. Each year, gifted children are recruited into state-sponsored schools focused on athletic performance rather than academics. How similar or different is the path to becoming a star athlete in your country?

MORNING *exercises*

In every Chinese city, with the early morning comes the spectacular sight of dozens, even hundreds, of men and women gathering in parks to practice *t'ai chi ch'uan*, 太极拳 *(tàijíquán)*, and other forms of exercise. Most practitioners are older people and retirees. Another phenomenon is "public-square dancing," 广场舞 *(guǎngchǎng wǔ)*, which typically takes place in the early morning or early evening in neighborhood parks or squares. Its participants, mostly middle-aged and retired women, believe in the health benefits of their practice, but the loud music they play has been controversial.

Women engaged in public-square dancing

Cuju (蹴鞠) *(cùjū)*, a game played as early as the Han dynasty (202 BCE–220 CE), is recognized as the earliest precursor of the modern sport of soccer. *Cuju* was initially played with a ball filled with feathers, then later played with an inflated ball. During the Tang (618–907 CE) and Song (960–1279 CE) dynasties, *cuju* was popular among all social classes and among both men and women; fields for playing *cuju* were reportedly numerous in the Tang and Song capitals of Chang'an and Bianliang. As in soccer, players were not allowed to touch the ball with their hands. Gao Qiu, a hooligan in the classic Chinese novel *Outlaws of the Marsh*, becomes a favorite of the emperor because of his extraordinary skills as a *cuju* player and goes on to perpetrate all sorts of nefarious deeds. As a result, one of the novel's heroes, who falls victim to Gao, is forced into becoming an outlaw.

Cuju

Gao Qiu showing off his footwork

diet & WEIGHT

With the improvement in living standards in China over recent decades, the consumption of calorie-rich foods, especially meat, has been on the rise. Obesity has quietly become a problem for many people in urban areas, especially children. The transformation in people's lifestyles has affected language as well: before the 1970s, one could say 你胖了 (Nǐ pàng le) (You've put on weight) as a compliment, but this is no longer the case.

Lesson Wrap-Up

The following sentences are arranged in a logical order. Combine the sentences into a coherent narrative. Substitute nouns with pronouns and change periods to commas where necessary. Avoid unnecessary repetitions of subject pronouns. Add the connective devices 又 (yòu), 所以 (suǒyǐ), 如果 (rúguǒ), and 可是 (kěshì) where appropriate.

高文中两年没运动了。高文中平常吃得很多。高文中越来越胖。

高文中问王朋怎么办。王朋说一个星期运动两三次，每次半个小时，肚子就会小了。高文中不知道做什么运动好。王朋告诉高文中可以跑步。王朋告诉高文中可以打网球。王朋告诉高文中可以打篮球。王朋告诉高文中可以游泳。高文中觉得，跑步冬天太冷。高文中觉得，跑步夏天太热。高文中觉得，跑步太难受。高文中觉得，打网球买网球拍太贵。高文中觉得，打网球买网球鞋太贵。高文中觉得，打篮球每次都得打电话约人，太麻烦。高文中觉得，游泳太危险。高文中怕淹死。

王朋没有办法了。高文中可能还得胖下去。

You're a freshman who has been enjoying college life. You love your classes, professors, and new friends, but your hectic, unhealthy lifestyle has meant that you've put on fifteen pounds (磅) (bàng). You've been staying up late, helping yourself to multiple slices of pizza, and avoiding the gym. You decide to go to a wellness coach. The coach tries to find out about your habits and recommends various kinds of exercise. Respond to his/her suggestions: Do you like the recommendations? Will you able to follow them? You will jointly decide on a plan to get you back in shape.

Video

Make a short video introducing American football to a Chinese audience. What is the biggest difference between American football and soccer? How do the clothes and equipment for each sport compare? Are players allowed to manipulate the ball with their hands? How long is a game? Is football more popular among men or women? Do you have a favorite team? Who are some of the most famous players?

Supplemental Reading Practice

For additional reading practice that builds on the vocabulary introduced in this lesson, turn to the supplemental readings that begin on page 419.

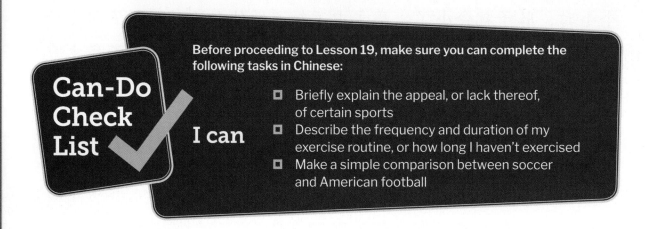

Can-Do Check List

I can

Before proceeding to Lesson 19, make sure you can complete the following tasks in Chinese:

- ☐ Briefly explain the appeal, or lack thereof, of certain sports
- ☐ Describe the frequency and duration of my exercise routine, or how long I haven't exercised
- ☐ Make a simple comparison between soccer and American football

旅行

Lǚxíng

TRAVEL

Learning Objectives

In this lesson, you will learn to:

- Talk about your plans for summer break
- Describe what kind of city Beijing is
- Describe your travel itinerary
- Ask for discounts, compare airfares and routes, and book airplane tickets
- Ask about seat assignments and request meal accommodations based on your dietary restrictions or preferences

Relate & Get Ready

In your own culture/community:

- How do students normally spend the summer?
- What town or city is the nearest cultural or political center? What are its special attractions?
- Where can people get good deals on airline tickets?
- How are discounts expressed and advertised?

Traveling to Beijing

Dialogue 1

Audio

Video

（暑假快要到了……）

李友，时间过得真快，马上就要放假了，我们的同学，有的去暑期班学习，有的去公司实习，有的回家打工，你有什么计划？

我还没有想好。你呢，王朋？

我暑假打算^a回北京去看父母。

是吗？我听说北京这个城市很有意思。

当然。北京是中国的首都，也是中国的政治、文化中心，有很多名胜古迹。

对啊，长城很有名。

还有，北京的好饭馆多得不得了[1]。

真的？我去过香港、台北，还没去过北京，要是能去北京就好了。

那你跟我一起回去吧，我当你的导游。

真的吗？那太好了！护照我已经有了，我得赶快办^b签证。

那我马上给旅行社打电话订飞机票。

(Shǔjià kuài yào dào le . . .)

Lǐ Yǒu, shíjiān guò de zhēn kuài, mǎshàng jiù yào

fàng jià le, wǒmen de tóngxué, yǒude qù shǔqī

bān xuéxí, yǒude qù gōngsī shíxí, yǒude huí jiā dǎ

gōng, nǐ yǒu shénme jìhuà?

Wǒ hái méiyǒu xiǎng hǎo. Nǐ ne, Wáng Péng?

Wǒ shǔjià dǎsuàn[a] *huí Běijīng qù kàn fùmǔ.*

Shì ma? Wǒ tīngshuō Běijīng zhè ge chéngshì hěn

yǒu yìsi.

Dāngrán. Běijīng shì Zhōngguó de shǒudū, yě shì

Zhōngguó de zhèngzhì, wénhuà zhōngxīn, yǒu hěn

duō míngshèng gǔjì.

Duì a, Chángchéng hěn yǒumíng.

Hái yǒu, Běijīng de hǎo fànguǎn duō de bùdéliǎo[1].

Zhēn de? Wǒ qù guo Xiānggǎng, Táiběi, hái méi

qù guo Běijīng, yàoshi néng qù Běijīng jiù hǎo le.

Nà nǐ gēn wǒ yìqǐ huí qu ba, wǒ dāng nǐ de dǎoyóu.

Zhēn de ma? Nà tài hǎo le! Hùzhào wǒ yǐjīng

yǒu le. Wǒ děi gǎnkuài bàn[b] *qiānzhèng.*

Nà wǒ mǎshàng gěi lǚxíngshè dǎ diànhuà dìng

fēijī piào.

Language Notes

a 打算 *(dǎsuàn)* **vs.** 计划 *(jìhuà)*

打算 *(dǎsuàn)* is synonymous with 计划 *(jìhuà)*, but the former is more colloquial.

b 办 *(bàn)*

To apply for a certificate or an official document, you can use this verb, especially in spoken Chinese, e.g.: 办护照 *(bàn hùzhào)* (to apply for a passport), 办签证 *(bàn qiānzhèng)* (to apply for a visa), 办学生证 *(bàn xuéshēng zhèng)* (to apply for a student ID), 办手续 *(bàn shǒuxù)* (to do paperwork), and 办结婚证 *(bàn jiéhūn zhèng)* (to apply for a marriage license).

Vocabulary

No.	Word	Pinyin	Part of Speech	Definition
1	马上	mǎshàng	adv	immediately, right away
2	放假	fàng jià	vo	go on vacation, have time off
	放	fàng	v	to let go, to set free
	假	jià	n	vacation, holiday
3	公司	gōngsī	n	company
4	实习	shíxí	v	to intern
5	打工	dǎ gōng	vo	to work at a temporary job (often part time)
6	计划	jìhuà	n/v	plan; to plan
7	暑假	shǔjià	n	summer vacation
8	打算	dǎsuàn	v/n	to plan; plan
9	父母	fùmǔ	n	parents, father and mother
10	首都	shǒudū	n	capital city
11	政治	zhèngzhì	n	politics
12	文化	wénhuà	n	culture
13	名胜古迹	míngshèng gǔjì		famous scenic spots and historic sites
14	有名	yǒumíng	adj	famous, well-known
15	导游	dǎoyóu	n	tour guide
16	护照	hùzhào	n	passport
17	签证	qiānzhèng	n	visa

Your friend wore this shirt to school after a study-abroad semester. What does it tell you about his trip to China?

GET Real WITH CHINESE

No.	Word	Pinyin	Part of Speech	Definition
18	旅行社	*lǚxíngshè*	n	travel agency
19	订	*dìng*	v	to reserve, to book (a ticket, a hotel room, etc.)
20	长城	*Chángchéng*	pn	the Great Wall
21	香港	*Xiānggǎng*	pn	Hong Kong
22	台北	*Táiběi*	pn	Taipei

你暑假打算去什么地方旅行?

Nǐ shǔjià dǎsuàn qù shénme dìfang lǚxíng?

Where do you plan to travel over summer break?

AFRICA

ASIA

EUROPE

我打算去 ＿＿＿＿＿＿＿＿。

Wǒ dǎsuàn qù ＿＿＿＿＿＿＿ .

How About You?

See index for corresponding vocabulary or research another term.

Grammar

不得了 (bùdéliǎo) (extremely)

The expression 不得了 (bùdéliǎo) (extremely), which often follows the structure "adjective + 得 (de)," indicates a high degree, in the speaker's judgment, of the attribute signified by the adjective. For example, if one cannot stand the summer heat in a certain place, one can say:

A   那个地方夏天热得不得了。

Nà ge dìfang xiàtiān rè de bùdéliǎo.

Summer is unbearably hot in that place.

If the Great Wall was extremely crowded, you could say:

B   长城上的人多得不得了。

Chángchéng shàng de rén duō de bùdéliǎo.

There were an incredible number of people on the Great Wall.

Verbs like 想 (xiǎng), 喜欢 (xǐhuan), and 爱 (ài) can also be followed by "得 (de) + 不得了 (bùdéliǎo)."

C   海伦的孩子真可爱，大家喜欢得不得了。

Hǎilún de háizi zhēn kě'ài, dàjiā xǐhuan de bùdéliǎo.

Helen's kid is so adorable. Everyone just loves him.

More exercises

EXERCISES

Rewrite the sentences by replacing 极了 with 不得了 and adding 得 where appropriate. Use exercise 1 as an example.

1   在高速公路上开车让小高紧张极了。

→ 在高速公路上开车让小高紧张得不得了。

2   那个商店的家具贵极了。

3   有的人觉得国际足球比赛好看极了。

Language Practice

<table>
<tr><td>A</td><td colspan="2">**Planning ahead**</td><td>INTERPERSONAL</td></tr>
</table>

In pairs, form a question-and-answer about each other's plans for a particular time, e.g.:

tonight

你今天晚上打算做什么？

Nǐ jīntiān wǎnshang dǎsuàn zuò shénme?

1   the coming weekend

2   summer break

3   next semester

4   next year

<table>
<tr><td>B</td><td>INTERPERSONAL</td><td>**Survey says**</td><td>PRESENTATIONAL</td></tr>
</table>

Interview your classmates to find out more about their opinions and experiences. Then report the results of your survey to the class by using "我的同学有的人……，有的人……" (*Wǒ de tóngxué yǒude rén . . . , yǒude rén . . .*). Each student should choose a different topic to inquire about. Possible topics include: your classmates' thoughts on Chinese pronunciation, Chinese grammar, or Chinese characters; their allergies, living arrangements, or travel plans; or their favorite cuisines, fruits, colors, sports, or beverages, e.g.:

我的同学有的人喜欢喝可乐，有的人喜欢喝咖啡。

Wǒ de tóngxué yǒude rén xǐhuan hē kělè, yǒude rén xǐhuan hē kāfēi.

Geography buff

In pairs, form a question-and-answer to quiz each other about the capitals of different countries, e.g.:

Q: 中国的首都是哪一个城市？

Zhōngguó de shǒudū shì nǎ yí ge chéngshì?

A: 中国的首都是北京。

Zhōngguó de shǒudū shì Běijīng.

1 美国

Měiguó

3 日本

Rìběn

5 加拿大

Jiā'nádà

(Canada)

7 澳大利亚

Àodàlìyà

(Australia)

2 英国

Yīngguó

4 韩国

Hánguó

(South Korea)

6 墨西哥

Mòxīgē

(Mexico)

Places to go, people to meet

You must have people that you adore or dislike. Share your sentiments with the class.

可爱

kě'ài

海伦的儿子可爱得不得了。

Hǎilún de érzi kě'ài de bùdéliǎo.

1 帅

shuài

3 漂亮

piàoliang

5 酷

kù

7 懒

lǎn

2 聪明

cōngming

4 用功

yònggōng

6 坏

huài

What about places? Where do you like and dislike visiting?

1 漂亮
piàoliang

2 好玩（儿）
hǎowán(r)

3 安静
ānjìng

4 干净
gānjìng

5 人多
rén duō

6 热
rè

7 冷
lěng

8 危险
wēixiǎn

9 吵
chǎo

E | **When I get older** | INTERPERSONAL

Survey your classmates to find out their aspirations for the future.

你以后想当什么？老师、导游、律师，
还是医生？

Nǐ yǐhòu xiǎng dāng shénme? Lǎoshī, dǎoyóu, lǜshī, háishi yīshēng?

F | INTERPERSONAL | **Globetrotter** | PRESENTATIONAL

In pairs, recap what you know about Beijing, then find one or two other cities in the world that are similar to it in certain ways. What do they have in common? If you could travel to any city in the world during your next vacation, where would you go? Why? What attractions would you especially want to see? Present your choice of destination and your reasons for selecting it to your class, either in writing on a poster or in a video shared on social media.

Planning an Itinerary

Dialogue 2

Audio

Video

（王朋给旅行社打电话订机票……）

天一旅行社，你好。

你好。请问六月初[a]到北京的机票多少钱？

您要买单程票还是往返票？

我要买两张往返票。

你想买哪家航空公司的？

哪家的便宜，就买哪[2]家的。

请等等，我查一下……好几家航空公司
都有航班[b]。中国国际航空公司，一千五[3]，
直飞。西北航空公司正在打折[c]，差不多
一千四百六十，可是要转机。

西北只比国航[d]便宜四十几块钱[4]，我还是
买国航吧。

哪一天走[e]？哪一天回来？

六月十号走，七月十五号回来。现在可以
订位子吗？

可以。你们喜欢靠窗户的还是靠走道的？

靠走道的。对了[f]，我朋友吃素，麻烦帮她
订一份素餐。

没问题……您在北京要订旅馆、租车吗？

不用，谢谢！

(*Wáng Péng gěi lǚxíngshè dǎ diànhuà dìng jīpiào . . .*)

Tiān Yī lǚxíngshè, nǐ hǎo.

Nǐ hǎo. Qǐng wèn liùyuè chū^a dào Běijīng de jīpiào duōshao qián?

Nín yào mǎi dānchéng piào háishi wǎngfǎn piào?

Wǒ yào mǎi liǎng zhāng wǎngfǎn piào.

Nǐ xiǎng mǎi nǎ jiā hángkōng gōngsī de?

Nǎ jiā de piányi, jiù mǎi nǎ² jiā de.

Qǐng děng deng, wǒ chá yixià . . . Hǎo jǐ jiā hángkōng gōngsī dōu yǒu hángbān^b. Zhōngguó Guójì Hángkōng Gōngsī, yì qiān wǔ³, zhífēi. Xīběi Hángkōng Gōngsī zhèngzài dǎ zhé^c, chàbuduō yì qiān sì bǎi liùshí, kěshì yào zhuǎn jī.

Xīběi zhǐ bǐ Guóháng^d piányi sìshí jǐ kuài qián⁴, wǒ háishi mǎi Guóháng ba.

Nǎ yì tiān zǒu^e? Nǎ yì tiān huí lai?

Liùyuè shí hào zǒu, qīyuè shíwǔ hào huí lai. Xiànzài kěyǐ dìng wèizi ma?

Kěyǐ. Nǐmen xǐhuan kào chuānghu de háishi kào zǒudào de?

Kào zǒudào de. Duì le^f, wǒ péngyou chī sù, máfan bāng tā dìng yí fèn sùcān.

Méi wèntí . . . Nín zài Běijīng yào dìng lǚguǎn, zū chē ma?

Búyòng, xièxie!

Language Notes

a 初 (*chū*), 中 (*zhōng*), and 底 (*dǐ*)

月初 (*yuè chū*) is the first few days of the month, 月中 (*yuè zhōng*) is the middle of the month, and 月底 (*yuè dǐ*) is the final days of the month. You can also say 年初 (*nián chū*) (beginning of the year), 年中 (*nián zhōng*) (middle of the year), and 年底 (*nián dǐ*) (end of the year). The words 初 (*chū*) (beginning), 中 (*zhōng*) (middle), and 底 (*dǐ*) (end, bottom) compound with 月 (*yuè*) or 年 (*nián*), but are never used with 星期 (*xīngqī*).

b 航班 (*hángbān*) vs. 班机 (*bānjī*)

In Mainland China, people use 航班 (*hángbān*), whereas in Taiwan, people say 班机 (*bānjī*).

c 打折 (*dǎ zhé*)

Discounts are expressed differently in Chinese from English. In English the emphasis is on the amount that is given as a discount, e.g., ten percent off. In Chinese, however, the emphasis is on the post-discount amount. Therefore, ten percent off in Chinese would be rendered as 打九折 (*dǎ jiǔ zhé*), or ninety percent of the original price, and twenty-five percent off would be 打七五折 (*dǎ qī wǔ zhé*), or seventy-five percent of the original price. 打对折 (*dǎ duì zhé*) means that the discounted price is fifty percent of the original price.

d 国航 (*Guóháng*)

中国国际航空公司 (*Zhōngguó Guójì Hángkōng Gōngsī*) (Air China, lit. China International Airlines) is often shortened to 国航 (*Guóháng*).

e 走 (*zǒu*)

As you learned in Lesson 10, the basic meaning of 走 (*zǒu*) is "to walk." Here, 走 (*zǒu*) means to leave or to depart.

f 对了 (*duì le*)

This term is often used when one suddenly thinks of something. For instance, if a student is saying goodbye to his classmate, and all of a sudden it occurs to him that they need to study for a test the next day, the student can say: 明天见。……对了，明天考试，别忘了复习。 (*Míngtiān jiàn . . . Duì le, míngtiān kǎo shì, bié wàng le fùxí*) (See you tomorrow . . . Oh right, we have a test tomorrow. Don't forget to review.)

你去旅行的时候会带些什么东西？

Nǐ qù lǚxíng de shíhou huì dài xiē shénme dōngxi?

What would you bring with you when traveling?

我会带 ＿＿＿＿＿＿＿。

Wǒ huì dài ＿＿＿＿＿＿＿.

How About You?

See index for corresponding vocabulary or research another term.

Vocabulary

Audio

Flashcards

No.	Word	Pinyin	Part of Speech	Definition
1	初	*chū*	n	beginning
2	单程	*dānchéng*	n	one-way trip
3	往返	*wǎngfǎn*	v	make a round trip, go there and back
4	航空	*hángkōng*	n	aviation
5	查	*chá*	v	to check, to look into
6	航班	*hángbān*	n	scheduled flight
7	千	*qiān*	nu	thousand
8	直飞	*zhí fēi*		fly directly
9	打折	*dǎ zhé*	vo	to sell at a discount, to give a discount
10	转机	*zhuǎn jī*	vo	change planes
11	靠	*kào*	v	to lean on, to lean against, to be next to
12	窗户	*chuānghu*	n	window
13	走道	*zǒudào*	n	aisle
14	份	*fèn*	m	(measure word for meal orders, jobs)
15	素餐	*sùcān*	n	vegetarian meal
16	旅馆	*lǚguǎn*	n	hotel
17	租	*zū*	v	to rent
18	中国国际航空公司	*Zhōngguó Guójì Hángkōng Gōngsī*	pn	Air China
19	西北航空公司	*Xīběi Hángkōng Gōngsī*	pn	Northwest Airlines

GET
Real
WITH **CHINESE**

You decide to bypass the travel agent and book your trip from Beijing to Shanghai using an app. What flight options are available?

Chinese Chat

You're exchanging WeChat messages with a friend about the upcoming summer break. How would you complete the conversation?

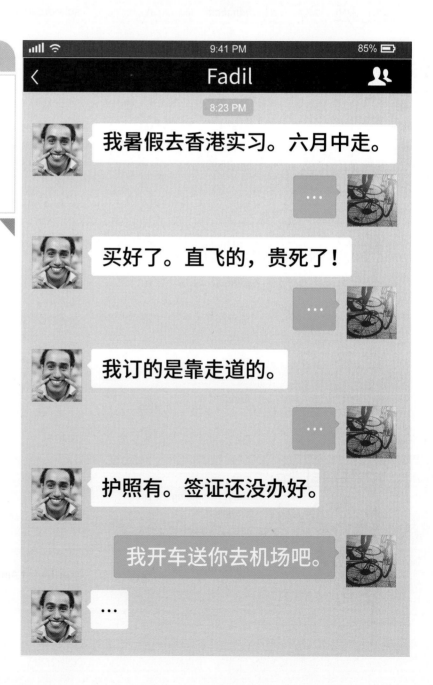

Fadil

8:23 PM

我暑假去香港实习。六月中走。

...

买好了。直飞的，贵死了！

...

我订的是靠走道的。

...

护照有。签证还没办好。

我开车送你去机场吧。

...

Grammar

2   Question pronouns as indefinite references (whoever, whatever, etc.)

The equivalent of the "question pronoun + -ever" expression in English is formed by repeating a question pronoun in two separate but related clauses in the same sentence. The first occurrence refers to an indefinite person, object, time, place, etc. The second occurrence then refers to that same person, object, time, place, etc.

A   谁想去，谁就去。

Shéi xiǎng qù, shéi jiù qù.

Whoever wants to go can go.

B   你吃什么，我就吃什么。

Nǐ chī shénme, wǒ jiù chī shénme.

I'll have whatever you're having.

C   哪双鞋便宜，就买哪双。

Nǎ shuāng xié piányi, jiù mǎi nǎ shuāng.

Buy whichever pair of shoes is the cheapest.

D   Q: 你想怎么走?

Ní xiǎng zěnme zǒu?

Which way do you want to take?

      A: 怎么近，怎么走。

Zěnme jìn, zěnme zǒu.

Let's take whichever's the shortest.

In this kind of sentence, sometimes the two occurrences of the question pronoun play the same grammatical role, i.e, both are subjects, as in (A); or both are objects, as in (B). Sometimes the two occurrences of the question pronoun perform different grammatical functions. In (C), for example, the first 哪双 (*nǎ shuāng*) is the subject whereas the second 哪双 (*nǎ shuāng*) is the object. The adverb 就 (*jiù*) often precedes the verb in the second clause, but not always, as in (E) and (F) below.

E

哪儿安静，我住哪儿。

Nǎr ānjìng, wǒ zhù nǎr.

I'll live wherever it's quiet.

F

Q: 他找谁帮他搬家具？

Tā zhǎo shéi bāng tā bān jiājù?

Who's he going to ask to help him move his furniture?

A: 谁身体棒，他找谁。

Shéi shēntǐ bàng, tā zhǎo shéi.

He'll ask whoever is strong.

More exercises

EXERCISES

In pairs, form a question-and answer and use the question pronouns as indefinite references to show you're being flexible or accommodating. Use exercise 1 as an example.

1 下个周末   去哪儿

→ **Student A** 下个周末我们去哪儿？

    Student B 你想去哪儿，我们就去哪儿。

2 今天晚饭   吃什么

3 明年暑假   做什么

Characterize it!

More characters

❶ ❷ ❸

| What do the characters mean? |
| What is the common radical? |
| What does the radical mean? |
| How does the radical relate to the overall meaning of the characters? |

You have already learned how to count in Chinese up to a thousand.

一	十	百	千
yī	*shí*	*bǎi*	*qiān*
1	10	100	1,000
one	ten	hundred	thousand

In Chinese, the next-largest unit after a thousand is not ❌ 十千, but 万 *(wàn)*. Even though long Arabic numbers are segmented into three-digit sets in writing and in print, such numbers have to be expressed in four-digit sets. The four-digit set of 万 *(wàn)* starts at the fifth digit from the right; the next four-digit set is that of 亿 *(yì)*. In the examples below, we have indicated such divisions as an aid.

Chinese	Pinyin	Chinese Mental Division	Arabic Number	English
（一）千	*(yì) qiān*	1000	1,000	thousand
（一）万	*(yí) wàn*	1:0000	10,000	ten thousand
十万	*shí wàn*	10:0000	100,000	hundred thousand
（一）百万	*(yì) bǎi wàn*	100:0000	1,000,000	million
（一）千万	*(yì) qiān wàn*	1000:0000	10,000,000	ten million
（一）亿/ （一）万万	*(yí) yì/* *(yí) wànwàn*	1:0000:0000	100,000,000	hundred million
十亿	*shí yì*	10:0000:0000	1,000,000,000	billion

A

12,345 (1⋮2345)

一万两千三百四十五

yí wàn liǎng qiān sān bǎi sìshíwǔ

B

25,000 (2⋮5000)

两万五千

liǎng wàn wǔ qiān

C

340,876 (34⋮0876)

三十四万〇八百七十六

sānshísì wàn líng bā bǎi qīshíliù

D

1,000,900,000 (10⋮0090⋮0000)

十亿〇九十万

shí yì líng jiǔshí wàn

More
exercises

EXERCISES

Say the following amounts of money in Chinese. Use exercise 1 as an example.

1   $1111.11

→ 一千一百一十一块一毛一分钱

2   $2202.59

3   $34560.05

---

4 | **Comparative sentences using 比 (bǐ) (II)**

In a sentence where 比 (bǐ) is used, a numeral + measure word combination can be placed after the adjective to indicate a disparity in numerical terms. [See also Grammar 1, Lesson 11.]

> X + 比 (bǐ) + Y + adjective + numeral + measure word + noun

A

我们班比你们班多四个学生。

Wǒmen bān bǐ nǐmen bān duō sì ge xuésheng.

Our class is larger than yours by four students.

B 这件衬衫比那件衬衫贵二十块钱。

Zhè jiàn chènshān bǐ nà jiàn chènshān guì èrshí kuài qián.

This shirt is twenty dollars more expensive than that shirt.

C 我的房租比你的便宜五百块。

Wǒ de fángzū bǐ nǐ de piányi wǔ bǎi kuài.

My rent is five hundred dollars cheaper than yours.

D 我表弟比我小三岁。

Wǒ biǎodì bǐ wǒ xiǎo sān suì.

My cousin is three years younger than I am.

EXERCISES

Based on the given information, join these sentences to describe the difference by inserting the adjectives in parentheses and 比 where appropriate. Use exercise 1 as an example.

More exercises

1 我们班有三十个学生，你们班有二十七个学生。（多）
　→ 我们班比你们班多三个学生。

2 小王今年十八岁，小高今年十九岁。（小）

3 蓝色的裤子三十号，绿色的裤子三十四号。（大）

Characterize it!

| What do the characters mean? |
| What is the common radical? |
| What does the radical mean? |
| How does the radical relate to the overall meaning of the characters? |

❶ 　❷ 　❸

More characters

Language Practice

| **Good deal** | INTERPERSONAL |

A furniture store is having a big sale. Compare the original prices and the sale prices. Then, in pairs, figure out what discount the store is offering on each item, e.g.:

Q: 这张床打几折?

Zhè zhāng chuáng dǎ jǐ zhé?

A: 这张床打八折。

Zhè zhāng chuáng dǎ bā zhé.

1 ~~$500~~ $400   2 ~~$500~~ $425   3 ~~$80~~ $40   4 ~~$120~~ $90

| **Up to you** | INTERPERSONAL |

Ms. Wang has just started dating Mr. Li. She wants to be nice and asks Mr. Li what he would like to do, where he would like to go, etc. Mr. Li also wants to be nice, so he leaves it up to Ms. Wang to decide. In pairs, role-play and see if you and your partner can settle on a day, time, place, and activity, e.g.:

Ms. Wang   你想去哪儿玩儿?

Nǐ xiǎng qù nǎr wánr?

Mr. Li   你想去哪儿玩儿,我们就去哪儿玩儿。

Nǐ xiǎng qù nǎr wánr, wǒmen jiù qù nǎr wánr.

1 Find out what he would like to do.

2 Find out what cuisine he prefers.

3 Find out when he would like to see a movie.

4 Find out which city he would like to travel to.

By the way

In pairs, role-play the following scenarios using 对了 (duì le).

1 You have just said goodbye to your friend, but suddenly it occurs to you that you need to borrow a Chinese book from him. What do you say?

2 You are talking to your mom on the phone to ask for more money, and she says yes. You thank her. It occurs to you that you should mention your plan to travel to China for the summer and ask for her opinion.

3 You are on the phone with your friend discussing booking plane tickets for both of you online. Before you hang up the phone, it occurs to you that you should ask for your friend's seat preferences.

Price-wise

In pairs, compare notes with your partner and find out the difference between what you pay for rent, security deposits, and utilities. Then report to the class.

1 房租

fángzū

2 押金

yājīn

3 水电费

shuǐ diàn fèi

Trip advisor

Divide the class into two groups: travelers and travel agents.

Travelers: As experienced travelers, what questions would you ask when making a flight reservation? Make your list as detailed as possible.

Travel Agents: As experienced travel agents, what questions would you ask customers booking flights? Make your list as detailed as possible.

After each group completes its list, the two groups should compare lists and see if any important questions have been left out. Then the whole class will decide which list is better.

A Chinese high-speed train

Rail travel

Rail remains the major means of domestic travel in China. During the Chinese New Year period, railroad stations across the country are overcrowded with travelers waiting for trains or seeking tickets. High-speed trains offer three classes of service: business class (商务座) (*shāngwù zuò*), which, as the most expensive, offers the most comfort; first class (一等座) (*yīděng zuò*); and second class (二等座) (*èrděng zuò*). There are no sleeping berths on high-speed trains. Old-fashioned "regular" trains offer four classes of service: hard seat (硬座) (*yìng zuò*), soft seat (软座) (*ruǎn zuò*), hard sleeper (硬卧) (*yìng wò*), and soft sleeper (软卧) (*ruǎn wò*).

The three oldest travel agencies in China are International Travel Agencies, 国际旅行社 (*Guójì Lǚxíngshè*) or 国旅 (*Guólǚ*); China Travel Agencies, 中国旅行社 (*Zhōngguó Lǚxíngshè*) or 中旅 (*Zhōnglǚ*); and Youth Travel Agencies, 青年旅行社 (*Qīngnián Lǚxíngshè*), or 青旅 (*Qīnglǚ*). While 国旅 (*Guólǚ*) and 中旅 (*Zhōng Lǚ*) mainly serve foreign tourists and overseas Chinese, respectively, 青旅 (*Qīnglǚ*) is primarily oriented toward Chinese citizens. The divisions among types of travel agency, however, have become less distinct in recent years. Nowadays, there are many prominent newer agencies, and it is also common for people to choose independent travel, 自助游 (*zìzhùyóu*) rather than arranging their trips through agencies.

Travel agencies

Airlines

Apart from Air China (中国国际航空公司) (*Zhōngguó Guójì Hángkōng Gōngsī*), China's major airlines also include China Eastern (中国东方航空) (*Zhōngguó Dōngfāng Hángkōng*), China Southern (中国南方航空) (*Zhōngguó Nánfāng Hángkōng*), and Hainan Airlines (海南航空) (*Hǎinán Hángkōng*). Additionally, there are more than a dozen airline companies specializing in regional routes and half a dozen low-cost carriers.

Attitudes toward travel

In traditional China, the general attitude toward travel was largely ambivalent. As fundamentally an agrarian people, the Chinese were, as expressed in the idiomatic phrase 安土重迁 (*ān tǔ zhòng qiān*), "attached to their native land and reluctant to move." Confucius even admonished that "One should not travel afar while one's parents are still alive, unless there are excellent reasons to do so," 父母在不远游，游必有方 (*fùmǔ zài bù yuǎn yóu, yóu bì yǒu fāng*). On the other hand, however, travel was perceived to be a crucial component of one's intellectual development, a view that is registered in the celebrated saying that a good scholar should "Read ten thousand volumes and travel ten thousand miles," 读万卷书，行万里路 (*dú wàn juàn shū, xíng wàn lǐ lù*). Indeed, many scholars in premodern China were well traveled, as they had to trek, many by boat along the Grand Canal, to take the civil service examinations in the imperial capital.

COMPARE & CONTRAST

1 Compare Beijing with the capital of your country in terms of location, population, political and cultural significance, and famous tourist sites.

2 You may be familiar with Washington, D.C., but how much do you know about Beijing? Both cities are full of monuments. Research the most significant memorial structures on the National Mall in Washington and in Tiananmen Square in Beijing. What historical events and figures do they commemorate? How are the two public spaces used?

Lesson Wrap-Up

Make It Flow

The following sentences are arranged in a logical order. Combine the sentences into a coherent narrative. Replace nouns with pronouns and change periods to commas where appropriate. Avoid unnecessary repetitions of subject pronouns. Add the connective devices 有的⋯有的⋯有的⋯ (*yǒu de . . . yǒu de . . . yǒu de . . .*), 也⋯也⋯ (*yě . . . yě . . .*), 不但⋯而且⋯ (*búdàn . . . érqiě . . .*), and ⋯以后 (*. . . yǐhòu*) where appropriate.

学校马上就要放暑假了。王朋的一些同学去暑期班学习。王朋的一些同学回家打工。王朋的一些同学去公司实习。王朋告诉李友他要回北京看父母。李友对北京很有兴趣。王朋给李友介绍说，北京是中国的首都。王朋给李友介绍说，北京是中国的政治中心。王朋给李友介绍说，北京是中国的文化中心。王朋给李友介绍说，北京有很多名胜古迹。王朋给李友介绍说，北京好吃的饭馆多得不得了。李友听了王朋的介绍。李友说要是她能去北京就好了。王朋让李友一起去。王朋说他当导游。李友很高兴。李友说她得赶快办签证。王朋说他马上订机票。

Presentation

Present a video or slideshow of a destination in China. Include sights you want to see. How is your destination perceived in China? What is it famous for? The class will vote on where to go.

Skit

You're flying to Hong Kong to visit your parents; your partner is a travel agent in Chinatown. Before calling the agent, list key information you'll need: time and city of departure, direct or indirect flight, passport and visa requirement, seat preference, etc. If you're the agent, what information will you need that is not mentioned above? Do travelers need a visa and a passport to enter Hong Kong?

Supplemental Reading Practice

For additional reading practice that builds on the vocabulary introduced in this lesson, turn to the supplemental readings that begin on page 419.

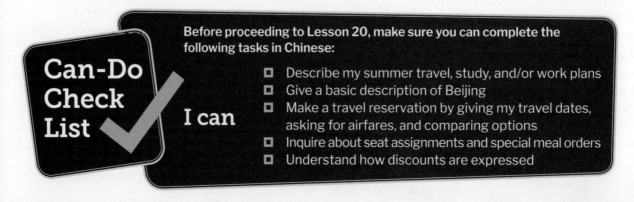

Can-Do Check List

I can

Before proceeding to Lesson 20, make sure you can complete the following tasks in Chinese:

- ☐ Describe my summer travel, study, and/or work plans
- ☐ Give a basic description of Beijing
- ☐ Make a travel reservation by giving my travel dates, asking for airfares, and comparing options
- ☐ Inquire about seat assignments and special meal orders
- ☐ Understand how discounts are expressed

在机场

Zài jīchǎng

AT THE AIRPORT

Learning Objectives	Relate & Get Ready

In this lesson, you will learn to:

- Check in at the airport
- Wish departing friends a safe journey and remind them to keep in touch
- Greet guests at the airport
- Compliment someone's language ability
- Ask about someone's health
- Take leave of someone

In your own culture/community:

- What do people say when seeing someone off on a trip?
- For travel over the summer, is road tripping a popular option?
- What do people say when greeting guests at the airport, train, or bus station?
- What local food should foreign guests try?

Checking in at the Airport

Dialogue 1

Audio

Video

（在国航的服务台……）

 小姐，这是我们的¹机票。

请把护照给我看看。你们有几件行李要托运？

两件。这个包不托运，我们带上飞机。

麻烦ᵃ您把箱子拿上来²。

小姐，没超重吧？

没有。这是你们的护照、机票，这是登机
牌ᵇ。请到五号登机口ᶜ上飞机。

谢谢。

……

哥哥，你们去北京了，就我一个人在这儿。

小红，别哭，我们几个星期就回来，你好
好儿地¹学英文，别乱跑。

不是几个星期就回来，是几个星期以后才
回来。

别担心，我姐姐小音会照顾你。

对，别担心。

飞机几点起飞？

中午十二点，还有两个多小时。

白英爱，你什么时候去纽约实习？

我不去纽约了。文中帮我在加州找了一份实习工作。

对，我们下个星期开车去加州。

是吗？一边儿开车，一边儿玩儿，太好了。

开车小心。祝你们玩儿得[1]高兴。

祝你们一路平安。到了北京以后[3]，别忘了给我们发个电子邮件。

好，那我们秋天见。

下个学期见。

再见！

Pinyin Dialogue

(Zài Guóháng de fúwùtái . . .)

 Xiǎojiě, zhè shì wǒmen de¹ jīpiào.

 Qǐng bǎ hùzhào gěi wǒ kàn kan. Nǐmen yǒu jǐ jiàn

xíngli yào tuōyùn?

 Liǎng jiàn. Zhè ge bāo bù tuōyùn, wǒmen dài

shàng fēijī.

 Máfan ᵃ nín bǎ xiāngzi ná shàng lai².

 Xiǎojiě, méi chāozhòng ba?

 Méiyǒu. Zhè shì nǐmen de hùzhào, jīpiào, zhè shì

dēngjīpái ᵇ. Qǐng dào wǔ hào dēngjīkǒu ᶜ

shàng fēijī.

 Xièxie.

. . .

 Gēge, nǐmen qù Běijīng le, jiù wǒ yí ge rén

zài zhèr.

 Xiǎo Hóng, bié kū, wǒmen jǐ ge xīngqī jiù huí lai,

nǐ hǎohāor de¹ xué Yīngwén, bié luàn pǎo.

 Bú shì jǐ ge xīngqī jiù huí lai, shì jǐ ge xīngqī yǐhòu

cái huí lai.

 Bié dān xīn, wǒ jiějie Xiǎoyīn huì zhàogu nǐ.

 Duì, bié dān xīn.

 Fēijī jǐ diǎn qǐfēi?

 Zhōngwǔ shí'èr diǎn, hái yǒu liǎng ge duō xiǎoshí.

 Bái Yīng'ài, nǐ shénme shíhou qù Niǔyuē shíxí?

 Wǒ bú qù Niǔyuē le. Wénzhōng bāng wǒ zài

Jiāzhōu zhǎo le yí fèn shíxí gōngzuò.

 Duì, wǒmen xià ge xīngqī kāi chē qù Jiāzhōu.

 Shì ma? Yìbiānr kāi chē, yìbiānr wánr, tài hǎo le.

 Kāi chē xiǎoxīn. Zhù nǐmen wánr de¹ gāoxìng.

 Zhù nǐmen yí lù píng'ān. Dào le Běijīng yǐhòu³,

bié wàng le gěi wǒmen fā ge diànzǐ yóujiàn.

 Hǎo, nà wǒmen qiūtiān jiàn.

 Xià ge xuéqī jiàn.

 Zàijiàn!

Language Notes

a 麻烦 *(máfan)*

When asking others for help, one polite way is to use 麻烦 *(máfan)* as a verb and begin the request with the phrase 麻烦你 *(máfan nǐ)* or 麻烦您 *(máfan nín)*, e.g.: 麻烦您今天晚上给我打一个电话 *(Máfan nín jīntiān wǎnshang gěi wǒ dǎ yí ge diàn huà)* (Could I trouble you to give me a call this evening?).

b 登机牌 *(dēngjīpái)*

In Chinese, a boarding pass can be referred to as either 登机牌 *(dēngjīpái)* (lit. boarding card) or 登机证 *(dēngjīzhèng)* (lit. boarding certificate).

c 登机口 *(dēngjīkǒu)*

In Mainland China, boarding gates are called 登机口 *(dēngjīkǒu)*. In Taiwan and Hong Kong, they are called 登机门 *(dēngjīmén)* and 闸口 *(zhákǒu)*, respectively.

Vocabulary

No.	Word	Pinyin	Part of Speech	Definition
1	行李	xíngli	n	luggage
2	托运	tuōyùn	v	to check (luggage)
3	包	bāo	n	bag, sack, bundle, package
4	箱子	xiāngzi	n	suitcase, box
5	超重	chāozhòng	v	to be overweight (of luggage, freight, etc.)
	超	chāo	v	to exceed, to surpass
6	登机牌	dēngjīpái	n	boarding pass
	牌	pái	n	plate, tablet, card
7	登机口	dēngjīkǒu	n	boarding gate
	口	kǒu	n	opening, entrance, mouth
8	哭	kū	v	to cry, to weep
9	地	de	p	(particle to link adverbial and verb) [See Grammar 1.]
10	照顾	zhàogu	v	to look after, to care for, to attend to
11	起飞	qǐfēi	v	(of airplanes) to take off
12	小心	xiǎoxīn	v	to be careful
13	一路平安	yí lù píng'ān		have a good trip, bon voyage

Audio

Flashcards

Chinese knots (中国结) (*Zhōngguójié*) like this can be given as gifts for good luck. When would be an appropriate occasion for you to give this knot to someone?

GET Real WITH CHINESE

坐飞机旅行，什么东西你不托运？

Zuò fēijī lǚxíng, shénme dōngxi nǐ bù tuōyùn?

What items do you not check in when traveling by plane?

How About You?

我不会托运 _____。

Wǒ bú huì tuōyùn _____.

See index for corresponding vocabulary or research another term.

Grammar

<u>1</u>   **Comparing 的 (de), 得 (de), and 地 (de)**

的 (de) usually follows an attributive, which can be formed by an adjective, a noun, or a verb phrase.

A   漂亮的女孩子

piàoliang de nǚ háizi

pretty girl

B   哥哥的公司

gēge de gōngsī

older brother's company

C   我的卧室

wǒ de wòshì

my bedroom

D   刚买的机票

gāng mǎi de jīpiào

a recently purchased plane ticket

E   妈妈给我们做的蛋糕

māma gěi wǒmen zuò de dàngāo

the cake Mom made for us

In most cases, 的 (de) is followed by a noun, as seen in (A) to (E), but it can also precede an adjective or verb if that adjective or verb serves as the subject or object in the sentence.

F   南京的热[是有名的]。

Nánjīng de rè [shì yǒumíng de].

Nanjing's hot weather [is well known].

G   他的死[让我们很难受]。

Tā de sǐ [ràng wǒmen hěn nánshòu].

His death [made us very sad].

地 (de) usually links an adverbial to a following verb. An adverbial can be an adjective, an adverb, or a set phrase, and is not always followed by 地 (de).

H	慢慢儿（地）吃	J	一直（地）走
	mànmānr de chī		*yìzhí de zǒu*
	eat slowly		to walk straight forward

I	很高兴地说	K	好好儿（地）玩儿
	hěn gāoxìng de shuō		*hǎohāor de wánr*
	to say happily		to have some real fun

得 (*de*) is used after a verb or an adjective to connect it with a descriptive complement or a complement of degree.

L	跑得很快	N	高兴得跳起来
	pǎo de hěn kuài		*gāoxìng de tiào qi lai*
	to run fast		to jump up with joy

M	做菜做得很好	O	危险得不得了
	zuò cài zuò de hěn hǎo		*wēixiǎn de bùdéliǎo*
	to cook well		unbelievably dangerous

Compare the following two sentences:

P 他高兴地唱着歌走回宿舍。

Tā gāoxìng de chàng zhe gē zǒu huí sùshè.

He sang happily on his way back to the dorm.

Q 他高兴得唱起歌来了。

Tā gāoxìng de chàng qǐ gē lai le.

He was so happy that he started to sing.

In (P), 高兴 (gāoxìng) is used to describe the manner of his singing. In (Q), 高兴 (gāoxìng) is the cause of his singing. Patterns for 的 (de), 地 (de), and 得 (de) are provided below.

Attributive + 的 (de) + noun
Adverbial + 地 (de) + verb
Verb/adjective + 得 (de) + adjective/verb

EXERCISES

Fill in the blanks with 的, 得, or 地 where appropriate. Use exercise 1 as an example.

1 公寓 _____ 房租贵 _____ 不得了。

→ 公寓的房租贵得不得了。

2 要是希望游泳游 _____ 又快又好，得每天好好儿 _____ 练习。

3 他托运 _____ 行李被慢慢 _____ 送上飞机。

---

2 | **The 把 (bǎ) construction (II)**

You can use 把 (bǎ) with a directional complement. The basic constructions are as follows.

把 (bǎ) **with simple directional complements:**

Pattern A
Subject + 把 + object + verb + 来/去
(bǎ)   (lai/qu)

| A | 请把你的床搬来。 |

Qǐng bǎ nǐ de chuáng bān lai.

Please move your bed here.

| B | 小王把冰茶拿去了。 |

Xiǎo Wáng bǎ bīngchá ná qu le.

Little Wang took the iced tea (with him).

Pattern B

Subject + 把 + object + verb + 上／下／进／出／回／过／起／开／到 + place word

(bǎ)　　　　　　　　　　　(shang/xia/jin/chu/hui/guo/qi/kai/dao)

C 你把孩子送回爷爷家。

Nǐ bǎ háizi sòng hui yéye jiā.

Take the child back to Grandpa's.

D 妈妈把椅子搬上楼了。

Māma bǎ yǐzi bān shang lóu le.

Mom took the chair upstairs.

Note that place words come after the verb and directional complement.

把 *(bǎ)* with compound directional complements:

Pattern A

Subject + 把 + object + verb + 上／下／进／出／回／过／起／开 + 来／去

(bǎ)　　　　　　　　　(shang/xia/jin/chu/hui/guo/qi/kai)　(lai/qu)

E 你把书拿起来。　　　　　**F** 小李把车开回去了。

Nǐ bǎ shū ná qi lai .　　　　　　*Xiǎo Lǐ bǎ chē kāi hui qu le.*

Pick up the book.　　　　　　　Little Li drove the car back.

Pattern B

Subject + 把 + object + verb + 上／下／进／出／回／过／起／到 + place word + 来／去

(bǎ)　　　　　　　　(shang/xia/jin/chu/hui/guo/qi/dao)　　　　(lai/qu)

G 麻烦把包拿上桌来。

Máfan bǎ bāo ná shang zhuō lai.

Please put the bag on the table.

| H | 他把刚买的桌子搬进房间来了。 |

Tā bǎ gang mǎi de zhuōzi bān jin fáng jiān lai le.

He moved the table that he had just bought into the room.

Note that the place word is inserted in the compound directional complement, between 上/下/进/出/回/过/起/到 (shang/xia/jin/chu/hui/guo/qi/dao) and 来/去 (lai/qu).

---

3 | ···的时候 (... de shíhou) **and** ···以后 (... yǐhòu) **compared**

With "Verb 1 + 的时候 (de shíhou), verb 2 ...," the second action and the first action take place simultaneously.

| A | 走的时候别忘了带些钱。 |

Zǒu de shíhou bié wàng le dài xiē qián.

Don't forget to take some money with you when you leave.

| B | 我看见他的时候，他正在打球。 |

Wǒ kàn jiàn tā de shíhou, tā zhèngzài dǎ qiú.

When I saw him, he was playing ball.

| C | 妹妹看短信的时候，一边看一边笑。 |

Mèimei kàn duǎnxìn de shíhou, yìbiān kàn yìbiān xiào.

When my little sister was reading the text messages, she laughed as she read along.

However, with "Verb 1 以后 (yǐhòu), verb 2 ...," the second action takes place after the first one.

| D | 他从家里走了以后，才想起来忘了带钱。 |

Tā cóng jiā li zǒu le yǐhòu, cái xiǎng qi lai wàng le dài qián.

He didn't realize until after he had left home that he'd forgotten to take some money with him.

The "···的时候 (*...de shíhou*)" structure describes two simultaneous actions. You may say in English, "When I get to China, I will eat Beijing roast duck," when you really mean, "After I get to China, I'll eat Beijing roast duck." In Chinese, that idea has to be conveyed with 以后 (*yǐhòu*):

E 我到中国以后要吃北京烤鸭。

Wǒ dào Zhōngguó yǐhòu yào chī Běijīng kǎoyā.

I will eat some Beijing roast duck after I arrive in China.

[烤鸭 *[kǎoyā]* [roast duck]. See Dialogue 2.]

[⊗ 我到中国的时候要吃北京烤鸭。]

(This sentence is incorrect because you won't eat Beijing roast duck until after you arrive in China.)

More exercises

EXERCISES

Fill in the blanks with ···的时候 or ···以后 where appropriate. Use exercise 1 as an example.

1　开车 ＿＿＿＿＿＿＿ 发短信太危险了。

　　→ 开车的时候发短信太危险了。

2　旅行 ＿＿＿＿＿＿＿ 小王不喜欢带太多行李。

3　大家约好打完球 ＿＿＿＿＿＿＿ 去喝咖啡。

Characterize it!

More characters

What do the characters mean?

What is the common radical?

What does the radical mean?

How does the radical relate to the overall meaning of the characters?

Language Practice

A | **Playing by the rules** | PRESENTATIONAL

Multitasking can be problematic. In pairs, use the visual prompts to figure out what the rules are in the various contexts provided, e.g.:

做功课的时候，不准/不能
看电视。

Zuò gōngkè de shíhou, bù zhǔn/bù néng kàn diànshì.

1

2

3

4

B | **Could I trouble you?** | INTERPERSONAL

In pairs, take turns asking for help from each other using 麻烦你 (*máfan nǐ*). Think of three or four things you would like your partner to help you with, e.g.:

Q: 麻烦你帮我准备考试，好吗？
Máfan nǐ bāng wǒ zhǔnbèi kǎoshì, hǎo ma?

A: 行，没问题。
Xíng, méi wèntí.

Big move

You (living on the second floor) and your housemate (living on the third floor) decided to switch rooms with each other. Based on the image below, describe which items need to be moved upstairs and downstairs. For things to be moved upstairs, you should say 把＿＿＿＿搬/拿上（楼）去 (Bǎ ＿＿＿＿ bān/ná shang [lóu] qu); for things to be moved downstairs, you should say 把＿＿＿＿搬/拿下（楼）来 (Bǎ ＿＿＿＿ bān/ná xia [lóu] lai).

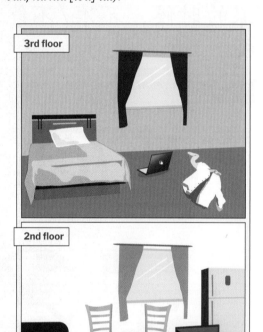

3rd floor

2nd floor

Before

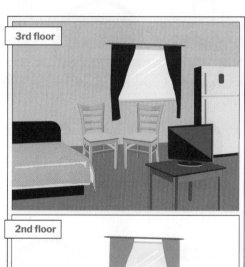
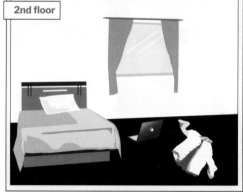

3rd floor

2nd floor

After

1

2

3

4

5

6

7

Positive energy

PRESENTATIONAL

In pairs, use the prompts to practice giving warm, occasion-appropriate wishes to your partner, e.g.:

On his/her birthday

生日快乐！

Shēngrì kuàilè!

1　Before he/she gets on a plane
2　On New Year's Day
3　Before he/she takes an examination
4　Before he/she goes on a fun date

Don't stress

PRESENTATIONAL

In pairs, use the prompts to practice giving reassurance to your partner about his/her vexing situation, e.g.:

Your friend is quite anxious before an exam.

别担心，明天的考试很简单。

Bié dān xīn, míngtiān de kǎoshì hěn jiǎndān.

1　Your friend hopes his/her dog will be cared for while he/she is away.
2　Your friend isn't sure if his/her date will like him/her.
3　Your friend is worried he/she won't be able to afford clothes at a store.
4　Your friend thinks that his/her baggage might be overweight.

In proper order

INTERPERSONAL

In pairs, form a question-and-answer to find out when Wang Peng takes a shower, takes his medicine, goes online, and cleans his room, e.g.:

Q: 王朋什么时候做功课？吃饭以前
还是吃饭以后？

Wáng Péng shénme shíhou zuò gōngkè? Chī fàn yǐqián háishi chī fàn yǐhòu?

A: 他吃了晚饭以后做功课。

Tā chī le wǎnfàn yǐhòu zuò gōngkè.

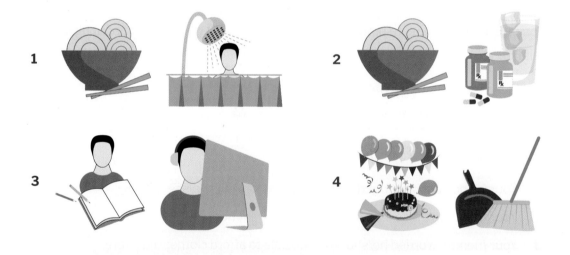

Don't do anything I wouldn't do

INTERPERSONAL

Survey each of your classmates about his/her summer plans and how long the activities he/she has planned will last. Remind him/her to keep in touch, and give appropriate good wishes before moving on to the next person.

Counter culture

Unlike Li You, you may not have a Chinese friend to accompany you on your trip to China and be your interpreter or tour guide. In pairs, make a list of questions and responses that may come in handy when you check in at a Chinese airline counter.

Chinese Chat

Your friend is going on a trip and is texting you to say goodbye. How would you respond?

Marian

我已经登机，飞机马上就起飞了。谢谢你开车送我来机场，回去路上开车小心。

7 minutes ago

...
6 minutes ago

对了，也请多照顾我的狗。我到了香港再给你发短信。暑假快乐！

3 minutes ago

...
1 minute ago

Type your message...

Arriving in Beijing

Dialogue 2

Audio

Video

（在北京首都机场……）

小朋！

爸，妈！

累坏了吧？

还好[4]。爸，妈，我给你们介绍一下，这是我的同学李友。

叔叔，阿姨[5a]，你们好。

欢迎你来北京。

李友，你的中文说得真好。

谢谢。是因为王朋教得好。

哪里，是因为你聪明。

哎，你们俩都聪明。

小朋，你好像瘦了点儿。是不是打工太忙，没有时间吃饭？

我没瘦。我常常运动，身体比以前棒多了。

小红怎么样？

她很好，英文水平提高了很多。

走吧，我们上车以后，再慢慢儿地聊吧。
爷爷、奶奶在烤鸭店等我们呢！

烤鸭店？

(Zài Běijīng Shǒudū Jīchǎng . . .)

 Xiǎo Péng!

 Bà, mā !

 Lèi huài le ba?

 Hái hǎo⁴. Bà, mā, wǒ gěi nǐmen jièshao yí xià, zhè

shì wǒ de tóngxué Lǐ Yǒu.

 Shūshu, āyí ⁵ ᵃ, nǐmen hǎo.

 Huānyíng nǐ lái Běijīng.

 Lǐ Yǒu, nǐ de Zhōngwén shuō de zhēn hǎo.

 Xièxie. Shì yīnwèi Wáng Péng jiāo de hǎo.

 Nǎli, shì yīnwèi nǐ cōngming.

 Āi, nǐmen liǎ dōu cōngming.

 Xiǎo Péng, nǐ hǎoxiàng shòu le diǎnr. Shì bu shì

dǎ gōng tài máng, méiyǒu shíjiān chī fàn?

 Wǒ méi shòu. Wǒ chángcháng yùndòng, shēntǐ bǐ

yǐqián bàng duō le.

 Xiǎo Hóng zěnmeyàng?

 Tā hěn hǎo, Yīngwén shuǐpíng tígāo le hěn duō.

 Zǒu ba, wǒmen shàng chē yǐhòu, zài mànmānr de

liáo ba. Yéye, nǎinai zài kǎoyā diàn děng wǒmen ne!

 Kǎoyā diàn?

Language Note

a 叔叔 (shūshu) **and** 阿姨 (āyí)

Young people often address a nonrelative as 叔叔
(shūshu) (uncle) or 阿姨 (āyí) (aunt) if the person
is approximately the same age as their parents. These
respectful forms of address can be applied even to
strangers. [See Grammar 5 for additional terms for kin.]

Vocabulary

Audio

Flashcards

No.	Word	Pinyin	Part of Speech	Definition
1	叔叔	*shūshu*	n	uncle [See Grammar 5.]
2	阿姨	*āyí*	n	aunt [See Grammar 5.]
3	欢迎	*huānyíng*	v	to welcome
4	瘦	*shòu*	adj	thin, skinny, lean
5	爷爷	*yéye*	n	paternal grandfather [See Grammar 5.]
6	奶奶	*nǎinai*	n	paternal grandmother [See Grammar 5.]
7	烤鸭	*kǎoyā*	n	roast duck
8	首都机场	*Shǒudū Jīchǎng*	pn	the Capital Airport (in Beijing)

等飞机的时候，
你常常做什么？

Děng fēijī de shíhou, nǐ chángcháng zuò shénme?

What do you often do when waiting for a flight?

我 _____ 。

Wǒ _____ .

How About You?

See index for corresponding vocabulary or research another term.

Grammar

4   还 *(hái)* + positive adjective

还 *(hái)* can be used before a positive adjective to indicate that something is acceptable but not truly outstanding.

A   **Q:** 你对那家旅馆的印象怎么样?

Nǐ duì nà jiā lǚguǎn de yìnxiàng zěnmeyàng?

What was your impression of that hotel?

     A: 还好。

Hái hǎo.

It's okay.

B   这个厨房还可以，挺干净的。

Zhè ge chúfáng hái kěyǐ, tǐng gānjìng de.

This kitchen is all right. It's pretty clean.

C   那套公寓还行，带家具。

Nà tào gōngyù hái xíng, dài jiājù.

That apartment is not too bad. It's furnished.

D   那个饭馆的红烧牛肉和家常豆腐
还不错。

Nà ge fànguǎn de hóngshāo niúròu hé jiācháng dòufu hái búcuò.

That restaurant's beef braised in soy sauce and home-style tofu
are pretty good.

More exercises

EXERCISES

In pairs, form a question-and-answer and indicate something is okay but not great.

Use exercise 1 as an example.

1   这个电影　　好看　可以

→ **Student A** 这个电影好看吗？

Student B 还可以。

2   这碗酸辣汤　好喝　可以

3   这盘饺子　　好吃　不错

4   这儿的地铁　方便　行

GET **Real** WITH **CHINESE**

This ad for an all-inclusive tour package promises a few tour highlights. What aspects of the trip are covered?

9天晶鑽北京江南

2016年3月1日起，逢週五抵達北京

成人 18歲以上	18歲以下不佔床（不包早餐）	18歲以下佔床（包早餐）	單人房附加費	指定自費節目（大小同價）
$99	$99	$399	$300	$150
酒店延住（雙人房/每晚）：$110			額外接/送機（2人起）：$	

不包括北京—南京高鐵$100，北京/南京機票$140（大小同價）

DAY 4 北京-南京（週一）

住宿國際品牌:
南京鉑爾曼酒店或同級
Pullman Nanjing

早餐後搭乘高鐵或飛機前往南京，遊覽【東水關城墙遺址】，接著遊覽莊嚴肅穆的【中山陵】，享用著名的南京特產風味--南京鹽水鴨，餐後夜遊【夫子廟】十裏秦淮河。當晚品嘗【煙波漁港】正宗淮揚風味（指定自費節目）。

（早，午，晚）

DAY 7 蘇州-杭州

住宿國際品牌:
杭州皇冠假日
Holiday Inn Crow

早餐後前往蘇州絲綢廠
"天寶之物" 絲綢繰絲
【乘船遊覽西湖】（指
魚）、【柳浪聞鶯】等
前往杭州龍井茶園，品
于杭幫菜博物館品嘗
費節目）。

DAY 杭州

5 | Kinship terms

The system of kinship terms in Chinese is rather complicated, especially because Chinese people distinguish between paternal and maternal relatives, older and younger siblings, etc. The following tables provide Chinese kinship terms. Note that [n] indicates northern usage, [s] indicates southern usage, and [f] indicates a more formal form of address.

Parents

English	Chinese	Pinyin
father, dad	爸爸	bàba
	父亲[f]	fùqin
mother, mom	妈妈	māmā
	母亲[f]	mǔqin

Grandparents

English	Chinese	Pinyin
[paternal] grandfather	爷爷	yéye
	祖父[f]	zǔfù
[paternal] grandmother	奶奶	nǎinai
	祖母[f]	zǔmǔ
[maternal] grandfather	姥爷[n]	lǎoye
	外公[s]	wàigōng
	外祖父[f]	wàizǔfù
[maternal] grandmother	姥姥[n]	lǎolao
	外婆[s]	wàipó
	外祖母[f]	wàizǔmǔ

Uncles and aunts

English	Chinese	Pinyin
father's older brother	伯伯	bóbo
	伯父[f]	bófù
father's older brother's wife	大妈	dàmā
	大娘[n]	dàniáng
	伯母[f]	bómǔ
father's younger brother	叔叔	shūshu
	叔父[f]	shūfù
father's younger brother's wife	婶婶	shěnshen
	婶儿[n]	shěnr
father's sister	姑姑	gūgu
	姑妈	gūmā
father's sister's husband	姑父[f]	gūfù
	姑丈	gūzhàng
mother's brother	舅舅	jiùjiu
mother's brother's wife	舅妈	jiùmā
mother's sister	姨[n]	yí
	阿姨	āyí
	姨妈	yímā
mother's sister's husband	姨父[f]	yífu
	姨丈	yízhàng

Brothers, sisters, and their spouses

English	Chinese	Pinyin
older brother	哥哥	*gēge*
older brother's wife	嫂子	*sǎozi*
	嫂嫂	*sǎosao*
older sister	姐姐	*jiějie*
older sister's husband	姐夫	*jiěfu*
younger brother	弟弟	*dìdi*
younger brother's wife	弟妹	*dìmèi*
younger sister	妹妹	*mèimei*
younger sister's husband	妹夫	*mèifu*

Cousins

English	Chinese	Pinyin
father's brother's son (older than you)	堂哥	*tánggē*
father's brother's son (younger than you)	堂弟	*tángdì*
father's brother's daughter (older than you)	堂姐	*tángjiě*
father's brother's daughter (younger than you)	堂妹	*tángmèi*
other male cousin (older than you)	表哥	*biǎogē*
other male cousin (younger than you)	表弟	*biǎodì*
other female cousin (older than you)	表姐	*biǎojiě*
other female cousin (younger than you)	表妹	*biǎomèi*

Children and their spouses

English	Chinese	Pinyin
son	儿子	érzi
son's wife	儿媳妇	érxífu
daughter	女儿	nǚ'ér
daughter's husband	女婿	nǚxu

Grandchildren

English	Chinese	Pinyin
son's son	孙子	sūnzi
son's daughter	孙女	sūnnǚ
daughter's son	外孙	wàisūn
daughter's daughter	外孙女	wàisūnnǚ

More exercises

EXERCISES

Identify kinship terms. Use exercise 1 as an example.

1   妈妈的姐姐我们叫阿姨。

2   妈妈的弟弟我们叫 _____。

3   爸爸的妈妈我们叫 _____。

Language Practice

| ! | **Being diplomatic** | INTERPERSONAL |

Your friend has returned from the store with a substantial amount of final-sale merchandise. She wants your opinion on what she's bought. You don't want to hurt her feelings, so you try to be tactful, e.g.:

Friend 你觉得我的大衣怎么样?

Nǐ juéde wǒ de dàyī zěnmeyàng?

You 我觉得你的大衣还不错/还行。

Wǒ juéde nǐ de dàyī hái búcuò/hái xíng.

1

2

3

Characterize it!

What do the characters mean?

What is the common radical?

What does the radical mean?

How does the radical relate to the overall meaning of the characters?

❶ 照 ❷ 烤 ❸ 烦 ❹ 烧 ❺ 灯

More characters

Puppy love

You've just adopted a puppy that you've decided to name 毛毛 *(Máomao)*. At the vet's office, you want to express your concerns that something is wrong with the puppy, e.g.:

thin

哎，我觉得毛毛好像瘦了。

Āi, wǒ juéde Máomao hǎoxiàng shòu le.

1 tired

2 fat

3 hungry

4 has a cold

5 has a fever

Bon voyage

In pairs, list the things that people say to each other when saying goodbye at the airport or train station, e.g. "Have a safe trip," "Give us a call when you get there," "I'll be back soon," and "Don't worry, I'll be fine." Then sequence the phrases in a logical order. Based on your list, role-play a seeing-off scenario.

Welcome

In pairs, list the things that people say to each other when greeting guests at the airport/train station, e.g. "Welcome to . . . ," "Thank you for picking me up," "You must be exhausted after a long trip," "I'm okay, not too tired," and "Let me help you with your luggage." Then sequence the phrases in a logical order. Based on your list, do a role-play between a guest and a person who comes to pick up the guest.

Chinese Chat

Li You just posted about her trip to Beijing on Instagram. What were some of the highlights?

Instagram

 李友   20min

            o o o

❤ 75 likes

李友 到了北京以后，每天都有人请吃饭。中国菜真好吃，我特别爱吃素饺子！北京城里、城外都好玩儿极了，我觉得最有意思的名胜古迹是长城。

20 MINUTES AGO

| Comment

文化

Continue
to explore

FLYING
domestic

On domestic flights in China, each passenger is allowed to check only one piece of luggage for free. Snacks or meals are often served on domestic flights.

In addition to 一路平安 *(yí lù píng'ān)* (lit. be peaceful and safe all the way), other expressions in Chinese can be used to wish someone a good journey: 旅途愉快 *(lǚtú yúkuài)* and 旅途快乐 *(lǚtú kuàilè)* mean "happy travels" (lit. be happy on the road), and 一路顺风 *(yí lù shùnfēng)* literally means "to travel with a favorable wind all the way." While this expression is frequently heard at railroad stations, some people choose not to use it at airports, for fear of jinxing the flight.

A structure impressive in both size and design, Beijing Daxing International Airport (the capital's second international airport) opened in 2019. It was designed with sustainability in mind, and the airport's economic zone earned a LEED Platinum Certification. Daxing Airport is one of the world's largest airports, and it is expected to become the world's busiest airport in the future.

This signboard at Shanghai Hongqiao International Airport shows a selection of popular domestic destinations, including Sanya (三亚) *(Sānyà)*, famous for its sandy beaches, and Chengdu (成都) *(Chéngdū)*, renowned for its spicy food. Which of these places would you like to visit, and why?

COMPARE & CONTRAST

Despite the destructive impact on traditional Chinese culture of twentieth-century social upheavals, especially the Cultural Revolution (1966–1976), the importance of family and family values has not changed for the Chinese people. In Dialogue 2 of the lesson, Wang Peng's mother says to her son after not seeing him for nearly a year, 你好像瘦了点儿 *(Nǐ hǎoxiàng shòu le diǎnr)* (You seem to have lost some weight). That is not true, according to Wang Peng. What is true, however, is the mother's love for the son and concern for his health. Would your mother say something like that in a similar situation? What are the typical expressions of love from your parents when you see them after an extended separation?

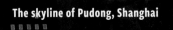

The skyline of Pudong, Shanghai

The skyline of Chaoyang District, Beijing, with the CCTV Headquarters at center

Beijing roast duck

Originally a delicacy on imperial menus, Beijing roast duck boasts a history several centuries long. Now it is arguably the food item most emblematic of the culinary culture of northern China. Indeed, its reputation is well reflected in the Chinese saying that no visit to Beijing is complete without a trip to the Great Wall and a meal at a roast duck restaurant. The most famous roast duck restaurant in Beijing is 全聚德 (*Quánjùdé*), which was established in 1864.

Lesson Wrap-Up

Rearrange the following sentences into a logical sequence. Then combine the sentences into a coherent narrative. Substitute nouns with pronouns and change periods to commas where necessary. Avoid unnecessary repetitions of identical subject pronouns. Add the connective devices 和 (hé), 因为…也…所以… (yīnwèi…yě…suǒyǐ…), 也 (yě), and 祝 (zhù) where appropriate.

__1__ 王朋和李友要去北京。

_____ 王朋和李友要到五号登机口上飞机。

_____ 王朋让妹妹好好儿学英文。

_____ 高文中说小音会照顾王红。

_____ 白英爱和高文中下个星期要去加州。

_____ 白英爱祝王朋和李友一路平安。

_____ 这几个好朋友要秋天再见。

_____ 王朋和李友在机场托运了两件行李。

_____ 王红来送王朋和李友。

_____ 高文中来送王朋和李友。

_____ 白英爱来送王朋和李友。

_____ 王红的爸爸、妈妈在北京。

_____ 王红的哥哥也要去北京。

_____ 王红哭了。

_____ 白英爱告诉李友高文中在加州给她找了一个实习的工作。

_____ 王朋祝他们玩儿得高兴。

Off to China

You're going to study in China for a semester and are at the Air China counter at the airport. A ground representative for Air China helps you check in and asks to see your ticket and passport. You search for them and in a moment of panic, think you might have left them at home. Luckily, they are in your bag under a Chinese textbook. He/she asks how many pieces of baggage you are checking. You answer that question. You also want to know if your luggage is overweight. You are reassured that it is not, and receive your passport back and the boarding pass. You want to know the gate number and boarding time. After the Air China representative gives you the information, you thank him/her. He/she wishes you a safe trip.

Welcome to China!

Your host father, Mr. Wang, is holding a placard with your name written on it outside the arrival gate. You greet Mr. Wang and introduce yourself. Mr. Wang welcomes you to Beijing. You have brought your host family a small gift and you give it to Mr. Wang, who thanks you and compliments you on your Chinese. You are too modest to accept Mr. Wang's praise. You ask him if his home is far from the airport. Mr. Wang says it is not close, but it's very convenient by subway. You tell him you have two bags, so Mr. Wang decides to get a taxi. Since it's nearly dinner time, Mr. Wang is taking you to the most famous Peking duck restaurant in the capital!

Supplemental Reading Practice

For additional reading practice that builds on the vocabulary introduced in this lesson, turn to the supplemental readings that begin on page 419.

Can-Do Check List ✓ **I can**

Before proceeding to the next volume, make sure you can complete the following tasks in Chinese:

- ☐ Check in for a flight and check my luggage
- ☐ Wish others a safe journey
- ☐ Greet out-of-town guests at the airport
- ☐ Compliment someone's language ability
- ☐ Express concern about someone's health
- ☐ Remind people to move on to the next engagement

Keeping It Casual (Lessons 16–20)

Before you progress to the next volume, we'll review how some of the functional expressions from Lessons 16–20 are used in casual Chinese. After you complete the review, note any other casual expressions you would like to learn; then share the list with your teacher.

<u>1</u> | 一言为定 *(yì yán wéi dìng)* **(it's a deal, it's decided)**

Say 一言为定 *(yì yán wéi dìng)* when you and your friends or business partners have reached a decision. It indicates that you and the other parties pledge to remember and honor the decision.

A   **Gao Wenzhong**

明年我们去中国，怎么样？

Míngnián wǒmen qù Zhōngguó, zěnmeyàng?

We'll go to China next year. How about it?

     Bai Ying'ai

好啊！

Hǎo a!

That's great.

     Gao Wenzhong

一言为定。

Yì yán wéi dìng.

That settles it.

B   **Wang Peng**

考完试我们出去玩儿，好吗？

Kǎo wán shì wǒmen chū qu wánr, hǎo ma?

After the exam let's go out and have some fun, all right?

     Li You

太好了。你开车？

Tài hǎo le. Nǐ kāi chē?

Wonderful! Will you drive?

     Wang Peng

没问题。

Méi wèntí.

No problem.

     Li You

一言为定。

Yì yán wéi dìng.

It's a deal.

     Wang Peng

一言为定。

Yì yán wéi dìng.

Deal.

2 | Good, very good, excellent, and extraordinary

Here are some expressions to convey varying degrees of approval, in progressive order of intensity.

A　他的中文不错。

Tā de Zhōngwén búcuò.

His Chinese is quite good.

B　他的中文很好。

Tā de Zhōngwén hěn hǎo.

His Chinese is very good.

C　他的中文好得很。

Tā de Zhōngwén hǎo de hěn.

His Chinese is very, very good.

D　他的中文非常好。

Tā de Zhōngwén fēicháng hǎo.

His Chinese is unusually good.

E　他的中文好极了。

Tā de Zhōngwén hǎo jí le.

His Chinese is fantastic.

F　他的中文好得不得了。

Tā de Zhōngwén hǎo de bùdéliǎo.

His Chinese is extraordinary.

3 | Greetings

Say these to greet people in different contexts.

A　您好，老师！

Nín hǎo, lǎoshī!

Hello, professor!

B　王先生，早上好！

Wáng xiānsheng, zǎoshang hǎo!

Good morning, Mr. Wang!

C　早！

Zǎo!

Good morning!

In daily life, however, a common way to greet an acquaintance is by asking a casual question about what that person is doing at the moment:

D 老李，上课去呀？

Lǎo Lǐ, shàng kè qu ya?

Old Li, going to class? (It looks like Old Li is going to class.)

E 小王，回家呀？

Xiǎo Wáng, huí jiā ya?

Little Wang, going home? (Upon seeing someone wrapping up his/her things and leaving the office, or someone on his/her way home, for instance.)

F 爸，回来了？

Bà, huí lai le?

Dad, you're home? (Upon seeing one's father walking in the door, for instance.)

4   Farewells

Say these to bid someone farewell.

A 再见!

Zàijiàn!

Bye!

B 明天见!

Míngtiān jiàn!

See you tomorrow!

C 回头见!

Huí tóu jiàn!

See you later!

D 慢走!

Màn zǒu!

Take it easy! (Lit. Walk slowly!)

Mealtime expressions

Say these upon finishing a meal before others or before everyone starts eating.

A	慢吃！

Màn chī!

Take your time (to enjoy the meal)!

B	慢用！

Màn yòng!

Enjoy the meal!

The Chinese-English index is alphabetized according to *pinyin*. Words containing the same Chinese characters are first grouped together. Homonyms appear in the order of their tonal pronunciation (i.e., first tones first, second tones second, third tones third, fourth tones fourth, and neutral tones last).

Simplified	Traditional	Pinyin	Part of Speech	English	Lesson
			A		
啊		*a*	p	(a sentence-final particle of exclamation, interrogation, etc.)	6
阿姨		*āyí*	n	aunt	20
艾	哎	*āi*	excl	(exclamatory particle to express surprise or dissatisfaction)	13
爱	愛	*ài*	v	to love, to like, to be fond of	14
安静	安靜	*ānjìng*	adj	quiet	17
			B		
把		*bǎ*	m	(measure word for things with handles, for handfuls of things)	14
把		*bǎ*	prep	(indicating disposition, arrangement, or settlement of something)	15
爸爸		*bàba*	n	father, dad	2
吧		*ba*	p	(a sentence-final particle)	5
白英爱	白英愛	*Bái Yīng'ài*	pn	(a personal name)	2
百		*bǎi*	nu	hundred	9
班		*bān*	n	class	14
搬		*bān*	v	to move	16
半		*bàn*	nu	half, half an hour	3
半天		*bàntiān*		half a day, a long time	18
办	辦	*bàn*	v	to handle, to do	11

Simplified	Traditional	Pinyin	Part of Speech	English	Lesson
办法	辦法	bànfǎ	n	method, way (of doing something)	15
办公室	辦公室	bàngōngshì	n	office	6
帮	幫	bāng	v	to help	6
棒		bàng	adj	fantastic, super [colloq.]	18
包		bāo	n	bag, sack, bundle, package	20
保险	保險	bǎoxiǎn	n/adj	insurance; secure	15
抱		bào	v	to hold or carry in the arms	18
报纸	報紙	bàozhǐ	n	newspaper	17
杯		bēi	m	(measure word for things contained in a cup or glass)	5
北		běi	n	north	13
北京		Běijīng	pn	Beijing	1
被		bèi	prep	by	18
本		běn	m	(measure word for books)	14
鼻子		bízi	n	nose	14
笔	筆	bǐ	n	pen	7
比		bǐ	prep/v	compared with (comparison marker); to compare	11
比赛	比賽	bǐsài	n/v	game, match, competition; to compete	18
遍		biàn	m	(measure word for complete courses of an action or instances of an action)	15
表姐		biǎojiě	n	older female cousin	14
别	別	bié	adv	don't	6
别人	別人	biérén	n	other people, another person	4
冰茶	冰茶	bīngchá	n	iced tea	12
冰箱		bīngxiāng	n	refrigerator	15
病人		bìngrén	n	patient	15

Simplified	Traditional	Pinyin	Part of Speech	English	Lesson
不		*bù*	adv	not, no	1
不错	不錯	*búcuò [bùcuò]**	adj	pretty good	4
不但…，而且…		*búdàn…, érqiě… [bùdàn…, érqiě…]*	conj	not only …, but also …	11
不过	不過	*búguò [bùguò]*	conj	however, but	9
不好意思		*bù hǎoyìsi*		to feel embarrassed	10
不用		*bú yòng [bù yòng]*		need not	9

			C		
才		*cái*	adv	not until, only then	5
菜	菜	*cài*	n	dish, cuisine	3
餐厅	餐廳	*cāntīng*	n	dining room, cafeteria	8
厕所	廁所	*cèsuǒ*	n	restroom, toilet	15
茶	茶	*chá*	n	tea	5
查		*chá*	v	to check, to look into	19
差不多	差不多	*chàbuduō*	adv/adj	almost, nearly; similar	17
常常		*chángcháng*	adv	often	4
常老师	常老師	*Cháng lǎoshī*	pn	Teacher Chang	6
长城	長城	*Chángchéng*	pn	the Great Wall	19
长短	長短	*chángduǎn*	n	length	9
场	場	*chǎng*	n	field	13
唱歌（儿）	唱歌（兒）	*chàng gē(r)*	vo	to sing (a song)	4
超重		*chāozhòng*	v	to be overweight (of luggage, freight, etc.)	20
吵		*chǎo*	v/adj	to quarrel; noisy	17
衬衫	襯衫	*chènshān*	n	shirt	9

For vocabulary items starting with 不 or 一, we have included the *pinyin* with the stand-alone tone of these two characters in square brackets. However, the *pinyin* listed first indicates how the characters are conventionally pronounced as a lexical unit.

Simplified	Traditional	Pinyin	Part of Speech	English	Lesson
成		*chéng*	v	to become	16
城市		*chéngshì*	n	city	10
吃		*chī*	v	to eat	3
吃坏	吃壞	*chī huài*	vc	to get sick because of bad food	15
宠物	寵物	*chǒngwù*	n	pet	17
初		*chū*	n	beginning	19
出去		*chūqu*	vc	to go out	10
出租		*chūzū*	v	to rent out	17
出租汽车	出租汽車	*chūzū qìchē*	n	taxi	10
厨房	廚房	*chúfáng*	n	kitchen	17
除了…以外		*chúle . . . yǐwài*	conj	in addition to, besides	8
穿		*chuān*	v	to wear, to put on	9
窗户	窗戶	*chuānghu*	n	window	19
春天		*chūntiān*	n	spring	11
次		*cì*	m	(measure word for frequency)	13
聪明	聰明	*cōngming*	adj	smart, bright, clever	14
从	從	*cóng*	prep	from	13
错	錯	*cuò*	adj	wrong	12

D

Simplified	Traditional	Pinyin	Part of Speech	English	Lesson
打车	打車	*dǎ chē*	vo	to take a taxi	10
打电话	打電話	*dǎ diànhuà*	vo	to make a phone call	6
打工		*dǎ gōng*	vo	to work at a temporary job (often part time)	19
打球		*dǎ qiú*	vo	to play ball	4
打扫	打掃	*dǎsǎo*	v	to clean up (a room, apartment or house)	16

mplified	Traditional	Pinyin	Part of Speech	English	Lesson
丁算		*dǎsuàn*	v/n	to plan; plan	19
丁折		*dǎ zhé*	vo	to sell at a discount, to give a discount	19
丁针	打針	*dǎ zhēn*	vo	to get an injection	15
大		*dà*	adj	big, old	3
大哥		*dàgē*	n	eldest/oldest brother	2
大家		*dàjiā*	pr	everybody	7
大姐		*dàjiě*	n	eldest/oldest sister	2
大小		*dàxiǎo*	·n	size	9
大学生	大學生	*dàxuéshēng*	n	college student	2
节	帶	*dài*	v	to bring, to take, to carry, to come with	12
单程	單程	*dānchéng*	n	one-way trip	19
旦心	擔心	*dān xīn*	vo	to worry	18
蛋糕		*dàngāo*	n	cake	14
旦是		*dànshì*	conj	but	6
当	當	*dāng*	v	to serve as, to be	17
当然	當然	*dāngrán*	adv	of course	18
导游	導遊	*dǎoyóu*	n	tour guide	19
到		*dào*	v	to go to, to arrive	6
的		*de*	p	(a possessive or descriptive particle)	2
地		*de*	p	(particle to link adverbial and verb)	20
得		*de*	p	(a structural particle)	7
得		*děi*	av	must, to have to	6
登机口	登機口	*dēngjīkǒu*	n	boarding gate	20
登机牌	登機牌	*dēngjīpái*	n	boarding pass	20

Simplified	Traditional	Pinyin	Part of Speech	English	Lesso
等		*děng*	v	to wait, to wait for	6
第		*dì*	prefix	(prefix for ordinal numbers)	7
弟弟		*dìdi*	n	younger brother	2
地方		*dìfang*	n	place	13
地铁	地鐵	*dìtiě*	n	subway	10
地图	地圖	*dìtú*	n	map	13
点	點	*diǎn*	m	o'clock (lit. dot, point, thus "points on the clock")	3
点菜	點菜	*diǎn cài*	vo	to order food	12
点（儿）	點（兒）	*diǎn(r)*	m	a little, a bit, some	5
电	電	*diàn*	n	electricity	16
电脑	電腦	*diànnǎo*	n	computer	8
电视	電視	*diànshì*	n	television	4
电影	電影	*diànyǐng*	n	movie	4
电子邮件	電子郵件	*diànzǐ yóujiàn*	n	email/electronic mail	10
订	訂	*dìng*	v	to reserve, to book (a ticket, a hotel room, etc.)	19
东	東	*dōng*	n	east	13
东京	東京	*Dōngjīng*	pn	Tokyo	13
东西	東西	*dōngxi*	n	things, objects	9
冬天		*dōngtiān*	n	winter	11
懂	懂	*dǒng*	v	to understand	7
都		*dōu*	adv	both, all	2
豆腐		*dòufu*	n	tofu, bean curd	12
肚子		*dùzi*	n	belly, abdomen, stomach	15
对	對	*duì*	adj	right, correct	4

Simplified	Traditional	Pinyin	Part of Speech	English	Lesson
对不起	對不起	*duìbuqǐ*	v	sorry	5
多		*duō*	adv	how many/much, to what extent	3
多		*duō*	adj	many, much	7
多少		*duōshao*	qpr	how much/how many	9

<table><tbody><tr><td colspan="6" align="center">E</td></tr></tbody></table>

Simplified	Traditional	Pinyin	Part of Speech	English	Lesson
饿	餓	*è*	adj	hungry	12
儿子	兒子	*érzi*	n	son	2
二姐		*èrjiě*	n	second oldest sister	2

<table><tbody><tr><td colspan="6" align="center">F</td></tr></tbody></table>

Simplified	Traditional	Pinyin	Part of Speech	English	Lesson
发短信	發短信	*fā duǎnxìn*	vo	to send a text message (lit. to send a short message)	10
发烧	發燒	*fā shāo*	vo	to have a fever	15
发音	發音	*fāyīn*	n	pronunciation	8
饭	飯	*fàn*	n	meal, (cooked) rice	3
饭馆（儿）	飯館（兒）	*fànguǎn(r)*	n	restaurant	12
饭卡	飯卡	*fànkǎ*	n	meal card	12
饭桌	飯桌	*fànzhuō*	n	dining table	17
方便		*fāngbiàn*	adj	convenient	6
房间	房間	*fángjiān*	n	room	16
房租		*fángzū*	n	rent	17
放		*fàng*	v	to put, to place	12
放假		*fàng jià*	vo	go on vacation, have time off	19
非常		*fēicháng*	adv	very, extremely, exceedingly	11
飞机	飛機	*fēijī*	n	airplane	10
（飞）机场	（飛）機場	*(fēi)jīchǎng*	n	airport	10

Simplified	Traditional	Pinyin	Part of Speech	English	Lesson
费	費	*fèi*	v	to spend, to take (effort)	16
费	費	*fèi*	n	fee, expenses	17
分		*fēn*	m	(measure word for 1/100 of a kuai [equivalent of a cent])	9
分钟	分鐘	*fēnzhōng*	n	minute	17
份		*fèn*	m	(measure word for meal orders, jobs)	19
封		*fēng*	m	(measure word for letters)	8
服务员	服務員	*fúwùyuán*	n	waiter, attendant	12
附近		*fùjìn*	n	vicinity, neighborhood, nearby area	17
父母		*fùmǔ*	n	parents, father and mother	19
付钱	付錢	*fù qián*	vo	to pay money	9
复习	復習	*fùxí*	v	to review	7

G					
干净	乾淨	*gānjìng*	adj	clean	17
赶快	趕快	*gǎnkuài*	adv	right away, quickly, in a hurry	15
感冒		*gǎnmào*	v	to have a cold	15
刚	剛	*gāng*	adv	just	12
刚才	剛才	*gāngcái*	t	just now, a moment ago	11
高速公路		*gāosù gōnglù*	n	highway	10
高文中		*Gāo Wénzhōng*	pn	(a personal name)	2
高小音		*Gāo Xiǎoyīn*	pn	(a personal name)	5
高兴	高興	*gāoxìng*	adj	happy, pleased	5
告诉	告訴	*gàosu*	v	to tell	8
哥哥		*gēge*	n	older brother	2

Simplified	Traditional	Pinyin	Part of Speech	English	Lesson
个	個	gè/ge	m	(measure word for many common everyday objects)	2
给	給	gěi	v	to give	5
给	給	gěi	prep	to, for	6
跟		gēn	prep	with	6
更		gèng	adv	even more	11
公共汽车	公共汽車	gōnggòng qìchē	n	bus	10
公司		gōngsī	n	company	19
公寓		gōngyù	n	apartment	17
公园	公園	gōngyuán	n	park	11
功课	功課	gōngkè	n	homework, schoolwork	7
工作		gōngzuò	n/v	job; to work	2
狗		gǒu	n	dog	14
够	夠	gòu	adj	enough	12
谷歌		Gǔgē	pn	Google	13
拐	拐	guǎi	v	to turn	13
广告	廣告	guǎnggào	n	advertisement	17
贵	貴	guì	adj	honorable, expensive	1
国际	國際	guójì	adj	international	18
过	過	guò	v	to live (a life), to observe (a holiday), to celebrate (a festival), to pass	14
过敏	過敏	guòmǐn	v	to be allergic to	15
过	過	guo	p	(particle used after a verb to indicate a past experience)	13

H

Simplified	Traditional	Pinyin	Part of Speech	English	Lesson
还	還	hái	adv	also, too, as well	3

Simplified	Traditional	Pinyin	Part of Speech	English	Lesson
还是	還是	*háishi*	conj	or	3
孩子		*háizi*	n	child	2
海伦	海倫	*Hǎilún*	pn	Helen	14
寒假		*hánjià*	n	winter vacation	10
汉字	漢字	*Hànzì*	n	Chinese characters	7
航班		*hángbān*	n	scheduled flight	19
航空		*hángkōng*	n	aviation	19
好		*hǎo*	adj	fine, good, nice, OK, it's settled	1
好吃		*hǎochī*	adj	delicious	12
好几	好幾	*hǎo jǐ*		quite a few	15
好久		*hǎo jiǔ*		a long time	4
好玩儿	好玩兒	*hǎowánr*	adj	fun, amusing, interesting	11
好像	好像	*hǎoxiàng*	v	to seem, to be like	12
号	號	*hào*	m	(measure word for a position in a numerical series, day of the month)	3
号	號	*hào*	n	size	9
号码	號碼	*hàomǎ*	n	number	16
喝		*hē*	v	to drink	5
和		*hé*	conj	and	2
合适	合適	*héshì*	adj	suitable	9
黑		*hēi*	adj	black	9
很		*hěn*	adv	very	3
红	紅	*hóng*	adj	red	9
红绿灯	紅綠燈	*hónglǜdēng*	n	traffic light	13

Simplified	Traditional	Pinyin	Part of Speech	English	Lesson
红烧	紅燒	hóngshāo	v	to braise in soy sauce (to red-cook)	12
后来	後來	hòulái	t	later	8
后天	後天	hòutiān	t	the day after tomorrow	16
护照	護照	hùzhào	n	passport	19
花	花	huā	v	to spend	10
花	花	huā	n	flower	14
滑冰	滑冰	huá bīng	vo	to ice skate	11
欢迎	歡迎	huānyíng	v	to welcome	20
还	還	huán	v	to return (something)	17
换	換	huàn	v	to exchange, to change	9
黄	黃	huáng	adj	yellow	9
黄瓜	黃瓜	huánggua	n	cucumber	12
回家		huí jiā	vo	to go home	5
回来	回來	huí lai	vc	to come back	6
回去		huí qu	vc	to go back, to return	11
会	會	huì	mv	can, know how to	8
会	會	huì	mv	will	11
活动	活動	huódòng	n	activity	13
或者		huòzhě	conj	or	10

		J			
极	極	jí	adv	extremely	12
几	幾	jǐ	nu	how many, some, a few	2
记得	記得	jìde	v	to remember	16
计划	計劃	jìhuà	v/n	to plan; plan	19

Simplified	Traditional	Pinyin	Part of Speech	English	Lesson
家		jiā	n	family, home	2
家常		jiācháng	n	home-style	12
家具	傢俱	jiājù	n	furniture	17
加州		Jiāzhōu	pn	California	11
检查	檢查	jiǎnchá	v	to examine	15
简单	簡單	jiǎndān	adj	simple	18
件		jiàn	m	(measure word for shirts, dresses, jackets, coats, etc.)	9
见	見	jiàn	v	to see	3
见面	見面	jiàn miàn	vo	to meet up, to meet with	6
健康		jiànkāng	adj/n	healthy; health	15
教		jiāo	v	to teach	7
脚	腳	jiǎo	n	foot	18
饺子	餃子	jiǎozi	n	dumplings (with vegetable and/or meat filling)	12
叫		jiào	v	to be called, to call	1
教室		jiàoshì	n	classroom	8
接		jiē	v	to catch, to meet, to welcome	14
节	節	jié	m	(measure word for class periods)	6
姐姐		jiějie	n	older sister	2
介绍	介紹	jièshào	v	to introduce	5
今年		jīnnián	t	this year	3
今天		jīntiān	t	today	3
紧张	緊張	jǐnzhāng	adj	nervous, anxious	10
近		jìn	adj	near	13
进	進	jìn	v	to enter	5

Simplified	Traditional	Pinyin	Part of Speech	English	Lesson
进来	進來	*jìn lai*	vc	to come in	5
九月		*jiǔyuè*	n	September	3
就		*jiù*	adv	precisely, exactly	6
就		*jiù*	adv	just, only (indicating a small number)	16
觉得	覺得	*juéde*	v	to feel, to think	4
K					
咖啡		*kāfēi*	n	coffee	5
咖啡色		*kāfēisè*	n	brown, coffee color	9
开车	開車	*kāi chē*	vo	to drive a car	10
开会	開會	*kāi huì*	vo	to have a meeting	6
开始	開始	*kāishǐ*	v/n	to begin, to start; beginning	7
看		*kàn*	v	to watch, to look, to read	4
看病		*kàn bìng*	vo	to see a doctor	15
考试	考試	*kǎo shì*	vo/n	to give or take a test; test	6
烤鸭	烤鴨	*kǎoyā*	n	roast duck	20
靠		*kào*	v	to lean on, to lean against, to be next to	19
渴		*kě*	adj	thirsty	12
可爱	可愛	*kě'ài*	adj	cute, lovable	14
可乐	可樂	*kělè*	n	cola	5
可能		*kěnéng*	mv/adj	may; possible	17
可是		*kěshì*	conj	but	3
可以		*kěyǐ*	mv	can, may	5
刻		*kè*	m	quarter (of an hour)	3
课	課	*kè*	n	class, course, lesson	6

Simplified	Traditional	Pinyin	Part of Speech	English	Lesson
课文	課文	*kèwén*	n	text of a lesson	7
客气	客氣	*kèqi*	adj	polite	6
客厅	客廳	*kètīng*	n	living room	17
空（儿）	空（兒）	*kòng(r)*	n	free time	6
口		*kǒu*	m	(measure word for number of family members)	2
哭		*kū*	v	to cry, to weep	20
酷		*kù*	adj	cool (appearance, behavior)	7
裤子	褲子	*kùzi*	n	pants	9
块	塊	*kuài*	m	(measure word for the basic Chinese monetary unit [equivalent of a dollar])	9
快		*kuài*	adj/adv	fast, quick; quickly	5
快乐	快樂	*kuàilè*	adj	happy	10
L					
来	來	*lái*	v	to come	5
蓝	藍	*lán*	adj	blue	10
篮球	籃球	*lánqiú*	n	basketball	18
懒	懶	*lǎn*	adj	lazy	15
老师	老師	*lǎoshī*	n	teacher	1
了		*le*	p	(a dynamic particle)	5
累		*lèi*	adj	tired	8
冷		*lěng*	adj	cold	11
离	離	*lí*	prep	away from	13
梨		*lí*	n	pear	14
里边	裡邊	*lǐbian*	n	inside	13
礼物	禮物	*lǐwù*	n	gift, present	14

Simplified	Traditional	Pinyin	Part of Speech	English	Lesson
李友		Lǐ Yǒu	pn	(a personal name)	1
力气	力氣	lìqi	n	strength, effort	16
俩	倆	liǎ	nu+m	two [colloq.]	16
连	連	lián	prep	even	17
脸	臉	liǎn	n	face	14
练习	練習	liànxí	v	to practice	6
凉拌	涼拌	liángbàn	v	(of food) cold "blended", cold tossed	12
两	兩	liǎng	nu	two, a couple of	2
聊天（儿）	聊天（兒）	liáo tiān(r)	vo	to chat	5
另外		lìngwài	conj	furthermore, in addition	17
楼	樓	lóu	n	multi-storied building, floor (of a multi-level building)	14
路		lù	n	route, road	10
路口		lùkǒu	n	intersection	13
录音	錄音	lùyīn	n/vo	sound recording; to record	7
旅馆	旅館	lǚguǎn	n	hotel	19
旅行		lǚxíng	v	to travel	16
旅行社		lǚxíngshè	n	travel agency	19
绿	綠	lǜ	adj	green	10
律师	律師	lǜshī	n	lawyer	2
乱	亂	luàn	adv	randomly, arbitrarily, messily	15
M					
妈妈	媽媽	māma	n	mother, mom	2
麻烦	麻煩	máfan	adj	troublesome	10
马上	馬上	mǎshàng	adv	immediately, right away	19

Simplified	Traditional	Pinyin	Part of Speech	English	Lesson
吗	嗎	*ma*	qp	(question particle)	1
买	買	*mǎi*	v	to buy	9
卖完	賣完	*mài wán*	vc	to be sold out	12
慢		*màn*	adj	slow	7
忙		*máng*	adj	busy	3
毛		*máo*	m	(measure word for 1/10 of a kuai [equivalent of a dime])	9
没	沒	*méi*	adv	not	2
没关系	沒關係	*méi guānxi*		it doesn't matter	12
每		*měi*	pr	every, each	10
美国	美國	*Měiguó*	pn	America	1
美式		*Měishì*	adj	American-style	18
美元		*Měiyuán*	n	American dollar (USD)	17
妹妹		*mèimei*	n	younger sister	2
米饭	米飯	*mǐfàn*	n	cooked rice	12
面试	面試	*miànshì*	v/n	to interview; interview (for a job or school admission)	11
名胜古迹	名勝古蹟	*míngshèng gǔjì*		famous scenic spots and historic sites	19
明天		*míngtiān*	t	tomorrow	3
名字		*míngzi*	n	name	1

N

Simplified	Traditional	Pinyin	Part of Speech	English	Lesson
拿		*ná*	v	to take, to get	13
哪		*nǎ/něi*	qpr	which	6
哪里	哪裡	*nǎli*	pr	where	7
哪儿	哪兒	*nǎr*	qpr	where	5
那		*nà*	pr	that	2

Simplified	Traditional	Pinyin	Part of Speech	English	Lesson
那		nà	conj	in that case, then	4
那里	那裡	nàli	pr	there	17
那么	那麼	nàme	pr	(indicating degree) so, such	11
那儿	那兒	nàr	pr	there	8
奶奶		nǎinai	n	paternal grandmother	20
男		nán	adj	male	2
南		nán	n	south	13
难	難	nán	adj	difficult	7
难受	難受	nánshòu	adj	hard to bear, uncomfortable	18
呢		ne	qp	(question particle)	1
能		néng	mv	can, to be able to	8
你		nǐ	pr	you	1
年级	年級	niánjí	n	grade in school	6
念		niàn	v	to read aloud	7
您		nín	pr	you (honorific for 你)	6
牛肉		niúròu	n	beef	12
纽约	紐約	Niǔyuē	pn	New York	1
暖和		nuǎnhuo	adj	warm	11
女		nǚ	adj	female	2
女儿	女兒	nǚ'ér	n	daughter	2
P					
怕		pà	v	to fear, to be afraid of	18
拍		pāi	n	racket	18
盘	盤	pán	n	plate, dish	12

Simplified	Traditional	Pinyin	Part of Speech	English	Lesson
旁边	旁邊	*pángbiān*	n	side	13
胖		*pàng*	adj	fat	18
跑步		*pǎo bù*	vo	to jog	18
朋友		*péngyou*	n	friend	3
篇		*piān*	m	(measure word for essays, articles, etc.)	8
便宜		*piányi*	adj	cheap, inexpensive	9
片		*piàn*	m	(measure word for tablets, slices, etc.)	15
票		*piào*	n	ticket	10
漂亮	漂亮	*piàoliang*	adj	pretty	5
瓶		*píng*	m/n	(measure word for bottled liquid, etc.)	5
平常		*píngcháng*	adv	usually	7
苹果	蘋果	*píngguǒ*	n	apple	14

		Q			
起床	起床	*qǐ chuáng*	vo	to get up	8
起飞	起飛	*qǐfēi*	v	(of airplanes) to take off	20
千		*qiān*	nu	thousand	19
签证	簽證	*qiānzhèng*	n	visa	19
钱	錢	*qián*	n	money	9
前		*qián*	n	forward, ahead	13
前面		*qiánmiàn*	n	ahead, in front of	13
青菜	青菜	*qīngcài*	n	green, leafy vegetable	12
清楚		*qīngchu*	adj	clear	12
请	請	*qǐng*	v	please (polite form of request), to treat or to invite (somebody)	1

Simplified	Traditional	Pinyin	Part of Speech	English	Lesson
请客	請客	qǐng kè	vo	to invite someone (to dinner, coffee, etc.), to play the host	4
秋天		qiūtiān	n	autumn, fall	11
去		qù	v	to go	4
去年		qùnián	t	last year	14
R					
然后	然後	ránhòu	adv	then	10
让	讓	ràng	v	to allow or cause (somebody to do something)	10
热	熱	rè	adj	hot	11
人		rén	n	people, person	1
人民币	人民幣	rénmínbì	n	renminbi (RMB, Chinese currency)	17
认识	認識	rènshi	v	to be acquainted with, to recognize	3
日本		Rìběn	pn	Japan	13
日记	日記	rìjì	n	diary	8
日文		Rìwén	pn	Japanese (language)	13
容易		róngyì	adj	easy	7
肉		ròu	n	meat	12
如果…的话	如果…的話	rúguǒ…de huà	conj	if	9
S					
沙发	沙發	shāfā	n	sofa	17
商店		shāngdiàn	n	store, shop	9
上		shàng	v	to go [colloq.]	13
上菜	上菜	shàng cài	vo	to serve food	12
上次		shàng cì		last time	15

Simplified	Traditional	Pinyin	Part of Speech	English	Lesson
上大学	上大學	shàng dàxué	vo	to attend college/university	18
上个	上個	shàng ge		previous, last	7
上海		Shànghǎi	pn	Shanghai	12
上课	上課	shàng kè	vo	to go to a class, to start a class, to be in class	7
上网	上網	shàng wǎng	vo	to go online, to surf the internet	8
上午		shàngwǔ	t	morning	6
谁	誰	shéi	qpr	who, whom	2
身体	身體	shēntǐ	n	body, health	15
什么	什麼	shénme	qpr	what	1
生病		shēng bìng	vo	to get sick	15
生词	生詞	shēngcí	n	new words, vocabulary	7
生日		shēngrì	n	birthday	3
师傅	師傅	shīfu	n	master worker	12
十八		shíbā	nu	eighteen	3
十二		shí'èr	nu	twelve	3
时候	時候	shíhou	n	(a point in) time, moment, (a duration of) time	4
时间	時間	shíjiān	n	time	6
实习	實習	shíxí	v	to intern	19
是		shì	v	to be	1
试	試	shì	v	to try	9
事（儿）	事（兒）	shì(r)	n	matter, affair, event	3
收		shōu	v	to receive, to accept	9
手		shǒu	n	hand	18
手机	手機	shǒujī	n	cell phone	10

Simplified	Traditional	Pinyin	Part of Speech	English	Lesson
首都		*shǒudū*	n	capital city	19
首都机场	首都機場	*Shǒudū Jīchǎng*	pn	the Capital Airport (in Beijing)	20
瘦		*shòu*	adj	thin, skinny, lean	20
售货员	售貨員	*shòuhuòyuán*	n	shop assistant, salesclerk	9
书	書	*shū*	n	book	4
书店	書店	*shūdiàn*	n	bookstore	13
书架	書架	*shūjià*	n	bookcase, bookshelf	17
书桌	書桌	*shūzhuō*	n	desk	17
舒服		*shūfu*	adj	comfortable	11
叔叔		*shūshu*	n	uncle	20
属	屬	*shǔ*	v	to belong to	14
暑假		*shǔjià*	n	summer vacation	19
暑期		*shǔqī*	n	summer term	14
刷卡		*shuā kǎ*	vo	to pay with a credit card	9
帅	帥	*shuài*	adj	handsome	7
双	雙	*shuāng*	m	(measure word for a pair)	9
水		*shuǐ*	n	water	5
水果		*shuǐguǒ*	n	fruit	14
水平		*shuǐpíng*	n	level, standard	18
睡觉	睡覺	*shuì jiào*	vo	to sleep	4
说	說	*shuō*	v	to say, to speak	6
说话	說話	*shuō huà*	vo	to talk	7
送		*sòng*	v	to see off or out, to take (someone somewhere)	10
送		*sòng*	v	to give as a gift	14

Simplified	Traditional	Pinyin	Part of Speech	English	Lesson
素		*sù*	adj	vegetarian (lit. plain)	12
素餐		*sùcān*	n	vegetarian meal	19
宿舍		*sùshè*	n	dormitory	8
酸		*suān*	adj	sour	12
酸辣汤	酸辣湯	*suānlàtāng*	n	hot-and-sour soup	12
算了		*suàn le*		forget it, never mind	4
虽然	雖然	*suīrán*	conj	although	9
岁	歲	*suì*	n	year (of age)	3
所以		*suǒyǐ*	conj	so	4
		T			
他		*tā*	pr	he, him	2
她		*tā*	pr	she, her	2
它		*tā*	pr	it	9
台北		*Táiběi*	pn	Taipei	19
太…了		*tài … le*		too, extremely	3
汤姆	湯姆	*Tāngmǔ*	pn	Tom	14
糖醋鱼	糖醋魚	*tángcùyú*	n	sweet-and-sour fish	12
躺下		*tǎng xià*	vc	to lie down	15
套		*tào*	m	(measure word for things that come in a set/sets)	17
特别	特別	*tèbié*	adv	especially	10
疼死		*téng sǐ*	adj + c	really painful	15
踢		*tī*	v	to kick	18
提高		*tígāo*	v	to improve, to raise, to heighten	18
天		*tiān*	n	day	3

Simplified	Traditional	Pinyin	Part of Speech	English	Lesson
天气	天氣	*tiānqì*	n	weather	11
甜		*tián*	adj	sweet	12
条	條	*tiáo*	m	(measure word for pants and long, thin objects)	9
跳舞		*tiào wǔ*	vo	to dance	4
听	聽	*tīng*	v	to listen	4
听说	聽說	*tīngshuō*	v	to be told, to hear of	13
挺		*tǐng*	adv	very, rather	9
同		*tóng*	adj	same	16
同学	同學	*tóngxué*	n	classmate	3
图书馆	圖書館	*túshūguǎn*	n	library	5
托运	托運	*tuōyùn*	v	to check (luggage)	20

W

Simplified	Traditional	Pinyin	Part of Speech	English	Lesson
外国	外國	*wàiguó*	n	foreign country	4
玩（儿）	玩（兒）	*wán(r)*	v	to have fun, to play	5
碗		*wǎn*	n	bowl	12
晚		*wǎn*	adj	late	7
晚饭	晚飯	*wǎnfàn*	n	dinner, supper	3
晚上		*wǎnshang*	t	evening, night	3
王红	王紅	*Wáng Hóng*	pn	a personal name	14
王朋		*Wáng Péng*	pn	(a personal name)	1
往		*wǎng*	prep	towards	13
往返		*wǎngfǎn*	v	make a round trip, go there and back	19
网球	網球	*wǎngqiú*	n	tennis	18
网上	網上	*wǎng shang*		on the Internet	11

Simplified	Traditional	Pinyin	Part of Speech	English	Lesso
忘		*wàng*	v	to forget	12
危险	危險	*wēixiǎn*	adj	dangerous	18
喂		*wéi/wèi*	interj	(on the phone) Hello!, Hey!	6
位		*wèi*	m	(polite measure word for people)	6
位子		*wèizi*	n	seat	12
味精		*wèijīng*	n	monosodium glutamate (MSG)	12
为了	為了	*wèile*	prep	for the sake of	18
为什么	為什麼	*wèishénme*	qpr	why	3
卫生间	衛生間	*wèishēngjiān*	n	bathroom	17
文化		*wénhuà*	n	culture	19
问	問	*wèn*	v	to ask (a question)	1
问题	問題	*wèntí*	n	question, problem	6
我		*wǒ*	pr	I, me	1
我们	我們	*wǒmen*	pr	we, us	3
卧室	臥室	*wòshì*	n	bedroom	17
午饭	午飯	*wǔfàn*	n	lunch, midday meal	8
舞会	舞會	*wǔhuì*	n	dance party, ball	14
X					
西		*xī*	n	west	13
西北航空公司		*Xīběi Hángkōng Gōngsī*	pn	Northwest Airlines	19
西瓜		*xīgua*	n	watermelon	14
希望	希望	*xīwàng*	v/n	to hope; hope	8
喜欢	喜歡	*xǐhuan*	v	to like	3
洗澡		*xǐ zǎo*	vo	to take a bath/shower	8

implified	Traditional	Pinyin	Part of Speech	English	Lesson
下车	下車	xià chē	vo	to get off (a bus, train, etc.)	10
下个	下個	xià ge		next	6
下午		xiàwǔ	t	afternoon	6
下雪		xià xuě	vo	to snow	11
下雨		xià yǔ	vo	to rain	11
夏天		xiàtiān	n	summer	11
先		xiān	adv	first	10
先生		xiānsheng	n	Mr., husband, teacher	1
线	線	xiàn	n	line	10
现在	現在	xiànzài	t	now	3
香港		Xiānggǎng	pn	Hong Kong	19
箱子		xiāngzi	n	suitcase, box	20
想		xiǎng	av	to want to, would like to	4
想		xiǎng	v	to think	16
想起来	想起來	xiǎng qi lai	vc	to remember, to recall	16
像	像	xiàng	v	to be like, to look like, to take after	14
小		xiǎo	adj	small, little	4
小白菜	小白菜	xiǎo báicài	n	baby bok choy	12
小姐		xiǎojiě	n	Miss, young lady	1
小时	小時	xiǎoshí	n	hour	15
小心		xiǎoxīn	v	to be careful	20
笑		xiào	v	to laugh at, to laugh, to smile	8
些		xiē	m	(measure word for an indefinite amount), some	12
鞋		xié	n	shoes	9

Simplified	Traditional	Pinyin	Part of Speech	English	Lesson
写	寫	*xiě*	v	to write	7
谢谢	謝謝	*xièxie*	v	to thank	3
新		*xīn*	adj	new	8
新年		*xīnnián*	n	new year	10
信		*xìn*	n	letter (correspondence)	8
信用卡		*xìnyòngkǎ*	n	credit card	9
星期		*xīngqī*	n	week	3
星期四		*xīngqīsì*	n	Thursday	3
行		*xíng*	v	all right, OK	6
行李		*xíngli*	n	luggage	20
姓		*xìng*	v/n	(one's) family name is . . .; family name	1
兴趣	興趣	*xìngqù*	n	interest	17
休息		*xiūxi*	v	to take a break, to rest	15
学	學	*xué*	v	to study, to learn	7
学期	學期	*xuéqī*	n	school term, semester, quarter	8
学生	學生	*xuésheng*	n	student	1
学习	學習	*xuéxí*	v	to study, to learn	7
学校	學校	*xuéxiào*	n	school	5
Y					
压	壓	*yā*	v	to press, to hold down, to weigh down	18
押金		*yājīn*	n	security deposit	17
呀		*ya*	p	(interjectory particle used to soften a question)	5
淹死		*yān sǐ*	vc	to drown	18

implified	Traditional	Pinyin	Part of Speech	English	Lesson
盐	鹽	*yán*	n	salt	12
颜色	顔色	*yánsè*	n	color	9
演		*yǎn*	v	to show (a film), to perform	16
眼睛		*yǎnjing*	n	eye	14
痒	癢	*yǎng*	adj	itchy	15
养	養	*yǎng*	v	to raise	17
样子	樣子	*yàngzi*	n	style	9
药	藥	*yào*	n	medicine	15
药店	藥店	*yàodiàn*	n	pharmacy	15
要		*yào*	v	to want	5
要		*yào*	mv	will, to be going to; to want to, to have a desire to	6
要不然		*yàobùrán*	conj	otherwise	15
要是		*yàoshi*	conj	if	6
爷爷	爺爺	*yéye*	n	paternal grandfather	20
也		*yě*	adv	too, also	1
夜里	夜裡	*yè lǐ*	n	at night	15
衣服		*yīfu*	n	clothes	9
医生	醫生	*yīshēng*	n	doctor, physician	2
医院	醫院	*yīyuàn*	n	hospital	15
一定		*yídìng [yīdìng]*	adj/adv	certain, definite; certainly, definitely	14
一共		*yígòng [yīgòng]*	adv	altogether	9
一路平安		*yí lù píng'ān [yī lù píng'ān]*		have a good trip, bon voyage	20
一下		*yí xià [yī xià]*	n+m	once, a bit	5

Simplified	Traditional	Pinyin	Part of Speech	English	Lesson
一样	一樣	yíyàng [yīyàng]	adj	same, alike	9
一边	一邊	yìbiān [yībiān]	adv	simultaneously, at the same time	8
一房一厅	一房一廳	yì fáng yì tīng [yī fáng yī tīng]		one bedroom and one living room	17
一起	一起	yìqǐ [yīqǐ]	adv	together	5
一言为定	一言為定	yì yán wéi dìng [yī yán wéi dìng]		that settles it, that's settled, it's decided	16
一直		yìzhí [yīzhí]	adv	straight, continuously	13
以后	以後	yǐhòu	t	after, from now on, later on	6
以前		yǐqián	t	before	8
以为	以為	yǐwéi	v	to assume erroneously	14
已经	已經	yǐjīng	adv	already	8
椅子		yǐzi	n	chair	17
因为	因為	yīnwèi	conj	because	3
音乐	音樂	yīnyuè	n	music	4
音乐会	音樂會	yīnyuèhuì	n	concert	8
饮料	飲料	yǐnliào	n	beverage	14
印象	印象	yìnxiàng	n	impression	16
应该	應該	yīnggāi	mv	should, ought to	18
英国	英國	Yīngguó	pn	Britain	3
英文	英文	Yīngwén	n	the English language	2
用		yòng	v	to use	8
用功		yònggōng	adj	hard-working, diligent, studious	14
游泳		yóu yǒng	vo	to swim	18
有		yǒu	v	to have, to exist	2
有的		yǒude	pr	some	4

mplified	Traditional	Pinyin	Part of Speech	English	Lesson
有名		*yǒumíng*	adj	famous, well-known	19
有意思		*yǒu yìsi*	adj	interesting	4
又		*yòu*	adv	again	11
右		*yòu*	n	right	13
鱼	魚	*yú*	n	fish	12
语法	語法	*yǔfǎ*	n	grammar	7
预报	預報	*yùbào*	v/n	to forecast; forecast	11
预习	預習	*yùxí*	v	to preview	7
圆	圓	*yuán*	adj	round	14
元		*yuán*	m	(measure word for the basic Chinese monetary unit), *yuan*	17
远	遠	*yuǎn*	adj	far	13
愿意	願意	*yuànyì*	mv	to be willing	18
约	約	*yuē*	v	to make an appointment	11
月		*yuè*	n	month	3
越来越	越來越	*yuè lái yuè*	adv	more and more	15
运动	運動	*yùndòng*	n	sports	13
运动服	運動服	*yùndòngfú*	n	sportswear, athletic clothing	18
		Z			
在		*zài*	prep	at, in, on	5
在		*zài*	v	to be present, to be at (a place)	6
再		*zài*	adv	again	9
再见	再見	*zàijiàn*	v	goodbye, see you again	3
再说	再說	*zàishuō*	conj	moreover	15

Simplified	Traditional	Pinyin	Part of Speech	English	Lesson
糟糕		zāogāo	adj	in a terrible mess, how terrible	11
早		zǎo	adj	early	7
早饭	早飯	zǎofàn	n	breakfast	8
早上		zǎoshang	t	morning	7
怎么	怎麼	zěnme	qpr	how, how come	7
怎么样	怎麼樣	zěnmeyàng	qpr	Is it OK? How is that? How does that sound?	3
站		zhàn	m	(measure word for bus stops, train stops, etc.)	10
张	張	zhāng	m	(measure word for flat objects such as paper, pictures, etc.)	7
长	長	zhǎng	v	to grow, to appear	14
长大	長大	zhǎng dà	vc	to grow up	14
找		zhǎo	v	to look for	4
找（钱）	找（錢）	zhǎo (qián)	v(o)	to give change	9
照顾	照顧	zhàogu	v	to look after, to care for, to attend to	20
照片		zhàopiàn	n	picture, photo	2
这	這	zhè	pr	this	2
这么	這麼	zhème	pr	so, this (late, etc.)	7
这儿	這兒	zhèr	pr	here	9
真		zhēn	adv	really	7
整理		zhěnglǐ	v	to put in order	16
正在		zhèngzài	adv	in the middle of (doing something)	8
政治		zhèngzhì	n	politics	19
枝		zhī	m	(measure word for long, thin, inflexible objects such as pens, pencils, etc.)	7

Simplified	Traditional	Pinyin	Part of Speech	English	Lesson
知道		zhīdao	v	to know	8
直飞	直飛	zhí fēi		fly directly	19
只		zhǐ	adv	only	4
纸	紙	zhǐ	n	paper	7
中		zhōng	adj	medium, middle	9
中国	中國	Zhōngguó	pn	China	1
中国城	中國城	Zhōngguóchéng	n	Chinatown	13
中国国际航空公司	中國國際航空公司	Zhōngguó Guójì Hángkōng Gōngsī	pn	Air China	19
中间	中間	zhōngjiān	n	middle	13
中文		Zhōngwén	n	the Chinese language	6
中午		zhōngwǔ	t	noon	8
中心		zhōngxīn	n	center	13
中学	中學	zhōngxué	n	middle school, secondary school	14
钟头	鐘頭	zhōngtóu	n	hour	14
种	種	zhǒng	m	(measure word for kinds, sorts, types)	9
重		zhòng	adj	heavy, serious	14
周末	週末	zhōumò	n	weekend	4
祝		zhù	v	to wish (well)	8
住		zhù	v	to live (in a certain place)	14
专业	專業	zhuānyè	n	major (in college), specialty	8
转机	轉機	zhuǎn jī	vo	change planes	19
准		zhǔn	v	to allow, to be allowed	17
准备	準備	zhǔnbèi	v	to prepare	6

Simplified	Traditional	Pinyin	Part of Speech	English	Lesson
桌子		zhuōzi	n	table	12
字		zì	n	character	7
自己		zìjǐ	pr	oneself	10
走		zǒu	v	to go by way of, to walk	10
走道		zǒudào	n	aisle	19
走路		zǒu lù	vo	to walk	17
租		zū	v	to rent	19
足球		zúqiú	n	soccer, football	18
嘴		zuǐ	n	mouth	14
最		zuì	adv	most, (of superlative degree) -est	14
最好		zuìhǎo	adv	had better	15
最后	最後	zuìhòu		final, last	10
最近		zuìjìn	t	recently	8
昨天		zuótiān	t	yesterday	4
左		zuǒ	n	left	13
做		zuò	v	to do	2
做饭	做飯	zuò fàn	vo	to cook, to prepare a meal	17
坐		zuò	v	to sit	5
坐		zuò	v	to travel by	10

e English-Chinese index is organized based on the alphabetical order of the English definitions. For ease of
erence, indefinite articles and definite articles are omitted when they are the beginning of a phrase.

nglish	Simplified	Traditional	Pinyin	Part of Speech	Lesson
A					
ctivity	活动	活動	*huódòng*	n	13
dvertisement	广告	廣告	*guǎnggào*	n	17
ter, from now on, ter on	以后	以後	*yǐhòu*	t	6
fternoon	下午	下午	*xiàwǔ*	t	6
gain	再	再	*zài*	adv	9
gain	又	又	*yòu*	adv	11
head, in front of	前面	前面	*qiánmiàn*	n	13
ir China	中国国际航空公司	中國國際航空公司	*Zhōngguó Guójì Hángkōng Gōngsī*	pn	19
rplane	飞机	飛機	*fēijī*	n	10
rport	（飞）机场	（飛）機場	*(fēi)jīchǎng*	n	10
isle	走道	走道	*zǒudào*	n	19
l right, OK	行	行	*xíng*	v	6
low, be allowed	准	准	*zhǔn*	v	17
low or cause omebody to do omething)	让	讓	*ràng*	v	10
most, nearly; similar	差不多	差不多	*chàbuduō*	adv/adj	17
ready	已经	已經	*yǐjīng*	adv	8
lso, too, as well	还	還	*hái*	adv	3
lthough	虽然	雖然	*suīrán*	conj	9

English	Simplified	Traditional	Pinyin	Part of Speech	Lesson
altogether	一共		yígòng	adv	9
America	美国	美國	Měiguó	pn	1
American-style	美式		Měishì	adj	18
American dollar (USD)	美元		Měiyuán	n	17
and	和		hé	conj	2
apartment	公寓		gōngyù	n	17
apple	苹果	蘋果	píngguǒ	n	14
ask (a question)	问	問	wèn	v	1
assume erroneously	以为	以為	yǐwéi	v	14
at, in, on	在		zài	prep	5
at night	夜里	夜裡	yè lǐ	n	15
aunt	阿姨		āyí	n	20
autumn, fall	秋天		qiūtiān	n	11
aviation	航空		hángkōng	n	19
away from	离	離	lí	prep	13
B					
baby bok choy	小白菜	小白菜	xiǎo báicài	n	12
bag, sack, bundle, package	包		bāo	n	20
Bai Ying'ai	白英爱	白英愛	Bái Yīng'ài	pn	2
basketball	篮球	籃球	lánqiú	n	18
bathroom	卫生间	衛生間	wèishēngjiān	n	17
be	是		shì	v	1
be acquainted with, recognize	认识	認識	rènshi	v	3
be allergic to	过敏	過敏	guòmǐn	v	15

English	Simplified	Traditional	Pinyin	Part of Speech	Lesson
e called, call	叫		jiào	v	1
e careful	小心		xiǎoxīn	v	20
e like, look like, ake after	像	像	xiàng	v	14
e overweight (of ggage, freight, etc.)	超重		chāozhòng	v	20
e present, be at place)	在		zài	v	6
e sold out	卖完	賣完	mài wán	vc	12
e told, hear of	听说	聽說	tīngshuō	v	13
e willing	愿意	願意	yuànyì	mv	18
ecause	因为	因為	yīnwèi	conj	3
ecome	成		chéng	v	16
edroom	卧室	臥室	wòshì	n	17
eef	牛肉		niúròu	n	12
efore	以前		yǐqián	t	8
egin, start; beginning	开始	開始	kāishǐ	v/n	7
eginning	初		chū	n	19
eijing	北京		Běijīng	pn	1
elly, abdomen, tomach	肚子		dùzi	n	15
elong to	属	屬	shǔ	v	14
everage	饮料	飲料	yǐnliào	n	14
ig, old	大		dà	adj	3
irthday	生日		shēngrì	n	3
lack	黑		hēi	adj	9
lue	蓝	藍	lán	adj	10
oarding gate	登机口	登機口	dēngjīkǒu	n	20

English	Simplified	Traditional	Pinyin	Part of Speech	Lesson
boarding pass	登机牌	登機牌	*dēngjīpái*	n	20
body, health	身体	身體	*shēntǐ*	n	15
book	书	書	*shū*	n	4
bookcase, bookshelf	书架	書架	*shūjià*	n	17
bookstore	书店	書店	*shūdiàn*	n	13
both, all	都		*dōu*	adv	2
bowl	碗		*wǎn*	n	12
braise in soy sauce (to red-cook)	红烧	紅燒	*hóngshāo*	v	12
breakfast	早饭	早飯	*zǎofàn*	n	8
bring, take, carry, come with	带	帶	*dài*	v	12
Britain	英国	英國	*Yīngguó*	pn	3
brown, coffee color	咖啡色		*kāfēisè*	n	9
bus	公共汽车	公共汽車	*gōnggòng qìchē*	n	10
busy	忙		*máng*	adj	3
but	可是		*kěshì*	conj	3
but	但是		*dànshì*	conj	6
buy	买	買	*mǎi*	v	9
by	被		*bèi*	prep	18
C					
cake	蛋糕		*dàngāo*	n	14
California	加州		*Jiāzhōu*	pn	11
can, able to	能		*néng*	mv	8
can, know how to	会	會	*huì*	mv	8
can, may	可以		*kěyǐ*	mv	5

English	Simplified	Traditional	Pinyin	Part of Speech	Lesson
Capital Airport (in Beijing)	首都机场	首都機場	*Shǒudū Jīchǎng*	pn	20
capital city	首都		*shǒudū*	n	19
catch, meet, welcome	接		*jiē*	v	14
cell phone	手机	手機	*shǒujī*	n	10
center	中心		*zhōngxīn*	n	13
certain, definite; certainly, definitely	一定		*yídìng*	adj/adv	14
chair	椅子		*yǐzi*	n	17
change planes	转机	轉機	*zhuǎn jī*	vo	19
character	字		*zì*	n	7
chat	聊天（儿）	聊天（兒）	*liáo tiān(r)*	vo	5
cheap, inexpensive	便宜		*piányi*	adj	9
check, look into	查		*chá*	v	19
check (luggage)	托运	托運	*tuōyùn*	v	20
child	孩子		*háizi*	n	2
China	中国	中國	*Zhōngguó*	pn	1
Chinatown	中国城	中國城	*Zhōngguóchéng*	n	13
Chinese characters	汉字	漢字	*Hànzì*	n	7
Chinese language	中文		*Zhōngwén*	n	6
city	城市		*chéngshì*	n	10
class	班		*bān*	n	14
class, course, lesson	课	課	*kè*	n	6
classmate	同学	同學	*tóngxué*	n	3
classroom	教室		*jiàoshì*	n	8
clean	干净	乾淨	*gānjìng*	adj	17

English	Simplified	Traditional	Pinyin	Part of Speech	Lesso
clean up (a room, apartment or house)	打扫	打掃	dǎsǎo	v	16
clear	清楚		qīngchu	adj	12
clothes	衣服		yīfu	n	9
coffee	咖啡		kāfēi	n	5
cola	可乐	可樂	kělè	n	5
cold	冷		lěng	adj	11
college student	大学生	大學生	dàxuéshēng	n	2
color	颜色	顔色	yánsè	n	9
come	来	來	lái	v	5
come back	回来	回來	huí lai	vc	6
come in	进来	進來	jìn lai	vc	5
comfortable	舒服		shūfu	adj	11
company	公司		gōngsī	n	19
compared with (comparison marker), to compare	比		bǐ	prep/v	11
computer	电脑	電腦	diànnǎo	n	8
concert	音乐会	音樂會	yīnyuèhuì	n	8
convenient	方便		fāngbiàn	adj	6
cook, prepare a meal	做饭	做飯	zuò fàn	vo	17
cooked rice	米饭	米飯	mǐfàn	n	12
cool (appearance, behavior)	酷		kù	adj	7
credit card	信用卡		xìnyòngkǎ	n	9
cry, weep	哭		kū	v	20
cucumber	黄瓜	黃瓜	huánggua	n	12

English	Simplified	Traditional	Pinyin	Part of Speech	Lesson
...ulture	文化		*wénhuà*	n	19
...ute, lovable	可爱	可愛	*kě'ài*	adj	14

English	Simplified	Traditional	Pinyin	Part of Speech	Lesson
...ance	跳舞		*tiào wǔ*	vo	4
...ance party, ball	舞会	舞會	*wǔhuì*	n	14
...angerous	危险	危險	*wēixiǎn*	adj	18
...aughter	女儿	女兒	*nǚ'ér*	n	2
...ay	天		*tiān*	n	3
...ay after tomorrow	后天	後天	*hòutiān*	t	16
...elicious	好吃		*hǎochī*	adj	12
...esk	书桌	書桌	*shūzhuō*	n	17
...iary	日记	日記	*rìjì*	n	8
...ifficult	难	難	*nán*	adj	7
...ining room, cafeteria	餐厅	餐廳	*cāntīng*	n	8
...ining table	饭桌	飯桌	*fànzhuō*	n	17
...inner, supper	晚饭	晚飯	*wǎnfàn*	n	3
...ish, cuisine	菜	菜	*cài*	n	3
...o	做		*zuò*	v	2
...octor, physician	医生	醫生	*yīshēng*	n	2
...og	狗		*gǒu*	n	14
...on't	别	別	*bié*	adv	6
...ormitory	宿舍		*sùshè*	n	8
...rink	喝		*hē*	v	5
...rive a car	开车	開車	*kāi chē*	vo	10

English	Simplified	Traditional	Pinyin	Part of Speech	Lesson
drown	淹死		yān sǐ	vc	18
dumplings (with vegetable and/or meat filling)	饺子	餃子	jiǎozi	n	12
(dynamic particle)	了		le	p	5
E					
early	早		zǎo	adj	7
east	东	東	dōng	n	13
easy	容易		róngyì	adj	7
eat	吃		chī	v	3
eighteen	十八		shíbā	nu	3
eldest/oldest brother	大哥		dàgē	n	2
eldest/oldest sister	大姐		dàjiě	n	2
electricity	电	電	diàn	n	16
email/electronic mail	电子邮件	電子郵件	diànzǐ yóujiàn	n	10
English language	英文	英文	Yīngwén	n	2
enough	够	夠	gòu	adj	12
enter	进	進	jìn	v	5
especially	特别	特別	tèbié	adv	10
even	连	連	lián	prep	17
even more	更		gèng	adv	11
evening, night	晚上		wǎnshang	t	3
every, each	每		měi	pr	10
everybody	大家		dàjiā	pr	7
examine	检查	檢查	jiǎnchá	v	15

English	Simplified	Traditional	Pinyin	Part of Speech	Lesson
exchange, change	换	換	huàn	v	9
exclamatory particle (to express surprise or dissatisfaction)	哎	哎	āi	excl	13
extremely	极	極	jí	adv	12
eye	眼睛		yǎnjing	n	14
F					
face	脸	臉	liǎn	n	14
family, home	家		jiā	n	2
famous, well-known	有名		yǒumíng	adj	19
famous scenic spots and historic sites	名胜古迹	名勝古蹟	míngshèng gǔjì	n	19
fantastic, super [colloq.]	棒		bàng	adj	18
far	远	遠	yuǎn	adj	13
fast, quick; quickly	快		kuài	adj/adv	5
fat	胖		pàng	adj	18
father, dad	爸爸		bàba	n	2
fear, be afraid of	怕		pà	v	18
fee, expenses	费	費	fèi	n	17
feel, think	觉得	覺得	juéde	v	4
feel embarrassed	不好意思		bù hǎoyìsi		10
female	女		nǚ	adj	2
field	场	場	chǎng	n	13
final, last	最后	最後	zuìhòu		10
fine, good, nice, OK, it's settled	好		hǎo	adj	1
first	先		xiān	adv	10

English	Simplified	Traditional	Pinyin	Part of Speech	Lesson
fish	鱼	魚	yú	n	12
flower	花	花	huā	n	14
fly directly	直飞	直飛	zhí fēi		19
foot	脚	腳	jiǎo	n	18
for the sake of	为了	為了	wèile	prep	18
forecast; forcast	预报	預報	yùbào	v/n	11
foreign country	外国	外國	wàiguó	n	4
forget	忘		wàng	v	12
forget it, never mind	算了		suàn le		4
forward, ahead	前		qián	n	13
free time	空（儿）	空（兒）	kòng(r)	n	6
friend	朋友		péngyou	n	3
from	从	從	cóng	prep	13
fruit	水果		shuǐguǒ	n	14
fun, amusing, interesting	好玩儿	好玩兒	hǎowánr	adj	11
furniture	家具	傢俱	jiājù	n	17
furthermore, in addition	另外		lìngwài	conj	17

<table>
<tr><td colspan="6" align="center">G</td></tr>
</table>

English	Simplified	Traditional	Pinyin	Part of Speech	Lesson
game, match, competition; to compete	比赛	比賽	bǐsài	n/v	18
Gao Wenzhong	高文中		Gāo Wénzhōng	pn	2
Gao Xiaoyin	高小音		Gāo Xiǎoyīn	pn	5
get an injection	打针	打針	dǎ zhēn	vo	15
get off (a bus, train, etc.)	下车	下車	xià chē	vo	10

English	Simplified	Traditional	Pinyin	Part of Speech	Lesson
et sick	生病		shēng bìng	vo	15
et sick because f bad food	吃坏	吃壞	chī huài	vc	15
et up	起床	起床	qǐ chuáng	vo	8
ft, present	礼物	禮物	lǐwù	n	14
ve	给	給	gěi	v	5
ve as a gift	送		sòng	v	14
ve change	找（钱）	找（錢）	zhǎo (qián)	v(o)	9
ve or take a test; test	考试	考試	kǎo shì	vo/n	6
o	去		qù	v	4
o [colloq.]	上		shàng	v	13
o back, return	回去		huí qu	vc	11
o by way of, walk	走		zǒu	v	10
o home	回家		huí jiā	vo	5
o on vacation, have me off	放假		fàng jià	vo	19
o online, surf the ternet	上网	上網	shàng wǎng	vo	8
o out	出去		chūqu	vc	10
o to, arrive	到		dào	v	6
o to a class, start a ass, be in class	上课	上課	shàng kè	vo	7
oodbye, see you again	再见	再見	zàijiàn	v	3
oogle	谷歌		Gǔgē	pn	13
rade in school	年级	年級	niánjí	n	6
rammar	语法	語法	yǔfǎ	n	7
reat Wall	长城	長城	Chángchéng	pn	19
reen	绿	綠	lǜ	adj	10

English	Simplified	Traditional	Pinyin	Part of Speech	Lesso
green, leafy vegetable	青菜	青菜	*qīngcài*	n	12
grow, appear	长	長	*zhǎng*	v	14
grow up	长大	長大	*zhǎng dà*	vc	14
H					
had better	最好		*zuìhǎo*	adv	15
half, half an hour	半		*bàn*	nu	3
half a day, a long time	半天		*bàntiān*		18
hand	手		*shǒu*	n	18
handle, do	办	辦	*bàn*	v	11
handsome	帅	帥	*shuài*	adj	7
happy	快乐	快樂	*kuàilè*	adj	10
happy, pleased	高兴	高興	*gāoxìng*	adj	5
hard to bear, uncomfortable	难受	難受	*nánshòu*	adj	18
hard-working, diligent, studious	用功		*yònggōng*	adj	14
have, exist	有		*yǒu*	v	2
have a cold	感冒		*gǎnmào*	v	15
have a fever	发烧	發燒	*fā shāo*	vo	15
have a good trip, bon voyage	一路平安		*yí lù píng'ān*		20
have a meeting	开会	開會	*kāi huì*	vo	6
have fun, play	玩（儿）	玩（兒）	*wán(r)*	v	5
he, him	他		*tā*	pr	2
healthy; health	健康		*jiànkāng*	adj/n	15
heavy, serious	重		*zhòng*	adj	14

English	Simplified	Traditional	Pinyin	Part of Speech	Lesson
elen	海伦	海倫	*Hǎilún*	pn	14
ello!, Hey! on the phone)	喂		*wéi/wèi*	interj	6
elp	帮	幫	*bāng*	v	6
ere	这儿	這兒	*zhèr*	pr	9
ghway	高速公路		*gāosù gōnglù*	n	10
old or carry in he arms	抱		*bào*	v	18
ome-style	家常		*jiācháng*	n	12
omework, schoolwork	功课	功課	*gōngkè*	n	7
ong Kong	香港		*Xiānggǎng*	pn	19
onorable, expensive	贵	貴	*guì*	adj	1
ope; hope	希望	希望	*xīwàng*	v/n	8
ospital	医院	醫院	*yīyuàn*	n	15
ot	热	熱	*rè*	adj	11
ot-and-sour soup	酸辣汤	酸辣湯	*suānlàtāng*	n	12
otel	旅馆	旅館	*lǚguǎn*	n	19
our	钟头	鐘頭	*zhōngtóu*	n	14
our	小时	小時	*xiǎoshí*	n	15
ow, how come	怎么	怎麼	*zěnme*	qpr	7
ow many, some, a few	几	幾	*jǐ*	nu	2
ow many/much, o what extent	多		*duō*	adv	3
ow much/many	多少		*duōshao*	qpr	9
owever, but	不过	不過	*búguò*	conj	9
undred	百		*bǎi*	nu	9
ungry	饿	餓	*è*	adj	12

English	Simplified	Traditional	Pinyin	Part of Speech	Lesson
		I			
I, me	我		wǒ	pr	1
ice skate	滑冰	滑冰	huá bīng	vo	11
iced tea	冰茶	冰茶	bīngchá	n	12
if	要是		yàoshi	conj	6
if	如果…的话	如果…的話	rúguǒ…de huà	conj	9
immediately, right away	马上	馬上	mǎshàng	adv	19
impression	印象	印象	yìnxiàng	n	16
improve, raise, heighten,	提高		tígāo	v	18
in a terrible mess, how terrible	糟糕		zāogāo	adj	11
in addition to, besides	除了…以外		chúle…yǐwài	conj	8
in that case, then	那		nà	conj	4
in the middle of (doing something)	正在		zhèngzài	adv	8
(indicating degree) so, such	那么	那麼	nàme	pr	11
(indicating disposition, arrangement, or settlement of something)	把		bǎ	prep	15
inside	里边	裡邊	lǐbian	n	13
insurance; secure	保险	保險	bǎoxiǎn	n/adj	15
interest	兴趣	興趣	xìngqù	n	17
interesting	有意思		yǒu yìsi	adj	4
(interjectory particle used to soften a question)	呀		ya	p	5
intern	实习	實習	shíxí	v	19

English	Simplified	Traditional	Pinyin	Part of Speech	Lesson
international	国际	國際	*guójì*	adj	18
intersection	路口		*lùkǒu*	n	13
interview, interview (for a job or school admission)	面试	面試	*miànshì*	v/n	11
introduce	介绍	介紹	*jièshào*	v	5
invite someone (to dinner, coffee, etc.), play the host	请客	請客	*qǐng kè*	vo	4
is it OK? How is that? How does that sound?	怎么样	怎麼樣	*zěnmeyàng*	qpr	3
it	它		*tā*	pr	9
it doesn't matter	没关系	沒關係	*méi guānxi*		12
itchy	痒	癢	*yǎng*	adj	15

<table>
<tr><td colspan="6" align="center">J</td></tr>
</table>

English	Simplified	Traditional	Pinyin	Part of Speech	Lesson
Japan	日本		*Rìběn*	pn	13
Japanese (language)	日文		*Rìwén*	pn	13
job; to work	工作		*gōngzuò*	n/v	2
jog	跑步		*pǎo bù*	vo	18
just	刚	剛	*gāng*	adv	12
just, only (indicating a small number)	就		*jiù*	adv	16
just now, a moment ago	刚才	剛才	*gāngcái*	t	11

<table>
<tr><td colspan="6" align="center">K</td></tr>
</table>

English	Simplified	Traditional	Pinyin	Part of Speech	Lesson
kick	踢		*tī*	v	18
kitchen	厨房	廚房	*chúfáng*	n	17
know	知道		*zhīdao*	v	8

English	Simplified	Traditional	Pinyin	Part of Speech	Lesson
		L			
last time	上次		shàng cì		15
last year	去年		qùnián	t	14
late	晚		wǎn	adj	7
later	后来	後來	hòulái	t	8
laugh at, laugh, smile	笑		xiào	v	8
lawyer	律师	律師	lǜshī	n	2
lazy	懒	懶	lǎn	adj	15
lean on, lean against, be next to	靠		kào	v	19
left	左		zuǒ	n	13
length	长短	長短	chángduǎn	n	9
letter (correspon-dence)	信		xìn	n	8
level, standard	水平		shuǐpíng	n	18
Li You	李友		Lǐ Yǒu	pn	1
library	图书馆	圖書館	túshūguǎn	n	5
lie down	躺下		tǎng xià	vc	15
like	喜欢	喜歡	xǐhuan	v	3
line	线	線	xiàn	n	10
listen	听	聽	tīng	v	4
little, a bit, some	点（儿）	點（兒）	diǎn(r)	m	5
live (a life), observe (a holiday), celebrate (a festival), pass	过	過	guò	v	14
live (in a certain place)	住		zhù	v	14
living room	客厅	客廳	kètīng	n	17
long time	好久		hǎo jiǔ		4

English	Simplified	Traditional	Pinyin	Part of Speech	Lesson
look after, care for, attend to	照顾	照顧	zhàogu	v	20
look for	找		zhǎo	v	4
love, like, be fond of	爱	愛	ài	v	14
luggage	行李		xíngli	n	20
lunch, midday meal	午饭	午飯	wǔfàn	n	8
M					
major (in college), specialty	专业	專業	zhuānyè	n	8
make a phone call	打电话	打電話	dǎ diànhuà	vo	6
make a round trip, go there and back	往返		wǎngfǎn	v	19
make an appointment	约	約	yuē	v	11
male	男		nán	adj	2
many, much	多		duō	adj	7
map	地图	地圖	dìtú	n	13
master worker	师傅	師傅	shīfu	n	12
matter, affair, event	事（儿）	事（兒）	shì(r)	n	3
may; possible	可能		kěnéng	mv/adj	17
meal, (cooked) rice	饭	飯	fàn	n	3
meal card	饭卡	飯卡	fànkǎ	n	12
measure word for a pair)	双	雙	shuāng	m	9
measure word for a position in a numerical series, day of the month)	号	號	hào	m	3
measure word for an indefinite amount), some	些		xiē	m	12
measure word for books)	本		běn	m	14

English	Simplified	Traditional	Pinyin	Part of Speech	Lesson
(measure word for bottled liquid, etc.)	瓶		*píng*	m/n	5
(measure word for bus stops, train stops, etc.)	站		*zhàn*	m	10
(measure word for class periods)	节	節	*jié*	m	6
(measure word for complete courses of an action or instances of an action)	遍		*biàn*	m	15
(measure word for essays, articles, etc.)	篇		*piān*	m	8
(measure word for flat objects such as paper, pictures, etc.)	张	張	*zhāng*	m	7
(measure word for frequency)	次		*cì*	m	13
(measure word for kinds, sorts, types)	种	種	*zhǒng*	m	9
(measure word for letters)	封		*fēng*	m	8
(measure word for long, thin, inflexible objects such as pens, pencils, etc.)	枝		*zhī*	m	7
(measure word for many common everyday objects)	个	個	*gè/ge*	m	2
(measure word for meal orders, jobs)	份		*fèn*	m	19
(measure word for number of family members)	口		*kǒu*	m	2
(measure word for pants and long, thin objects)	条	條	*tiáo*	m	9
(measure word for people [polite])	位		*wèi*	m	6
(measure word for shirts, dresses, jackets, coats, etc.)	件		*jiàn*	m	9
(measure word for tablets, slices, etc.)	片		*piàn*	m	15

English	Simplified	Traditional	Pinyin	Part of Speech	Lesson
measure word for the basic Chinese monetary unit (equivalent of a dollar])	块	塊	*kuài*	m	9
measure word for the basic Chinese monetary unit), *yuan*	元		*yuán*	m	17
measure word for things contained in a cup or glass)	杯		*bēi*	m	5
measure word for things that come in a set/sets)	套		*tào*	m	17
measure word for things with handles, for handfuls of things)	把		*bǎ*	m	14
measure word for 1/100 of a kuai (equivalent of a cent])	分		*fēn*	m	9
measure word for 1/10 of a kuai [equivalent of a dime])	毛		*máo*	m	9
meat	肉		*ròu*	n	12
medicine	药	藥	*yào*	n	15
medium, middle	中		*zhōng*	adj	9
meet up/with	见面	見面	*jiàn miàn*	vo	6
method, way (of doing something)	办法	辦法	*bànfǎ*	n	15
middle	中间	中間	*zhōngjiān*	n	13
middle school, secondary school	中学	中學	*zhōngxué*	n	14
minute	分钟	分鐘	*fēnzhōng*	n	17
Miss, young lady	小姐		*xiǎojiě*	n	1
money	钱	錢	*qián*	n	9
monosodium glutamate (MSG)	味精		*wèijīng*	n	12
month	月		*yuè*	n	3

English	Simplified	Traditional	Pinyin	Part of Speech	Lesson
more and more	越来越	越來越	*yuè lái yuè*	adv	15
moreover	再说	再說	*zàishuō*	conj	15
morning	上午		*shàngwǔ*	t	6
morning	早上		*zǎoshang*	t	7
most, (of superlative degree) -est	最		*zuì*	adv	14
mother, mom	妈妈	媽媽	*māma*	n	2
mouth	嘴		*zuǐ*	n	14
move	搬		*bān*	v	16
movie	电影	電影	*diànyǐng*	n	4
Mr., husband, teacher	先生		*xiānsheng*	n	1
multi-story building, floor (of a multi-level building)	楼	樓	*lóu*	n	14
music	音乐	音樂	*yīnyuè*	n	4
must, have to	得		*děi*	av	6

N

English	Simplified	Traditional	Pinyin	Part of Speech	Lesson
name	名字		*míngzi*	n	1
near	近		*jìn*	adj	13
need not	不用		*bú yòng*		9
nervous, anxious	紧张	緊張	*jǐnzhāng*	adj	10
new	新		*xīn*	adj	8
new words, vocabulary	生词	生詞	*shēngcí*	n	7
new year	新年		*xīnnián*	n	10
New York	纽约	紐約	*Niǔyuē*	pn	1
newspaper	报纸	報紙	*bàozhǐ*	n	17

English	Simplified	Traditional	Pinyin	Part of Speech	Lesson
next one	下个	下個	xià ge		6
noon	中午		zhōngwǔ	t	8
north	北		běi	n	13
Northwest Airlines	西北航空公司		Xīběi Hángkōng Gōngsī	pn	19
nose	鼻子		bízi	n	14
not	没	沒	méi	adv	2
not, no	不		bù	adv	1
not only …, but also …	不但⋯，而且⋯		búdàn …, érqiě …	conj	11
not until, only then	才		cái	adv	5
now	现在	現在	xiànzài	t	3
number	号码	號碼	hàomǎ	n	16

O

English	Simplified	Traditional	Pinyin	Part of Speech	Lesson
o'clock (lit. dot, point, thus "points on the clock")	点	點	diǎn	m	3
(of airplanes) take off	起飞	起飛	qǐfēi	v	20
of course	当然	當然	dāngrán	adv	18
(of food) cold "blended", cold tossed	凉拌	涼拌	liángbàn	v	12
office	办公室	辦公室	bàngōngshì	n	6
often	常常		chángcháng	adv	4
older brother	哥哥		gēge	n	2
older female cousin	表姐		biǎojiě	n	14
older sister	姐姐		jiějie	n	2
on the Internet	网上	網上	wǎng shang		11
once, a bit	一下		yí xià	n+m	5

English	Simplified	Traditional	Pinyin	Part of Speech	Lesson
one bedroom and one living room	一房一厅	一房一廳	yì fáng yì tīng		17
(one's) family name is ...; family name	姓		xìng	v/n	1
oneself	自己		zìjǐ	pr	10
one-way trip	单程	單程	dānchéng	n	19
only	只		zhǐ	adv	4
or	还是	還是	háishi	conj	3
or	或者		huòzhě	conj	10
order food	点菜	點菜	diǎn cài	vo	12
other people, another person	别人	別人	biérén	n	4
otherwise	要不然		yàobùrán	conj	15

<table>
<tr><td colspan="6" align="center">P</td></tr>
</table>

English	Simplified	Traditional	Pinyin	Part of Speech	Lesson
pants	裤子	褲子	kùzi	n	9
paper	纸	紙	zhǐ	n	7
parents, father and mother	父母		fùmǔ	n	19
park	公园	公園	gōngyuán	n	11
(particle to link adverbial and verb)	地		de	p	20
(particle used after a verb to indicate a past experience)	过	過	guo	p	13
passport	护照	護照	hùzhào	n	19
paternal grandfather	爷爷	爺爺	yéye	n	20
paternal grandmother	奶奶		nǎinai	n	20
patient	病人		bìngrén	n	15
pay money	付钱	付錢	fù qián	vo	9
pay with a credit card	刷卡		shuā kǎ	vo	9

English	Simplified	Traditional	Pinyin	Part of Speech	Lesson
...ear	梨		*lí*	n	14
...en	笔	筆	*bǐ*	n	7
...eople, person	人		*rén*	n	1
...et	宠物	寵物	*chǒngwù*	n	17
...harmacy	药店	藥店	*yàodiàn*	n	15
...icture, photo	照片		*zhàopiàn*	n	2
...ace	地方		*dìfang*	n	13
...an; plan	打算		*dǎsuàn*	v/n	19
...an; plan	计划	計劃	*jìhuà*	v/n	19
...ate, dish	盘	盤	*pán*	n	12
...ay ball	打球		*dǎ qiú*	vo	4
...ease (polite form of ...equest), to treat or to ...vite (somebody)	请	請	*qǐng*	v	1
...olite	客气	客氣	*kèqi*	adj	6
...olitics	政治		*zhèngzhì*	n	19
...ossessive or ...escriptive particle)	的		*de*	p	2
...ractice	练习	練習	*liànxí*	v	6
...recisely, exactly	就		*jiù*	adv	6
...refix for ordinal ...umbers)	第		*dì*	prefix	7
...repare	准备	準備	*zhǔnbèi*	v	6
...ress, hold down, ...veigh down	压	壓	*yā*	v	18
...retty	漂亮	漂亮	*piàoliang*	adj	5
...retty good	不错	不錯	*búcuò*	adj	4
...review	预习	預習	*yùxí*	v	7

English	Simplified	Traditional	Pinyin	Part of Speech	Lesso
previous one	上个	上個	shàng ge		7
pronunciation	发音	發音	fāyīn	n	8
put, place	放		fàng	v	12
put in order	整理		zhěnglǐ	v	16
Q					
quarrel; noisy	吵		chǎo	v/adj	17
quarter (of an hour)	刻		kè	m	3
(question particle)	吗	嗎	ma	qp	1
(question particle)	呢		ne	qp	1
question, problem	问题	問題	wèntí	n	6
quiet	安静	安静	ānjìng	adj	17
quite a few	好几	好幾	hǎo jǐ		15
R					
racket	拍		pāi	n	18
rain	下雨		xià yǔ	vo	11
raise	养	養	yǎng	v	17
randomly, arbitrarily, messily	乱	亂	luàn	adv	15
read aloud	念		niàn	v	7
really	真		zhēn	adv	7
really painful	疼死		téng sǐ	adj+c	15
receive, accept	收		shōu	v	9
recently	最近		zuìjìn	t	8
red	红	紅	hóng	adj	9
refrigerator	冰箱		bīngxiāng	n	15

English	Simplified	Traditional	Pinyin	Part of Speech	Lesson
remember	记得	記得	*jìde*	v	16
remember, recall	想起来	想起來	*xiǎng qi lai*	vc	16
renminbi (RMB, Chinese currency)	人民币	人民幣	*rénmínbì*	n	17
rent	房租		*fángzū*	n	17
rent	租		*zū*	v	19
rent out	出租		*chūzū*	v	17
reserve, book (a ticket, hotel room, etc.)	订	訂	*dìng*	v	19
restaurant	饭馆（儿）	飯館（兒）	*fànguǎn(r)*	n	12
restroom, toilet	厕所	廁所	*cèsuǒ*	n	15
return	还	還	*huán*	v	17
review	复习	復習	*fùxí*	v	7
right	右		*yòu*	n	13
right, correct	对	對	*duì*	adj	4
right away, quickly, in a hurry	赶快	趕快	*gǎnkuài*	adv	15
roast duck	烤鸭	烤鴨	*kǎoyā*	n	20
room	房间	房間	*fángjiān*	n	16
round	圆	圓	*yuán*	adj	14
route, road	路		*lù*	n	10
S					
salt	盐	鹽	*yán*	n	12
same, alike	一样	一樣	*yíyàng*	adj	9
same, alike	同		*tóng*	adj	16
say, speak	说	說	*shuō*	v	6
scheduled flight	航班		*hángbān*	n	19

English	Simplified	Traditional	Pinyin	Part of Speech	Lesson
school	学校	學校	xuéxiào	n	5
school term, semester, quarter	学期	學期	xuéqī	n	8
seat	位子		wèizi	n	12
second oldest sister	二姐		èrjiě	n	2
security deposit	押金		yājīn	n	17
see	见	見	jiàn	v	3
see a doctor	看病		kàn bìng	vo	15
see off or out, take (someone somewhere)	送		sòng	v	10
seem, be like	好像	好像	hǎoxiàng	adv	12
sell at a discount, give a discount	打折		dǎ zhé	vo	19
send a text message (lit. send a short message)	发短信	發短信	fā duǎnxìn	vo	10
(sentence-final particle of exclamation, interrogation, etc.)	啊		a	p	6
(sentence-final particle)	吧		ba	p	5
September	九月		jiǔyuè	p	3
serve as, to be	当	當	dāng	v	17
serve food	上菜	上菜	shàng cài	vo	12
Shanghai	上海		Shànghǎi	pn	12
she, her	她		tā	pr	2
shirt	衬衫	襯衫	chènshān	n	9
shoes	鞋		xié	n	9
shop assistant, salesclerk	售货员	售貨員	shòuhuòyuán	n	9
should, ought to	应该	應該	yīnggāi	mv	18
show (a film), perform	演		yǎn	v	16

nglish	Simplified	Traditional	Pinyin	Part of Speech	Lesson
ide	旁边	旁邊	*pángbiān*	n	13
mple	简单	簡單	*jiǎndān*	adj	18
multaneously, t the same time	一边	一邊	*yìbiān*	adv	8
ng (a song)	唱歌（儿）	唱歌（兒）	*chàng gē(r)*	vo	4
t	坐		*zuò*	v	5
ze	大小		*dàxiǎo*	n	9
ze	号	號	*hào*	n	9
eep	睡觉	睡覺	*shuì jiào*	vo	4
ow	慢		*màn*	adj	7
mall, little	小		*xiǎo*	adj	4
mart, bright, clever	聪明	聰明	*cōngming*	adj	14
now	下雪		*xià xuě*	vo	11
o	所以		*suǒyǐ*	conj	4
o, this (late, etc.)	这么	這麼	*zhème*	pr	7
occer, football	足球		*zúqiú*	n	18
ofa	沙发	沙發	*shāfā*	n	17
ome	有的		*yǒude*	pr	4
on	儿子	兒子	*érzi*	n	2
orry	对不起	對不起	*duìbuqǐ*	v	5
ound recording; ecord	录音	錄音	*lùyīn*	n/vo	7
our	酸		*suān*	adj	12
outh	南		*nán*	n	13
pend	花	花	*huā*	v	10
pend, take (effort)	费	費	*fèi*	v	16

English	Simplified	Traditional	Pinyin	Part of Speech	Lesson
sports	运动	運動	yùndòng	n	13
sportswear, athletic clothing	运动服	運動服	yùndòngfú	n	18
spring	春天		chūntiān	n	11
store, shop	商店		shāngdiàn	n	9
straight, continuously	一直		yìzhí	adv	13
strength, effort	力气	力氣	lìqi	n	16
(structural particle)	得		de	p	7
student	学生	學生	xuésheng	n	1
study, learn	学	學	xué	v	7
study, learn	学习	學習	xuéxí	v	7
style	样子	樣子	yàngzi	n	9
subway	地铁	地鐵	dìtiě	n	10
suitable	合适	合適	héshì	adj	9
suitcase, box	箱子		xiāngzi	n	20
summer	夏天		xiàtiān	n	11
summer term	暑期		shǔqī	n	14
summer vacation	暑假		shǔjià	n	19
sweet	甜		tián	adj	12
sweet-and-sour fish	糖醋鱼	糖醋魚	tángcùyú	n	12
swim	游泳		yóu yǒng	vo	18

T

English	Simplified	Traditional	Pinyin	Part of Speech	Lesson
table	桌子		zhuōzi	n	12
Taipei	台北		Táiběi	pn	19
take, get	拿		ná	v	13

English	Simplified	Traditional	Pinyin	Part of Speech	Lesson
take a bath/shower	洗澡		xǐ zǎo	vo	8
take a break, to rest	休息		xiūxi	v	15
take a taxi	打车	打車	dǎ chē	vo	10
talk	说话	說話	shuō huà	vo	7
taxi	出租汽车	出租汽車	chūzū qìchē	n	10
tea	茶	茶	chá	n	5
teach	教		jiāo	v	7
teacher	老师	老師	lǎoshī	n	1
Teacher Chang	常老师	常老師	Cháng lǎoshī	pn	6
television	电视	電視	diànshì	n	4
tell	告诉	告訴	gàosu	v	8
tennis	网球	網球	wǎngqiú	n	18
text of a lesson	课文	課文	kèwén	n	7
thank	谢谢	謝謝	xièxie	v	3
that	那		nà	pr	2
that settles it, that's settled, it's decided	一言为定	一言為定	yì yán wéi dìng		16
then	然后	然後	ránhòu	adv	10
there	那儿	那兒	nàr	pr	8
there	那里	那裡	nàli	pr	17
thin, skinny, lean	瘦		shòu	adj	20
things, objects	东西	東西	dōngxi	n	9
think	想		xiǎng	v	16
thirsty	渴		kě	adj	12
this	这	這	zhè	pr	2

English	Simplified	Traditional	Pinyin	Part of Speech	Lesson
this year	今年		*jīnnián*	t	3
thousand	千		*qiān*	nu	19
Thursday	星期四		*xīngqīsì*	n	3
ticket	票		*piào*	n	10
time	时间	時間	*shíjiān*	n	6
time (a point in), moment, time (a duration of)	时候	時候	*shíhou*	n	4
tired	累		*lèi*	adj	8
to, for	给	給	*gěi*	prep	6
today	今天		*jīntiān*	t	3
tofu, bean curd	豆腐		*dòufu*	n	12
together	一起	一起	*yìqǐ*	adv	5
Tokyo	东京	東京	*Dōngjīng*	pn	13
Tom	汤姆	湯姆	*Tāngmǔ*	pn	14
tomorrow	明天		*míngtiān*	t	3
too, also	也		*yě*	adv	1
too, extremely	太…了		*tài … le*		3
tour guide	导游	導遊	*dǎoyóu*	n	19
towards	往		*wǎng*	prep	13
traffic light	红绿灯	紅綠燈	*hónglǜdēng*	n	13
travel	旅行		*lǚxíng*	v	16
travel agency	旅行社		*lǚxíngshè*	n	19
travel by	坐		*zuò*	v	10
troublesome	麻烦	麻煩	*máfan*	adj	10
try	试	試	*shì*	v	9

English	Simplified	Traditional	Pinyin	Part of Speech	Lesson
turn	拐	拐	*guǎi*	v	13
twelve	十二		*shí'èr*	nu	3
two [colloq.]	俩	倆	*liǎ*	nu+m	16
two, a couple of	两	兩	*liǎng*	nu	2

English	Simplified	Traditional	Pinyin	Part of Speech	Lesson
uncle	叔叔		*shūshu*	n	20
understand	懂	懂	*dǒng*	v	7
use	用		*yòng*	v	8
usually	平常		*píngcháng*	adv	7

		V			
vegetarian (lit. plain)	素		*sù*	adj	12
vegetarian meal	素餐		*sùcān*	n	19
very	很		*hěn*	adv	3
very, extremely, exceedingly	非常		*fēicháng*	adv	11
very, rather	挺		*tǐng*	adv	9
vicinity, neighborhood, nearby area	附近		*fùjìn*	n	17
visa	签证	簽證	*qiānzhèng*	n	19

		W			
wait, wait for	等		*děng*	v	6
waiter, attendant	服务员	服務員	*fúwùyuán*	n	12
walk	走路		*zǒu lù*	vo	17
Wang Hong	王红	王紅	*Wáng Hóng*	pn	14
Wang Peng	王朋		*Wáng Péng*	pn	1
want	要		*yào*	v	5

English	Simplified	Traditional	Pinyin	Part of Speech	Lesson
want to, would like to	想		xiǎng	av	4
warm	暖和		nuǎnhuo	adj	11
watch, look, read	看		kàn	v	4
water	水		shuǐ	n	5
watermelon	西瓜		xīgua	n	14
we, us	我们	我們	wǒmen	pr	3
wear, put on	穿		chuān	v	9
weather	天气	天氣	tiānqì	n	11
week	星期		xīngqī	n	3
weekend	周末	週末	zhōumò	n	4
welcome	欢迎	歡迎	huānyíng	v	20
west	西		xī	n	13
what	什么	什麼	shénme	qpr	1
where	哪儿	哪兒	nǎr	qpr	5
where	哪里	哪裡	nǎli	pr	7
which	哪		nǎ/něi	qpr	6
who, whom	谁	誰	shéi	qpr	2
why	为什么	為什麼	wèishénme	qpr	3
will	会	會	huì	mv	11
will, be going to; want to, have a desire to	要		yào	mv	6
window	窗户	窗戶	chuānghu	n	19
winter	冬天		dōngtiān	n	11
winter vacation	寒假		hánjià	n	10

English	Simplified	Traditional	Pinyin	Part of Speech	Lesson
wish (well)	祝		*zhù*	v	8
with	跟		*gēn*	prep	6
work at a temporary job (often part time)	打工		*dǎ gōng*	vo	19
worry	担心	擔心	*dān xīn*	vo	18
write	写	寫	*xiě*	v	7
wrong	错	錯	*cuò*	adj	12
Y					
year (of age)	岁	歲	*suì*	n	3
yellow	黄	黃	*huáng*	adj	9
yesterday	昨天		*zuótiān*	t	4
you	你		*nǐ*	pr	1
you (honorific for 你)	您		*nín*	pr	6
younger brother	弟弟		*dìdi*	n	2
younger sister	妹妹		*mèimei*	n	2

Lesson 11   L11-1

Noun:	天气，公园
Verb:	下雪，约，滑冰，预报，办
Modal Verb:	会
Adjective:	冷，暖和
Adverb:	更
Preposition:	比
Conjunction:	不但…，而且…
Time Word:	刚才
Others:	网上

L11-2

Noun:	冬天，夏天，春天，秋天
Pronoun:	那么
Verb:	下雨，面试，回去
Adjective:	好玩儿，糟糕，热，舒服
Adverb:	非常，又
Proper Noun:	加州

Lesson 12   L12-1

Noun:	饭馆（儿），位子，服务员，桌子，盘，饺子，家常，豆腐，肉，碗，酸辣汤，味精，盐，小白菜，青菜，冰茶
Measure Word:	些
Verb:	点菜，放，卖完，上菜
Adjective:	素，渴，够，饿
Adverb:	好像，刚

L12-2

Noun:	师傅，糖醋鱼，牛肉，鱼，黄瓜，米饭，饭卡
Verb:	红烧，凉拌，忘，带
Adjective:	好吃，甜，酸，错，清楚
Adverb:	极
Others:	没关系
Proper Noun:	上海

Lesson 13

L13-1

Noun: 中心，运动场，旁边，活动，中间，书店，地方，里边

Verb: 上，听说

Adjective: 远，近

Preposition: 离

L13-2

Noun: 中国城，地图，南，路口，西，东，北，前，红绿灯，右，左，前面

Measure Word: 次

Verb: 拿，拐

Adverb: 一直

Preposition: 从，往

Particle: 过

Others: 哎

Proper Noun: 谷歌，日文，东京，日本

Lesson 14

L14-1

Noun: 舞会，表姐，中学，礼物，饮料，水果，花，苹果，梨，西瓜，楼

Measure Word: 本，把

Verb: 过，送，爱，住，接

Adjective: 重

Proper Noun: 王红

L14-2

Noun: 钟头，暑期班，狗，脸，眼睛，鼻子，嘴，蛋糕

Verb: 以为，长，属，像，长大

Adjective: 聪明，用功，可爱，圆

Adverb: 一定，最

Time Word: 去年

Proper Noun: 海伦，汤姆

Vocabulary Index (by Lesson and Grammar Category), Volume 2 383

Lesson 15

L15-1

Noun:	病人，医院，肚子，夜里，厕所，冰箱，药，小时，办法
Measure Word:	片，遍
Verb:	看病，发烧，躺下，检查，吃坏，打针
Adverb:	最好
Preposition:	把
Others:	疼死，好几

L15-2

Noun:	身体，药店，保险
Verb:	生病，感冒，过敏，休息
Adjective:	痒，健康，懒
Adverb:	赶快，越来越，乱
Conjunction:	要不然，再说
Others:	上次

Lesson 16

L16-1

Noun:	印象，力气
Verb:	成，演，费
Adjective:	同
Adverb:	就
Time Word:	后天
Others:	俩，一言为定

L16-2

Noun:	号码，房间，电
Verb:	记得，想，想起来，搬，打扫，整理，旅行

Lesson 17

L17-1

Noun:	报纸，广告，附近，公寓，分钟，卧室，厨房，卫生间，客厅，家具
Measure Word:	套
Verb:	吵，做饭，出租，走路
Adverb:	可能
Preposition:	连

L17-2

Noun:	沙发，饭桌，椅子，书桌，书架，房租，美元，人民币，费，押金，宠物，兴趣
Measure Word:	元
Pronoun:	那里
Verb:	当，还，准，养
Adjective:	干净，安静
Adverb:	差不多
Conjunction:	另外
Others:	一房一厅

Lesson 18

L18-1

Noun:	网球，拍，篮球
Verb:	怕，跑步，游泳，淹死
Modal Verb:	愿意
Adjective:	胖，简单，难受，危险
Adverb:	当然

L18-2

Noun:	水平，足球，比赛，脚，手，运动服
Verb:	上大学，提高，踢，抱，压，担心
Modal Verb:	应该
Adjective:	国际，美式，棒
Preposition:	为了，被
Others:	半天

Lesson 19

L19-1

Noun:	公司，计划，暑假，父母，首都，政治，文化，导游，护照，签证，旅行社
Verb:	放假，实习，打工，打算，订
Adjective:	有名
Adverb:	马上
Others:	名胜古迹
Proper Noun:	长城，香港，台北

L19-2

Noun:	初，单程，航空，航班，窗户，走道，素餐，旅馆
Measure Word:	份
Numeral:	千
Verb:	往返，查，打折，转机，靠，租
Others:	直飞
Proper Noun:	中国国际航空公司，西北航空公司

Lesson 20

L20-1

Noun:	行李，包，箱子，登机牌，登机口
Verb:	托运，超重，哭，照顾，起飞，小心
Particle:	地
Others:	一路平安

L20-2

Noun:	叔叔，阿姨，爷爷，奶奶，烤鸭
Verb:	欢迎
Adjective:	瘦
Proper Noun:	首都机场

The How About You? vocabulary index is sequenced according to the order of the corresponding images, horizontally from left to right.

English	Simplified	Traditional	Pinyin	Part of Speech
Lesson 11: Dialogue 1				
windy	刮大风	刮大風	guā dà fēng	vo
cloudy	多云	多雲	duō yún	
sunny	出太阳（了）	出太陽（了）	chū tàiyang (le)	vo
Lesson 11: Dialogue 2				
play games on the Internet	上网玩儿游戏	上網玩兒遊戲	shàng wàng wánr yóuxì	
wash clothes	洗衣服		xǐ yīfu	vo
clean the room	打扫房间	打掃房間	dǎsǎo fángjiān	vo
Lesson 12: Dialogue 1				
small steamed bun	小笼包	小籠包	xiǎolóngbāo	n
fried noodles	炒面	炒麵	chǎomiàn	n
mapo tofu	麻婆豆腐		mápó dòufu	n
Lesson 12: Dialogue 2				
curry	咖喱		gālí	n
ramen	拉面	拉麵	lāmiàn	n
fried rice	炒饭	炒飯	chǎofàn	n
Lesson 13: Dialogue 1				
to an art gallery	去美术馆看展览	去美術館看展覽	qù měishùguǎn kàn zhǎnlǎn	
to exercise at the gym	去健身房运动	去健身房運動	qù jiànshēnfáng yùndòng	
to the music hall	去音乐厅看演出	去音樂廳看演出	qù yīnyuètīng kàn yǎnchū	

English	Simplified	Traditional	Pinyin	Part of Speech
Lesson 13: Dialogue 2				
southeast	东南	東南	*dōngnán*	n
southwest	西南		*xīnán*	n
northeast	东北	東北	*dōngběi*	n
northwest	西北		*xīběi*	n
Lesson 14: Dialogue 1				
banana	香蕉	香蕉	*xiāngjiāo*	n
strawberry	草莓	草莓	*cǎoméi*	n
grapes	葡萄	葡萄	*pútao*	n
Lesson 14: Dialogue 2				
cookies	饼干	餅乾	*bǐnggān*	n
balloon	气球	氣球	*qìqiú*	n
popcorn	爆米花	爆米花	*bàomǐhuā*	n
Lesson 15: Dialogue 1				
lower back pain	腰疼		*yāo téng*	
cough	咳嗽		*késòu*	v
have a runny nose	流鼻涕		*liú bítì*	vo
Lesson 15: Dialogue 2				
peanuts	花生	花生	*huāshēng*	n
cats	猫	貓	*māo*	n
pollen	花粉	花粉	*huāfěn*	n
Lesson 16: Dialogue 1				
go fishing	钓鱼	釣魚	*diào yú*	vo
go for a drive	开车兜风	開車兜風	*kāi chē dōu fēng*	
have a picnic	野餐		*yěcān*	v

English	Simplified	Traditional	Pinyin	Part of Speech
Lesson 16: Dialogue 2				
fix the car	修车	修車	*xiū chē*	vo
do volunteer work	做义工	做義工	*zuò yìgōng*	vo
mow the lawn	割草	割草	*gē cǎo*	vo
Lesson 17: Narrative				
coffee table	咖啡桌		*kāfēizhuō*	n
barstools	吧台凳	吧檯凳	*bātáidèng*	n
recliner	躺椅		*tǎngyǐ*	n
Lesson 17: Dialogue				
bird	鸟	鳥	*niǎo*	n
guinea pig	天竺鼠		*tiānzhúshǔ*	n
turtle	乌龟	烏龜	*wūguī*	n
Lesson 18: Dialogue 1				
play baseball	打棒球		*dǎ bàngqiú*	vo
play ice hockey	打冰球		*dǎ bīngqiú*	vo
do skateboarding	玩儿滑板	玩兒滑板	*wánr huábǎn*	vo
Lesson 18: Dialogue 2				
table tennis competition	乒乓球比赛	乒乓球比賽	*pīngpāngqiú bǐsài*	n
gymnastics competition	体操比赛	體操比賽	*tǐcāo bǐsài*	n
car-racing competition	赛车比赛	賽車比賽	*sàichē bǐsài*	n
Lesson 19: Dialogue 1				
Africa	非洲		*Fēizhōu*	pn
Asia	亚洲	亞洲	*Yàzhōu*	pn
Europe	欧洲	歐洲	*Ōuzhōu*	pn

English	Simplified	Traditional	Pinyin	Part of Speech
Lesson 19: Dialogue 2				
driver's license	驾（驶执）照	駕（駛執）照	*jià(shǐ zhí)zhào*	n
camera	照相机	照相機	*zhàoxiàngjī*	n
cash	现金	現金	*xiànjīn*	n
Lesson 20: Dialogue 1				
keys	钥匙	鑰匙	*yàoshi*	n
jewelry	珠宝首饰	珠寶首飾	*zhūbǎo shǒushì*	n
tablet computer	平板电脑	平板電腦	*píngbǎn diànnǎo*	n
Lesson 20: Dialogue 2				
charge one's cell phone	给手机充电	給手機充電	*gěi shǒujī chōng diàn*	
go shopping at duty-free shops	逛免税商店	逛免稅商店	*guàng miǎnshuì shāngdiàn*	vo
take and post a selfie	自拍打卡		*zì pāi dǎ kǎ*	

Lesson 11 Dialogue 1

Tomorrow's Weather
Will Be Even Better!

（高小音跟弟弟高文中聊到天氣……）

高小音： 今天天氣比[1]昨天好，不下雪了[2]。

高文中： 我約了朋友明天去公園滑冰，不知道天氣會[3]怎麼樣，冷不冷？

高小音： 我剛才看了網上的天氣預報，明天天氣比今天更好。不但不會下雪，而且[a]會暖和一點兒[4]。

高文中： 是嗎？太好了！

高小音： 你約了誰去滑冰？

高文中： 白英愛。

高小音： 你約了白英愛？可是她今天早上坐飛機去紐約了。

高文中： 真的啊？那我明天怎麼辦？

高小音： 你還是在家看電視吧！

Dialogue 2

The Weather
Here Is Awful!

（高文中在網上找白英愛聊天兒。）

高文中： 英愛，紐約那麼好玩兒，你怎麼在網上，沒出去？

白英愛： 這兒的天氣非常糟糕。

高文中： 怎麼了[a]？

白英愛： 昨天下大雨，今天又[5]下雨了。

高文中： 這個週末這兒天氣很好，你快一點兒回來吧。

白英愛： 這個週末紐約也會暖和一點兒。我下個星期有一個面試，還不能回去。

高文中： 我在加州找了一個工作，你也去吧。加州冬天不冷，夏天不熱，春天和秋天更舒服。

白英愛： 加州好是好[6]，可是我更喜歡紐約。

Lesson 12 (Dialogue 1)

Dining Out

（在飯館兒……）

服務員：請進，請進。

李友：　人怎麼這麼[a]多？好像一個位子[b]都沒[1]有了。

王朋：　服務員，請問，還有沒有位子？

服務員：有，有，有。那張桌子沒有人。

……

服務員：兩位想吃點兒什麼？

李友：　王朋，你點菜吧。

王朋：　好。先給我們兩盤餃子，要素的。

服務員：除了餃子以外，還要什麼？

王朋：　李友，你說呢？

李友：　還要一盤家常豆腐，不要放肉，我吃素。

服務員：我們的家常豆腐沒有肉。

李友：　還要兩碗[c]酸辣湯，請別放味精，少[2]放點兒鹽。有小白菜嗎？

服務員：對不起，小白菜剛[3]賣完[4]。

王朋：　那就不要青菜了。

服務員：那喝點兒什麼呢？

王朋：　我要一杯冰茶。李友，你喝什麼？

李友：　我很渴，請給我一杯可樂，多放點兒冰。

服務員：好，兩盤餃子，一盤家常豆腐，兩碗酸辣湯，一杯冰茶，一杯可樂，多放冰。還要別的嗎？

李友：　不要別的了，這些夠[d]了。服務員，我們都餓了，請上菜快一點兒[e]。

服務員：沒問題，菜很快就能做好[5]。

Dialogue 2

At the Dining Hall

（今天是星期四，學生餐廳有中國菜，師傅是上海人。）

王朋：師傅[a]，請問今天晚飯有什麼好吃的？

師傅：我們今天有糖醋魚，甜甜的[6]、酸酸的，好吃極了[b]，你買一個吧。

王朋：好。今天有沒有紅燒牛肉？

師傅：沒有。你已經要魚了，別吃肉了。來[7]個涼拌黃瓜吧？

王朋：好。再來一碗米飯。一共多少錢？

師傅：糖醋魚，四塊五，涼拌黃瓜，一塊七；一碗米飯，五毛錢。一共六塊七。

王朋：師傅，糟糕，我忘了帶飯卡了。這是十塊錢。

師傅：找你三塊三。

王朋：師傅，錢你找錯了，多找了我一塊錢。

師傅：對不起，我沒有看清楚。

王朋：沒關係[c]。

師傅：下個星期四再來。

王朋：好，再見。

Lesson 13

Dialogue 1

Where Are You
Off To?

（白英愛剛下課……）

常老師：小白，下課了？上哪兒去[a]？

白英愛：您好，常老師。我想去學校的電腦中心，不知道怎麼走，聽說就在運動場旁邊[1]。

常老師：電腦中心沒有[2]運動場那麼[3]遠。你知道學校圖書館在哪裡[b]嗎？

白英愛：知道，離王朋的宿舍不遠。

常老師：電腦中心離圖書館很近，就在圖書館和學生活動中心中間。

白英愛：常老師，您去哪兒呢？

常老師：我想到學校書店去買書[4]。

白英愛：書店在什麼地方[c]？

常老師：就在學生活動中心裡邊。我們一起走吧。

白英愛：好。

（高文中找王朋去中國城吃飯……）

高文中：我們去中國城吃中國飯吧！

王朋：　我沒去過[5]中國城，不知道中國城在哪兒。

高文中：沒問題[a]，你開車，我告訴你怎麼走。

王朋：　你有谷歌地圖嗎？拿給我看看[6]。

高文中：手機在宿舍里，我忘了帶了。

王朋：　沒有地圖，走錯了怎麼辦？

高文中：沒有地圖沒關係，中國城我去過很多次，不用地圖也能找到[7]。你從這兒一直往南開，到第三個路口，往西一拐[b]就[8]到了。

王朋：　哎，我不知道東南西北[c]。

高文中：那你一直往前開，到第三個紅綠燈，往右一拐就到了。

（到了第三個路口……）

王朋：　不對，不對。你看，這個路口只能往左拐，不能往右拐。

高文中：那就是下一個路口。往右拐，再往前開。到了，到了，你看見了嗎？前面有很多中國字。

王朋：　那不是中文，那是日文，我們到了小東京了。

高文中：是嗎？那我們不吃中國飯了，吃日本飯吧！

Dialogue 1

Let's Go to
a Party!

（李友給王朋打電話。）

李友： 王朋，你做什麼呢[1]？

王朋： 我看書呢。

李友： 今天高小音過生日[a]，晚上我們在她
家開舞會，你能去嗎？

王朋： 能去。幾點？

李友： 七點。我們先吃飯，吃完飯再唱歌
跳舞。

王朋： 有哪些人？

李友： 小音和她的男朋友，小音的表姐[b]，
白英愛， 你妹妹王紅，聽說還有
小音的中學同學。

王朋： 你要送給小音什麼生日禮物？

李友： 我買了一本書送給她。

王朋： 那我帶什麼東西？

李友： 飲料或者水果都可以。

王朋： 那我帶一些飲料，再買一把花兒。

李友： 小音愛吃水果，我再買一些蘋果、
梨和西瓜吧。

王朋： 你住的地方[2]離小音家很遠，水果
很重，我開車去接你，我們一起
去吧。

李友： 好，我六點半在樓下等你。

（在高小音家……）

高小音：　王朋，李友，快進來。

李友：　　小音，祝你生日快樂！這是送給你的生日禮物。

高小音：　謝謝！……太好了！我一直想買這書。帶這麼多東西，你們太客氣了

王紅：　　哥哥，李友，你們來了[a]。

李友：　　啊[b]。小紅，你怎麼樣？

王紅：　　我很好。每天都在學英文。

王朋：　　小紅，你每天練習英文練習多長時間[3]？

王紅：　　三個半鐘頭[c]。還看兩個鐘頭的英文電視。

高文中：　哎，你們兩個是什麼時候到的[4]？

李友：　　剛到。

高文中：　白英愛沒跟你們一起來嗎？

李友：　　她還[5]沒來？我以為[d]她已經來了。

高小音：　王朋，李友，來，我給你們介紹一下，這是我表姐海倫，這是她的兒子湯姆。

王朋：　　你好，海倫。

海倫：　　你好，王朋。文中和小音都說你又聰明[e]又用功[6]。

王朋：　　哪裡，哪裡。你的中文說得真好，是在哪兒學的？

海倫：　　在暑期班[f]學的。

王朋：　　哎，湯姆長[g]得真可愛！你們看，他笑了。他幾歲了？

海倫：　　剛一歲，是去年生的，屬狗。

李友：　　你們看，他的臉圓圓的，眼睛大大的，鼻子高高的，嘴不大也不小，長得很像海倫。

王紅：　　媽媽這麼漂亮，兒子長大一定也很帥。

高小音：　來，來，來，我們吃蛋糕吧。

高文中：　等等白英愛吧。她最愛吃蛋糕。

Lesson 15 （Dialogue 1）

My Stomach Is
Killing Me!

（病人去醫院看病……）

高文中： 醫生，我肚子疼死[1]了。

醫生： 你昨天吃什麼東西了？

高文中： 我姐姐上個星期過生日，蛋糕沒吃
完。昨天晚上我吃了幾口[2]，夜裡
肚子就疼起來[2]了，今天早上上了
好幾次[3]廁所。

醫生： 你把[4]蛋糕放在哪兒了？

高文中： 放在冰箱里了。

醫生： 放了幾天了？

高文中： 五、六天[a]了。

醫生： 發燒嗎？

高文中： 不發燒。

醫生： 你躺下。先檢查一下。

……

醫生： 你吃蛋糕把肚子吃壞了。

高文中： 得打針嗎？

醫生： 不用打針，吃這種藥[b]就可以。一天
三次，一次兩片。

高文中： 醫生，一天吃幾次？請您再說一遍。

醫生： 一天三次，一次兩片。

高文中： 好！飯前[c]吃還是飯後吃？

醫生： 飯前飯後都可以。不過，你最好二十
四小時不要吃飯。

高文中： 那我要餓死了。不行，這個辦法
不好！

（王朋這幾天好像生病了……）

李友： 王朋，你怎麼了？眼睛怎麼紅紅的，感冒了嗎？

王朋： 沒感冒。我也不知道怎麼了，最近這幾天身體很不舒服。眼睛又紅又癢。

李友： 你一定是對[5]什麼過敏了。

王朋： 我想也是，所以去藥店買了一些藥。已經吃了四、五種了，花了不少錢，都沒有用。

李友： 把你買的藥拿出來給我看看。

王朋： 這些就是。

李友： 這些藥沒有用。為什麼不去看病？你沒有健康保險嗎？

王朋： 我有保險。可是我這個學期功課很多，看病太花時間。

李友： 那你也得趕快去看病[a]。要不然病會越來越[6]重。

王朋： 我想再吃點兒別的藥試試[b]。我上次生病，沒去看醫生[a]，休息了兩天，最後也好了。

李友： 不行，不行，你太懶了。再說[7]，你不能自己亂吃藥。走，我跟你看病去。

Lesson 16

王朋跟李友在同[a]一個學校學習，他們認識已經快半年了。王朋常常幫李友練習說中文。他們也常常一起出去玩兒，每次都玩兒得[1]很高興。李友對王朋的印象[b]很好，王朋也很喜歡李友，他們成了好朋友。

王朋： 這個週末學校演一個中國電影[c]，我們一起去看，好嗎？

李友： 好啊！不過，聽說看電影的人很多，買得到[2]票嗎？

王朋： 票已經買好了，我費了很大的力氣才買到。

李友： 好極了！我早[d]就想看中國電影了。還有別人跟我們一起去嗎？

王朋： 沒有，就[3]我們倆[e]。

李友： 好。什麼時候？

王朋： 後天晚上八點。

李友： 看電影以前，我請你吃晚飯。

王朋： 太好了！一言為定[f]。

（費先生給李友打電話……）

費先生：喂，請問李友小姐在嗎？

李友：　我就是。請問你是哪一位？

費先生：我姓費，你還記得^a我嗎？

李友：　姓費？

費先生：你還記得上個月高小音的生日舞會
　　　　嗎？我就是最後請你跳舞的那個人。
　　　　你再想想。想起來了嗎？

李友：　對不起，我想不起來。

費先生：我是高小音的中學同學。

李友：　是嗎？你是怎麼知道我的電話號碼
　　　　的？

費先生：是小音告訴我的。

李友：　費先生，你有事嗎？

費先生：這個週末你有空兒嗎？我想請你去
　　　　跳舞。

李友：　這個週末不行，下個星期我有三個
　　　　考試。

費先生：沒關係，下個週末怎麼樣？你考完
　　　　試，我們好好兒^b玩兒玩兒。

李友：　下個週末也不行，我要從宿舍搬出
　　　　去⁴，得打掃、整理房間。

費先生：你看下下個週末，好不好？

李友：　對不起，下下個週末更不行了，我
　　　　要跟我的男朋友去紐約旅行。

費先生：……那……

李友：　費先生，對不起，我的手機沒電了。
　　　　再見！

費先生：喂……喂……

王朋在學校的宿舍住了兩個學期了[1]。他覺得宿舍太吵，睡不好覺，房間太小，連電腦都[2]放不下[3]，再說也沒有地方可以做飯，很不方便，所以準備下個學期搬出去住。他找房子找了一個多[4]月了，可是還沒有找到合適的。剛才他從報紙上看到了一個廣告，說學校附近有一套公寓出租，離學校很近，走路只要五分鐘，很方便。公寓有一個[a]臥室，一個廚房，一個衛生間[b]，一個客廳，還帶傢俱。王朋覺得這套公寓可能對他很合適。

（王朋打電話問租房子的事兒……）

王朋：喂，請問你們是不是[a]有公寓出租？

房東：有啊，一房一廳[b]，非常乾淨，還帶傢俱。

王朋：有什麼傢俱？

房東：客廳裡有一套沙發、一張飯桌跟四把椅子。臥室裡有一張床、一張書桌和一個書架。

王朋：你們那裡安靜不安靜？

房東：非常安靜。

王朋：每個月房租多少錢？

房東：八百五十元。

王朋：八百五十美元？人民幣差不多是……有一點兒貴，能不能便宜點兒？

房東：那你不用付水電費。

王朋：要不要付押金？

房東：要多付一個月的房租當押金，搬出去的時候還給你。另外，我們公寓不准養寵物。

王朋：沒關係，我對養寵物沒有興趣[c]，什麼寵物都[5]不養。

房東：那太好了。你今天下午來看看吧。

王朋：好。

Lesson 18

Dialogue 1

Getting in Shape

（高文中跟王朋聊天兒……）

高文中：　你看，我的肚子越來越大了。

王朋：　　你平常吃得那麼多，又[a]不運動，
　　　　　當然越來越胖了。

高文中：　那怎麼辦呢？

王朋：　　如果怕胖，你一個星期運動兩、三
　　　　　次，每次半個小時，肚子就會小了。

高文中：　我兩年沒運動了[1]，做什麼運動呢？

王朋：　　最簡單的運動是跑步。

高文中：　冬天那麼冷，夏天那麼熱，跑步太
　　　　　難受[2]了。

王朋：　　你打網球吧。

高文中：　打網球得買網球拍、網球鞋，你知
　　　　　道，網球拍、網球鞋貴極了！

王朋：　　找幾個人打籃球吧。買個籃球很便
　　　　　宜。

高文中：　那每次都得打電話約人，麻煩死了。

王朋：　　你去游泳吧。不用找人，也不用花
　　　　　很多錢，什麼時候去都可以。

高文中：　游泳？我怕水，太危險了，淹死了
　　　　　怎麼辦？

王朋：　　我也沒辦法了。你不願意運動，那
　　　　　就胖下去[3]吧。

王朋的妹妹王紅剛從北京來,要在美國上^a大學,現在住在高小音家裡學英文。為了^b提高英文水平,她每天都看兩個小時的電視⁴。

高小音: 快把電視打開,足球比賽開始了。

王紅: 是嗎?我也喜歡看足球賽^c。……這是什麼足球^d啊?怎麼不是圓的?

高小音: 這不是國際^e足球,這是美式足球。

王紅: 足球應該用腳踢,為什麼那個人用手抱著⁵跑呢?

高小音: 美式足球可以用手。

王紅: 你看,你看,那麼多人都壓在一起下面的人不是要被⁶壓壞^f了嗎?

高小音: 別擔心,他們的身體都很棒,而且還穿特別的運動服,沒問題。

王紅: 我看了半天^g也看不懂。還是看別的吧。

高小音: 你在美國住半年就會喜歡了。我男朋友看美式足球的時候,常常連飯都忘了吃。

Lesson 19　Dialogue 1

Traveling to Beijing

(暑假快要到了……)

王朋: 李友,時間過得真快,馬上就要放假了,我們的同學,有的去暑期班學習,有的去公司實習,有的回家打工,你有什麼計劃?

李友: 我還沒有想好。你呢,王朋?

王朋: 我暑假打算^a回北京去看父母。

李友: 是嗎?我聽說北京這個城市很有意思。

王朋: 當然。北京是中國的首都,也是中國的政治、文化中心,有很多名勝古蹟。

李友: 對啊,長城很有名。

王朋: 還有,北京的好飯館多得不得了¹。

李友: 真的?我去過香港、台北,還沒去過北京,要是能去北京就好了。

王朋: 那你跟我一起回去吧,我當你的導遊。

李友: 真的嗎?那太好了!護照我已經有了,我得趕快辦^b簽證。

王朋: 那我馬上給旅行社打電話訂飛機票。

Dialogue 2 Planning an Itinerary	

旅行社： 天一旅行社，你好。

王朋： 你好。請問六月初[a]到北京的機票多
少錢？

旅行社： 您要買單程票還是往返票？

王朋： 我要買兩張往返票。

旅行社： 你想買哪家航空公司的？

王朋： 哪家的便宜，就買哪[2]家的。

旅行社： 請等等，我查一下⋯⋯好幾家航空
公司都有航班[b]。中國國際航空公司，
一千五[3]，直飛。西北航空公司正在
打折[c]，差不多一千四百六十，可是
要轉機。

王朋： 西北只比國航[d]便宜四十幾塊錢[4]，我
還是買國航吧。

旅行社： 哪一天走[e]？哪一天回來？

王朋： 六月十號走，七月十五號回來。現在
可以訂位子嗎？

旅行社： 可以。你們喜歡靠窗戶的還是靠走道
的？

王朋： 靠走道的。對了[f]，我朋友吃素，麻煩
幫她訂一份素餐。

旅行社： 沒問題⋯⋯您在北京要訂旅館、租車
嗎？

王朋： 不用，謝謝！

（在國航的服務台……）

王朋：	小姐，這是我們的[1]機票。
航空公司：	請把護照給我看看。你們有幾件行李要托運？
王朋：	兩件。這個包不托運，我們帶上飛機。
航空公司：	麻煩[a]您把箱子拿上來[2]。
王朋：	小姐，沒超重吧？
航空公司：	沒有。這是你們的護照、機票，這是登機牌[b]。請到五號登機口[c]上飛機。
李友和王朋：	謝謝。

……

王紅：	哥哥，你們去北京了，就我一個人在這兒。
王朋：	小紅，別哭，我們幾個星期就回來，你好好兒地[1]學英文，別亂跑。
王紅：	不是幾個星期就回來，是幾個星期以後才回來。
高文中：	別擔心，我姐姐小音會照顧你。
李友：	對，別擔心。
白英愛：	飛機幾點起飛？
王朋：	中午十二點，還有兩個多小時。
李友：	白英愛，你什麼時候去紐約實習？
白英愛：	我不去紐約了。文中幫我在加州找了一份實習工作。
高文中：	對，我們下個星期開車去加州。
李友：	是嗎？一邊兒開車，一邊兒玩兒，太好了。
王朋：	開車小心。祝你們玩兒得[1]高興。
白英愛：	祝你們一路平安。到了北京以後[3]，別忘了給我們發個電子郵件。
王朋：	好，那我們秋天見。
高文中：	下個學期見。
白英愛和王紅：	再見！

（在北京首都機場……）

王父：小朋！

王朋：爸，媽！

王母：累壞了吧？

王朋：還好[4]。爸，媽，我給你們介紹一下，這是我的同學李友。

李友：叔叔，阿姨[5a]，你們好。

王父：歡迎你來北京。

王母：李友，你的中文說得真好。

李友：謝謝。是因為王朋教得好。

王朋：哪裡，是因為你聰明。

王父：哎，你們倆都聰明。

王母：小朋，你好像瘦了點兒。是不是打工太忙，沒有時間吃飯?

王朋：我沒瘦。我常常運動，身體比以前棒多了。

王母：小紅怎麼樣？

王朋：她很好，英文水平提高了很多。

王父：走吧，我們上車以後，再慢慢兒地聊吧。爺爺、奶奶在烤鴨店等我們呢！

李友：烤鴨店？

Lesson 11

Dialogue 1

Tomorrow's Weather
Will Be Even Better!

(Gao Xiaoyin and her younger brother Gao Wenzhong are discussing the weather . . .)

Gao Xiaoyin:	Today's weather is better than yesterday's. It's no longer snowing anymore.
Gao Wenzhong:	I asked a friend to go ice skating with me in the park tomorrow. I wonder what the weather is going to be like. Will it be cold?
Gao Xiaoyin:	I just looked up the forecast on the Internet. Tomorrow's weather will be even better than today's. Not only will it not snow, it'll be a bit warmer, too.
Gao Wenzhong:	Really? Great!
Gao Xiaoyin:	Who did you ask to go ice skating with?
Gao Wenzhong:	Bai Ying'ai.
Gao Xiaoyin:	You asked Bai Ying'ai? But she flew to New York this morning.
Gao Wenzhong:	Really? Then what do I do tomorrow?
Gao Xiaoyin:	Why don't you stay home and watch TV?

Dialogue 2

The Weather
Here Is Awful!

(Gao Wenzhong is chatting with Bai Ying'ai online.)

Gao Wenzhong:	Ying'ai, New York is so much fun. How come you're online and not out and about?
Bai Ying'ai:	The weather here is awful.
Gao Wenzhong:	How come?
Bai Ying'ai:	Yesterday it poured. It rained again today.
Gao Wenzhong:	The weather here is great this weekend. You'd better come back as soon as you can.
Bai Ying'ai:	It's going to be warmer in New York this weekend. I have an interview next week, I can't come back just yet.
Gao Wenzhong:	I found a job in California. Go with me. It's not cold in the winter in California, or hot in the summer. Spring and fall are even more comfortable.
Bai Ying'ai:	California is great, but I like New York more.

Lesson 12

Dialogue 1

Dining Out

(In a restaurant . . .)

Waiter:	Come in! Please come in!
Li You:	How come there are so many people? It looks like there isn't a single seat left.
Wang Peng:	Waiter, are there any tables left?
Waiter:	Yes, yes. That table is not taken.

. . .

Waiter:	What would you like to order?
Li You:	Wang Peng, why don't you order?
Wang Peng:	All right. To start, give us two plates of dumplings—vegetarian ones.
Waiter:	What else would you like besides dumplings?
Wang Peng:	Li You, what do you say?
Li You:	Home-style tofu with no meat in it. I'm vegetarian.
Waiter:	Our home-style tofu has no meat in it.
Li You:	Also, two bowls of hot and sour soup with no MSG. Not too salty. Do you have baby bok choy?
Waiter:	I'm sorry. We've just sold out of the baby bok choy.
Wang Peng:	Then we'll do without green vegetables.
Waiter:	What would you like to drink?
Wang Peng:	I'd like a glass of iced tea. Li You, what would you like to drink?
Li You:	I'm really thirsty. Please give me a cola, with lots of ice.
Waiter:	OK. Two plates of dumplings, home-style tofu, two hot-and-sour soups, a glass of iced tea, and a cola with lots of ice. Anything else?
Li You:	That's good, that's enough. Waiter, we're both really hungry. Could you please bring out the food as soon as possible?
Waiter:	No problem. The dishes will be done in no time.

Dialogue 2

At the Dining Hall

(It's Thursday. The student cafeteria is serving Chinese food. The chef is from Shanghai.)

Wang Peng:	Chef, what do you have for dinner today that's tasty?
Chef:	We've got sweet-and-sour fish. It's a little sweet and a little sour. It's delicious. Why don't you get that?
Wang Peng:	Great. Do you have beef braised in soy sauce today?
Chef:	No, we don't. You've already got fish, so there's no need to have meat. How about a cucumber salad?
Wang Peng:	All right. I'd also like a bowl of rice. How much is everything together?
Chef:	Sweet-and-sour fish is $4.50, cucumber salad is $1.70, and one bowl of rice is fifty cents. All together, it's $6.70.
Wang Peng:	Shoot, Chef. I forgot my meal card. Here's $10.
Chef:	$3.30 is your change.
Wang Peng:	Chef, you've given the wrong change. You gave me one dollar extra.
Chef:	I'm sorry. I didn't see it clearly.
Wang Peng:	That's all right.
Chef:	Come again next Thursday.
Wang Peng:	OK. Bye.

(Bai Ying'ai has just gotten out of class . . .)

Teacher Chang: Are classes over, Little Bai? Where are you off to?

Bai Ying'ai: Hello, Teacher Chang. I want to go to the school computer center, but I don't know how to get ther I heard it's next to the sports field.

Teacher Chang: The computer center is not as far as the sports fie Do you know where the school library is?

Bai Ying'ai: I do. It's not far from Wang Peng's dorm.

Teacher Chang: The computer center is near the library. It's betwe the library and the student activity center.

Bai Ying'ai: Teacher Chang, where are you headed?

Teacher Chang: I'd like to get some books at the school bookstore

Bai Ying'ai: Where's the bookstore?

Teacher Chang: It's in the student activity center. We can walk together.

Bai Ying'ai: OK.

(Gao Wenzhong takes Wang Peng to Chinatown to eat . . .)

Gao Wenzhong: Let's go to Chinatown to have some Chinese food

Wang Peng: I've never been to Chinatown. I don't know where it is.

Gao Wenzhong: No problem. You drive, and I'll tell you how to get there.

Wang Peng: You have Google Maps, right? Let me take a look.

Gao Wenzhong: Shoot, my phone's in the dorm. I forgot to bring it.

Wang Peng: Without a map, what do we do if we go the wrong way?

Gao Wenzhong: We're fine without a map. I've been to Chinatown bunch of times, I don't need a map to get there. G south from here. At the third intersection, turn we and we'll be there.

Wang Peng: Oh, I don't have a sense of direction.

Gao Wenzhong: Then drive straight ahead. At the third traffic light turn right, and you'll be there.

(At the third intersection . . .)

Wang Peng: This isn't right. See, you can only turn left here. You can't turn right.

Gao Wenzhong: Then it'll be the next block. Turn right. Keep going further. We're here! See, there are lots of Chinese characters out in front.

Wang Peng: That's not Chinese, that's Japanese. We're in Littl Tokyo.

Gao Wenzhong: Really? Then let's not eat Chinese food, let's eat Japanese food instead!

Lesson 14 (Dialogue 1)

Let's Go to
a Party!

(Li You calls Wang Peng.)

Li You:	Wang Peng, what are you doing?
Wang Peng:	I'm reading.
Li You:	Today is Gao Xiaoyin's birthday. Tonight we're having a dance party at her place. Can you go?
Wang Peng:	Yes. What time?
Li You:	Seven o'clock. We'll eat first. After dinner we'll sing and dance.
Wang Peng:	Who will be there?
Li You:	Xiaoyin and her boyfriend, Xiaoyin's cousin, Bai Ying'ai, your sister Wang Hong, and Xiaoyin's middle school classmates, I hear.
Wang Peng:	What birthday gift are you giving Xiaoyin?
Li You:	I bought a book to give her.
Wang Peng:	What should I bring?
Li You:	Either beverages or fruit would do.
Wang Peng:	Then I'll bring some beverages. I'll also get some flowers.
Li You:	Xiaoyin loves fruit. I'll get some apples, pears, and a watermelon.
Wang Peng:	Your place is very far from Xiaoyin's house, and the fruit will be heavy. I'll come pick you up. Let's go together.
Li You:	OK, I'll wait for you downstairs at six-thirty.

(At Gao Xiaoyin's house . . .)

Gao Xiaoyin:	Wang Peng, Li You, come in.
Li You:	Happy birthday, Xiaoyin. This is a birthday gift for you.
Gao Xiaoyin:	Thank you! . . I always wanted to buy this book. You've brought so many things with you. You're really too kind.
Wang Hong:	Brother! Li You! You're here.
Li You:	Xiao Hong, how are you?
Wang Hong:	I'm good. I've been studying English every day.
Wang Peng:	Xiao Hong, how much time do you spend practicir English every day?
Wang Hong:	Three and a half hours, plus I watch two hours of English-language TV.
Gao Wenzhong:	When did you two get here?
Li You:	Just now.
Gao Wenzhong:	Didn't Bai Ying'ai come with you?
Li You:	She's still not here? I thought she'd already gotten here.
Gao Xiaoyin:	Wang Peng, Li You, let me introduce you. This is my cousin Helen. This is her son, Tom.
Wang Peng:	Hello, Helen.
Helen:	Hello, Wang Peng. Wenzhong and Xiaoyin say that you're very smart and very hardworking.
Wang Peng:	You flatter me. Your Chinese is great. Where did you learn it?
Helen:	At summer school.
Wang Peng:	Hey, Tom is really cute. Look, he's smiling now. How old is he?
Helen:	He just turned one. He was born last year, the year of the dog.
Li You:	Look, he's got a round face, big eyes, and a straigh nose. His mouth is not too big, and not too small. He looks just like Helen.
Wang Hong:	With such a gorgeous mom, the son will definitely be very handsome.
Gao Xiaoyin:	Come, let's eat the cake.
Gao Wenzhong:	Why don't we wait for Bai Ying'ai? She loves cake.

Lesson 15

Dialogue 1

My Stomach Is Killing Me!

(A patient is at a hospital for treatment . . .)

Gao Wenzhong: Doctor, my stomach is killing me!

Doctor: What did you have to eat yesterday?

Gao Wenzhong: It was my sister's birthday last week. We didn't finish the cake. Last night I had a few bites. My stomach began to hurt at night, and this morning I went to the bathroom several times.

Doctor: Where did you put the cake?

Gao Wenzhong: In the refrigerator.

Doctor: How long had it been there?

Gao Wenzhong: About five or six days.

Doctor: Do you have a fever?

Gao Wenzhong: No, I don't.

Doctor: Please lie down. Let me check.

. . .

Doctor: You upset your stomach by eating that cake.

Gao Wenzhong: Do I need an injection?

Doctor: No, you don't need an injection. Just take this medicine, three times a day, two pills at a time.

Gao Wenzhong: Doctor, how many times a day? Could you please repeat that?

Doctor: Three times a day, two pills at a time.

Gao Wenzhong: All right. Before or after meals?

Doctor: Either before or after meals is fine, but you'd better not eat anything for twenty-four hours.

Gao Wenzhong: Then I'll be starving. That's not a good idea. That's not a good remedy!

Dialogue 2

Allergies

(The past few days, Wang Peng has seemed to be sick . . .)

Li You: Wang Peng, what's the matter? How come your eyes are red? Did you catch a cold?

Wang Peng: No, I didn't catch a cold. I don't know what's wrong with me. I haven't been feeling well the last few days. My eyes are red and itchy.

Li You: You must be allergic to something.

Wang Peng: I think so, too. That's why I went to the pharmacy and got some medicine. I've taken four or five kinds and spent quite a bit of money, but none of them has been effective.

Li You: Take out the medicines you bought. Let me take a look.

Wang Peng: Here you are.

Li You: These medicines are useless. Why didn't you go to the doctor? Don't you have health insurance?

Wang Peng: I do have health insurance. I have too much home-work this semester. Going to the doctor takes too much time.

Li You: Even so, you still need to go see a doctor as soon as possible. Otherwise, you'll get sicker and sicker.

Wang Peng: I'd like to try some other medicines first. Last time I was sick I didn't go to the doctor. After a couple of days' rest, I was fine.

Li You: No way, no way, you're too lazy. Besides, you can't just randomly take medicine by yourself. Let's go. I'll go to the doctor with you.

Lesson 16 ⟨ Dialogue 1 ⟩

Seeing a Movie

Wang Peng and Li You go to the same school. They have known each other for almost six months now. Wang Peng often helps Li You practice speaking Chinese. They also often go out for fun, and they always have a good time. Li You has a very good impression of Wang Peng, and Wang Peng likes Li You very much, too. So they've become good friends.

Wang Peng:	This weekend they're showing a Chinese film at school. How about we go together?
Li You:	Okay! But I hear that many people are going to see the film. Will we be able to get tickets?
Wang Peng:	I already got the tickets. It took a lot of effort.
Li You:	Fantastic. I've wanted to see a Chinese film for a long time. Anyone else going with us?
Wang Peng:	No one else. Just the two of us.
Li You:	OK. When?
Wang Peng:	The day after tomorrow, eight o'clock.
Li You:	Before the movie, I'll take you to dinner.
Wang Peng:	Great! It's a deal.

⟨ Dialogue 2 ⟩

Turning Down an Invitation

(Mr. Fei calls Li You . . .)

Mr. Fei:	Hello, is Miss Li You there?
Li You:	This is she. Who is this, please?
Mr. Fei:	My name is Fei. Do you remember me?
Li You:	Mr. Fei?
Mr. Fei:	Do you still remember Gao Xiaoyin's birthday party last month? I was the last person to ask you to dance. Think again. Do you remember now?
Li You:	I'm sorry. I can't recall.
Mr. Fei:	I was Gao Xiaoyin's high school classmate.
Li You:	Is that so? How did you get my number?
Mr. Fei:	Xiaoyin gave it to me.
Li You:	Mr. Fei, can I help you?
Mr. Fei:	Are you free this weekend? I'd like to ask you out to dance.
Li You:	This weekend won't do. Next week I have three tests.
Mr. Fei:	No problem. What about the following weekend? After your tests are over, we'll go have a good time.
Li You:	Next weekend won't work, either. I'm moving out of the dorm. I have to clean my room.
Mr. Fei:	How about two weeks from now?
Li You:	I'm sorry, two weeks from now would be even more impossible. I'm going on a trip to New York with my boyfriend.
Mr. Fei:	In that case . . .
Li You:	Mr. Fei, I'm sorry, my cell phone is out of power. Bye.
Mr. Fei:	Hello . . . hello . . .

Lesson 17

Narrative

Finding a Better Place

Wang Peng has been living in the school dorm for two semesters. He thinks that the dorm is too noisy, and he can't sleep well. His room is too small, and he can't even fit a computer there. Besides, he has nowhere to cook. It's really inconvenient, so he plans to move out next semester. He has been looking for a place for a month now, but he hasn't found anything suitable yet. He just saw an ad in the newspaper saying there's an apartment for rent. It's very close to school, only a five-minute walk—very convenient. The apartment includes a bedroom, a kitchen, a bathroom, and a living room, and it's furnished. Wang Peng thinks this apartment may be just right for him.

Dialogue

Calling about an Apartment for Rent

(Wang Peng makes a call to ask about renting an apartment . . .)

Wang Peng: Hi, do you have an apartment for rent?

Landlord: Yes, we do. One bedroom with a living room. It's very clean, and also furnished.

Wang Peng: What kind of furniture does it have?

Landlord: In the living room there are a sofa set, a dining table, and four chairs. The bedroom has a bed, a desk, and a bookcase.

Wang Peng: Is it quiet over there?

Landlord: Extremely quiet.

Wang Peng: How much is the monthly rent?

Landlord: Eight hundred and fifty dollars.

Wang Peng: Eight hundred and fifty U.S. dollars? In renminbi that's almost . . . That's a little bit expensive. Could you come down a little bit?

Landlord: All right. You won't have to pay for the utilities.

Wang Peng: Do I have to pay a deposit?

Landlord: An extra month's rent as a security deposit, which will be returned to you when you move out. And another thing, no pets are allowed in our apartments.

Wang Peng: That doesn't matter. I'm not interested in keeping pets. I don't have pets of any kind.

Landlord: Great. Why don't you come over this afternoon and take a look?

Wang Peng: OK.

Lesson 18

Dialogue 1

Getting in Shape

(Gao Wenzhong and Wang Peng are chatting . . .)

Gao Wenzhong: Look, my gut is getting bigger and bigger.

Wang Peng: You usually overeat, and on top of that you don't exercise; of course you're putting on more and more weight.

Gao Wenzhong: What should I do?

Wang Peng: If you're afraid of being overweight, you should exercise two or three times a week, for half an hou each time. Then your belly will get smaller.

Gao Wenzhong: I haven't exercised for two years. What kind of exercise should I do?

Wang Peng: The simplest exercise is jogging.

Gao Wenzhong: It's so cold in winter, and so hot in summer. Joggin is too uncomfortable.

Wang Peng: How about playing tennis?

Gao Wenzhong: Then I'd have to get a tennis racket and tennis shoes. You know tennis rackets and tennis shoes are very expensive!

Wang Peng: How about getting a few people together to play basketball? Buying a basketball is very inexpensiv

Gao Wenzhong: Then every time I'd have to call people and arrang to meet. That's way too much hassle.

Wang Peng: Then why don't you swim? There's no need to loo for people, it wouldn't cost much money, and you could go any time.

Gao Wenzhong: Swimming? I'm afraid of water. That's too danger-ous. What if I drown?

Wang Peng: There's nothing I can do [to help]. If you're not willi to exercise, then keep packing on the pounds.

Dialogue 2

Watching American Football

Wang Peng's younger sister, Wang Hong, just came from Beijing. She will be going to college in the United States. Right now she is staying at Gao Xiaoyin's place, studying English. To improve her English, she watches two hours of TV every day.

Gao Xiaoyin: Hurry, turn the TV on. The football game is starting

Wang Hong: Really? I like watching football games too...What kind of football is this? How come it's not round?

Gao Xiaoyin: This is not international football, this is American football.

Wang Hong: To play football you should kick (the ball) with your feet. Why is that guy running with the ball in his hand

Gao Xiaoyin: In American football you can use your hands.

Wang Hong: Look! All those people are piling on top of each other. Wouldn't the people underneath be crushec to pieces?

Gao Xiaoyin: Don't worry, they're really strong. Besides, they we special sports clothing, so everything's fine.

Wang Hong: I've been watching for a while and I still don't get it Let's watch something else.

Gao Xiaoyin: You only have to live in America for half a year before you will begin to like American football. When my boyfriend is watching a football game, often he will even forget to eat.

Lesson 19

Dialogue 1

Traveling to Beijing

(It's almost summer break . . .)

Wang Peng:	Li You, time flies. It'll be break soon. Some of our class-mates are going to summer school; some of them are going to intern at different companies. Some will go home and work. What are your plans?
Li You:	I haven't decided. What about you, Wang Peng?
Wang Peng:	I plan to go back to Beijing to see my parents.
Li You:	Really? I hear that Beijing is a really interesting city.
Wang Peng:	Of course. Beijing is China's capital, and it's also China's political and cultural center with lots of famous historic sites.
Li You:	That's right. The Great Wall is very famous.
Wang Peng:	And there are tons of great restaurants in Beijing.
Li You:	Really? I've been to Hong Kong and Taipei, but I've never been to Beijing. I wish I could go to Beijing.
Wang Peng:	Why don't you go with me? I could be your guide.
Li You:	Really? That would be great! I already have a passport. I'll have to apply for a visa at once.
Wang Peng:	I'll get the plane tickets online right away.
Li You:	It's not secure to make payments online. Let's rather call a travel agency instead.

Dialogue 2

Planning an Itinerary

(Wang Peng calls a travel agency to make flight reservations . . .)

Travel Agent:	Tianyi Travel Agency, good morning.
Wang Peng:	Good morning. How much is a ticket to Beijing for the beginning of June?
Travel Agent:	One-way or roundtrip?
Wang Peng:	Two roundtrip tickets.
Travel Agent:	Which airline?
Wang Peng:	I'll take whichever airline is the least expensive.
Travel Agent:	Please wait a moment. Let me check. Quite a few airlines fly there. Air China, $1,500, direct flight. Northwest Airlines is having a sale. About $1,460, but you have to change planes.
Wang Peng:	Northwest Airlines is only $40 cheaper than Air China. I'll go with Air China.
Travel Agent:	What are the dates for departure and return?
Wang Peng:	Departing on June 10, returning on July 15. Can I reserve seats now?
Travel Agent:	Yes, you can. Do you prefer window or aisle seats?
Wang Peng:	Aisle seats. Oh, that's right, my friend is a vegetarian. Could you please order vegetarian meals for her?
Travel Agent:	No problem. While in Beijing, do you need to make reservations for a hotel or car rental?
Wang Peng:	No, thank you.

(At the Air China Counter . . .)

Wang Peng:	Miss, these are our tickets.
Airline staff:	Please show me your passports. How many piece of checked luggage do you have?
Wang Peng:	Two. We won't check this bag. We'll take it on boa
Airline staff:	Please put the suitcases up here.
Li You:	Miss, they are not over the weight limit, I hope.
Airline staff:	No, they're not. Here are your passports and ticke These are your boarding passes. Please go to Gat 5 to board the plane.
Li You and Wang Peng:	Thank you.

. . .

Wang Hong:	You're both leaving for Beijing. I'll be all alone here
Wang Peng:	Xiao Hong, don't cry. We'll be back in just a few weeks. Work hard on your English. Don't go runnir around.
Wang Hong:	Be back in a few weeks? Won't be back till a few weeks later!
Gao Wenzhong:	Don't worry. My sister Xiaoyin will take good care of you.
Li You:	That's right. Don't worry.
Bai Ying'ai:	When does the plane leave?
Wang Peng:	12:00 noon. There are two hours left.
Li You:	Bai Ying'ai, when are you going to New York for your internship?
Bai Ying'ai:	I'm not going to New York anymore. Wenzhong helped me get an internship in California.
Gao Wenzhong:	That's right. We're driving to California next week.
Li You:	Really? Driving and sightseeing at the same time, that's really wonderful.
Wang Peng:	Drive carefully. Have fun!
Bai Ying'ai:	Have a safe trip. Don't forget to email us after you arrive in Beijing.
Wang Peng:	OK. See you in the fall then.
Gao Wenzhong:	See you next semester.
Bai Ying'ai and Wang Hong:	Goodbye!

Dialogue 2

Arriving in Beijing

(At Beijing Capital International Airport . . .)

Dad: Xiao Peng!

Wang Peng: Dad, Mom!

Mom: You must be really tired.

Wang Peng: Not really. Dad, Mom, let me introduce you . . . This is my classmate Li You.

Li You: Uncle, Aunt, how do you do?

Dad: Welcome to Beijing.

Mom: Li You, you speak Chinese wonderfully.

Li You: Thank you. It's because Wang Peng is a good teacher.

Wang Peng: You flatter me. It's because you're smart.

Dad: Hey, you're both smart.

Mom: Xiao Peng, you seem to have lost some weight. Is it because you were too busy working and had no time to eat?

Wang Peng: Mom, I haven't lost any weight. I exercise a lot. I'm much stronger than before.

Mom: How is Xiao Hong?

Wang Peng: She's great. Her English has really improved.

Dad: Let's go. We'll talk at leisure after we get in the car. Grandpa and Grandma are waiting for us at the roast duck restaurant.

Li You: Roast duck restaurant?

SUPPLEMENTAL READING PRACTICE

补充阅读与练习

Simplified Characters

Novice High to Intermediate Low

CHENG & TSUI

© 2025 Cheng & Tsui Co., Inc.

All rights reserved. No part of this publication may be reproduced or transmitted in any form or by any means, electronic or mechanical, including photocopying, recording, scanning, or any information storage or retrieval system, without written permission from the publisher.

President & CEO
Jill Cheng

VP, Product Development
Amy Baron

Executive Managing Editor
Kaesmene Harrison Banks

Associate Curriculum Manager
Lei Wang

Development
Yingchun Guan, Ning Ma, Tamsin True-Alcalá

Copyediting
Jingge Li

Manager, Digital Product
Dory Schultz

Design and Production
Liv Cosgrove, Jimmy Fahy

Photo Credits: p.422, Max Studio/Shutterstock.com; Danita Delimont/Shutterstock.com; zhengzaishuru/Shutterstock.com; Openfinal/Shutterstock.com; **p.425**, axz700/Shutterstock.com; **p.426**, Inspired By Maps/Shutterstock.com; **p.429**, humphery/Shutterstock.com; **p.430**, Robert Way/Shutterstock.com; md.alaminrahman/Shutterstock.com; icemanphotos/Shutterstock.com; santypan/Shutterstock.com; aphotostory/Shutterstock.com; Diego Grandi/Shutterstock.com; **p.433**, I Wei Huang/Shutterstock.com; **p.434**, Robert CHG/Shutterstock.com; yuda chen/Shutterstock.com; **p.437**, Jack.Q/Shutterstock.com; **p.438**, pixiaomo/Shutterstock.com; **p.441**, Robert Way/Shutterstock.com; **p.442**, TimeImage Production/Shutterstock.com; **p.445**, riekephotos/Shutterstock.com; **p.446**, Tom Wang/Shutterstock.com; doyz86/Shutterstock.com; Fotoldee/Shutterstock.com; Aygun Ali/Shutterstock.com; **p.449**, Ocean Wong/Shutterstock.com; **p.450**, mooinblack/Shutterstock.com; **p.453**, Yu Chun Christopher Wong/Shutterstock.com; **p.454**, naKornCreate/Shutterstock.com; doyz86/Shutterstock.com; Fotoldee/Shutterstock.com; Aygun Ali/Shutterstock.com; **p.457**, Sleeping cat/Shutterstock.com; **p.458**, Toxa2x2/Shutterstock.com; Gulshan Gulabli/Shutterstock.com; GANJIRO KUMA/Shutterstock.com; 13ree.design/Shutterstock.com; Janis Abolins/Shutterstock.com; WonderfulPixel/Shutterstock.com; Illust_monster/Shutterstock.com; **p.461**, lazy dragon/Shutterstock.com

Every effort has been made to accurately credit the copyright owners of materials reproduced in this text. Omissions brought to our attention will be corrected in subsequent editions.

Contents

A Note on Grammar: 的

The following supplemental readings sometimes use verb phrases or other phrases before 的, as attributives to modify the subjects that follow, since this is a prevalent structure in Chinese prose. This grammar is explained in detail in L14. One example of this kind is 我认识的一个朋友 (wǒ rènshi de yí ge péngyou; a friend I know).

 Indicates interactive exercises on Cheng & Tsui FluencyLink™

北京的四季

北京在中国的北方，春夏秋冬四季分明。北京的冬天比较长，春天和秋天比较短。夏天的时间比冬天短，比春秋长。

春天的时候，北京经常刮大风，一天的温差也有点儿大。因为早上比较冷，人们常常穿两三件衣服。到了中午，天气就暖和得只能穿一件衬衫了。晚上也比较冷，人们又得穿很多衣服。

六月到八月是北京的夏天。夏天的时候，北京不但非常热，而且常常下大雨。所以，夏天外出以前，最好看一下天气预报。

北京的秋天天气很好，不冷也不热。那时候的北京不常刮风，也不常下雨，很舒服。北京的秋天也很漂亮。不过，北京的秋天跟春天一样短，只有两个多月。

十一月的时候，北京的冬天就开始了。北京的冬天很冷，有的时候会下雪。不过，那时候的北京也有很多好玩儿的。比如，很多北京人冬天的时候喜欢去公园滑冰。下雪的时候，人们也会出去堆雪人、打雪仗、滑雪。

No.	Word	Pinyin	Part of Speech	Definition
1	四季	sìjì	n	the four seasons
2	北方	běifāng	n	the north, the northern part of a country
3	分明	fēnmíng	adj	distinct
4	比较	bǐjiào	adv	relatively, comparatively
5	经常	jīngcháng	adv	frequently, often
6	刮风	guā fēng	vo	to be windy (lit. to blow wind)
7	温差	wēnchā	n	difference in temperature
8	外出	wàichū	v	to go outside
9	最好	zuìhǎo	adv	had better
10	多	duō	nu	somewhat more than
11	比如	bǐrú	conj	for example
12	堆雪人	duī xuěrén	vo	to build a snowman
13	打雪仗	dǎ xuězhàng	vo	to have a snowball fight
14	滑雪	huá xuě	vo	to ski

➤ Reading Comprehension

A **Skimming and Scanning:** Skim the reading and try to get a basic sense of the content and purpose of the text. If a question asks about a specific detail, scan the text for key words to help answer that question. [INTERPRETIVE]

1 What is the main idea of this passage?

(a) Winter is the worst season in Beijing.

(b) Beijing is a good travel destination year-round.

(c) The weather in Beijing is significantly different for each of the four seasons.

2 How is Beijing's summer described in this reading?

(a) rainy but comfortable   **(b)** very hot and rainy   **(c)** hot and not very rainy

B Comprehension Check: Mark the following statements true or false. INTERPRETIVE

1 Spring and autumn are shorter than winter and summer in Beijing. **T F**

2 In the spring, the temperature varies greatly over the course of a day. **T F**

3 It frequently rains in summer and autumn. **T F**

4 It's too cold to spend time outside in the winter. **T F**

Cultural and Societal Context

Ice skating is a winter pastime with a long history in China. Its roots date back to the Song dynasty (960-1279), and it became popular as a leisure activity both among the general public and within the imperial court during the Qing dynasty (1644-1911). Today, ice skating most often takes place at indoor rinks. However, the unique flavor and atmosphere of old Beijing can only be truly experienced on outdoor natural ice rinks, like the frozen ponds or lakes in parks. These ice rinks are open to the public and are often divided into separate areas for general entertainment, beginning skaters, and speed skaters, allowing people of all different ages and skill levels to enjoy the ice together.

➤ Reflection

A Discussion: Ask and answer the following questions with your classmates. INTERPERSONAL

1 你家那儿夏天的天气跟北京夏天的天气一样吗？

2 你家那儿四季分明吗？四季的时间一样长吗？

B Research and Reflect: Investigate one of the questions below. Present your thoughts and findings in Chinese, using the supplemental vocabulary and/or consulting a dictionary for additional words as needed. PRESENTATIONAL

1 在北京，人们春天的时候喜欢做什么？夏天，秋天，和冬天呢？如果你去北京玩儿，你想什么时候去？

2 中国或者别的国家 (guójiā; country) 还有哪个城市跟北京一样四季分明？你喜欢四季分明的天气吗？为什么？

C Further Exploration: Extend your knowledge by looking into the following questions.

1 How does the climate of a city or region influence patterns of life and community activities? What are some interesting innovations that have taken place in China or elsewhere in response to the challenges and opportunities brought about by climate?

2 Look into the history of Beijing's climate and air quality. How has it changed over the years? Choose another city you are familiar with. How has that city's climate and air quality changed over the years? Are there similarities between the changes in Beijing and in the city that you chose?

➢ **Pinyin of the Text**

Běijīng de sìjì

Běijīng zài Zhōngguó de běifāng, chūn xià qiū dōng sìjì fēnmíng. Běijīng de dōngtiān bǐjiào cháng, chūntiān hé qiūtiān bǐjiào duǎn. Xiàtiān de shíjiān bǐ dōngtiān duǎn, bǐ chūn qiū cháng.

Chūntiān de shíhou, Běijīng jīngcháng guā dà fēng, yì tiān de wēnchā yě yǒudiǎnr dà. Yīnwèi zǎoshang bǐjiào lěng, rénmen chángcháng chuān liǎng sān jiàn yīfu. Dào le zhōngwǔ, tiānqì jiù nuǎnhuo de zhǐ néng chuān yí jiàn chènshān le. Wǎnshang yě bǐjiào lěng, rénmen yòu děi chuān hěn duō yīfu.

Liùyuè dào bāyuè shì Běijīng de xiàtiān. Xiàtiān de shíhou, Běijīng búdàn fēicháng rè, érqiě chángcháng xià dà yǔ. Suǒyǐ, xiàtiān wàichū yǐqián, zuìhǎo kàn yí xià tiānqì yùbào.

Běijīng de qiūtiān tiānqì hěn hǎo, bù lěng yě bú rè. Nà shíhou de Běijīng bù cháng guā fēng, yě bù cháng xià yǔ, hěn shūfu. Běijīng de qiūtiān yě hěn piàoliang. Búguò, Běijīng de qiūtiān gēn chūntiān yíyàng duǎn, zhǐyǒu liǎng ge duō yuè.

Shíyīyuè de shíhou, Běijīng de dōngtiān jiù kāishǐ le. Běijīng de dōngtiān hěn lěng, yǒude shíhou huì xià xuě. Búguò, nà shíhou de Běijīng yě yǒu hěn duō hǎowánr de. Bǐrú, hěn duō Běijīng rén dōngtiān de shíhou xǐhuan qù gōngyuán huá bīng. Xià xuě de shíhou, rénmen yě huì chūqu duī xuěrén, dǎ xuězhàng, huá xuě.

People having fun with ice sleds at a skating rink in Beijing

机器人餐厅

最近几年，中国的一些城市出现了机器人餐厅。这些餐厅的"服务员"都是机器人，做饭的"师傅"也是机器人。有的机器人餐厅的饭菜非常便宜，比如：一碗米饭两块钱，一盘凉拌黄瓜六块钱，一盘家常豆腐十二块钱，一盘红烧牛肉十八块钱。在北京和上海，在机器人餐厅吃饭比在有的路边摊吃还便宜。

机器人餐厅刚出现的时候，人们都觉得很有意思，很多人排队去吃。有些人觉得这些餐厅上菜快，做的菜也很好吃。可是，也有些人觉得这些机器人餐厅的菜不好吃。有的时候，如果机器人服务员坏了，上菜就会变得很慢。

现在，有几家机器人餐厅已经因为一些问题关门了。也许，机器人餐厅的技术还是不够成熟。也许，人们还是更喜欢有真人服务的餐厅。

上海一家机器人餐厅的服务员

➤ Supplemental Vocabulary

No.	Word	Pinyin	Part of Speech	Definition
1	机器人	jīqìrén	n	robot
2	出现	chūxiàn	v/n	to appear, to emerge; appearance, emergence
3	比如	bǐrú	conj	for example
4	路边摊	lù biān tān	n	streetside booth, food stall
5	还	hái	adv	even more
6	排队	pái duì	vo	to line up, to queue
7	坏了	huài le		broken, not working
8	变	biàn	v	to change, to become
9	家	jiā	m	(measure word for store, restaurant, company, or other enterprise)
10	关门	guān mén	vo	to be closed, to close the doors (here meaning permanently closed)
11	也许	yěxǔ	adv	maybe
12	技术	jìshù	n	technology
13	还是	háishi	adv	still, nonetheless
14	成熟	chéngshú	adj	mature
15	真	zhēn	adj	real

➤ Reading Comprehension

A Skimming and Scanning: Skim the reading and try to get a basic sense of the content and purpose of the text. If a question asks about a specific detail, scan the text for key words to help answer that question. INTERPRETIVE

1 When and where do the circumstances described in the reading take place?

(a) starting from this year, in Beijing

(b) for several decades, in Shanghai

(c) the past several years, in cities around China

2 Which of the following topics is mentioned in the reading?

(a) prices of dishes   **(b)** how to indicate allergies   **(c)** how to ask for the check

B Comprehension Check: Mark the following statements true or false. INTERPRETIVE

1 The type of restaurant described in the reading has robot waiters but human chefs.　　　　　　　　　　　　　　　　　　　　　　　　T　F

2 According to the reading, it is quite expensive to eat in a robot restaurant.　　　T　F

3 Service in a robot restaurant can become slow sometimes.　　　T　F

4 The end of the reading offers two possible reasons for the closing of some robot restaurants.　　　　　　　　　　　　　　　　　　　T　F

Cultural and Societal Context

Over the past few decades, the Chinese economy has gradually transitioned from focusing on low-cost, labor-intensive manufacturing jobs (as the "world's factory") towards developing a new model of high-tech products and domestically oriented service industries. The growth of China's own tech companies and technological adoptions is essential to this economic transition. Since the 2000s, some globally notable advancements have taken place in the Chinese tech landscape, including mobile payment systems, batteries for electric vehicles, and 5G and 6G networks. China has also become the world's largest user of industrial robots.

➤ Reflection

A Discussion: Ask and answer the following questions with your classmates. INTERPERSONAL

1 你想去一家机器人餐厅试一下吗？你觉得机器人做的饭会好吃吗？

2 你觉得机器人餐厅的出现是好事吗？为什么？你觉得以后会有更多的机器人餐厅吗？

B Research and Reflect: Investigate one of the questions below. Present your thoughts and findings in Chinese, using the supplemental vocabulary and/or consulting a dictionary for additional words as needed. PRESENTATIONAL

1 请介绍一家有机器人服务的餐厅。你可以介绍这家餐厅在哪儿，有什么菜，大家觉得那儿的服务怎么样。这家餐厅可以在中国，也可以不在中国。

2 除了餐厅以外，中国还有什么服务行业 (hángyè; industry) 用机器人？这些行业怎么用机器人？

C Further Exploration: Extend your knowledge by looking into the following questions. Note that the Cultural and Societal Context segment may have some helpful information to get you started.

1 One of the pressing topics in today's global workplace is the automation of jobs through artificial intelligence and robotics. How does the rise of automation technologies influence the practices and perceptions of various professions and skills? Investigate and compare related trends in at least two areas of the world.

2 What are some rapidly developing technologies in today's China? How have they affected perceptions and everyday life in Chinese society? How would you compare technological shifts (such as those in transportation, e-commerce, and communications) and their societal impacts in China to where you live? Please use concrete examples and evidence to support any conclusions.

➤ **Pinyin of the Text**

Jīqìrén cāntīng

Zuìjìn jǐ nián, Zhōngguó de yì xiē chéngshì chūxiàn le jīqìrén cāntīng. Zhè xiē cāntīng de "fúwùyuán" dōu shì jīqìrén, zuò fàn de "shīfu" yě shì jīqìrén. Yǒude jīqìrén cāntīng de fàn cài fēicháng piányi, bǐrú: yì wǎn mǐfàn liǎng kuài qián, yì pán liángbàn huánggua liù kuài qián, yì pán jiācháng dòufu shí'èr kuài qián, yì pán hóngshāo niúròu shíbā kuài qián. Zài Běijīng hé Shànghǎi, zài jīqìrén cāntīng chī fàn bǐ zài yǒude lù biān tān chī hái piányi.

Jīqìrén cāntīng gāng chūxiàn de shíhou, rénmen dōu juéde hěn yǒu yìsi, hěn duō rén pái duì qù chī. Yǒu xiē rén juéde zhè xiē cāntīng shàng cài kuài, zuò de cài yě hěn hǎo chī. Kěshì, yě yǒu xiē rén juéde zhè xiē jīqìrén cāntīng de cài bù hǎo chī. Yǒude shíhou, rúguǒ jīqìrén fúwùyuán huài le, shàng cài jiù huì biàn de hěn màn.

Xiànzài, yǒu jǐ jiā jīqìrén cāntīng yǐjīng yīnwèi yì xiē wèntí guān mén le. Yěxǔ, jīqìrén cāntīng de jìshù háishi bú gòu chéngshú. Yěxǔ, rénmen háishi gèng xǐhuan yǒu zhēn rén fúwù de cāntīng.

Workers in Jiujiang, China operating intelligent machines to fill LED product orders

大东的小家

去外国旅行过春节

2月7日

大东
北京人，
喜欢看书，
也喜欢旅行！

更多旅行日记

中国

外国

今年春节，我和家人去美国旅行了。这是我们第一次在外国过春节！我们的第一站是美国的第二大城市——洛杉矶。

以前我们听说，美国的中国城过年的时候有很多活动，非常好玩儿。所以到了洛杉矶以后，我们先去了那儿的中国城。一到中国城，我们就看到了很多人，还有很多商店挂了红灯笼、贴了春联，非常热闹。我们在一个商店里买糖葫芦的时候，售货员告诉我们前面就是中国城的中心，春节的时候有很多庆祝活动和好看的表演。我们走到那儿以后，看到有人唱中文歌，有人跳中国舞，还有舞龙舞狮表演，特别有意思！

看完表演以后，我们去了一个北京饭馆吃饭。因为过年，我们点了红烧肉、糖醋鱼、家常豆腐和饺子。我们都觉得有的菜很地道，可是有的菜不好吃，跟我们在中国吃到的很不一样。不过，过年的时候能在外国吃到这些菜，我们都觉得挺高兴的。

逛完中国城以后，我们在谷歌地图上看到小东京就在南边，离中国城很近，走走就能到。我们就去那儿逛到了晚上，买了一些日本的东西，还去一个日本饭馆吃了晚饭。我觉得小东京虽然没有中国城那么大，但是也挺好玩儿的。

➢ Supplemental Vocabulary

No.	Word	Pinyin	Part of Speech	Definition
1	旅行	lǚxíng	v	to travel
2	过	guò	v	to observe (a holiday), to celebrate (a festival) [过年: to celebrate the new year]
3	春节	Chūnjié	pn	Spring Festival, Chinese New Year
4	洛杉矶	Luòshānjī	pn	Los Angeles
5	挂	guà	v	to hang
6	灯笼	dēnglong	n	lantern
7	贴	tiē	v	to paste, to glue
8	春联	chūnlián	n	Spring Festival couplets
9	热闹	rènao	adj	lively, bustling
10	糖葫芦	tánghúlu	n	traditional Chinese snack consisting of candied hawthorn or other fruits on a bamboo skewer
11	庆祝	qìngzhù	n/v	celebration; to celebrate
12	表演	biǎoyǎn	n	performance
13	舞龙舞狮	wǔ lóng wǔ shī	n	dragon dance and lion dance
14	地道	dìdao	adj	authentic
15	逛	guàng	v	to walk around (for shopping, leisure, etc.)

➢ Reading Comprehension

A Skimming and Scanning: Skim the reading and try to get a basic sense of the content and purpose of the text. INTERPRETIVE

1 To which genre of writing does this reading belong?

(a) social commentary   **(b)** travelogue   **(c)** cultural analysis

Comprehension Check: Mark the following statements true or false. INTERPRETIVE

1 This was the first time that the author celebrated the Spring Festival abroad.   **T   F**

2 The author didn't think that any of the dishes they tried in Los Angeles's Chinatown tasted authentic.   **T   F**

3 The author sang songs and danced in Chinatown to celebrate the new year.   **T   F**

4 In Los Angeles, Little Tokyo is close to Chinatown.   **T   F**

Cultural and Societal Context

Chinatowns around the world carry a storied history deeply rooted in the global Chinese diaspora. The first Chinatowns in North America were formed in the mid-19th century and were tight-knit ethnic communities initially created in response to the harsh discrimination most Chinese faced during that period. Over time, these communities have transformed into cultural crossroads, blending tradition with modern and local influences. Despite some Chinatowns facing challenges like gentrification that threaten to alter their community and culture, Chinatowns generally remain vibrant and are known for their lively markets, authentic eateries, engaging cultural events, and more.

➤ Reflection

A Discussion: Ask and answer the following questions with your classmates. INTERPERSONAL

1 你以前庆祝过春节吗？如果你庆祝过春节，你在哪儿庆祝的？怎么庆祝的？

2 你去过中国城或者小东京吗？如果去过，你觉得那儿好玩儿吗？如果没去过，你想去看看吗？为什么？

B Research and Reflect: Investigate one of the questions below. Present your thoughts and findings in Chinese, using the supplemental vocabulary and/or consulting a dictionary for additional words as needed. PRESENTATIONAL

1 为什么很多中国人过春节的时候喜欢吃鱼？哪些地方的人过春节的时候喜欢吃饺子，为什么？人们还喜欢吃什么别的东西，为什么？

2 中国人过春节的时候还有哪些习俗 (xísú; customs)？不同 (tóng; same) 地方的习俗一样吗？

C Further Exploration: Extend your knowledge by looking into the following questions. Note that the Cultural and Societal Context segment may have some helpful information to get you started.

1 The Lunar New Year is celebrated in many Asian countries. Which nations celebrate Lunar New Year, and what names are used to refer to the festival? What factors have contributed to the widespread celebration of the Lunar New Year across many Asian countries? Consider the influence of cultural, historical, economic and political factors.

2 What cultural and historical significance do ethnic enclaves like Chinatown and Little Tokyo hold? Explore their role in preserving and celebrating the cultural heritage of their respective ethnic groups, their influence on aspects such as community identity and culinary heritage, and the impact such places can have on both residents and visitors.

➢ **Pinyin of the Text**

Qù wàiguó lǚxíng guò Chūnjié

Jīnnián Chūnjié, wǒ hé jiārén qù Měiguó lǚxíng le. Zhè shì wǒmen dì yī cì zài wàiguó guò Chūnjié! Wǒmen de dì yī zhàn shì Měiguó de dì èr dà chéngshì — Luòshānjī.

Yǐqián wǒmen tīngshuō, Měiguó de Zhōngguóchéng guò nián de shíhou yǒu hěn duō huódòng, fēicháng hǎowánr. Suǒyǐ dào le Luòshānjī yǐhòu, wǒmen xiān qù le nàr de Zhōngguóchéng. Yí dào Zhōngguóchéng, wǒmen jiù kàn dào le hěn duō rén, hái yǒu hěn duō shāngdiàn guà le hóng dēnglong, tiē le chūnlián, fēicháng rènao. Wǒmen zài yí ge shāngdiàn lǐ mǎi tánghúlu de shíhou, shòuhuòyuán gàosu wǒmen qiánmiàn jiù shì Zhōngguóchéng de zhōngxīn, Chūnjié de shíhou yǒu hěn duō qìngzhù huódòng hé hǎokàn de biǎoyǎn. Wǒmen zǒu dào nàr yǐhòu, kàn dào yǒu rén chàng Zhōngwén gē, yǒu rén tiào Zhōngguó wǔ, hái yǒu wǔ lóng wǔ shī biǎoyǎn, tèbié yǒu yìsi!

Kàn wán biǎoyǎn yǐhòu, wǒmen qù le yí ge Běijīng fànguǎn chī fàn. Yīnwèi guò nián, wǒmen diǎn le hóngshāo ròu, tángcùyú, jiācháng dòufu hé jiǎozi. Wǒmen dōu juéde yǒude cài hěn dìdao, kěshì yǒude cài bù hǎochī, gēn wǒmen zài Zhōngguó chī dào de hěn bù yíyàng. Búguò, guò nián de shíhou néng zài wàiguó chī dào zhè xiē cài, wǒmen dōu juéde tǐng gāoxìng de.

Guàng wán Zhōngguóchéng yǐhòu, wǒmen zài Gǔgē Dìtú shang kàn dào Xiǎo Dōngjīng jiù zài nánbian, lí Zhōngguóchéng hěn jìn, zǒu zou jiù néng dào. Wǒmen jiù qù nàr guàng dào le wǎnshang, mǎi le yì xiē Rìběn de dōngxi, hái qù yí ge Rìběn fànguǎn chī le wǎnfàn. Wǒ juéde Xiǎo Dōngjīng suīrán méiyǒu Zhōngguóchéng nàme dà, dànshì yě tǐng hǎowánr de.

People walking around in London's Chinatown

重要的生日

每个人都有自己的生日，不过每个生日的意义不一样。哪几个生日中国人觉得很重要呢？

第一个是周岁，也就是一岁的生日。孩子过周岁生日的时候，家人常常会准备很多种东西让他们抓，也就是抓周。孩子要抓的每种东西都代表一种工作，所以他们抓到什么东西，就代表长大以后可能做什么工作。

一周岁的小孩抓周

代表长寿的寿桃

代表长寿的生日在中国文化里也很重要，常常会有大的庆祝活动。六十、八十、九十、一百岁的生日都代表长寿。庆祝这些生日的时候，家人常常会给长寿的人准备寿宴。寿宴除了菜、蛋糕和长寿面以外，也常常会有寿桃。如果你去参加寿宴，可能会听到人们跟过生日的人说"祝您福如东海，寿比南山"。

除了这些生日以外，有的人觉得本命年的生日、逢十的生日、还有逢九的生日也很重要。

➤ Supplemental Vocabulary

No.	Word	Pinyin	Part of Speech	Definition
1	重要	*zhòngyào*	adj	important
2	意义	*yìyì*	n	meaning, significance
3	周岁	*zhōusuì*	n	a child's first birthday, a full year of age
4	抓	*zhuā*	v	to grab
5	抓周	*zhuā zhōu*	n/v	first-birthday grab
6	代表	*dàibiǎo*	v	to represent
7	可能	*kěnéng*	mv/adj	may; possible
8	长寿	*chángshòu*	n/adj	long life, longevity; long-lived
9	文化	*wénhuà*	n	culture
10	庆祝	*qìngzhù*	n/v	celebration; to celebrate
11	寿宴	*shòuyàn*	n	birthday feast to celebrate longevity
12	面	*miàn*	n	noodles
13	寿桃	*shòutáo*	n	longevity peach bun
14	参加	*cānjiā*	v	to participate, to join, to take part in
15	福如东海，寿比南山	*fúrúdōnghǎi, shòubǐnánshān*	idiom	happiness as vast as the East Sea and longevity as everlasting as the South Mountain
16	本命年	*běnmìngnián*	n	one's zodiac year
17	逢	*féng*	v	to fall on, to occur on [逢十: 10, 20, 30, etc.; 逢九: 9, 19, 29, etc.]

➤ Reading Comprehension

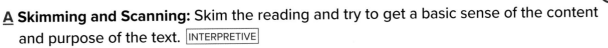

A **Skimming and Scanning:** Skim the reading and try to get a basic sense of the content and purpose of the text. INTERPRETIVE

1 Which topic is not covered in the reading?

(a) milestone birthdays in Chinese culture

(b) features of certain birthday celebrations in China

(c) items that would be considered inauspicious to give as birthday presents in China

1 In China, certain birthdays are considered more important than others. **T F**

2 The item a child grabs on their first birthday represents what their personality will be like. **T F**

3 Chinese people often celebrate significant birthdays for older people. **T F**

4 The reading mentions a special kind of soup that is usually eaten during birthday celebrations. **T F**

Cultural and Societal Context

Some Chinese people may choose to celebrate their birthday twice in one year— once on their birthday according to the Gregorian calendar, and once on their birthday according to the 农历 (nónglì; traditional Chinese lunar calendar). Because the 农历 does not align exactly with the Gregorian calendar, the date of one's 农历 birthday falls on different dates from year to year. Today, many of the younger generation only celebrate birthdays according to the Gregorian calendar because it is easier to memorize the date, but there are still some older people that choose to only celebrate their birthday according to the 农历.

> # Reflection

A Discussion: Ask and answer the following questions with your classmates. INTERPERSONAL

1 你觉得哪些生日最重要？为什么？

2 你怎么庆祝自己的生日？你会吃什么东西？

B Research and Reflect: Investigate one of the questions below. Present your thoughts and findings in Chinese, using the supplemental vocabulary and/or consulting a dictionary for additional words as needed. PRESENTATIONAL

1 小孩子抓周的时候，家人常常会准备哪些东西？这些东西代表什么工作？

2 给别人庆祝生日的时候，中国人喜欢说哪些祝福语 (zhùfú yǔ; well-wishes)？

Further Exploration: Extend your knowledge by looking into the following questions.

1 The reading mentions that longevity peach buns (寿桃) are a common food to have at a birthday feast (寿宴). What is the association between peaches and longevity in Chinese culture? Are there any foods in your culture that represent longevity?

2 Historically, birthday celebrations were not always common in many cultures. What is the history of birthday celebrations in your culture? How does it compare to the history of birthday celebrations in Chinese culture?

➤ **Pinyin of the Text**

Zhòngyào de shēngrì

Měi ge rén dōu yǒu zìjǐ de shēngrì, búguò měi ge shēngrì de yìyì bù yíyàng. Nǎ jǐ ge shēngrì Zhōngguó rén juéde hěn zhòngyào ne?

Dì yī ge shì zhōusuì, yě jiù shì yí suì de shēngrì. Háizi guò zhōusuì shēngrì de shíhou, jiārén chángcháng huì zhǔnbèi hěn duō zhǒng dōngxi ràng tāmen zhuā, yě jiù shì zhuā zhōu. Háizi yào zhuā de měi zhǒng dōngxi dōu dàibiǎo yì zhǒng gōngzuò, suǒyǐ tāmen zhuā dào shénme dōngxi, jiù dàibiǎo zhǎng dà yǐhòu kěnéng zuò shénme gōngzuò.

Dàibiǎo chángshòu de shēngrì zài Zhōngguó wénhuà lǐ yě hěn zhòngyào, chángcháng huì yǒu dà de qìngzhù huódòng. Liùshí, bāshí, jiǔshí, yìbǎi suì de shēngrì dōu dàibiǎo chángshòu. Qìngzhù zhè xiē shēngrì de shíhou, jiārén chángcháng huì gěi chángshòu de rén zhǔnbèi shòuyàn. Shòuyàn chúle cài, dàngāo hé chángshòu miàn yǐwài, yě chángcháng huì yǒu shòutáo. Rúguǒ nǐ qù cānjiā shòuyàn, kěnéng huì tīng dào rénmen gēn guò shēngrì de rén shuō "zhù nín fúrúdōnghǎi, shòubǐnánshān".

Chúle zhè xiē shēngrì yǐwài, yǒude rén juéde běnmìngnián de shēngrì, féng shí de shēngrì, hái yǒu féng jiǔ de shēngrì yě hěn zhòngyào.

A grandmother celebrating her 90th birthday with her grandchildren

在中国看病和在美国看病

　　一般来说，在中国看病和在美国看病非常不一样。在中国，很多人生病的时候一般会先去医院挂号，看门诊。挂号的时候，病人需要告诉医院自己想看哪一个科室。看门诊的时候，病人每次看的医生不一定一样。有的时候，因为想找到最合适的医生，病人会去好几家医院看病。在美国，很多人生病的时候一般会先去看自己的家庭医生。家庭医生做完检查以后，如果觉得有需要，才会推荐病人去看专科医生。

在北京一家医院挂号的人们

　　另外，在中国，人们看完医生以后常常会在医院里付钱拿药。在美国，人们常常会去离自己家不远的药店拿药。在中国，除了西药以外，医生有的时候还会开一些中药。美国的医生一般不开中药，不过有的时候会推荐病人去做针灸。

　　最后，在美国看病有医疗保险非常重要。如果没有保险，看医生和买药常常会特别贵。有的时候，看过敏、感冒、吃坏肚子这些小病都会花很多钱。在中国有医疗保险也非常重要。现在，很多中国人都有医疗保险。

No.	Word	Pinyin	Part of Speech	Definition
1	一般来说	yìbān lái shuō		generally speaking
	一般	yìbān	adv	generally
2	挂号	guà hào	vo	to register and make an appointment (at a hospital)
3	门诊	ménzhěn	n	outpatient clinic
4	需要	xūyào	v/n	to need, to require; need
5	科室	kēshì	n	department (usually of a hospital)
6	家	jiā	m	(measure word for hospital, store, restaurant, company, or other enterprise)
7	家庭	jiātíng	n	family [家庭医生: family doctor, primary care physician]
8	推荐	tuījiàn	v/n	to recommend; recommendation
9	专科	zhuānkē	n	specialized subject [专科医生: medical specialist]
10	另外	lìngwài	conj	furthermore, in addition
11	西药	xīyào	n	Western medicine (pharmaceutical drugs)
12	开	kāi	v	to prescribe
13	中药	zhōngyào	n	Chinese medicine (herbal medicines)
14	针灸	zhēnjiǔ	n	acupuncture
15	医疗	yīliáo	n	medical care
16	重要	zhòngyào	adj	important

➤ Reading Comprehension

A Skimming and Scanning: Skim the reading and try to get a basic sense of the content and purpose of the text. INTERPRETIVE

1 Number each topic below to indicate the paragraph in which it is mentioned.

_____ medical insurance

_____ where to get prescribed medications

_____ how to find doctors

B Comprehension Check: Mark the following statements true or false. [INTERPRETIVE]

1 Patients in China usually have one doctor that they see for most of their medical concerns.　　**T　F**

2 In China, patients often get prescription medications at the hospital.　　**T　F**

3 According to the reading, doctors in the U.S. sometimes recommend acupuncture treatment.　　**T　F**

Cultural and Societal Context

Traditional Chinese medicine (TCM) or 中医 (zhōngyī) includes both herbal medicines and therapies such as acupuncture and cupping. Despite waves of backlash against it during the 20th century, traditional medicine continues to be practiced in modern Chinese healthcare. Typically, physicians in Chinese hospitals are trained in Western medicine but may prescribe herbal medicines as supplements, often as ready-to-use tablets or pills known as "patent medicine" (中成药, zhōng chéng yào). Some hospitals specialize in Chinese medicine, but physicians there generally practice Western medicine as well. In addition to prescription medications for ailments, there are numerous TCM products available as over-the-counter medicines or tonics. The most famous TCM brand in China is Tong Ren Tang (同仁堂, Tóngréntáng), which originated from a Beijing pharmacy founded in 1669. Tong Ren Tang is now a multi-branch modern enterprise and one of China's primary producers of TCM products.

➢ Reflection

A Discussion: Ask and answer the following questions with your classmates. [INTERPERSONAL]

1 如果你感冒了，你会去看病吗？你觉得一般来说大学生看病方便吗？

2 如果你生病了，可是明天有考试，你会怎么做？

B Research and Reflect: Investigate one of the questions below. Present your thoughts and findings in Chinese, using the supplemental vocabulary and/or consulting a dictionary for additional words as needed. [PRESENTATIONAL]

1 请再介绍一些在中国看病的信息 (xìnxī; information)。比如 (bǐrú; for example)，人们会先看病再付钱，还是先付钱再看病？人们能在网上挂号和看病吗？

2 一般来说，中国的大学生在遇到 (yù dào; to encounter, to experience) 心理 (xīnlǐ; mental) 健康问题的时候，会去看医生吗？别的地方的大学生呢？

C Further Exploration: Extend your knowledge by looking into the following questions. Note that the Cultural and Societal Context segment may have some helpful information to get you started.

1 Affordable medical care is an important topic all around the world. What are some practices, policies, and public opinions related to medical care in today's China? Have there been major changes in recent years? Compare the current medical care system in China to the system in another place of your choice.

2 Research how and when modern Western medicine began to be practiced in China, and how traditional Chinese medicine continued to evolve as a popular form of medical treatment at the same time. How does traditional Chinese medicine coexist with Western medicine in today's China? What are some notable products, practices, or perspectives related to Chinese medicine?

➤ **Pinyin of the Text**

Zài Zhōngguó kàn bìng hé zài Měiguó kàn bìng

Yìbān lái shuō, zài Zhōngguó kàn bìng hé zài Měiguó kàn bìng fēicháng bù yíyàng. Zài Zhōngguó, hěn duō rén shēng bìng de shíhou yìbān huì xiān qù yīyuàn guà hào, kàn ménzhěn. Guà hào de shíhou, bìngrén xūyào gàosu yīyuàn zìjǐ xiǎng kàn nǎ yí ge kēshì. Kàn ménzhěn de shíhou, bìngrén měi cì kàn de yīshēng bù yídìng yíyàng. Yǒude shíhou, yīnwèi xiǎng zhǎo dào zuì héshì de yīshēng, bìngrén huì qù hǎo jǐ jiā yīyuàn kàn bìng. Zài Měiguó, hěn duō rén shēng bìng de shíhou yìbān huì xiān qù kàn zìjǐ de jiātíng yīshēng. Jiātíng yīshēng zuò wán jiǎnchá yǐhòu, rúguǒ juéde yǒu xūyào, cái huì tuījiàn bìngrén qù kàn zhuānkē yīshēng.

Lìngwài, zài Zhōngguó, rénmen kàn wán yīshēng yǐhòu chángcháng huì zài yīyuàn lǐ fù qián ná yào. Zài Měiguó, rénmen chángcháng huì qù lí zìjǐ jiā bù yuǎn de yàodiàn ná yào. Zài Zhōngguó, chúle xīyào yǐwài, yīshēng yǒude shíhou hái huì kāi yì xiē zhōngyào. Měiguó de yīshēng yìbān bù kāi zhōngyào, búguò yǒude shíhou huì tuījiàn bìngrén qù zuò zhēnjiǔ.

Zuìhòu, zài Měiguó kàn bìng yǒu yīliáo bǎoxiǎn fēicháng zhòngyào. Rúguǒ méiyǒu bǎoxiǎn, kàn yīshēng hé mǎi yào chángcháng huì tèbié guì. Yǒude shíhou, kàn guòmǐn, gǎnmào, chī huài dùzi zhè xiē xiǎo bìng dōu huì huā hěn duō qián. Zài Zhōngguó yǒu yīliáo bǎoxiǎn yě fēicháng zhòngyào. Xiànzài, hěn duō Zhōngguó rén dōu yǒu yīliáo bǎoxiǎn.

A Tong Ren Tang storefront in Beijing

恋爱综艺为什么这么受欢迎?

高书文

在恋综《最好的印象》里约会的大学生王可苹(左)和白朋(右)

最近几年,恋爱综艺(也就是恋综)在中国很受欢迎。现在除了有素人恋综和明星恋综以外,还有明星和素人约会的恋综。另外,有些大学生还会自己在学校里做"恋综"。那为什么有这么多人喜欢看这种节目呢?我们来听听几位平常喜欢看恋综的观众是怎么说的。

一位名叫文文的单身大学生告诉我们,"我可以单身,但是我喜欢的CP(英文'couple'的缩写)一定要在一起!"她说她看到节目里别人约会,自己也觉得很甜。她看到节目里的人出去旅行,就觉得自己好像也去"旅行"了。跟文文比,刚工作的小东更喜欢看恋综里

> 我可以单身,但是我喜欢的CP一定要在一起!

的那些"冲突"。他说:"那些冲突有的时候是因为谁得打扫和整理房间,有的时候是因为俩人都想跟同一个人约会……非常有意思!"他还说在恋综里他能找到跟自己很像的人,找到共鸣,而且还可以从节目里学到些东西,让自己的EQ更高。

因为这几年恋综很受欢迎,有的素人上完节目以后自己也成了"明星"。这让观众觉得,现在有的素人上恋综就是想给观众一个好印象,所以他们约会的时候就像演电影一样,不够真实。另外,这几年恋综越来越多,广电总局会不会觉得这是个问题?恋综还能受欢迎几年?现在,我们还不知道。

➤ Supplemental Vocabulary

No.	Word	Pinyin	Part of Speech	Definition
1	恋爱	liàn'ài	n/v	love, romantic relationship; to be in love
2	综艺	zōngyì	n	entertainment show (a broad category including reality TV, variety programs, etc.)
3	受欢迎	shòu huānyíng	adj	popular
4	素人	sùrén	n	ordinary person (non-celebrity)
5	明星	míngxīng	n	celebrity, star
6	约会	yuēhuì	n/v	date; to have a date
7	另外	lìngwài	conj	furthermore, in addition
8	节目	jiémù	n	program, show
9	观众	guānzhòng	n	audience, viewers, spectators
10	单身	dānshēn	adj	single
11	缩写	suōxiě	n/v	abbreviation; to abbreviate
12	要	yào	mv	need to, should, must
13	冲突	chōngtū	n	conflict, clash
14	共鸣	gòngmíng	n/v	resonance; to resonate
15	真实	zhēnshí	adj	true, real, genuine
16	广电总局	Guǎngdiàn Zǒngjú	pn	National Radio and Television Administration (in China)

➤ Reading Comprehension

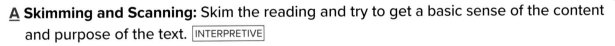

A Skimming and Scanning: Skim the reading and try to get a basic sense of the content and purpose of the text. INTERPRETIVE

1 What genre of nonfiction writing does this reading belong to, and where might you come across it?

   (a) movie teaser in a newspaper

   (b) cultural commentary in a magazine

   (c) coffee shop review in a travel guide

<u>B</u> **Comprehension Check:** Mark the following statements true or false. INTERPRETIVE

1 This article focuses specifically on celebrity dating shows. **T   F**

2 Wenwen likes watching the conflicts unfold in dating shows. **T   F**

3 The author predicts that dating shows will remain popular for many more years. **T   F**

Cultural and Societal Context

China's thriving entertainment industry produces a plethora of reality and variety shows to cater to the diverse interests of its audience. These shows encompass various genres, ranging from dating shows to escape room shows to rap competitions. Their devoted fans have given rise to many internet slang words and memes. One example of fandom internet language is 我可以单身，但是我喜欢的CP一定要在一起. This expression is commonly used by CP粉 (CP fěn; fans of character pairings and celebrity couples) to emphasize how important their favored pairings are to them. The terms CP and 粉 are also examples of the prevalence of English abbreviations and transliterations in Chinese internet language, particularly among younger generations.

➤ Reflection

<u>A</u> **Discussion:** Ask and answer the following questions with your classmates. INTERPERSONAL

1 你看过恋爱综艺节目或者别的真人秀 (zhēn rén xiù; reality show) 吗？你喜欢看真人秀吗？为什么？

2 如果有机会 (jīhuì; opportunity)，你想不想上真人秀 (zhēn rén xiù; reality show)？为什么？

<u>B</u> **Research and Reflect:** Investigate one of the questions below. Present your thoughts and findings in Chinese, using the supplemental vocabulary and/or consulting a dictionary for additional words as needed. PRESENTATIONAL

1 哪几种综艺节目现在在中国最受欢迎？如果你们国家 (guójiā; country) 也有这几种节目，它们和中国的节目有什么一样和不一样的地方？如果没有，你觉得这几种节目在你们国家会受欢迎吗？

2 请介绍几个中文网络流行语 (wǎngluò liúxíngyǔ; internet slang)，说说它们是什么意思、可以怎么用。

C Further Exploration: Extend your knowledge by looking into the following questions.

1 Consider the psychology of reality shows — how does watching them impact people's perceptions of self, relationships, and societal norms? What emotional factors contribute to their appeal?

2 The National Radio and Television Administration (广电总局) has played a key role in shaping the media landscape in China. One example is its support for including ordinary citizens in programs, which contributes to a more diverse representation of society in entertainment. Is there a comparable institution in your country? What do you see as the advantages and disadvantages of such regulatory bodies?

➢ Pinyin of the Text

Liàn'ài zōngyì wèishéme zhème shòu huānyíng?

Gāo Shūwén

Zuìjìn jǐ nián, liàn'ài zōngyì (yě jiù shì liàn zōng) zài Zhōngguó hěn shòu huānyíng. Xiànzài chúle yǒu sùrén liàn zōng hé míngxīng liàn zōng yǐwài, hái yǒu míngxīng hé sùrén yuēhuì de liàn zōng. Lìngwài, yǒu xiē dàxuéshēng hái huì zìjǐ zài xuéxiào lǐ zuò "liàn zōng". Nà wèishéme yǒu zhème duō rén xǐhuan kàn zhè zhǒng jiémù ne? Wǒmen lái tīng ting jǐ wèi píngcháng xǐhuan kàn liàn zōng de guānzhòng shì zěnme shuō de.

Yí wèi míng jiào Wénwen de dānshēn dàxuéshēng gàosu wǒmen, "Wǒ kěyǐ dānshēn, dànshì wǒ xǐhuan de CP (Yīngwén 'couple' de suōxiě) yídìng yào zài yìqǐ!" Tā shuō tā kàn dào jiémù lǐ biérén yuēhuì, zìjǐ yě juéde hěn tián. Tā kàn dào jiémù lǐ de rén chūqu lǚxíng, jiù juéde zìjǐ hǎoxiàng yě qù "lǚxíng" le. Gēn Wénwen bǐ, gāng gōngzuò de Xiǎo Dōng gèng xǐhuan kàn liàn zōng lǐ de nà xiē "chōngtū". Tā shuō, "Nà xiē chōngtū yǒude shíhou shì yīnwèi shéi děi dǎsǎo hé zhěnglǐ fángjiān, yǒude shíhou shì yīnwèi liǎ rén dōu xiǎng gēn tóng yí ge rén yuēhuì . . . Fēicháng yǒu yìsi!" Tā hái shuō zài liàn zōng lǐ tā néng zhǎo dào gēn zìjǐ hěn xiàng de rén, zhǎo dào gòngmíng, érqiě hái kěyǐ cóng jiémù lǐ xué dào xiē dōngxi, ràng zìjǐ de EQ gèng gāo.

Yīnwèi zhè jǐ nián liàn zōng hěn shòu huānyíng, yǒude sùrén shàng wán jiémù yǐhòu zìjǐ yě chéng le "míngxīng". Zhè ràng guānzhòng juéde, xiànzài yǒude sùrén shàng liàn zōng jiù shì xiǎng gěi guānzhòng yí ge hǎo yìnxiàng, suǒyǐ tāmen yuēhuì de shíhou jiù xiàng yǎn diànyǐng yíyàng, bú gòu zhēnshí. Lìngwài, zhè jǐ nián liàn zōng yuè lái yuè duō, Guǎngdiàn Zǒngjú huì bú huì juéde zhè shì ge wèntí? Liàn zōng hái néng shòu huānyíng jǐ nián? Xiànzài, wǒmen hái bù zhīdào.

A cameraman shoots a street scene for a Chinese reality TV show in Hong Kong

Renting an Apartment

图书馆 | 餐厅 | 宿舍 | 商店 | 医院 | 学生活动中心

京美大学的宿舍怎么样?

　　同学们进了大学以后,宿舍就成了很多人的第二个家。下面是京美大学宿舍的一些信息,希望对大家有帮助。

　　本科生宿舍楼的每个房间里都有四张床,可以住四个人。学校给每位同学都配备了一个书架、一张书桌、一把椅子,还有一个衣柜。宿舍的每层楼都有公共的盥洗室、卫生间、浴室等。同学们在盥洗室里可以洗漱、洗衣服。公共浴室的热水供应时间是7:00-9:00和15:20-23:00。

　　研究生公寓楼里的每套公寓都有一个客厅、一个卫生间和两间卧室,每间卧室可以住两个人。公寓里配备了家具,24小时都可以上网,而且24小时供应热水,洗澡很方便。虽然研究生可以在外面租房子,不过有很多研究生喜欢住学校的公寓,因为离教室很近。另外,虽然公寓里没有厨房,不能做饭,可是在学校的餐厅吃饭很方便,学校附近也有很多饭馆。

➢ Supplemental Vocabulary

No.	Word	Pinyin	Part of Speech	Definition
1	信息	*xìnxī*	n	information
2	对...有帮助	*duì ... yǒu bāngzhù*		is helpful for/towards . . .
3	本科生	*běnkēshēng*	n	undergraduate student
4	配备	*pèibèi*	v	to equip, to provide
5	衣柜	*yīguì*	n	wardrobe, closet
6	层	*céng*	m	(measure word for stories of a building)
7	盥洗室	*guànxǐ shì*	n	washroom (sinks only)
8	浴室	*yùshì*	n	shower room
9	等	*děng*	p	and so forth, etc.
10	洗漱	*xǐshù*	v	to wash up, to wash one's face and brush one's teeth
11	洗	*xǐ*	v	to wash
12	供应	*gōngyìng*	v	to supply
13	研究生	*yánjiūshēng*	n	graduate student
14	间	*jiān*	m	(measure word for rooms)
15	租	*zū*	v	to rent

➢ Reading Comprehension

<u>A</u> **Skimming and Scanning:** Skim the reading and try to get a basic sense of the content and purpose of the text. [INTERPRETIVE]

1 What is the main purpose of this reading?

    (a) to provide information about housing options at Jingmei University

    (b) to tell students about dorm culture and rules

    (c) to provide tips for renting apartments off campus

B Comprehension Check: Mark the following statements true or false. INTERPRETIVE

1 The intended audience for this reading is the faculty at Jingmei University.   **T   F**

2 Each dorm room has four beds.   **T   F**

3 Each dorm room has its own bathroom.   **T   F**

4 Each apartment for graduate students includes a shared living room.   **T   F**

5 Both dorms and apartments provide hot water for bathing 24 hours a day.   **T   F**

Cultural and Societal Context

In Chinese university dormitories, it is typical for four people to share a room, usually furnished with bunk beds or loft beds in order to conserve space. While having four students share a room is a common situation, it is possible for dorm rooms to accommodate six, eight, or even ten people. Students who live in the same building are generally the same gender, and rooms are typically assigned so that roommates share the same major. Living in dormitories is more affordable than renting an apartment off campus, so most college students choose to live on campus. Generally, universities do not allow undergraduate students to rent off-campus accommodations.

> # Reflection

A Discussion: Ask and answer the following questions with your classmates. INTERPERSONAL

1 你喜欢住在学校，还是自己在外面租房子？为什么？

2 你觉得京美大学的宿舍或者公寓怎么样？你觉得住在那儿方便吗？

B Research and Reflect: Investigate one of the questions below. Present your thoughts and findings in Chinese, using the supplemental vocabulary and/or consulting a dictionary for additional words as needed. PRESENTATIONAL

1 中国的大学生住宿舍的多还是住在学校外面的多？为什么？

2 你们那儿的大学宿舍跟中国的大学宿舍有哪些一样和不一样的地方？你觉得住在哪儿更方便？

<u>C</u> **Further Exploration:** Extend your knowledge by looking into the following questions. Note that the Cultural and Societal Context segment may have some helpful information to get you started.

1 Compare college students' accommodations across different countries. What are similarities and differences in dormitory culture and in the way dormitories are managed? What might be some reasons for these differences or similarities?

2 Choose three universities: one in China, and the other two in other countries of your choice. What is the cost of on-campus housing at each of those universities? Are the costs fairly similar, or quite different? Why?

➤ **Pinyin of the Text**

Jīngměi Dàxué de sùshè zěnmeyàng?

Tóngxuémen jìn le dàxué yǐhòu, sùshè jiù chéng le hěn duō rén de dì èr ge jiā. Xiàmiàn shì Jīngměi Dàxué sùshè de yì xiē xìnxī, xīwàng duì dàjiā yǒu bāngzhù.

Běnkēshēng sùshè lóu de měi ge fángjiān lǐ dōu yǒu sì zhāng chuáng, kěyǐ zhù sì ge rén. Xuéxiào gěi měi wèi tóngxué dōu pèibèi le yí ge shūjià, yì zhāng shūzhuō, yì bǎ yǐzi, háiyǒu yí ge yīguì. Sùshè de měi céng lóu dōu yǒu gōnggòng de guànxǐ shì, wèishēngjiān, yùshì děng. Tóngxuémen zài guànxǐ shì lǐ kěyǐ xǐshù, xǐ yīfu. Gōnggòng yùshì de rè shuǐ gōngyìng shíjiān shì 7:00-9:00 hé 15:20-23:00.

Yánjiūshēng gōngyù lóu lǐ de měi tào gōngyù dōu yǒu yí ge kètīng, yí ge wèishēngjiān hé liǎng jiān wòshì, měi jiān wòshì kěyǐ zhù liǎng ge rén. Gōngyù lǐ pèibèi le jiājù, èrshísì xiǎoshí dōu kěyǐ shàng wǎng, érqiě èrshísì xiǎoshí gōngyìng rè shuǐ, xǐ zǎo hěn fāngbiàn. Suīrán yánjiūshēng kěyǐ zài wàimiàn zū fángzi, búguò yǒu hěn duō yánjiūshēng xǐhuan zhù xuéxiào de gōngyù, yīnwèi lí jiàoshì hěn jìn. Lìngwài, suīrán gōngyù lǐ méiyǒu chúfáng, bù néng zuò fàn, kěshì zài xuéxiào de cāntīng chī fàn hěn fāngbiàn, xuéxiào fùjìn yě yǒu hěn duō fànguǎn.

A university dormitory in Guangzhou City

"三大球"和"三小球"

在中国最受欢迎的球类运动有"三大球"和"三小球"。三大球是足球，篮球和排球。三小球是乒乓球，羽毛球和网球。

三大球中的篮球和足球在中国是观众最多的运动。很多中国球迷喜欢看美国NBA的篮球比赛，英国的足球联赛，还有每四年一次的足球世界杯。中国也有自己的篮球和足球联赛。很多城市都有自己的联赛球队。这些联赛球队都有很多球迷。

正在看足球比赛的上海球迷

在三大球的国际比赛中，中国女排是成绩最好的球队，拿过好几次世界冠军。她们的第一个世界冠军是在1981年拿的。中国女足也是国际比赛成绩很好的球队。不过，中国的足球球迷虽然很多，平常看女足比赛的人还不太多。现在，越来越多的人觉得女足应该有更多的球迷。

在三小球运动中，中国乒乓球队和羽毛球队的水平一直很高，拿过很多次世界冠军。在中国喜欢打乒乓球和羽毛球的人也特别多。而且，人们常常说乒乓球是中国的"国球"。中国的第一个世界冠军就是1959年在乒乓球比赛里拿到的。最近二十几年，中国的网球运动水平也越来越高，中国有了自己的网球世界冠军。在中国喜欢打网球和看网球比赛的人也越来越多了。

➤ Supplemental Vocabulary

No.	Word	Pinyin	Part of Speech	Definition
1	受欢迎	shòu huānyíng	adj	popular
2	类	lèi	n	category, type
3	排球	páiqiú	n	volleyball
4	乒乓球	pīngpāngqiú	n	ping pong, table tennis
5	羽毛球	yǔmáoqiú	n	badminton
6	观众	guānzhòng	n	audience, viewers, spectators
7	球迷	qiúmí	n	(ball) sports fans
8	联赛	liánsài	n	sports league
9	世界杯	Shìjiè Bēi	pn	World Cup (here, the FIFA World Cup)
10	队	duì	n	team
11	女排	nǚ pái	n	women's volleyball (team)
12	成绩	chéngjì	n	score, achievement
13	世界	shìjiè	n	world
14	冠军	guànjūn	n	champion, first-place winner
15	女足	nǚ zú	n	women's soccer (team)
16	国球	guó qiú	n	national ball sport

➤ Reading Comprehension

A **Skimming and Scanning:** Skim the reading and try to get a basic sense of the content and purpose of the text. If a question asks about a specific detail, scan the text for key words to help answer that question. INTERPRETIVE

1 Which paragraph does not mention any of the three "big ball" sports?

(a) the second paragraph   (b) the third paragraph   (c) the fourth paragraph

2 What is the main purpose of the first paragraph?

(a) to rank the three most popular ball sports

(b) to introduce six of the most popular ball sports in China

(c) to state which ball sports China excels at

1 According to the reading, Chinese audiences often watch American football.   **T   F**

2 The reading refers to 1981 as the only time when the Chinese women's volleyball team won a world championship.   **T   F**

3 According to the reading, Chinese athletes won world championships in all the three "small ball" sports before the 1990s.   **T   F**

Cultural and Societal Context

The performance of Chinese athletes in international competitions has broad significance in contemporary China as an indicator of national strength. One reason for this is the historical association between physical weakness and national weakness that arose during China's "Century of Humiliation," a period of time that began with the First Opium War (1839-1842) and during which China experienced a succession of devastating foreign invasions. Modern sports milestones in China include ping pong player Rong Guotuan being recognized as a world champion in 1959 (China's first such accomplishment), the Chinese women's volleyball team's victory in the Women's World Cup in 1981, and the 2008 Beijing Olympics (the first time China hosted the Olympics). To the Chinese public, these events symbolize a rejuvenation of the national spirit.

➤ Reflection

A Discussion: Ask and answer the following questions with your classmates. INTERPERSONAL

1 你平常喜欢看体育 (tǐyù; sports) 比赛吗？如果不喜欢，你平常喜欢看什么？为什么？

2 你觉得喜欢一个球队的球迷会常常做什么？

B Research and Reflect: Investigate one of the questions below. Present your thoughts and findings in Chinese, using the supplemental vocabulary and/or consulting a dictionary for additional words as needed. PRESENTATIONAL

1 在你们国家 (guójiā; country) 哪些运动最受欢迎？为什么这些运动特别受欢迎？

2 中国有什么运动拿过很多世界冠军？你们国家 (guójiā; country) 呢？你觉得一个国家有多少世界冠军重要 (zhòngyào; important) 吗？

C **Further Exploration:** Extend your knowledge by looking into the following questions. Note that the Cultural and Societal Context segment may have some helpful information to get you started.

1 How do sports help shape local, regional, and national communities? What are the connections between professional and community sports? Research these questions based on one or two examples in China, and draw comparisons to sports and community bonding in situations you are familiar with.

2 How are women's sports practiced and perceived in China and in your country, or in other areas of the world? Are there noteworthy issues related to diversity, equity, and inclusivity when it comes to women's sports, or women's participation in sports? Have there been efforts or movements to resolve these issues? Find one or two specific examples related to these questions.

➤ **Pinyin of the Text**

"Sān dà qiú" hé "sān xiǎo qiú"

Zài Zhōngguó zuì shòu huānyíng de qiú lèi yùndòng yǒu "sān dà qiú" hé "sān xiǎo qiú". Sān dà qiú shì zúqiú, lánqiú hé páiqiú. Sān xiǎo qiú shì pīngpāngqiú, yǔmáoqiú hé wǎngqiú.

Sān dà qiú zhōng de lánqiú hé zúqiú zài Zhōngguó shì guānzhòng zuì duō de yùndòng. Hěn duō Zhōngguó qiúmí xǐhuan kàn Měiguó NBA de lánqiú bǐsài, Yīngguó de zúqiú liánsài, hái yǒu měi sì nián yí cì de zúqiú Shìjiè Bēi. Zhōngguó yě yǒu zìjǐ de lánqiú hé zúqiú liánsài. Hěn duō chéngshì dōu yǒu zìjǐ de liánsài qiú duì. Zhè xiē liánsài qiú duì dōu yǒu hěn duō qiúmí.

Zài sān dà qiú de guójì bǐsài zhōng, Zhōngguó nǚ pái shì chéngjì zuì hǎo de qiú duì, ná guò hǎo jǐ cì shìjiè guànjūn. Tāmen de dì yī ge shìjiè guànjūn shì zài yī jiǔ bā yī nián ná de. Zhōngguó nǚ zú yě shì guójì bǐsài chéngjì hěn hǎo de qiú duì. Búguò, Zhōngguó de zúqiú qiúmí suīrán hěn duō, píngcháng kàn nǚ zú bǐsài de rén hái bú tài duō. Xiànzài, yuè lái yuè duō de rén juéde nǚ zú yīnggāi yǒu gèng duō de qiúmí.

Zài sān xiǎo qiú yùndòng zhōng, Zhōngguó pīngpāngqiú duì hé yǔmáoqiú duì de shuǐpíng yìzhí hěn gāo, ná guò hěn duō cì shìjiè guànjūn. Zài Zhōngguó xǐhuan dǎ pīngpāngqiú hé yǔmáoqiú de rén yě tèbié duō. Érqiě, rénmen chángcháng shuō pīngpāngqiú shì Zhōngguó de "guó qiú". Zhōngguó de dì yī ge shìjiè guànjūn jiù shì yī jiǔ wǔ jiǔ nián zài pīngpāngqiú bǐsài lǐ ná dào de. Zuìjìn èrshí jǐ nián, Zhōngguó de wǎngqiú yùndòng shuǐpíng yě yuè lái yuè gāo, Zhōngguó yǒu le zìjǐ de wǎngqiú shìjiè guànjūn. Zài Zhōngguó xǐhuan dǎ wǎngqiú hé kàn wǎngqiú bǐsài de rén yě yuè lái yuè duō le.

Chinese women's volleyball team coach Lang Ping talks to players at an international match. Lang Ping is a legendary athlete in China and was a core player in the women's volleyball team that won the world championship in 1981.

中国游学项目现在开始申请

　　同学们，今年暑假的中国游学项目现在开始申请了。快来跟我们一起一边旅行，一边学中文吧！

游学计划：

　　今年游学项目的时间是：7月12日——8月1日。学生们上午在大学里学中文，下午去不同的地方和景点参观。第一个星期，我们先去中国的政治和文化中心——北京，参观长城等名胜古迹。第二个星期，我们会去中国最大的经济中心——上海。除了东方明珠等有名的景点以外，我们还会去参观上海最大的科技园。最后一个星期，我们会去"一国两制"下的香港看看，参观几个大的国际公司。

衣食住行：

　　每位学生都会收到一件国际文化中心的衬衫，大家还需要自己准备些夏天的衣服。学生们会住在北京、上海和香港的大学宿舍里，每天一起在学校的餐厅或者外面的饭馆吃饭。如果有食物过敏或者素餐要求，可以告诉我们。我们中心会帮大家订中国国际航空公司直飞中国的往返机票。另外，来中国以前，每位学生需要办好护照和中国签证，还需要买旅行保险。

　　对我们的游学项目有兴趣的同学，请在4月10日以前给京美大学国际文化中心发邮件申请！

Further Exploration: Extend your knowledge by looking into the following questions.

1 Explore Chinese social etiquette that might be important to know if you visit China. For example, you might look into expectations around dining, attire, behavior in public, etc.

2 Look up what travel documents are needed to visit Mainland China, Hong Kong, Macau, and Taiwan, and what the processes for obtaining those documents are like.

➢ Pinyin of the Text

Zhōngguó yóuxué xiàngmù xiànzài kāishǐ shēnqǐng

Tóngxuémen, jīnnián shǔjià de Zhōngguó yóuxué xiàngmù xiànzài kāishǐ shēnqǐng le. Kuài lái gēn wǒmen yìqǐ yìbiān lǚxíng, yìbiān xué Zhōngwén ba!

Yóuxué jìhuà:
Jīnnián yóuxué xiàngmù de shíjiān shì: qī yuè shí'èr rì—bā yuè yī rì. Xuéshengmen shàngwǔ zài dàxué lǐ xué Zhōngwén, xiàwǔ qù bù tóng de dìfang hé jǐngdiǎn cānguān. Dì yī ge xīngqī, wǒmen xiān qù Zhōngguó de zhèngzhì hé wénhuà zhōngxīn—Běijīng, cānguān Chángchéng děng míngshèng gǔjì. Dì èr ge xīngqī, wǒmen huì qù Zhōngguó zuì dà de jīngjì zhōngxīn—Shànghǎi. Chúle Dōngfāng Míngzhū děng yǒumíng de jǐngdiǎn yǐwài, wǒmen hái huì qù cānguān Shànghǎi zuì dà de kējì yuán. Zuìhòu yí ge xīngqī, wǒmen huì qù "yì guó liǎng zhì" xià de Xiānggǎng kàn kan, cānguān jǐ ge dà de guójì gōngsī.

Yī-shí-zhù-xíng:
Měi wèi xuésheng dōu huì shōu dào yí jiàn Guójì Wénhuà Zhōngxīn de chènshān, dàjiā hái xūyào zìjǐ zhǔnbèi xiē xiàtiān de yīfu. Xuéshengmen huì zhù zài Běijīng, Shànghǎi hé Xiānggǎng de dàxué sùshè lǐ, měi tiān yìqǐ zài xuéxiào de cāntīng huòzhě wàimiàn de fànguǎn chī fàn. Rúguǒ yǒu shíwù guòmǐn huòzhě sùcān yāoqiú, kěyǐ gàosu wǒmen. Wǒmen zhōngxīn huì bāng dàjiā dìng Zhōngguó Guójì Hángkōng Gōngsī zhí fēi Zhōngguó de wǎngfǎn jīpiào. Lìngwài, lái Zhōngguó yǐqián, měi wèi xuésheng xūyào bàn hǎo hùzhào hé Zhōngguó qiānzhèng, hái xūyào mǎi lǚxíng bǎoxiǎn.

Duì wǒmen de yóuxué xiàngmù yǒu xìngqù de tóngxué, qǐng zài sì yuè shí rì yǐqián gěi Jīngměi Dàxué Guójì Wénhuà Zhōngxīn fā yóujiàn shēnqǐng!

Chinese and international students gather at an event organized by the University of Hong Kong

怎么在北京大兴 国际机场坐飞机

01 往返机场

往返大兴机场最快的办法是坐北京地铁大兴机场线。旅客也可以在北京西站坐火车，20–35分钟就可以到达大兴机场。旅客还可以坐机场巴士，或者打出租车。在机场也有公司提供接送和租车服务。

02 到航站楼

坐国内出发航班请到航站楼三楼，坐国际出发航班请到四楼。

03 办登机牌

旅客可以在机场找航空公司办登机牌和行李托运，有的时候也可以自己在网上办登机牌。

04 安检

安检以前，请把护照或者别的证件准备好。安检的时候，请把电脑和手机拿出来。

05 到登机口

虽然大兴机场的航站楼很大，但是从航站楼的中心到每个登机口最远只有600米，走路只用8分钟。

06 等候航班

如果等候航班的时间很长，旅客可以在机场里买东西，吃饭，或者休息一下。过夜的旅客还可以找地方睡觉。大兴机场里有很多商店，餐厅和旅馆。

➤ Supplemental Vocabulary

No.	Word	Pinyin	Part of Speech	Definition
1	大兴	Dàxīng	pn	Daxing, a place name
2	旅客	lǚkè	n	traveler, passenger
3	火车	huǒchē	n	train
4	到达	dàodá	v/n	to arrive; arrival
5	巴士	bāshì	n	bus
6	提供	tígōng	v	to provide, to offer
7	航站楼	hángzhànlóu	n	(airport) terminal
8	国内	guó nèi	n	domestic (lit. inside the country)
9	出发	chūfā	v/n	to depart; departure
10	安检	ānjiǎn	n	security check
11	证件	zhèngjiàn	n	certificate, document
12	米	mǐ	m	meter
13	等候	děnghòu	v	to wait, to wait for
14	过夜	guò yè	v	to stay overnight

➤ Reading Comprehension

<u>A</u> **Skimming and Scanning:** Skim the reading and try to get a basic sense of the content and purpose of the text. If a question asks about a specific detail, scan the text for key words to help answer that question. INTERPRETIVE

1 What information about Beijing Daxing International Airport does this infographic include? Select all that apply.

  (a) how to get there

  (b) where to go for international departures

  (c) how to get from one terminal to another

2 What does the reading say about getting to one's gate in Daxing Airport?

  (a) The airport is large, so there is a shuttle that runs between the gates.

  (b) Although the airport is large, it doesn't take long to walk to any given gate.

  (c) It's easy to get lost, but there are maps in many places that you can refer to.

B Comprehension Check: Mark the following statements true or false. [INTERPRETIVE]

1 The subway is the fastest way to get from the city of Beijing to Daxing Airport. **T F**

2 Boarding gates for domestic flights are on the third floor of Daxing Airport. **T F**

3 Passengers can stay overnight at hotels in Daxing Airport. **T F**

Cultural and Societal Context

The notable qualities of Daxing Airport go beyond its sheer size and structural design and include a number of advanced technologies to help make the airport experience more streamlined. Some examples of this include 5G coverage throughout the entire airport, facial recognition technology to verify identity at checkpoints, and support for the use of electronic bag tags. These digital luggage tags are equipped with RFID chips, and when passengers check in on a designated airline's app, they can use their smartphones or NFC devices provided by the airlines to immediately transmit the flight information to their luggage tags, making the destination of the luggage clear. In some cases, the electronic bag tags can also be linked to 5G cameras, allowing luggage to be monitored throughout the duration of the trip.

➤ Reflection

A Discussion: Ask and answer the following questions with your classmates. [INTERPERSONAL]

1 你知道附近有什么机场吗？大家平常怎么往返机场？

2 如果你得在机场等好几个小时才能转机，在机场的时候你会做什么？你希望机场能提供哪些服务？

B Research and Reflect: Investigate one of the questions below. Present your thoughts and findings in Chinese, using the supplemental vocabulary and/or consulting a dictionary for additional words as needed. [PRESENTATIONAL]

1 北京大兴国际机场提供的哪些服务最受欢迎 (shòu huānyíng; popular)？你觉得哪些服务很酷？

2 请介绍几个在全世界 (quán shìjiè; the whole world) 有名的机场和它们的特色 (tèsè; feature)。

C Further Exploration: Extend your knowledge by looking into the following questions.

1 Beijing Daxing International Airport has a very unique design. Who designed it? What is the relationship between the desired functions/features of Daxing Airport and its design? You may compare the design features of Daxing Airport to another airport you are familiar with or have researched.

2 Explore the history of airports in China. Why is the development of airports important to a country?

➢ **Pinyin of the Text**

Zěnme zài Běijīng Dàxīng Guójì Jīchǎng zuò fēijī

01 Wǎngfǎn jīchǎng
Wǎngfǎn Dàxīng Jīchǎng zuì kuài de bànfǎ shì zuò Běijīng Dìtiě Dàxīng Jīchǎng Xiàn. Lǚkè yě kěyǐ zài Běijīng Xī Zhàn zuò huǒchē, èrshí dào sānshíwǔ fēnzhōng jiù kěyǐ dàodá Dàxīng Jīchǎng. Lǚkè hái kěyǐ zuò jīchǎng bāshì, huòzhě dǎ chūzūchē. Zài jīchǎng yě yǒu gōngsī tígōng jiē sòng hé zū chē fúwù.

02 Dào hángzhànlóu
Zuò guó nèi chūfā hángbān qǐng dào hángzhànlóu sān lóu, zuò guójì chūfā hángbān qǐng dào sì lóu.

03 Bàn dēngjīpái
Lǚkè kěyǐ zài jīchǎng zhǎo hángkōng gōngsī bàn dēngjīpái hé xíngli tuōyùn, yǒude shíhou yě kěyǐ zìjǐ zài wǎng shang bàn dēngjīpái.

04 Ānjiǎn
Ānjiǎn yǐqián, qǐng bǎ hùzhào huòzhě bié de zhèngjiàn zhǔnbèi hǎo. Ānjiǎn de shíhou, qǐng bǎ diànnǎo hé shǒujī ná chu lai.

05 Dào dēngjīkǒu
Suīrán Dàxīng Jīchǎng de hángzhànlóu hěn dà, dànshì cóng hángzhànlóu de zhōngxīn dào měi ge dēngjīkǒu zuì yuǎn zhǐ yǒu liùbǎi mǐ, zǒu lù zhǐ yòng bā fēnzhōng.

06 Děnghòu hángbān
Rúguǒ děnghòu hángbān de shíjiān hěn cháng, lǚkè kěyǐ zài jīchǎng lǐ mǎi dōngxi, chī fàn, huòzhě xiūxi yí xià. Guò yè de lǚkè hái kěyǐ zhǎo dìfang shuì jiào. Dàxīng Jīchǎng lǐ yǒu hěn duō shāngdiàn, cāntīng hé lǚguǎn.

Aerial view of Beijing Daxing International Airport